ACPL ITEM
DISCARDED

D1706896

62
Sou~~....~~, ~~.~~~~..~~ ~~u~~~~..~~.
Fourier array imaging

CAUTION
Computer Disk Inside
Do NOT Demagnetize

DO NOT REMOVE
CARDS FROM POCKET

ALLEN COUNTY PUBLIC LIBRARY
FORT WAYNE, INDIANA 46802

You may return this book to any agency, branch,
or bookmobile of the Allen County Public Library.

DEMCO

Fourier Array Imaging

Mehrdad Soumekh

State University of New York at Buffalo

P T R Prentice Hall
Englewood Cliffs, New Jersey 07632

Library of Congress Cataloguing-in-Publication Data
Soumekh., Mehrdad.
   Fourier array imaging / Mehrdad Soumekh.
     p. cm.
   Includes bibliographical references and index.
   ISBN 0-13-063769-6
   1. Signal processing. 2. Imaging systems. 3. Fourier
transformations. I. Title.
TK5102.9.S67 1994
621.36'7'01512433--dc20

Allen County Public Library
900 Webster Street
PO Box 2270
Fort Wayne, IN 46801-2270

93-31547
         CIP

Editorial/production supervision: *Mary P. Rottino*
Cover design: *Jeanette Jacobs*
Buyer: *Alexis Heydt*
Acquisitions editor: *Karen Gettman*
Editorial assistant: *Barbara Alfieri*

> ### To My Family

©1994 by P T R Prentice Hall
Prentice-Hall, Inc.
A Paramount Communications Company
Englewood Cliffs, New Jersey 07632

LIMITS OF LIABILITY AND DISCLAIMER OF WARRANTY: Tha author and publisher of this book have used
their best efforts in preparing this book and software. These efforts include the development, research, and testing
of the theories and programs to determine their effectiveness. The author and publisher make no warranty of any
kind, expressed, or implied, with regard to these programs for the documentation contained in this book..
The author and publisher shall not be liable in any event incidental or consequential damages in connection
with, or arising out of, the furnishing, performance, or use of these programs.

The publisher offers discounts on this book when ordered in bulk quantities.
For more information, contact:

      Corporate Sales Department
      P T R Prentice Hall
      113 Sylvan Avenue
      Englewood Cliffs, NJ 07632
      Phone (201) 592-2863   Fax (201) 592-2249

Printed in the United States of America

10 9 8 7 6 5 4 3 2 1

ISBN 0-13-063769-6

Prentice-Hall International (UK) Limited, *London*
Prentice-Hall of Australia Pty. Limited, *Sydney*
Prentice-Hall Canada Inc., *Toronto*
Prentice-Hall Hispanoamericana, S.A., *Mexico*
Prentice-Hall of India Private Limited, *New Delhi*
Prentice-Hall of Japan, Inc., *Tokyo*
Simon & Schuster Asia Pte. Ltd., *Singapore*
Editora Prentice-Hall do Brasil, Ltda., *Rio de Janeiro*

NOTICE:
Warning of Copyright
Restrictions

The Copyright law of the United States
(Title 17, United States Code) governs the
reproduction, distribution, adaptation,
public performance, and public display of
copyrighted material.
Under certain conditions of the law, nonprofit libraries are authorized to lend, lease,
or rent copies of computer programs to
patrons on a nonprofit basis and for nonprofit purposes. Any person who makes an
unauthorized copy or adaptation of the
computer program, or redistributes the loan
copy, or publicly performs or displays the
computer program, except as permitted by
Title 17 of the United States Code, may be
liable for copyright infringement.
This institution reserves the right to refuse
to fulfill a loan request if, in its judgment,
fulfillment of the request would lead to
violation of the copyright law.

CONTENTS

Chapter 5   BLIND-VELOCITY SAR/ISAR IMAGING   352

Chapter 6   PASSIVE ARRAY IMAGING AND DETECTION   440

Chapter 7   BISTATIC ARRAY IMAGING   505

PREFACE

This book is intended to be a teaching and research monograph for electrical engineers in the areas of *array processing and multidimensional signal processing*, and engineers interested in the *study of inverse problems of imaging systems from a system and signal theory point of view*. In the past 40 years, a number of imaging modalities have been developed for radar, sonar, diagnostic medicine, geophysical exploration, and nondestructive testing. The reader may well have heard of such examples as surveillance radar, towed-array sonar, Computerized Tomography (CT), Magnetic Resonance Imaging (MRI), Positron Emission Tomography (PET), ultrasonic scanner, phased array, passive array, Synthetic Aperture Radar (SAR), etc. In designing and developing information processing tools for these imaging systems, one encounters diverse issues such as physical and mathematical modeling of the problem, signal processing, reconstruction, image analysis and segmentation, image storage, and electronic instrumentation.

The signal processing community within the electrical engineering profession has paid special attention to the problem of *reconstruction or interpolation from spatial frequency domain data* that arises in imaging systems such as CT and SAR. However, the topics of *multidimensional system modeling and signal processing for imaging systems* are far broader and richer than the interpolation problem. Based on the recently developed multidimensional system and signal theory, a signal processor can present innovative solutions for imaging systems, and even open ways to introduce new and powerful imaging modalities.

The genesis of this view can be found in the books of J. Goodman, *Introduction to Fourier Optics*, and A. Papoulis, *Systems and Transforms with Applications in Optics*. Goodman and Papoulis pioneered the use of powerful signal processing tools of Fourier analysis and linear system theory as the basis for presenting the principles of *analog* optical image formation. In this book, I have also utilized *Fourier analysis, linear system theory and phase modulation* to formulate image formation in *discrete* array imaging systems. The major difference between the mathematical foundation presented in this book and the works of Goodman and Papoulis is a principle that is referred to as *spatial Doppler phenomenon*. Based on the spatial Doppler principle, one can replace the Fresnel (or Fraunhofer) approximation-based analog processing performed using lenses for image formation with spatial and temporal discrete Fourier transforms on array data and an approximation-free inversion. The practical advantages of this include *high-resolution* imaging utilizing *large-aperture* arrays in *near field* as well as far field inverse problems.

The material presented in this book originates from my lecture notes for a graduate-level course in imaging systems. In this effort, I put emphasis on the study of *multidimensional signal processing issues and system analysis* associated with a class of array imaging problems that is governed by the principle of *coherent wave propagation in time and space*. This class of array imaging systems includes widely used imaging modalities in diagnostic medicine, radar, sonar and geophysical exploration. As a result, I was able to exploit the field of *signal processing for imaging systems* to train and prepare my own graduate students for their thesis work as well as other students interested in applications of signal processing.

As noted, a common mathematical principle, that is, the spatial Doppler phenomenon, provides the unifying theme for analyzing these array imaging systems. As background for this approach, a thorough understanding of *Fourier analysis* and *phase modulation* is needed. This requirement is certain to be met by signal processors, though someone with background in wave theory would also be able to follow the development in the text. Nevertheless, I have tried to present the material in the framework of signal analysis and basic communication theory, and, on some occasions, also provide a brief physical interpretation of a topic.

Chapter 1 introduces the spatial Doppler phenomenon in conjunction with the most primitive signal processing tools and systems that are used in array imaging. These include coherent receivers, pulsed and continuous-wave signaling, temporal Doppler phenomenon, and monostatic, quasi-monostatic, and bistatic transmitters/receivers. These systems and signal processing tools are used throughout the chapters that deal with array imaging problems. Chapter 2 introduces terminologies and tools for two-dimensional signal processing. Chapters 3-7 treat specific array imaging systems via the unifying framework of spatial Doppler processing. These imaging systems include phased array imaging, synthetic aperture array (SAR and ISAR) imaging, passive array imaging, and bistatic array imaging with emphasis on transmission imaging problems of diagnostic medicine and geophysical exploration. A major portion of the text is devoted to the analysis of resolution anticipated in an imaging system and to the constraints that are instrumental for selecting the parameters of an imaging system. These issues are addressed via Fourier analysis of the signals and images involved. The analysis also includes the hardware structure used for transmission and reception (data acquisition system) and the flow-chart (overall system block diagram) indicating how the acquired data are processed to yield the final reconstructed image. I have also attempted to describe some of the classical methods used for image formation in array imaging systems, and to relate them to the spatial Doppler-based imaging via certain approximations.

Acknowledgements

I am grateful to my students Jeong-Hee Choi, Srihanto Nugroho, and Hoongee Yang for their help. I am also thankful for the comments of many of the graduate students in my imaging course and, in particular, Susan Yang who taught me *matlab*. I am greatly indebted to Robert Dinger and his group at the Radar Branch of Naval Command, Control, and Ocean Surveillance Center, San Diego, for providing technical assistance as well as realistic radar data during my summer visiting faculty appointments in NCCOSC. I am particularly thankful for many technical discussions with Michael Pollock who also reviewed this manuscript. My work also benefited from my interaction as a summer visiting faculty with Gary Loos, Sergio Restaino, and other members of Interferometric Imaging Group at the Phillips Laboratory, Kirtland Air Force Base. During my appointment, I had the assistance and encouragement of Don Payne of Rockwell International. I am also grateful to Bill Zwolinski of Bell Aerospace, Textron, for his collaboration with me. I am thankful to Murat Tekalp of University of Rochester, and Ge Wang of Washington University for reviewing the manuscript. I also appreciate the efforts and comments of John Chiasson of University of Pittsburgh, and my University at Buffalo colleagues Patrick Dowd, Alfred Kriman, Steve Margolis, and Nasser Nasrabadi.

INTRODUCTION

Imaging Systems

The object of imaging systems is to *probe* targets and produce an *image* of the targets probed. Generally, one seeks to construct an image which represents the locations of discrete targets, or the spatial distribution of some continuous parameter that is related to the physical properties of a target such as reflectivity, absorption, and/or refraction index. In imaging problems that involve *dynamic* targets, one may also desire to observe the evolution of this image in time.

The problem of imaging is of interest in diagnostic medicine, radar, sonar, geophysical and celestial exploration, and nondestructive testing of industrial components. In imaging problems of diagnostic medicine, geophysical exploration, and industrial inspection, one is interested in *seeing* the structure inside a nontransparent target, for example, a tumor inside a patient's body or a crack inside an engine, via probing it in a noninvasive fashion, that is, without altering the target's original nature. In remote sensing problems of radar, sonar and geophysical/celestial exploration, one is interested in seeing targets that are not close enough to be identifiable/resolvable by the human eye.

Active imaging systems illuminate the target under study with a radiation source, called the *transmitter*. Common active imaging systems use sound waves (acoustic sources in sonar and geophysical exploration, and ultrasonic sources in diagnostic medicine) or part of the electromagnetic spectrum (X-ray in diagnostic medicine, and 200 MHz to 35 GHz band as well as segments of the lower and higher portions of this band in radar). This transmitted radiation interacts with the target. The resultant waves emanating from the target are recorded via a sensor or sensors which constitute a *receiver*. In *passive* imaging systems, the original illumination is provided by an unknown source that may reside inside or outside of the target.

*The problem of extracting the target's properties from the recorded signals is a multidimensional **inverse** problem. An inverse or black box problem is the study of a system from the knowledge of its response (recorded signals) to known (active) or unknown (passive) sources [4].*

For instance, the forward problem in linear time-invariant (LTI) circuits is to find the output from the knowledge of the input (source) and the impulse response (the system properties). The inverse problem in LTI systems is to determine the impulse response from the knowledge of the output to a known input.

*The first step in solving the inverse problem of an imaging system is to obtain an analytical expression relating the recorded signals, the source, and the target's properties. This is called the **system modeling** of the imaging system. A **practical** multidimensional system model for an imaging system should be an **accurate** representation of the source/target interaction. However, the model should also yield a **computationally manageable** inversion.*

Classical works in the field of optical processing and wave theory, such as Born and Wolf [1], Goodman [2], Morse and Feshbach [3], and Papoulis [5], have provided the basic principles for formulating the system model and inversion in most imaging systems. In particular, Goodman's and Papoulis's analyses of analog optical imaging systems are based on modeling lenses as linear shift-invariant systems. Then, using the Fresnel or Fraunhofer approximation, the process of image formation (inversion) can be examined within the simple framework of *Fourier* analysis: the signal appearing across a lense's aperture is related to the spatial Fourier decomposition of the desired image; by going through the lens, this signal is multiplied by a quadratic phase function; the desired image formed on a screen is the inverse spatial Fourier transform of the signal that appears on the other side of the lens.

The next step in the evolution of the imaging systems was the use of computers for discrete processing of signals. This is achieved by using discrete sensors within an aperture instead of the continuous aperture of a lens [6],[7]. A sampled aperture of sources or sensors is called an *array*. The signals recorded by an array of sensors are stored in a computer.

The computer adds the quadratic phase function in the spatial frequency domain via fast discrete Fourier transform algorithms and displays the resultant image. Such processing techniques or variations of them have been used for imaging with optical, microwave, acoustic, and ultrasonic sources.

The Book

The main theme of this book is to provide a common framework for system modeling, inversion, and parameter selection in array imaging systems. The fundamental principle behind this effort is what we refer to as the **spatial Doppler** *phenomenon.*

This concept is the same as the spatial Fourier processing used in optical imaging. The main distinction is that the image formation is achieved without any need for the Fresnel or Fraunhofer approximation. The need for the Fresnel or Fraunhofer approximation arises from the fact that the imaging system model depends on *nonlinear* phase functions of the measurement and target domains that prevent development of a computationally manageable inversion.

The spatial Doppler-based approach is a Fourier analysis of the multi-dimensional imaging system model that converts such nonlinear phase functions into linear phase functions of the measurement and target domains. This reduces the analysis of the multidimensional integrals that represent the system model into a one-to-one mapping in the spatial frequency domain of the desired image.

Chapter 1 is a review of one-dimensional signals and systems. The basic principles behind monostatic and quasi-monostatic echo imaging are discussed, and their data acquisition system and reconstruction algorithm are shown. Pulsed and continuous wave signaling for echo imaging and their utility in range-Doppler imaging are examined. Motion-induced temporal Doppler phenomenon and position-induced spatial Doppler phenomenon are analyzed. This analysis, which is the first step in presenting the spatial Doppler phenomenon, also provides the mathematical basis for analysis of *resolution* in array imaging systems.

Chapter 2 establishes notations and terminology for analysis of two-dimensional signals and systems. Section 2.4 provides an analysis on the Fourier properties of propagating waves. Sections 2.6 and 2.7 provide sampling constraints and reconstruction for the generalized two-dimensional sampling. These are crucial concepts for the *implementation* and discrete processing of algorithms in Fourier array imaging systems. These two sections, however, could be skipped by the readers who are only interested in the inverse problem in array imaging.

Chapter 3 deals with array imaging with physical arrays. The concept of phased arrays is reviewed. Dynamic focusing and generalized beamforming with application in medical imaging and surveillance radar imaging are discussed. A spatial Doppler-based system model and inversion for a phased array imaging system that utilizes beam-steering are developed. The theory of image formation with circular phased arrays is formulated in Section 3.8. An instructor could skip this section since most students find this topic difficult to follow. Resolution, reconstruction, and sampling constraints are outlined for phased array imaging. Figures are provided for the imaging system geometry, coherent data acquisition system, spatial frequency coverage of the available data, spatial Doppler phenomenon for a single target, and reconstruction flow chart. Phased array imaging with FM-CW signaling for retrieving flow velocity as well as reflectivity function in the spatial domain is examined.

Chapter 4 presents a spatial Doppler-based system model and inversion for position-induced pulsed synthetic aperture array imaging. Two other inverse methods that utilize Fresnel and plane wave approximations are examined and their relative merits are discussed. Temporal Doppler-induced (Doppler beam sharpened) synthetic aperture radar imaging with FM-CW signaling, bistatic synthetic aperture radar imaging, and spaceborne (circular array) synthetic aperture radar imaging are presented. Resolution, reconstruction and sampling constraints are developed for synthetic aperture array imaging. Figures are provided for the monostatic/bistatic synthetic aperture array imaging system geometry in ground-plane and slant-plane, coherent data acquisition system, spatial frequency coverage of the available data, spatial Doppler phenomenon for a single target, and reconstruction flow chart.

Chapter 5 deals with blind-velocity synthetic aperture radar (SAR) and Inverse (SAR) of moving targets in a stationary background (clutter). The concept of mean spatial Doppler shift is introduced as a measure for moving target indication (MTI) or airborne MTI (AMTI). Velocity estimation based on the measurements of mean spatial Doppler shift is presented. A procedure for removing clutter signature and its system diagram are outlined. Blind-velocity SAR/ISAR imaging is formulated in terms of temporal Doppler data and its associated difficulties are analyzed. Blind-velocity ISAR detection and imaging of multiple moving targets in heavy clutter is formulated. Methods for estimating the moving targets' parameters are presented. Section 5.8 presents results on imaging of an airborne DC-9 (a commercial aircraft) from its real ISAR data acquired over the San Diego Airport.

Chapter 6 establishes a spatial Doppler processing framework for dealing with passive array data. The interrelationship of physical passive arrays and synthetic active arrays are shown. Coherent wide-band and incoherent narrow-band passive array imaging are discussed. Passive bistatic (stereo) detection and imaging of targets are formulated. Passive synthetic aperture array imaging and passive inverse synthetic aperture array imaging of targets emitting narrow-band and wide-band signals are examined. Passive array imaging of celestial targets via Michelson interferometry and nonredundant aperture synthesis for this problem are discussed.

Chapter 7 deals with bistatic physical arrays. Linear bistatic arrays in echo mode are discussed, and their relationship to phased array and synthetic aperture array data are established (generalized array synthesis). Transmit mode linear bistatic arrays using wide-band and rotating narrow-band sources are analyzed. A geophysical imaging modality involving bistatic arrays is discussed. Geometrical optics approximation-based inversion for rotating parallel beam and fan beam sources and its relation to early computer assisted tomography systems are shown.

Projects given at the end of each chapter are concerned mainly with the computer programs for system modeling and inversion for array imaging systems. A floppy disk is provided that contains the source *matlab* programs for some of the these projects.

The Reader

This book is based on the materials taught in a graduate level electrical engineering course entitled *Principles of Medical & Radar Imaging* at the State University of New York at Buffalo since 1986. The required background for this course is the knowledge of signal processing, in particular, the Fourier transform analysis. Familiarity with sophomore level physics for engineers or junior level electromagnetics for electrical engineers is useful but not essential. Graduate electrical engineering students with interest in signal/image processing and systems make up the main enrollment of the course. Graduate students from mechanical engineering, geophysics, biophysics, physics, and mathematics as well as senior electrical engineering students and part-time graduate students from the local aerospace industry have also enrolled in the course.

The purpose of the book is to bring out some of the new array imaging findings that may be applicable in various imaging modalities of diagnostic medicine, radar, sonar, artificial (robot) vision, geophysical and celestial exploration, and nondestructive testing. The coherent array imaging principles presented in the book represent some of the most current and advanced materials in the field of array processing and imaging systems. The book begins with basic signal and image processing principles and gradually builds up the advanced materials. The book is self-contained. No other basic or advanced textbooks are necessary to be used with the book.

The assigned projects are intended to assist the students to observe imaging phenomenon by computer simulations and reconstructions. The software in the floppy disk is to provide a basis for the students to develop their own imaging programs as well as for the instructor to assign other projects. The contents of the book could be taught in one semester by emphasizing just the basic theory, or two semesters/quarters by expanding the role of assigned projects. In the latter case, the instructor could teach the first four chapters in the first semester/quarter. The second semester/quarter could begin with a brief review of the first four chapters and then cover the last three chapters.

REFERENCES

1. M. Born and E. Wolf, *Principles of Optics*, 6th edition, New York: Pergamon Press, 1983.

2. J. Goodman, *Introduction to Fourier Optics*, New York: McGraw-Hill, 1968.

3. P. M. Morse and H. Feshbach, *Methods of Theoretical Physics*, New York: McGraw-Hill, Parts 1 and 2, 1953.

4. A. Naylor and G. Sell, *Linear Operator Theory in Engineering and Science*, New York: Springer-Verlag, 1982.

5. A. Papoulis, *Systems and Transforms with Applications in Optics*, New York: McGraw-Hill, 1968.

6. M. I. Skolnik, *Introduction to Radar Systems*, New York: McGraw Hill, 1980.

7. B. D. Steinberg, *Principles of Aperture and Array System Design*, New York: Wiley, 1976.

Chapter 1

ONE-DIMENSIONAL SIGNALS

A *signal* (or a function) is an information-bearing measure. For instance, $p(t)$ is an information-bearing time domain signal; the variations of $p(t)$ with respect to the time domain t represent the information content of $p(t)$. Our study of array imaging systems is based on processing of time and space signals and their Fourier properties. This is for the purpose of translating the information contents of an imaging system's measured signals into the desired image information via computationally manageable and numerically accurate signal and image processing methods. *Fourier analysis* will be the main tool used to achieve this objective.

In this section, we briefly examine certain classes of signals and processing issues associated with time signals, for example, $p(t)$, and space signals, such as $f(x)$ and $s(u)$; we commonly use variables (t, τ) to identify the time domain, and (x, y, z, u, v) to denote spatial domain variables. For further details on one-dimensional signal processing, the reader is referred to the books [1]-[8].

1.1 FOURIER TRANSFORM

Fourier Integral

A time signal $p(t)$ has the following Fourier decomposition in terms of complex sinusoidal signals (inverse Fourier transform equation):

$$p(t) = \frac{1}{2\pi} \int_{-\infty}^{\infty} P(\omega) \, \exp(j\omega t) \, d\omega$$
$$= \mathcal{F}_{(\omega)}^{-1}[P(\omega)];$$

ω is the radian temporal frequency domain (units = radians/second), and $P(\omega)$ is called the Fourier transform of $p(t)$ and is found via (forward

Fourier transform equation):

$$P(\omega) = \int_{-\infty}^{\infty} p(t) \, \exp(-j\omega t) \, dt$$

$$= \mathcal{F}_{(t)}[p(t)].$$

- *The inverse Fourier transform is a representation/decomposition of $p(t)$ in terms of a **linear** combination (view the Fourier integral as a sum) of $P(\omega)$, $\omega \in (-\infty, \infty)$; the weight of $P(\omega)$ in this linear combination is $\exp(j\omega t) \frac{d\omega}{2\pi}$. Similarly, the forward Fourier integral provides a decomposition of $P(\omega)$ in terms of a linear combination of $p(t)$, $t \in (-\infty, \infty)$.*

Both integrals perform a *reversible* linear transfer of information: one from the time domain to the frequency domain, and the other from the frequency domain to the time domain. The term reversible is used to imply that after obtaining $P(\omega)$ from $p(t)$ via the forward Fourier transform, one can retrieve the original information contents of $p(t)$ from $P(\omega)$ using the inverse Fourier transform; that is, there is no loss of information in the Fourier integrals linear transformation:

Fourier transform is an information-preserving linear transformation.

A spatial domain signal, for example, $f(x)$, has a Fourier decomposition similar to the one shown for temporal signals; that is,

$$f(x) = \frac{1}{2\pi} \int_{-\infty}^{\infty} F(k_x) \, \exp(jk_x x) \, dk_x$$

$$= \mathcal{F}_{(k_x)}^{-1}[F(k_x)],$$

where k_x is the radian spatial frequency domain (units = radians/meter; the same as wavenumber), and

$$F(k_x) = \int_{-\infty}^{\infty} f(x) \, \exp(-jk_x x) \, dx$$

$$= \mathcal{F}_{(x)}[f(x)].$$

Example: A rectangular pulse (indicator) function in the u domain is defined by

$$i(u) \equiv \begin{cases} 1, & \text{if } u \in [-L, L]; \\ 0, & \text{otherwise.} \end{cases}$$

Note that $[-L, L]$ is the support region of $i(u)$. The spatial Fourier transform of this signal with respect to u is the sinc function in the k_u domain:

$$I(k_u) = 2L \; \frac{\sin(k_u L)}{k_u L}$$

$$= 2L \; \text{sinc}(k_u L).$$

Figure 1.1 shows a rectangular pulse and its Fourier transform.

The sinc function is a sinusoidal signal, that is, $\sin(k_u L)$, that is damped by an amplitude function, $\frac{1}{k_u}$, as $|k_u|$ approaches infinity. The sinc function has zero-crossings at

$$k_u = 2\pi \frac{n}{2L},$$

for $n = \pm 1, \pm 2, \pm 3, \ldots$. The spatial frequency region that resides between the first two zero-crossings of the sinc function on the two (positive and negative) sides of the k_u axis, that is,

$$k_u \in [2\pi \frac{-1}{2L}, 2\pi \frac{1}{2L}],$$

is called the *main lobe* of the sinc function. The two spatial frequency regions identified via

$$k_u \in [2\pi \frac{n-1}{2L}, 2\pi \frac{n}{2L}]$$

$$k_u \in [2\pi \frac{-n}{2L}, 2\pi \frac{1-n}{2L}],$$

are called the n-th *side lobes* of the sinc function.

- *In practical problems of signal processing and communication theory, the support of the sinc function is approximated by its main lobe and a few, for example, one or two, of its side lobes. This fact is extensively used to analyze finite aperture effects in array imaging systems, as we will see in the following chapters.*

A unit *delta* function, denoted by $\delta(\cdot)$, is defined to be the limit of a rectangular pulse as its duration goes to zero at the same rate that its height goes to infinity; that is,

$$\delta(u) \equiv \lim_{L \to 0} \frac{1}{2L} \; i(u).$$

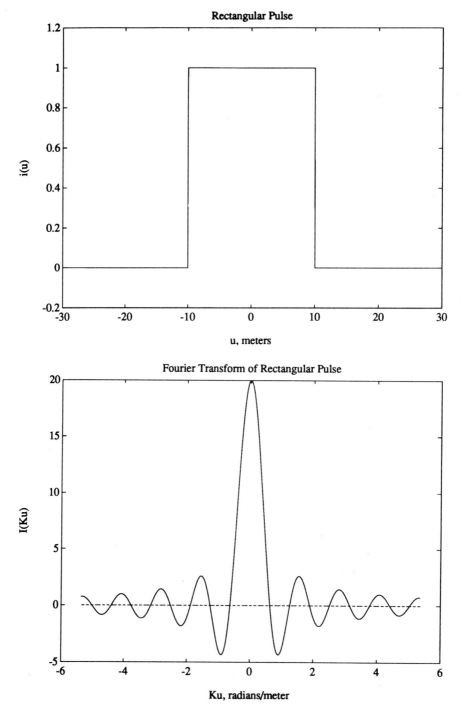

Figure 1.1 A rectangular pulse and its Fourier transform.

The Fourier transform of the delta function is a constant

$$\mathcal{F}_{(u)}[\delta(u)] = 1,$$

for all $k_u \in (-\infty, \infty)$.

Band-Limited Signals

$p(t)$ is said to be a band-limited signal if $P(\omega)$ is nonzero only within a finite region in the ω domain. Conversely, $P(\omega)$ is a band-limited signal if the support region of $p(t)$ on the time axis is finite. A signal cannot be band-limited in both the time and temporal frequency domains.

If

$$P(\omega) = 0 \quad \text{for } \omega \notin [-\omega_0, \omega_0],$$

where ω_0 is a constant, then $p(t)$ is a lowpass signal. If

$$P(\omega) = 0 \quad \text{for } \omega \notin [\omega_1, \omega_2],$$

where ω_1 and ω_2 are constants, then $p(t)$ is a bandpass signal. We will examine methods for representing and processing bandpass signals. Clearly, the class of lowpass signals is a special case of the class of bandpass signals with $\omega_0 \equiv \omega_2 = -\omega_1$.

1.2 PROPERTIES OF FOURIER TRANSFORM

Earlier, we emphasized the fact that Fourier transform (decomposition) is an information-preserving tool to transfer information from a domain to its Fourier counterpart domain (e.g., ω is the Fourier counterpart domain for t, and vice versa). One may ask why it is required to transform information via the Fourier transform or other means.

- *The utility of Fourier transform is in facilitating the analysis of linear shift-invariant systems and, in particular for our applications, system analysis for imaging systems.*

In this section, we outline some of the properties of Fourier transform that are extensively used to examine linear systems in control and communication theory. In addition to these properties, we will heavily exploit another Fourier transform property in formulating the analysis of array imaging systems. This property, which we refer to as the *spatial Doppler* phenomenon, will be introduced later in this chapter.

Linearity

Let $P_1(\omega)$ and $P_2(\omega)$ be the Fourier transforms for $p_1(t)$ and $p_2(t)$, respectively. We define $p(t)$ to be the following linear combination of $p_1(t)$ and $p_2(t)$:

$$p(t) \equiv a_1 p_1(t) + a_2 p_2(t),$$

where a_1 and a_2 are constants (i.e., time-invariant). Then, $P(\omega)$ is related to $P_1(\omega)$ and $P_2(\omega)$ via the same linear transformation in the ω domain; that is,

$$P(\omega) = a_1 P_1(\omega) + a_2 P_2(\omega).$$

Shifting

Let

$$s(t) \equiv p(t - t_0),$$

where t_0 is a constant. We say $s(t)$ is a shifted version of $p(t)$ by t_0 on the time axis. Then we have

$$S(\omega) = \exp(-j\omega t_0) \, P(\omega).$$

Figure 1.2 shows a shifted rectangular pulse and the real part of its Fourier transform. The dashed lines are the distributions of $|P(\omega)|$ and $-|P(\omega)|$; $|P(\omega)|$ is called the *envelope* or magnitude function for $S(\omega)$.

- *The envelope function of the shifted signal is invariant of the shift value t_0.*

- *The shift information is embedded in the sinusoidal signal $\exp(-j\omega t_0)$ that is a linear phase function of ω. Thus, a shift in one domain results in the addition of a* **linear** *phase function in the Fourier counterpart domain.*

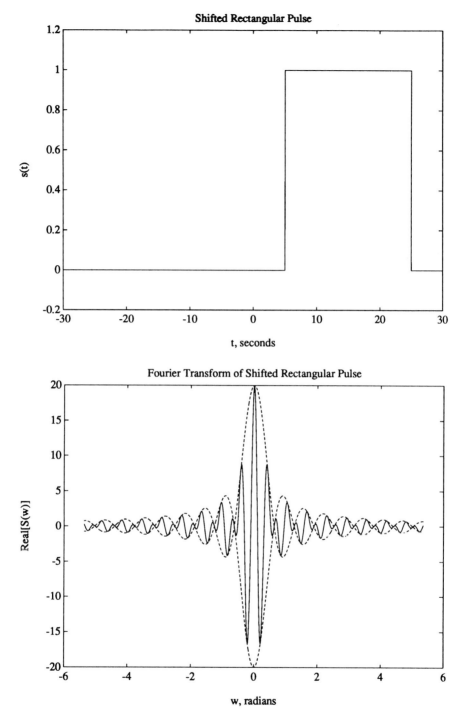

Figure 1.2 A shifted rectangular pulse and real part of its
Fourier transform.

Scaling

If

$$s(t) = p(at),$$

where a is a constant, then

$$S(\omega) = \frac{1}{|a|} P(\frac{\omega}{a}).$$

Shifting and time scaling properties will be examined further in Section 1.5.

Differentiation and Integration

If

$$s(t) \equiv \frac{d}{dt} p(t),$$

then

$$S(\omega) = j\omega P(\omega).$$

Conversely, if

$$s(t) \equiv \int_{-\infty}^{t} p(t) \ dt,$$

then,

$$S(\omega) = \frac{1}{j\omega} P(\omega).$$

Duality

Let $P(\omega)$ be the Fourier transform of $p(t)$. If

$$s(t) = P(2\pi t),$$

[note that $P(\cdot)$ can be a function of any variable] then

$$S(\omega) = p(\frac{-\omega}{2\pi}).$$

- *This property refers to the fact that whatever tools, principles, flexibilities, etc., that Fourier analysis brings to the study of signals and systems in a given domain (e.g., time), there exist dual forms of those tools, principles, flexibilities, etc., for the study of signals and systems in the Fourier counterpart domain (temporal frequency). Thus, all operational properties on a signal in any domain have an analogous form for the signal in the Fourier counterpart domain.*

Convolution

Convolution of two signals in the time domain, for example, $p(t)$ and $h(t)$, is defined by the following operation:

$$s(t) \equiv p(t) \; * \; h(t)$$

$$= \int_{-\infty}^{\infty} p(\tau) \, h(t - \tau) \, d\tau,$$

where $*$ denotes convolution in the time domain. In the frequency domain, this translates to the following relationship:

$$S(\omega) = P(\omega) \, H(\omega).$$

- *The utility of the convolution property is in simplifying the analysis of inverse as well as forward problems of linear shift-invariant systems that are governed by complicated integro-differential equations.*

The dual form of this property is that if

$$s(t) = p(t) \, h(t),$$

then

$$S(\omega) = \frac{1}{2\pi} \, P(\omega) \; * \; H(\omega)$$

$$= \frac{1}{2\pi} \int_{-\infty}^{\infty} p(\alpha) \, H(\omega - \alpha) \, d\omega,$$

where $*$ now denotes convolution in the frequency domain. See also Section 1.4.

Amplitude (Linear) Modulation

If

$$s(t) \equiv \exp(j\omega_c t)\, p(t),$$

where ω_c, called the *carrier frequency*, is a constant, then

$$S(\omega) = P(\omega - \omega_c).$$

Modulation property is the dual form of the time shifting property: a linear phase function in the time domain results in a shift transformation in the frequency domain. We say that $p(t)$ *amplitude* modulates the complex *sinusoidal carrier* at frequency ω_c to produce $s(t)$. Amplitude modulation (AM) is also referred to as *linear* modulation [2],[8]. Figure 1.3 shows the real part of an AM signal, which resulted from a rectangular pulse amplitude-modulating a sinusoidal carrier, and its Fourier transform.

Suppose $p(t)$ is a lowpass signal and the support band of $P(\omega)$ is $[-\omega_0, \omega_0]$. In this case, $s(t)$, that is, the amplitude-modulated signal, is a bandpass signal, and the support band of $S(\omega)$ is

$$[\omega_1, \omega_2] \equiv [\omega_c - \omega_0, \omega_c + \omega_0].$$

Finally, $p(t)$ can be recovered from the AM signal $s(t)$ via the following operation:

$$p(t) \equiv \exp(-j\omega_c t)\, s(t),$$

which is called *baseband conversion* (i.e., from a bandpass signal to a lowpass signal). We will examine the electronic structure used to perform this conversion and its application in array imaging systems in later sections.

Nonlinear Modulation

Nonlinear modulation corresponds to the following phase functional transformation that is known as *phase* modulation (PM):

$$s(t) \equiv \exp[j\,p(t)],$$

or this form, which is called *frequency* modulation (FM):

$$s(t) \equiv \exp\left[j \int_{-\infty}^{t} p(t)\, dt\right].$$

3 1833 02166 109 2

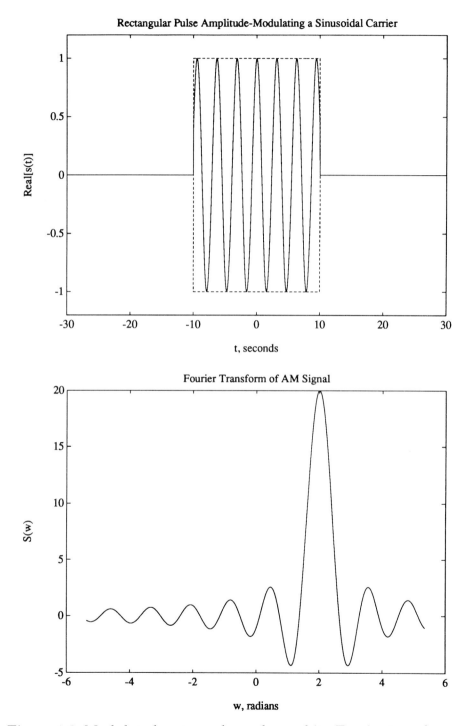

Figure 1.3 Modulated rectangular pulse and its Fourier transform.

In general, it is difficult to obtain a closed-form expression to relate $S(\omega)$ to $P(\omega)$ in nonlinear modulation. We will deal with PM/FM signals whose their Fourier transforms do have a closed-form expression and can easily be analyzed (an approach that we call spatial Doppler processing).

Consider a PM signal, for example, $s(t) = \exp[jp(t)]$. The *instantaneous (radian) frequency* of this signal is defined as

$$\omega_i(t) \equiv \frac{dp(t)}{dt}.$$

If $p(t) = \omega_c t$, that is, $s(t)$ is a complex sinusoid, then

$$\omega_i(t) = \omega_c,$$

which is a constant (time-invariant).

A *chirp* signal belongs to the class of PM waves that have the following form:

$$s(t) = \exp[j(\omega_c t + \alpha t^2)];$$

ω_c is called the *carrier frequency* and α is known as the *chirp rate*. The instantaneous frequency of a chirp signal is:

$$\omega_i(t) = \omega_c + 2\alpha t,$$

which increases linearly with time. Chirp pulses are widely used in imaging systems. The real part of a chirp signal and the real part of its Fourier transform are shown in Figure 1.4. Chirp signals will be discussed later in this chapter, and other examples of chirp pulses and their Fourier transforms will be given (see Figure 1.15).

Similarly, the instantaneous frequency of an FM wave

$$s(t) = \exp[j \int_{-\infty}^{t} p(t)\ dt],$$

is defined via

$$\omega_i(t) \equiv \frac{d}{dt} [\int_{-\infty}^{t} p(t)\ dt]$$

$$= p(t).$$

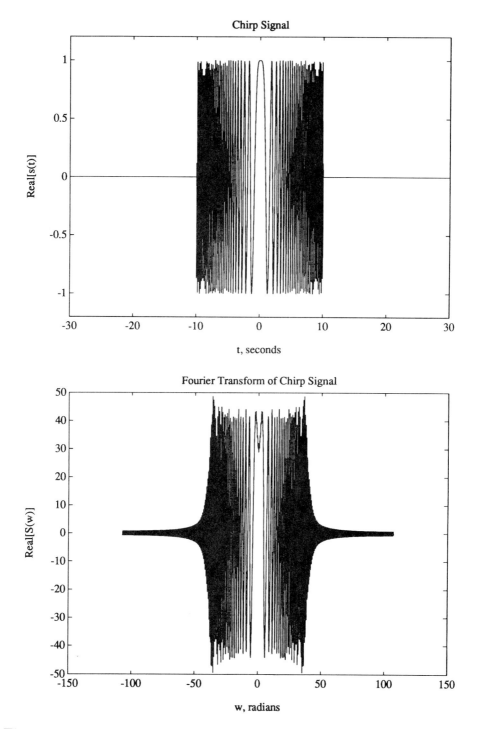

Figure 1.4 Real parts of a chirp pulse and its Fourier transform.

Single Frequency (Local) Interpretation of a PM Signal: Consider the Taylor series expansion for $p(t)$ around $t = t_0$ and its truncated version, that is,

$$p(t) = p(t_0) + (t - t_0) \left[\frac{dp(t)}{dt} \right]_{t=t_0} + \dots$$

$$= p(t_0) + (t - t_0) \, \omega_i(t_0) + \dots$$

$$\approx p(t_0) + (t - t_0) \, \omega_i(t_0).$$

Substituting the above approximation in the expression for $s(t)$ yields

$$s(t) \approx \exp[j\omega_i(t_0) \, t + j\theta_0],$$

where

$$\theta_0 \equiv p(t_0) - t_0 \, \omega_i(t_0).$$

- *The instantaneous frequency function can be used to provide a **local** interpretation for the spectral properties of a PM (or FM) signal. Within a small neighborhood of a fixed time t_0, a PM wave can be approximated via a **single** frequency sinusoidal signal with frequency $\omega_i(t_0)$ and a **constant** phase θ_0; the assumption that θ_0 is a constant is the reason why the above equation for $s(t)$ is an **approximation**.*

This interpretation can be used to obtain an approximation for the bandwidth of a PM signal, and to analyze the effects of filtering a PM wave; these are described next.

Bandwidth of a PM Signal: For a general PM (or FM) wave $s(t)$, let ω_1 and ω_2 be the minimum and maximum values of $\omega_i(t)$, respectively; that is,

$$\omega_1 \leq \omega_i(t) \leq \omega_2,$$

for all t within the support of $s(t)$ on the time axis. Then, under certain conditions [2],[8], the PM/FM wave $s(t)$ is *approximately* a band-limited signal, and the support band of $S(\omega)$ is

$$\Omega \equiv [\omega_1, \omega_2].$$

For instance, suppose $s(t)$ is a chirp signal within a finite time interval, for example,

$$s(t) = \begin{cases} \exp[j(\omega_c t + \alpha t^2)], & \text{if } t \in [t_1, t_2]; \\ 0, & \text{otherwise.} \end{cases}$$

In this case, the support band of $S(\omega)$ is approximately within $[\omega_1, \omega_2]$ where

$$\omega_1 \equiv \omega_c + 2\alpha t_1$$
$$\omega_2 \equiv \omega_c + 2\alpha t_2.$$

When $\alpha = 0$, $s(t)$ is a sinusoid that is amplitude-modulated by a rectangular pulse with support $[t_1, t_2]$ in the time domain. In this case, $S(\omega)$ is a sinc function that is shifted to $\omega = \omega_c$. The extent of the main lobe of the sinc function in the frequency domain is

$$2\omega_0 \equiv \frac{2\pi}{t_2 - t_1},$$

which is used to approximate the baseband bandwidth of $s(t)$. In fact, a better approximation for the bandwidth of a chirp signal ($\alpha \neq 0$) is

$$\Omega \equiv [\omega_1 - \omega_0, \omega_2 + \omega_0].$$

In most practical circumstances, α is sufficiently large such that

$$2\omega_0 \ll \omega_2 - \omega_1.$$

Thus, the contribution of $2\omega_0$ in the bandwidth of the chirp signal is negligible.

Recall that the Fourier transform of a Gaussian function is also a Gaussian function; that is, within a constant, we have

$$\mathcal{F}_{(t)}\left[\exp(-\frac{1}{2\sigma^2}t^2)\right] = \exp(-\frac{\sigma^2}{2}\omega^2).$$

If the Gaussian function is modulating a sinusoidal carrier, then we have

$$\mathcal{F}_{(t)}\left[\exp(j\omega_c t - \frac{1}{2\sigma^2}t^2)\right] = \exp[-\frac{\sigma^2}{2}(\omega - \omega_c)^2].$$

To find the Fourier transform of a chirp signal $s(t)$ with support $t \in [t_1, t_2]$, we can use the Gaussian Fourier pairs with

$$-\frac{1}{2\sigma^2} \equiv j\alpha.$$

This yields

$$S(\omega) \approx \begin{cases} \exp[-\frac{j}{4\alpha}(\omega - \omega_c)^2], & \text{if } \omega \in [\omega_1, \omega_2]; \\ 0, & \text{otherwise.} \end{cases}$$

Note that $S(\omega)$ is also a chirp signal with a finite duration. This can be observed in the example shown in Figure 1.4. Chirp signaling and its Fourier transform will be studied within the context of echo imaging in Section 1.7 and Figure 1.15.

Filtering a PM Signal: Let $s(t)$ be a PM (or FM) signal with instantaneous frequency $\omega_i(t)$. Suppose this PM wave is passed through a system that rejects the frequency components of $S(\omega)$ that reside outside a band, e.g., $[\omega_3, \omega_4]$. (Such a system, called a *bandpass filter*, is a special class of the linear shift-invariant systems, which is discussed in Section 1.4.) Thus, the Fourier transform of the output signal, call it $r(t)$, is

$$R(\omega) \equiv \begin{cases} S(\omega), & \text{if } \omega \in [\omega_3, \omega_4]; \\ 0, & \text{otherwise.} \end{cases}$$

In this case, within a small neighborhood of a fixed time t_0, we have

$$r(t) \approx \begin{cases} s(t) \approx \exp[j\omega_i(t_0)\, t + j\theta_0], & \text{if } \omega_i(t_0) \in [\omega_3, \omega_4]; \\ 0, & \text{otherwise.} \end{cases}$$

- *Frequency-selective filtering of a time domain PM/FM signal results in suppression of the time domain signal at the time points where the instantaneous frequency of the signal resides outside the pass-band of the frequency-selective filter. This is equivalent to a time-selective filtering where the pass-band region or regions of the time-selective filter vary with the original time domain signal's instantaneous frequency function.*

This fact will be used in the analysis of the spatial Doppler phenomenon in Section 1.12. For this discussion, we will revisit PM waves in Section 1.10, and introduce a special class of these signals that describe/represent coherent wave propagation in time and space.

Poisson Sum Formula

The evenly spaced train of unit impulse (delta) functions separated by, for example, Δ_t is defined to be

$$g(t) \equiv \sum_{n=-\infty}^{\infty} \delta(t - n\Delta_t).$$

This signal may also be expressed in terms of sinusoidal signals as follows:

$$g(t) = \frac{1}{\Delta_t} \sum_{n=-\infty}^{\infty} \exp(j\frac{2\pi n}{\Delta_t}t),$$

which is known as the Poisson sum formula. From this sum, one can see that the Fourier transform of the impulse train is another impulse train:

$$G(\omega) = \frac{2\pi}{\Delta_t} \sum_{n=-\infty}^{\infty} \delta(\omega - \frac{2\pi n}{\Delta_t}).$$

Sampling

The *delta-sampled* version of time intervals separated by Δ_t is

$$p_\delta(t) \equiv \sum_{n=-\infty}^{\infty}$$

$$= p(t)$$

$$= p(t)\ g$$

where $g(t)$ is the unit impulse tra following in the frequency domai

$$P_\delta(\omega) = \frac{1}{2\pi} P(\omega$$

$$= \frac{1}{\Delta_t} P(\omega)$$

$$= \frac{1}{\Delta_t} \sum_{n=-\infty}^{\infty} P(\omega - \frac{2\pi n}{\Delta_t}).$$

- *This implies that the Fourier transform of the delta-sampled signal is composed of repeated versions of $P(\omega)$ centered at $\frac{2\pi n}{\Delta_t}$.*

We call

$$P(\omega - \frac{2\pi n}{\Delta_t}) = \mathcal{F}_{(t)}\left[\, p(t)\ \exp(j\frac{2\pi n}{\Delta_t}t)\,\right],$$

which is the Fourier transform of $p(t)$ linearly modulating the n-th harmonic $\exp(j\frac{2\pi n}{\Delta_t}t)$, the n-th *linear harmonic* component.

Figure 1.5 shows a sampled rectangular pulse and a portion of its Fourier transform. The real parts of a sampled chirp signal and its Fourier transform are depicted in Figure 1.6.

Suppose $p(t)$ is a band-limited signal, and the support band of $P(\omega)$ is $[-\omega_0, \omega_0]$, with

$$\omega_0 \ \le \ \frac{2\pi}{2\Delta_t}.$$

In this case, the support regions for the repeated versions of $P(\omega)$ that make up $P_\delta(\omega)$ (the linear harmonic components), that is,

$$P(\omega - \frac{2\pi n}{\Delta_t}),$$

$n = 0, \pm 1, \pm 2, \ldots$, do not overlap with each other. In this case, the linear harmonic component corresponding to $n = 0$ defined in the frequency region

$$[\frac{-2\pi}{2\Delta_t}, \frac{2\pi}{2\Delta_t}],$$

is the distribution of $P(\omega)$.

Thus, one may recover $P(\omega)$ form the delta-sampled signal via the following windowing/filtering operation:

$$P(\omega) = H(\omega)\ P_\delta(\omega),$$

where $H(\omega)$ is a rectangular (indicator) function defined by

$$H(\omega) \equiv \begin{cases} \Delta_t, & \text{if } |\omega| \le \frac{2\pi}{2\Delta_t}; \\ 0, & \text{otherwise.} \end{cases}$$

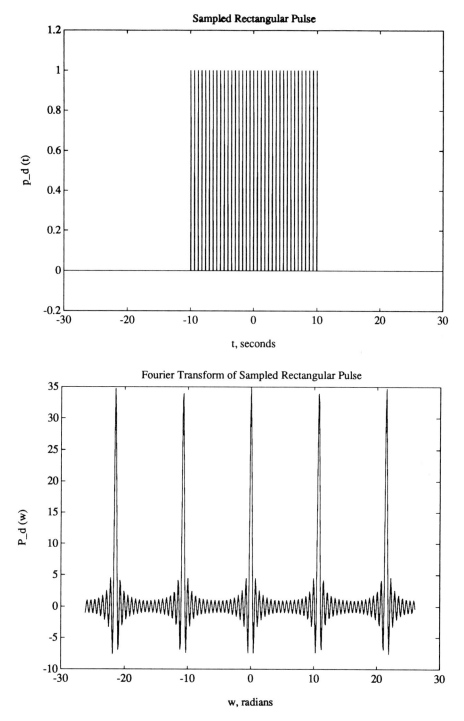

Figure 1.5 Sampled rectangular pulse and its Fourier transform.

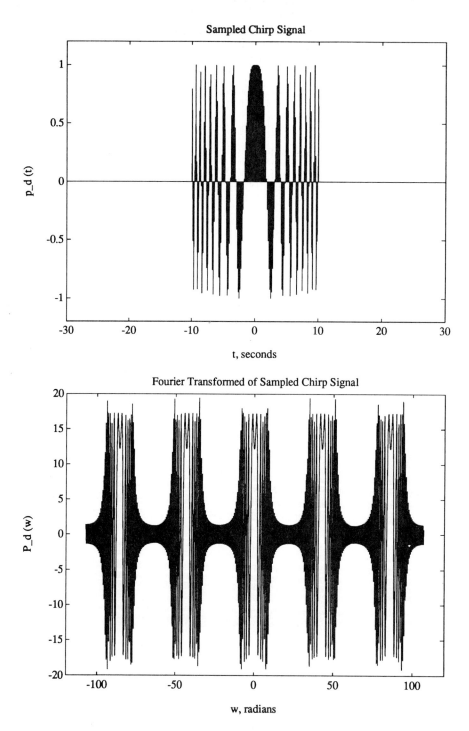

Figure 1.6 Sampled chirp pulse and its Fourier transform.

20

The above frequency-selective filtering is equivalent to the following operation in the time domain:

$$p(t) = \sum_{n=-\infty}^{\infty} p(n\Delta_t) \operatorname{sinc}\left[\frac{\pi(t - n\Delta_t)}{\Delta_t}\right].$$

This is called *reconstruction* or *interpolation* of the original signal from its delta-sampled signal.

The success of this operation hinges on the constraint

$$\omega_0 \leq \frac{2\pi}{2\Delta_t},$$

which is known as the *Nyquist* sampling criterion for *aliasing-free* or *error-free* reconstruction of $p(t)$ from the sampled data $p(n\Delta_t)$'s. The linear harmonic components $P(\omega - \frac{2\pi n}{\Delta_t})$, $n = \pm 1, \pm 2, \ldots$ (or $n \neq 0$), result in aliasing if the Nyquist criterion is not satisfied.

The issue of sampling and its dual form, that is, sampling in the frequency domain, and aliasing-free processing and reconstruction from the sampled signal will be extensively encountered in array imaging systems.

1.3 DISCRETE FOURIER TRANSFORM

Let $f(x)$ be a periodic signal composed of evenly spaced delta functions, for example,

$$f(x) = \sum_{\ell=-\infty}^{\infty} \underbrace{\sum_{n=-N/2}^{N/2-1} f_n \, \delta[x - (n + N\ell)\Delta_x]}_{One\ period},$$

where Δ_x is the spacing between two consecutive delta functions and $N\Delta_x$ is the period (see Figure 1.7). This model provides a link between a discrete sequence and evenly spaced samples of a continuous signal [6]. Using the forward and inverse Fourier integrals, one can show that

$$F(k_x) = 2\pi \sum_{\ell=-\infty}^{\infty} \sum_{m=-N/2}^{N/2-1} F_m \, \delta[k_x - (m + N\ell)\Delta_{k_x}],$$

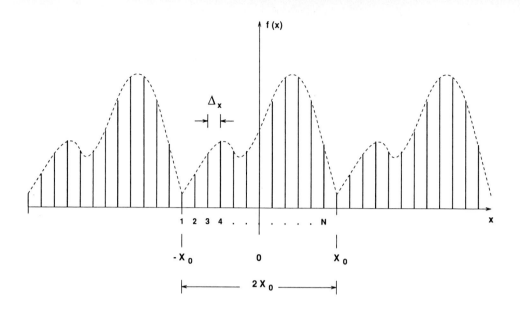

**Depiction of a Discrete Fourier Transform Pair:
The Spatial Domain Signal**

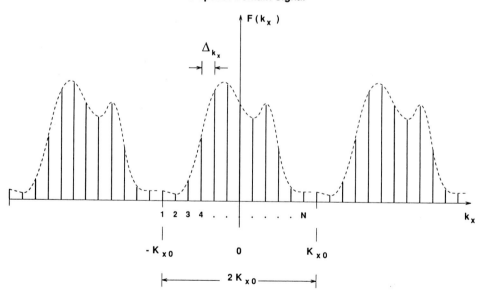

**Depiction of a Discrete Fourier Transform Pair:
The Spatial Frequency Domain Signal**

Figure 1.7 A discrete Fourier transform pair.

where

$$F_m = \sum_{n=-N/2}^{N/2-1} f_n \exp(-j\frac{2\pi}{N}mn)$$

$$f_n = \frac{1}{N} \sum_{m=-N/2}^{N/2-1} F_m \exp(j\frac{2\pi}{N}mn)$$

(1.1)

and

$$N \, \Delta_x \, \Delta_{k_x} \; = \; 2\pi.$$

(1.2)

Equations (1.1) and (1.2) are called the Discrete Fourier Transform (DFT) equations. It should be noted $F(k_x)$ *is also a periodic signal* that is composed of evenly spaced delta functions (see Figure 1.7).

- *In practice, we deal with continuous functions that are not band-limited in space/time and frequency domains. For storage and processing purposes in a computer, we represent (approximate) them via periodic functions that are made up of a finite number of evenly spaced delta functions (N sampled data). The main period of $f(x)$ [or $F(k_x)$] is assumed to be the region in the x (or k_x) domain, for example, $x \in [-X_0, X_0)$ [or $k_x \in [-K_{x0}, K_{x0})$], where most, for example, 95 percent, of its energy is concentrated (X_0 and K_{x0} are known constants). $[-X_0, X_0)$ and $[-K_{x0}, K_{x0})$ are called the* **effective** *support bandwidths of $f(x)$ and $F(k_x)$, respectively.*

Noting the fact that

$$2X_0 = N \, \Delta_x$$
$$2K_{x0} = N \, \Delta k_x,$$

we can write from (1.2) the following equations that are the Nyquist sampling rate (constraint) for representing/recovering a lowpass signal from its sampled data:

$$\Delta_x = \frac{\pi}{K_{x0}}$$
$$\Delta_{k_x} = \frac{\pi}{X_0}.$$

1.4 LINEAR SHIFT-INVARIANT SYSTEMS

A linear shift-invariant (LSI) system is uniquely identified by its impulse response, that is, the system's output when the input is a delta function. For instance, a time domain LSI (also called LTI, linear time-invariant) system with impulse response $h(t)$ produces the following output $p(t)$ for an arbitrary input $a(t)$:

$$p(t) = \int_{-\infty}^{\infty} a(\tau)\, h(t - \tau)\, d\tau$$
$$= a(t) \ast h(t),$$

where $\ast$ denotes convolution in the time domain. Furthermore, we have the following relationship in the temporal frequency domain for the convolution in the time domain:

$$P(\omega) = A(\omega)\, H(\omega).$$

Duality

If $R(k_u)$ is the output of an LSI system in the k_u domain with impulse response $I(k_u)$ when the input is $S(k_u)$, then

$$R(k_u) = S(k_u) \ast I(k_u)$$
$$r(u) = s(u)\, i(u),$$

where $\ast$ now denotes convolution in the k_u domain.

1.5 COORDINATE TRANSFORMATION

Let x' be a generalized (nonlinear) transformation of x defined via

$$x' \equiv g(x).$$

For simplicity of discussion, we assume $g(\cdot)$ is a one-to-one and differentiable transformation. The Jacobian of this transformation is defined by

$$J(x) \equiv |\frac{dx'}{dx}| = |\frac{dg(x)}{dx}|$$
$$J'(x') \equiv |\frac{dx}{dx'}| = \frac{1}{J(x)}$$

Consider an integrable signal $s(x)$ and its mapping in the x' domain:

$$s'(x') \equiv s(x).$$

Then, we have [3]

$$\int_{x_1'}^{x_2'} s'(x') \, dx' = \int_{x_1}^{x_2} s(x) \, J(x) \, dx$$

$$\int_{x_1'}^{x_2'} s'(x') \, J'(x') \, dx' = \int_{x_1}^{x_2} s(x) \, dx$$

where $x_1' = g(x_1)$ and $x_2' = g(x_2)$.

Linear Transformation

Consider the case when $g(\cdot)$ is a linear transformation, for example,

$$x' = g(x) = ax + x_0,$$

with the Jacobian

$$J(x) = |a|,$$

where a and x_0 are constants. Moreover, let

$$f'(x') = f(x).$$

From the Fourier transform equation, we have

$$F'(k_{x'}) = \int_{-\infty}^{\infty} f'(x') \, \exp(-j k_{x'} x') \, dx'.$$

Using the transformed integral relationship, we obtain

$$F'(k_{x'}) = \int_{-\infty}^{\infty} f(x) \, \exp[-j k_{x'}(ax + x_0)] \, |a| \, dx$$

$$= |a| \, \exp(-j k_{x'} \, x_0) \int_{-\infty}^{\infty} f(x) \, \exp(-j a \, k_{x'} x) \, dx \qquad (1.3)$$

$$= |a| \, \exp(-j k_{x'} \, x_0) \, F(a \, k_{x'}).$$

(1.3) provides a one-to-one relationship between Fourier components of $f(x)$ and its transformation $f'(x')$.

Delta Function Transformation

Suppose $g(\cdot)$ is a nonlinear transformation and

$$s(x) \equiv \delta(x - x_0),$$

where x_0 ,the location of the delta function on the x-axis, is a constant. The transformed version of this delta function in the x' domain is [3]

$$\begin{aligned} s'(x') &\equiv J(x)\ \delta\big[g(x) - g(x_0)\big] \\ &\equiv \frac{1}{J'(x')}\ \delta(x' - x_0'), \end{aligned}$$

where

$$x_0' \equiv g(x_0).$$

Now consider a unit impulse train in the x domain, for example,

$$s(x) \equiv \sum_{n=\infty}^{\infty} \delta(x - x_n),$$

where $x_n \equiv n\Delta_x$, $n = -\infty, \ldots, \infty$, represent the evenly spaced locations of the delta functions in the x domain. Using the transformed property of the delta function, the transformed version of the unit impulse train in the x' domain becomes

$$s'(x') = \frac{1}{J'(x')} \sum_{n=\infty}^{\infty} \delta(x' - x_n'),$$

where

$$\begin{aligned} x_n' &\equiv g(x_n) \\ &= g(n\Delta_x), \end{aligned}$$

are the locations of the delta functions in the x' domain.

- *If $g(\cdot)$ is not a linear transformation, then the impulses that make up $s'(x')$ are not evenly-space since x'_n's are not evenly positioned on the x'-axis, and the amplitude of the impulses are not the same since $J'(x')$ is not a constant.*

These properties will be used in Chapter 2 to examine the spectral distribution of unevenly spaced data and methods to interpolate from them.

1.6 COHERENT PROCESSING OF BANDPASS SIGNALS

We next examine a processing issue associated with the processing of bandpass signals in imaging systems. Using modulation theory, a bandpass signal, for example, $p(t)$, can be expressed in the following form (also known as *quadrature* representation [2]):

$$
\begin{aligned}
p(t) &\equiv a(t)\ \cos(\omega_c t + \theta) \\
&= \underbrace{a(t)\ \cos\theta}_{In-phase\ component}\ \cos\omega_c t - \underbrace{a(t)\ \sin\theta}_{Quadrature\ component}\ \sin\omega_c t \\
&= \frac{1}{2}\ a(t)\ [\ \exp(j\omega_c t + j\theta)\ + \exp(-j\omega_c t - j\theta)\ ],
\end{aligned}
$$

where ω_c, called the carrier frequency, is a constant, and $a(t)$ is a *lowpass* signal with its band defined by $[-\omega_0, \omega_0]$. This relationship translates to a shift operation in the frequency domain; that is,

$$
P(\omega) = \frac{1}{2}\ A(\omega - \omega_c)\ \exp(j\theta)\ +\ \frac{1}{2}\ A(\omega + \omega_c)\ \exp(-j\theta).
$$

Figure 1.8 shows a system, known as a coherent receiver [2],[8], for processing and storage of the information in a bandpass signal such as $p(t)$ or any linear combination of $p(t)$ [i.e., a sum of delayed versions of $p(t)$], and its equivalent complex representation, that is,

$$
p(t) = a(t)\ \exp[j(\omega_c t + \theta)].
$$

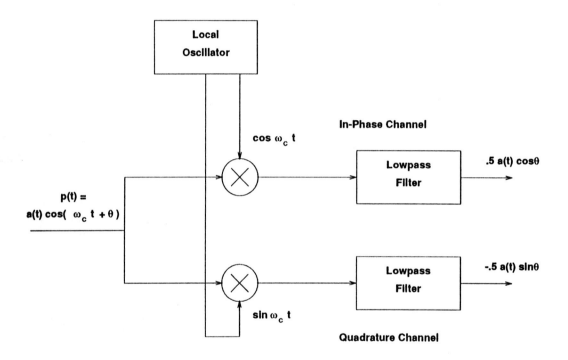

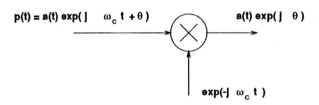

Figure 1.8 Coherent receiver for baseband conversion of bandpass signals.

- *The need for such processing, known as **baseband** (bandpass to low-pass) conversion, arises from the fact that an imaging system, via an electronic device called Analog to Digital (A/D) converter, must sample the incoming signal/information $p(t)$, or a linear combination of it, to be stored in a computer for further processing (inversion algorithm that yields the desired image). The Nyquist sampling rate for the lowpass signal $a(t)$ is commonly much smaller than the required sampling rate for the bandpass signal $p(t)$.*

The Nyquist sampling rate for processing $p(t)$ without baseband conversion is

$$\Delta_t \leq \frac{\pi}{\omega_c + \omega_0},$$

where $\omega_c + \omega_0$ is the highest frequency in $p(t)$. However, the Nyquist sampling rate for the baseband signal, that is, $a(t)$, is

$$\Delta_t \leq \frac{\pi}{\omega_0}.$$

The baseband conversion and delta sampling on $p(t)$ can be represented via the following:

$$\exp(j\theta)\, a_\delta(t) = \Big[\ \underbrace{p(t)\ \exp(-j\omega_c t)}_{Baseband\ conversion}\ \Big] \underbrace{\sum_{n=-\infty}^{\infty} \delta(t - n\Delta_t)}_{Delta\ sampling},$$

where $a_\delta(t)$ is the delta-sampled signal for $a(t)$ and $\Delta_t \leq \frac{\pi}{\omega_0}$. We may change the order of baseband conversion and delta sampling to obtain

$$\exp(j\theta)\, a_\delta(t) = \Big[p(t) \sum_{n=-\infty}^{\infty} \delta(t - n\Delta_t) \Big] \exp(-j\omega_c t).$$

- *This result indicates that we may **undersample** the bandpass signal $p(t)$ and yet recover its information at baseband, that is, $a(t)$, without aliasing via baseband conversion of the aliased signal.*

This is an important property for processing bandpass **spatial** signals. This is due to the fact that we do not have access to the *analog* or *continuous* form of spatial signals. For processing a bandpass spatial signal, we undersample the signal at its baseband rate and store it in a digital computer. Then, we perform baseband conversion on the aliased signal in the digital computer to retrieve the unaliased baseband signal. We will encounter these scenarios in synthetic aperture array imaging of a *squint* target in Chapter 4.

Theoretically, one may use either of the two methods, that is, baseband conversion followed by sampling or sampling followed by baseband conversion, on most *time* domain signals. However, the channels that the time signals propagate in are usually cluttered with other signals. For instance, in certain communication problems, a time domain signal has to be passed through various analog bandpass and lowpass filters before being sampled [2]. Thus, the practical processing of a temporal bandpass signal involves baseband conversion followed by sampling.

1.7 ONE-DIMENSIONAL ECHO IMAGING

We now examine an inverse problem encountered in radar, sonar, diagnostic medicine and geophysical exploration that is called echo imaging. (The term *imaging* is generally used to identify two or higher dimensional inverse problems though we also use it here for one-dimensional inverse problems.). The target model and transmitter/receiver structure given for this one-dimensional inverse problem will also be used for higher dimensional echo imaging problems.

Target Model

The target model in an inverse problem helps us to identify the target's physical properties that could be retrieved from the measurements. In echo imaging problems, one may model the target in two ways. One model assumes that the target region is composed of M *point* (zero-size) reflectors embedded in a homogeneous region, for example, air or water; the number of point targets, that is, M, could be finite or infinite.

Each target is identified by its reflection coefficient f_n that depends on its physical properties (e.g., index of refraction and density), and its coordinates x_n in the spatial x domain ($n = 1, 2, \ldots, M$). An example of such a target model is shown in Figure 1.9. This model is suited for radar problems where a target can be viewed as a combination of infinite point reflectors on its surface.

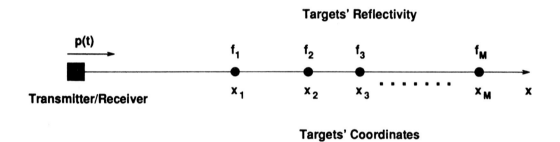

One-Dimensional Echo Imaging

Figure 1.9 System geometry for echo imaging.

The other target model assumes that the target is composed of several (e.g., M) homogenous *media*. This model describes the targets in diagnostic medicine (e.g., fat, tissue, water and blood are the homogenous media), and geophysical exploration (e.g., salt water, oil, sand and rock layers make up the homogeneous media). For this model, the *boundaries* of the homogeneous regions are located at x_n, $n = 1, 2, \ldots, M$. Moreover, f_n's represent the reflection coefficients at those boundaries. These coefficients depend on variations of a physical property known as *impedance* in two adjacent homogenous media.

- The **speed** of wave propagation in each homogeneous medium also depends on the physical properties of that medium and, thus, varies from one medium to another. In spite of this fact, the system model that will be shown later assumes that the propagation speed is a constant. This is not an appropriate approximation in most practical medical and geophysical echo imaging problems. However, the analysis of the type of errors introduced via the above-mentioned approximation and whether there exists methods to reduce those errors are not addressed in this book. Chapter 7 provides a more elaborate discussion of this issue.

System Model

The target region is irradiated by a transmitter located at $x = 0$ that sends a time-dependent signal $p(t)$. The transmitted signal $p(t)$ is said to be a *pulsed* signal if it has a finite duration in the time domain. The leading edge of the transmitted signal $p(t)$ reaches the first target at time $t_1 = \frac{x_1}{c}$, where c is the speed of wave propagation in the medium where the targets reside. Thus, the time-dependent signal that reaches the first target is

$$p(t - t_1).$$

After reflection from the first target, the signal

$$f_1 \ p(t - t_1),$$

travels backward (is echoed back) towards the transmitter/receiver and reaches $x = 0$ (the transmitter/receiver location) t_1 seconds later. Thus, the receiver, also located at $x = 0$, records the following signal:

$$s_1(t) \equiv f_1 \ p(t - t_1 - t_1)$$
$$= f_1 \ p(t - 2t_1).$$

The remaining portion of the signal that reaches the first target, that is,

$$p(t - t_1) - f_1 p(t - t_1) = (1 - f_1) \ p(t - t_1),$$

travels forward towards the second target. It is assumed that

$$|f_n| \ll 1,$$

for all available n, such that the signal transmitted forward can be approximated via

$$(1 - f_1)\, p(t - t_1) \approx p(t - t_1).$$

This implies that the signal experienced by the second target is the original transmitted signal delayed by $t_2 \equiv \frac{x_2}{c}$, that is, $p(t - t_2)$, and is *approximately* unaffected by the wave reflection at $x = x_1$. Using the analysis that we performed on the signal echoed from the first target, we can show that the receiver records the following signal that is due to reflection from the second target:

$$s_2(t) \equiv f_2\, p(t - 2t_2).$$

The receiver records the echoes from all reflectors from the target scene. This can be represented via the following signal that is the sum of all waves reflected from the targets:

$$
\begin{aligned}
s(t) &\equiv \sum_{n=1}^{M} s_n(t) \\
&= \sum_{n=1}^{M} f_n\, p(t - 2t_n),
\end{aligned}
\tag{1.4}
$$

where $t_n \equiv \frac{x_n}{c}$.

Monostatic and Quasi-Monostatic Transmitter/Receiver

An imaging geometry where the coordinates of the transmitter and receiver are identical is referred to as a **monostatic** *imaging system.* Figure 1.10 depicts the transmitter/receiver structure for a monostatic echo imaging system. Note that

$$2t_n = \frac{2x_n}{c},$$

is the round-trip time (delay) for the wave to reach the n-th target located at x_n and back to $x = 0$, that is, the receiver's coordinates. In *pulsed* echo imaging, the duration of the pulsed signal $p(t)$ is typically chosen to be shorter than the smallest round-trip time delay from the target region. Thus, the same hardware used for the signal transmission can be used as the receiver to record the echoed signals (see Figure 1.10).

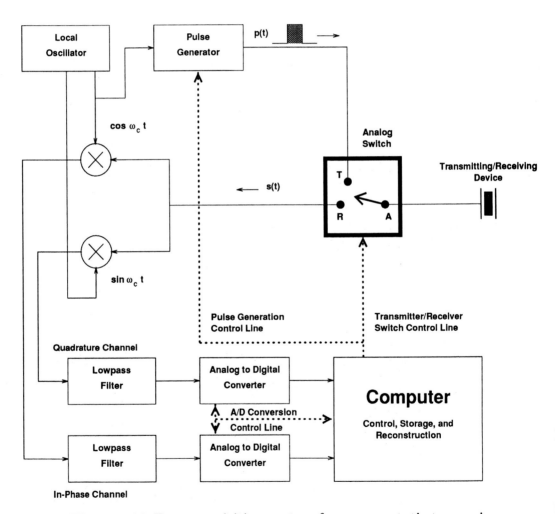

Figure 1.10 Data acquisition system for a monostatic transceiver.

In this setup, the transmitter and receiver use the same electronic circuitry via a switch: the switch connects the pulse generator to the transmitter/receiver device during the pulse duration (i.e., when the signal source is ON), and then switches the transmitter/receiver device to the coherent processor channel (i.e., when the signal source is OFF).

We denote the time duration of the pulsed signal with τ_0. A target is said to be too *close* to the transmitter/receiver to be detected when its round-trip delay is smaller than the pulse duration; that is,

$$\frac{2x_n}{c} < \tau_0.$$

In this case, all or a portion of the echoed signal from the n-th target, that is, $s_n(t)$, reaches the transmitter/receiver when the switch is set at the transmit mode. Thus, this portion of $s_n(t)$ cannot be recorded by the receiver.

It is possible to circumvent this problem by using a separate device (e.g., radar antenna) to receive the incoming echoed signals (see Figure 1.11). Generally, *an imaging geometry where the transmitter and receiver electronic circuitry are not identical is referred to as a* **bistatic** *imaging system.* However, the bistatic scenario for echo imaging shown in Figure 1.11 is commonly called *quasi-monostatic.* This is due to the fact that *the term bistatic is mainly used to identify imaging systems where the* **coordinates** *of the transmitter and receiver are not identical.*

- *Quasi-monostatic systems are useful for transmitting long duration signals, called* **Continuous Wave** *(CW) signaling. In those scenarios, the user simultaneously illuminates the target region and records the resulting echoed signals from the target.*

- *In radar imaging problems, a device called circulator [15] is also used in conjunction with a monostatic system for CW transmission and reception.*

The utility of pulsed signaling and CW signaling will become evident in our discussion on echo imaging of moving targets and temporal Doppler phenomenon.

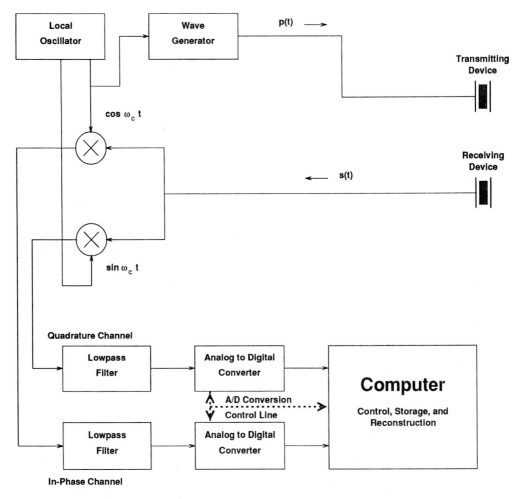

Figure 1.11 Data acquisition system for a quasi-monostatic transceiver.

Inversion

Our objective in this imaging problem is to identify the targets from the measurements of the signal $s(t)$. For this purpose, we rewrite the system model in (1.4) via the following time domain convolution (linear model):

$$s(t) = p(t) * f_0(x), \tag{1.5}$$

with

$$x \equiv \frac{ct}{2}, \tag{1.6}$$

(note that x *is a linear transformation of* t), where

$$f_0(x) \equiv \sum_{n=1}^{M} f_n \, \delta(x - x_n),$$

is a spatial domain signal that is composed of delta functions at the coordinates of the targets in the imaging scene; the amplitude of the delta function at $x = x_n$ is equal to the target's reflectivity at that point (see Figure 1.12).

Thus, our imaging problem is solved if we could retrieve $f_0(x)$ from $s(t)$. For this process, one has to *reverse* the system model convolution in (1.5) to recover $f_0(x)$ from the observed signal, that is, *deconvolve* the source function $p(t)$ from the measurement $s(t)$. This operation is called *source deconvolution*.

- *All imaging problems examined in this book involve* **linear** *system models, similar to a multidimensional convolution, relating the target information to the observed signal. The inverse or imaging problem is to seek a computationally manageable multidimensional signal processing method to perform the* **source deconvolution**.

The inversion or deconvolution in one-dimensional echo imaging is formulated via taking the temporal Fourier transform of both sides of (1.5) that yields

$$S(\omega) = P(\omega) \, F_0(k_x),$$

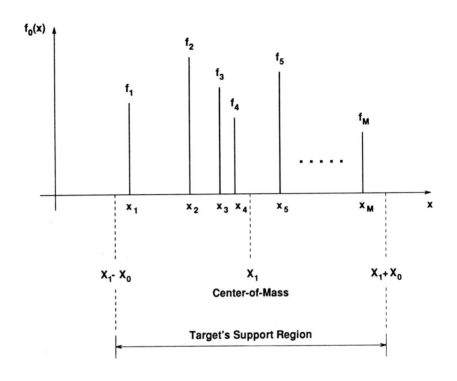

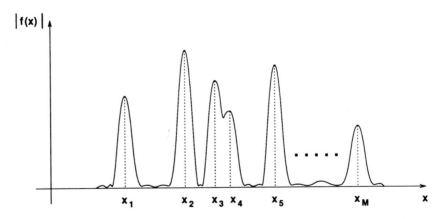

Figure 1.12 Reconstructed target function with an infinite bandwidth transmitted signal, $f_0(x)$, and a finite bandwidth transmitted signal, $|f(x)|$.

where, based on the linear transformation property of Fourier transform (1.3), k_x is a linear function of ω:

$$k_x \equiv \frac{2\omega}{c}. \tag{1.7}$$

Thus, we can write

$$F_0(k_x) = \frac{S(\omega)}{P(\omega)}, \tag{1.8}$$

provided that $P(\omega) \neq 0$ for all ω.

In practice, however, $p(t)$ is a bandpass signal of the following form (quadrature representation):

$$p(t) = a(t) \, \exp(j\omega_c t),$$

or, equivalently

$$P(\omega) = A(\omega - \omega_c),$$

where $A(\omega)$ is a baseband signal within $[-\omega_0, \omega_0]$ (effective bandwidth; see Figure 1.13). Due to the bandpass nature of $p(t)$, we are not capable f reconstructing $F_0(k_x)$ from the division in (1.8), that is, $\frac{S(\omega)}{P(\omega)}$. However, we are capable of reconstructing a bandpass filtered version of $f_0(x)$ that still contains useful target information. For this purpose, we first find the temporal Fourier transform of both sides of (1.4); this yields

$$S(\omega) = \sum_{n=1}^{M} f_n \, P(\omega) \, \exp(-j\omega \frac{2x_n}{c})$$
$$= P(\omega) \sum_{n=1}^{M} f_n \exp(-j\omega \frac{2x_n}{c}). \tag{1.9}$$

As we mentioned earlier, $p(t)$ is a bandpass signal. Suppose the support band of $P(\omega)$ is

$$[\omega_1, \omega_2] \equiv [\omega_c - \omega_0, \omega_c + \omega_0].$$

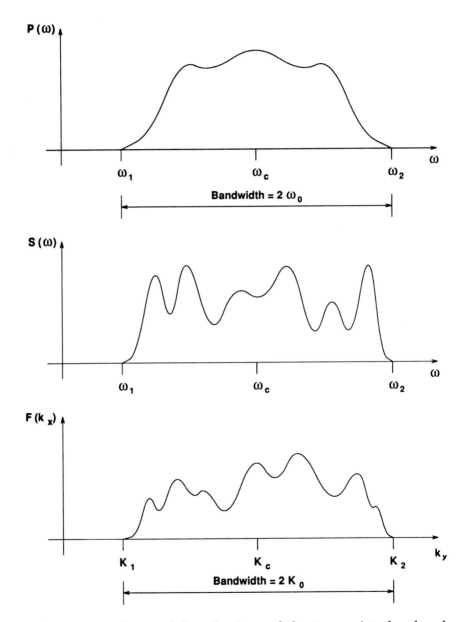

Figure 1.13 Spectral distributions of the transmitted, echoed, and reconstructed target signals.

From (1.9), we define the *target function* in the spatial frequency domain

$$k_x \equiv \frac{2\omega}{c},$$

by the following (see Figure 1.13):

$$F(k_x) \equiv \begin{cases} \frac{S(\omega)}{P(\omega)} = \sum_{n=1}^{N} f_n \exp(-jk_x\, x_n), & \text{if } K_1 < k_x < K_2; \\ 0, & \text{otherwise}, \end{cases} \quad (1.10)$$

where $K_1 \equiv \frac{2\omega_1}{c}$ and $K_2 \equiv \frac{2\omega_2}{c}$. Denote

$$\begin{aligned} K_0 &= \frac{K_2 - K_1}{2} = \frac{2\omega_0}{c} \\ K_c &= \frac{K_2 + K_1}{2} = \frac{2\omega_c}{c} \end{aligned} \quad (1.11)$$

- *One can observe from (1.10) and (1.11) that $f(x)$ is a bandpass signal with bandwidth $2K_0$ and carrier spatial frequency K_c.*

The inverse spatial Fourier transform of both sides of (1.10) yields

$$f(x) = \sum_{n=1}^{M} f_n\, 2K_0 \underbrace{\frac{\sin[K_0(x - x_n)]}{K_0(x - x_n)}}_{sinc\ pattern\ (amplitude\ function)} \underbrace{\exp[jK_c(x - x_n)]}_{sinusoidal\ carrier}.$$

$$(1.12)$$

- *If the effective bandwidth of the transmitted signal had been infinite, that is, $\omega_2 = -\omega_1 = \infty$, then* delta pulse in time

$$\begin{aligned} f(x) &= \sum_{n=1}^{M} f_n\, \delta(x - x_n) \\ &= f_0(x). \end{aligned}$$

Thus, all targets could have been identified uniquely no matter how closely they were positioned. In practice, a signal generator with an infinite effective bandwidth does not exist.

The support region of each sinc pattern in (1.12) is approximately equal to the extent of its first lobe in the x domain, that is,

$$\Delta x \equiv \frac{\pi}{K_0}. \tag{1.13}$$

We call Δx the *resolution* in the x domain. If the support region of each sinc pattern does not overlap with the other sinc patterns' support regions, that is,

$$x_n + \Delta x \ < \ x_{n+1} - \Delta x,$$

for all available n, then each sinc pattern and, consequently, each target is said to be *resolvable* or distinguishable, and we can write

$$|f(x)| \approx \sum_{n=1}^{M} f_n \ 2K_0 \ \left|\frac{\sin[K_0(x - x_n)]}{K_0(x - x_n)}\right|. \tag{1.14}$$

This is depicted in Figure 1.12.

The magnitude of the sinc pattern in (1.14), that is,

$$2K_0 \ \left|\frac{\sin(K_0 x)}{K_0 x}\right|,$$

is called the *point spread function* of the imaging system in the range, that is, x, domain. The approximate support of this sinc function in the x domain, that is, $\Delta_x = \frac{\pi}{K_0}$, is the measure of resolution of the imaging system [see (1.13)]. Clearly, the ideal point spread function is the delta function, which is, $\delta(x)$, that is the limit of the above sinc point spread function when $K_0 \to \infty$. The ideal point spread function $\delta(x)$ can never be achieved in practice. This, as we mentioned earlier, is due to the fact that $P(\omega)$ has a finite support in the temporal frequency domain.

- Δx *decreases, that is, the resolution improves, as* K_0 *or, equivalently, the bandwidth of* $p(t)$ *increases. However, the carrier* K_c *or* ω_c *has no role in determining the* **range resolution***. In our future discussion on two-dimensional imaging systems, we will see that the carrier frequency plays a role in the* **cross-range** *resolution.*

Matched Filtering

The division of $S(\omega)$ with $P(\omega)$ in (1.10), also known as *source decon-volution*, has the role of *phase synchronization* and *amplitude equalization* for the recognition of the targets. The phase synchronization does play a role in accurately identifying the targets' locations. However, the amplitude equalization results in a highpass window function in the temporal frequency domain. In the presence of additive noise, this window further amplifies the noise. Due to this fact, the division in (1.10) is not performed in practice.

A more practical processing technique used to implement the deconvolution in (1.10) is to multiply $S(\omega)$ with $P^*(\omega)$, where * denotes complex conjugation; that is, the inverse equation becomes

$$F_M(k_x) \equiv S(\omega) \, P^*(\omega), \tag{1.15}$$

with

$$k_x = \frac{2\omega}{c}.$$

The inverse Fourier transform of the above is

$$f_M(x) = s(t) \, * \, p^*(-t), \tag{1.16}$$

where $*$ denotes convolution in the time domain, p^* is the complex conjugate of p, and

$$x = \frac{ct}{2}. \tag{1.17}$$

We call $f_M(x)$ the *matched-filtered* target function.

- *The filter $P^*(\omega)$, also known as the **matched filter**, not only provides the desired phase synchronization but also amplifies the signal components at temporal frequencies where the signal is **relatively** stronger than the noise, an operation that is similar to the Wiener filtering [2].*

- *When $|a(t)|$ is a **rectangular pulse** with amplitude A_0, matched filtering becomes analogous to the classical estimation of a **constant**, A_0, received in the presence of uncorrelated noise with variance σ^2. In this problem, the optimum processor **averages** the, for example, K received* samples, $r_i = A_0 + n_i$, $i = 1, \ldots, K$. *The resultant scalar output is* $R \equiv \frac{1}{K} \sum_{i=1}^{K} r_i$ *that is equal to* A_0 *plus a noise with variance* $\frac{\sigma^2}{K}$.

- *When* $|a(t)|$ *is not a rectangular pulse and identified via the samples* a_i, $i = 1, \ldots, K$, *matched filtering is equivalent to a* **weighted averaging** *of the received samples; the weights are equal to the sampled values of* $|a(t|$, *that is,* a_i's. *In this case, the optimum processor's output is* $R \equiv \sum_{i=1}^{K} a_i r_i$, *which is also less sensitive to noise as compared to a* **single** *sample of the received signal.*

Substituting (1.10) in (1.15) yields

$$F_M(k_x) \equiv F(k_x) \, W(k_x),$$

where

$$W(k_x) \equiv |P(\omega)|^2,$$

with $k_x = \frac{2\omega}{c}$ is an amplitude (window) function in the spatial frequency domain k_x. The inverse Fourier transform of the above is

$$f_M(x) = f(x) \, * \, w(x),$$

where $*$ denotes convolution in the spatial domain x. Using (1.14) in the above, one obtains

$$|f_M(x)| \approx \sum_{n=1}^{M} f_n \, 2K_0 \, \left| \frac{\sin[K_0(x - x_n)]}{K_0(x - x_n)} \, * \, w(x) \right|$$

$$\equiv \sum_{n=1}^{M} f_n \, \text{psf}(x - x_n),$$

where

$$\text{psf}(x) \equiv 2K_0 \, \left| \frac{\sin(K_0 x)}{K_0 x} \, * \, w(x) \right|$$

is the point spread function of the imaging system with matched filtering.

In a practical imaging system where the measured data are corrupted with noise and numerical errors (e.g., aliasing errors that are due to the discrete Fourier transformation), $|f_M(x)|$ is used instead of $|f(x)|$ for target recognition and imaging. For notational simplicity, we drop the subscript of the matched-filtered target function and identify it as $|f(x)|$ in our discussion.

Figure 1.14a shows a rectangular pulse with duration .25 microsecond that is amplitude-modulating a 75 MHz sinusoidal carrier. This pulsed signal corresponds to a $p(t)$ transmitted at $t = 0$. On the same figure, an echoed version of $p(t)$ [i.e., $p(t - 2t_1)$ where $2t_1 = .6$ microsecond] that is matched filtered is shown. Figure 1.14b shows the Fourier transform of the rectangular pulse function, that is, a sinc function centered at the 75 MHz carrier frequency. Figure 1.14c shows the reconstructed magnitude based on matched filtering for three targets in air (with $c = 300000$ Km/second). The targets' parameters (reflectivity and range values) are: $(f_1, x_1) = (1., 90m)$; $(f_2, x_2) = (1., 120m)$; and $(f_3, x_3) = (.5, 225m)$. Note that the first two targets are barely ***resolvable*** from each other.

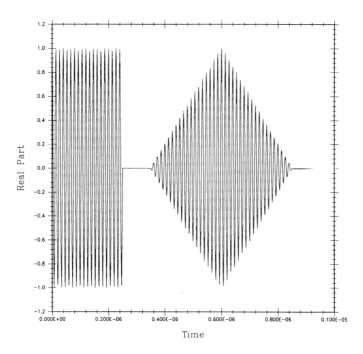

Figure 1.14a Rectangular pulse and its matched filtered pulse.

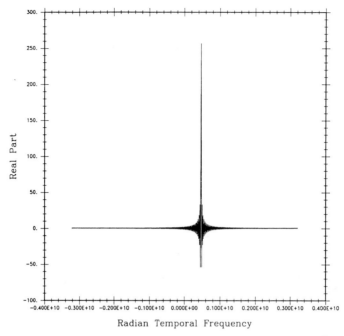

Figure 1.14b Rectangular pulse's Fourier transform.

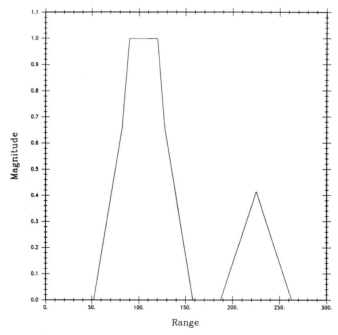

Figure 1.14c Echo imaging using a rectangular pulse.

The transmitted signal energy for a pulsed signal is defined to be

$$E_p \equiv \int_{-\infty}^{\infty} |p(t)|^2 \, dt$$

$$= \int_{-\infty}^{\infty} |a(t)|^2 \, dt.$$

When $|a(t)|$ is a rectangular with amplitude A_0 for $t \in [0, \tau_0]$, then the transmitted energy is

$$E_p = A_0^2 \, \tau_0,$$

which is proportional to the pulse duration. In this case, the energy of the echoed signal from the n-th target, that is, $s_n(t) = f_n p(t - 2t_n)$, is

$$S_n \equiv f_n^2 \, E_p$$

$$= f_n^2 \, A_0^2 \, \tau_0.$$

It can be shown [2] that as S_n increases, matched filtering provides improvement in the **output** signal-to-noise power ratio and, consequently, better target recognition. In particular, when $|a(t)|$ is a rectangular pulse, increasing the pulse duration, that is, τ_0, results in higher S_n values and more prominent targets in the reconstructed matched-filtered target function. This has implications in our next discussion on chirp signaling where increasing the pulse duration enables the user to obtain better range resolution as well as higher output signal-to-noise power ratio.

Chirp Pulse Signaling and Pulse Compression

Chirp pulses make up a special class of pulsed signals that are used in radar problems. An advantage of these signals is that they can possess long duration in both time and temporal frequency domains. The long duration in the frequency domain (bandwidth), as we mentioned earlier, provides better range resolution since

$$\Delta_x = \frac{\pi}{K_0} = \frac{\pi \, c}{2\omega_0},$$

where $[-\omega_0, \omega_0]$ is the support band for $A(\omega)$. The long duration in the time domain enables the user to transmit more energy to improve the *output* signal-to-noise power ratio [2].

When $a(t)$ is a rectangular pulse with duration τ_0, then its Fourier transform is a sinc function with its first zero-crossing at the following frequency:

$$\omega_0 \equiv \frac{2\pi}{\tau_0}, \tag{1.18}$$

which is also considered to be the support band for $A(\omega)$, that is, the bandwidth of $a(t)$ that dictates the range resolution. In this case, the range resolution becomes

$$\Delta_x = \frac{c\tau_0}{4}.$$

For the example shown in Figure 1.14c, this theoretical resolution is 18.75 m.

Clearly, when $a(t)$ is a rectangular pulse, we cannot achieve long duration in both time and temporal frequency domains since ω_0, the bandwidth, is inversely proportional to the pulse duration in the time domain, that is, τ_0. Chirp pulse signaling solves this problem via choosing the radiated signal to be a Frequency Modulated (FM) pulse

$$p(t) = \exp[j(\omega_c t + \alpha t^2)], \tag{1.19}$$

for $t \in [0, \tau_0]$, and zero otherwise, where $\alpha > 0$, call it the chirp rate, is a chosen constant. A chirp signal is a special class of phase modulated signals that is examined later in this chapter. The baseband signal for the chirp pulse is

$$a(t) = \exp(j\alpha t^2), \tag{1.20}$$

for $t \in [0, \tau_0]$, and zero otherwise. *Note that $|a(t)|$ is also a rectangular pulse in chirp signaling.* Thus, an increase in τ_0 results in a better output signal-to-noise power ratio for chirp signaling too.

The instantaneous frequency of $p(t)$ is defined via

$$\omega_i(t) \equiv \frac{d}{dt}[\omega_c t + \alpha t^2]$$
$$= \omega_c + 2\alpha t. \tag{1.21}$$

The unique feature of the chirp signal is that its instantaneous frequency linearly increases with t and is bounded by

$$\omega_c \leq \omega_i(t) \leq \omega_c + 2\alpha\tau_0.$$

Note that the upper bound for $\omega_i(t)$ increases with τ_0. The support band of the baseband signal [i.e., $a(t)$] in the frequency domain is approximately equal to

$$[-\frac{2\pi}{\tau_0}, \frac{2\pi}{\tau_0} + 2\alpha\tau_0].$$

Thus, the overall bandwidth of $a(t)$ is

$$2\omega_0 = 2\alpha\tau_0 + \frac{4\pi}{\tau_0}, \tag{1.22}$$

which yields the following range resolution

$$\Delta_x = \frac{\pi \ c}{2\omega_0}$$

$$= \frac{\pi \ c}{2\alpha\tau_0 + \frac{4\pi}{\tau_0}} \tag{1.23}$$

$$< \frac{c\tau_0}{4}$$

where $\frac{c\tau_0}{4}$ is the range resolution when $a(t)$ is a rectangular pulse (i.e., when $\alpha = 0$). By increasing α, one can increase this bandwidth and, thus, improve the range resolution.

- *By increasing the pulse duration τ_0 in chirp signaling, one can simultaneously increase (i) the overall transmitted power (or, equivalently, improve the* **output signal-to-noise power ratio***), and (ii) the bandwidth of the transmitted pulse (or, equivalently, improve the* **range resolution***). The same is not true in rectangular pulse signaling where increasing τ_0 to improve signal-to-noise power ratio results in a poorer range resolution.*

Note that the support band of $A(\omega)$ is not centered around $\omega = 0$. This can be resolved by redefining the pulsed signal via

$$p(t) = a(t) \ \exp[j(\omega_c + \alpha\tau_0)t], \tag{1.24}$$

thus,

$$a(t) = \exp(-j\alpha\tau_0 t + j\alpha t^2), \qquad (1.25)$$

for $t \in [0, \tau_0]$, and zero otherwise, that is, the carrier (center) frequency is $\omega_c + \alpha\tau_0$.

Finally, in the case of chirp signaling, the inversion that utilizes matched filtering, that is,

$$f(x) = s(t) * p^*(-t),$$

where $x \equiv \frac{ct}{2}$, is known as *pulse compression*. This is due to the fact that the time duration for the output signal is *smaller* than τ_0 (that is the time duration of the transmitted pulse). An example of a chirp pulse and its compressed version is shown in Figure 1.15a. This results in better resolution in the reconstructed signal, that is, $f(x = \frac{ct}{2})$. This should be anticipated from the fact that, unlike the rectangular pulse used for $a(t)$, the bandwidth of the chirp pulse $a(t)$ is not $\frac{2\pi}{\tau_0}$. This bandwidth is now expanded by the chirp rate α (see Figure 1.15b). A detailed analysis of chirp signaling and pulse compression is given in [10].

Figure 1.15a shows a chirp pulse with duration .25 microsecond with $\omega_c = 4\pi$ radians/second, and $\alpha = 500\pi$ X 10^{12} radians/second^2. This pulsed signal corresponds to a $p(t)$ transmitted at $t = 0$. On the same figure, an echoed version of $p(t)$ (i.e., $p(t - 2t_1)$ where $2t_1 = .6$ microsecond) that is matched filtered (compressed) is shown. Figure 1.15b shows the Fourier transform of the chirp pulse function that is approximately another chirp centered at the 2 MHz carrier frequency. (This fact was shown earlier in this chapter with the help of the Fourier properties of a Gaussian signal; see the discussion on Nonlinear Modulation in Section 1.2.)

Figure 1.15c shows the reconstructed magnitude based on matched filtering for three targets in air (with $c = 300000$ Km/second). The targets' parameters (reflectivity and range values) are: $(f_1, x_1) = (1., 90m)$; $(f_2, x_2) = (1., 120m)$; and $(f_3, x_3) = (.5, 225m)$. This corresponds to the echo imaging problem cited in Figure 1.14b. For the chirp pulse, the three targets are clearly resolvable. The range resolution from (1.23) can be found to be 1 m (as opposed to 18.75 m for the rectangular pulse).

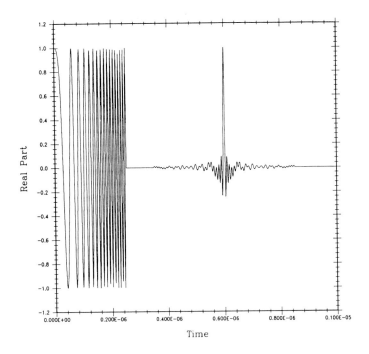

Figure 1.15a Chirp pulse and its matched filtered pulse.

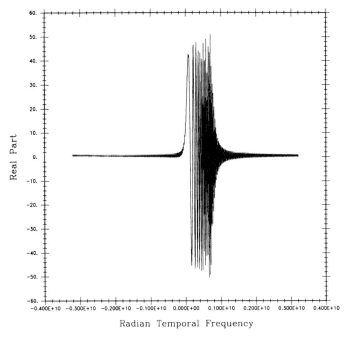

Figure 1.15b Chirp pulse's Fourier transform.

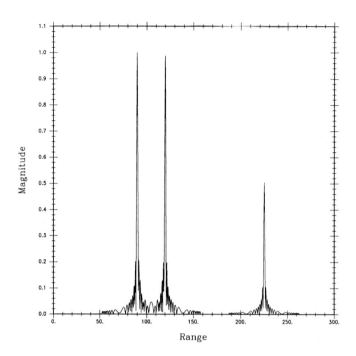

Figure 1.15c Echo imaging using a chirp pulse.

- *In imaging systems, we will encounter **chirp-type** signals in the spatial domain that are not introduced by the user similar to the above-mentioned time domain chirp signaling. These spatial domain chirp signals are generated due to the properties of propagating waves in the spatial domain. We will examine these in our discussion on spatial Doppler phenomenon later in this chapter.*

Signal Processing and Sampling Constraints

In our imaging problems, we encounter spatial domain and/or spatial frequency domain *bandpass* signals. *Appropriate processing and sampling of these signals is crucial for the success of theoretical inversion algorithms.* In this section, we examine this issue for the one-dimensional echo imaging.

Our objective in the echo imaging problem is to reconstruct the target's reflectivity function $f(x)$ from the measurement of the echoed signal $s(t)$. For this purpose, a coherent receiver is used to bring the information contents of $s(t)$ to baseband (see Figure 1.10 or 1.11); mathematically, this is modeled via the following operation:

$$s_b(t) \equiv s(t) \, \exp(-j\omega_c t). \tag{1.26}$$

We have for the Fourier transform of these signals the following relationship:

$$S_b(\omega) = S(\omega + \omega_c). \tag{1.27}$$

The resultant time domain baseband signal, that is, $s_b(t)$, is then sampled by an electronic device called Analog to Digital (A/D) converter. The A/D converter samples the baseband signal at N time points identified via $n\Delta_t$, $n = 0, 1, 2, \ldots, N-1$, where Δ_t, called the sampling interval, should satisfy the Nyquist criterion, that is,

$$\Delta_t \leq \frac{2\pi}{2\omega_0}, \tag{1.28}$$

where $[-\omega_0, \omega_0]$ is the support band for $S_b(\omega)$, to avoid aliasing.

The resultant sampled data, that is, $s_b(n\Delta_t)$'s, are sent to the input channel of a computer. The computer, which also serves as the *controller* of the A/D converter via sending a control signal to the A/D converter to sample $s_b(t)$ at the designated time points $n\Delta_t$, reads $s_b(n\Delta_t)$ from its input channel and stores it in its memory.

The inversion algorithm, which is programmed in the computer, now has the database for its image formation (target imaging). The process begins with a discrete Fourier transform (DFT) operation on the stored samples $s_b(n\Delta_t)$, $n = 0, 1, \ldots, N-1$. The resultant sequence are the samples of $S_b(\omega)$ at $\omega = m\Delta_\omega$, $m = \frac{-N}{2}, \ldots, 0, \ldots, \frac{N}{2} - 1$, where from the DFT equation (1.2)

$$\Delta_\omega \equiv \frac{2\pi}{N\Delta_t}. \tag{1.29}$$

However, we have from (1.27)

$$S_b(\omega) = S(\omega + \omega_c).$$

Thus, the transformed data (sequence) corresponds to the following samples: $S(m\Delta_\omega + \omega_c)$, $m = \frac{-N}{2}, \ldots, \frac{N}{2} - 1$.

The available samples of $S(\omega)$ provide us with the samples of $F(k_x)$ at $k_x = \frac{2(m\Delta_\omega + \omega_c)}{c}$, $m = \frac{-N}{2}, \ldots, \frac{N}{2} - 1$. As we mentioned before, this *bandpass* database may be used to identify point targets in the x domain via displaying $|f(x)|$. There is, however, one more catch. We have access only to a finite number of *sampled* values of $F(k_x)$, with sample spacing

$$\Delta_{k_x} \equiv \frac{2\Delta_\omega}{c}, \tag{1.30}$$

from the finite sampled measurements of $s_b(t)$. Thus, this database is not *aliased* provided that $F(k_x)$ is a band-limited signal or, equivalently, $f(x)$ is a space-limited signal. The latter mathematical condition translates into having a *target region* that has a finite extent.

- *In imaging systems, we usually deal with targets that are space-limited within a known region. If this is not the case, via a process known as **time gating** that is achieved by processing a certain portion (time interval) of the echoed signal, the target to be imaged can be modeled to be space-limited within a known region.*

Suppose it is known that the target region for our echo imaging problem is within a known spatial domain interval $[X_1 - X_0, X_1 + X_0]$ (see Figure 1.12); X_1 is the range of the *center* or *center-of-mass* of the target region, and $2X_0$ is the *size* of the target scene. Thus, we have to perform baseband conversion, now in the k_x domain (not in the time domain), on the available samples of $F(k_x)$ to end up with the samples of a signal that is not aliased. This is achieved via the following operation:

$$F_b(k_x) \equiv F(k_x) \ \exp(jk_x X_1). \tag{1.31}$$

(Note that the computer program performs this baseband translation on the sampled version of $F(k_x)$ that is acquired from the measurements of

$s(t)$.) This operation is simply a shift operation in the spatial domain that moves the origin to the center of the target region, that is, $x = X_1$. Clearly, we have

$$f_b(x) = f(x - X_1).$$

Figure 1.16 shows a block diagram for reconstruction in echo imaging.

We have to satisfy one final constraint to make sure that the available samples of $F_b(k_x)$, at $k_x = \frac{2(m\Delta_\omega + \omega_c)}{c}$, satisfy the Nyquist criterion in the k_x domain; that is,

$$\Delta_{k_x} \equiv \frac{2\Delta_\omega}{c} \leq \frac{2\pi}{2X_0}.$$

Suppose the time interval over which the echoed signal is observed is $[0, t_0]$, where

$$t_0 \equiv (N - 1)\Delta_t \approx N\Delta_t.$$

Thus, from the DFT equation (1.2), we have

$$\Delta_\omega = \frac{2\pi}{t_0}.$$

Substituting this in the Nyquist condition in the k_x domain yields

$$\frac{2}{ct_0} \leq \frac{1}{2X_0},$$

or

$$\frac{4X_0}{c} \leq t_0. \tag{1.32}$$

This condition is generally satisfied in one-dimensional echo imaging systems by the user. As we will see for multidimensional imaging problems, the user may be forced to **artificially** extend the observation time interval via a process known as **zero-padding** of the sampled echoed signal to increase the sampling rate for the temporally Fourier transformed data in the ω domain. This will be discussed in the specific imaging problems that we will encounter.

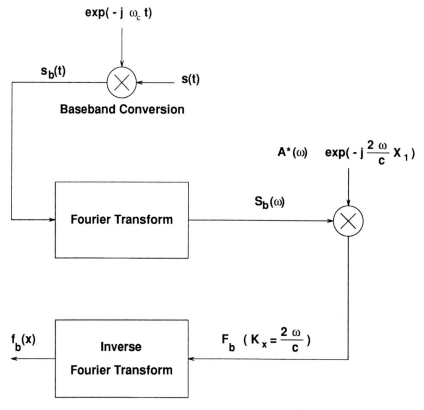

Figure 1.16 Reconstruction algorithm for echo imaging.

1.8 TEMPORAL DOPPLER PHENOMENON

System Model

Consider the one-dimensional echo imaging example that was cited in the previous section with the transmitted signal identified by its quadrature representation

$$p(t) = a(t) \ \exp(j\omega_c t).$$

Suppose the n-th target that is located at x_n is moving with a constant speed v_n $(n = 1, 2, \ldots, M)$. The coordinate of the n-th target at time t is

$$X_n(t) \equiv x_n \ - \ v_n t.$$

We denote the one-way propagation delay from the transmitter to the n-th moving target by $T_n(t)$; that is, the round-trip delay time is $2T_n(t)$. Thus, we have

$$T_n(t) = \frac{X_n[t - T_n(t)]}{c}, \qquad (1.33)$$

where

$$X_n[t - T_n(t)] = x_n \ - \ v_n[t - T_n(t)] \qquad (1.34)$$

is the coordinate of the target when the signal transmitted at time t reaches it.

Substituting (1.34) in (1.33) yields (with $v_n \ll c$)

$$\begin{aligned} T_n(t) &= \frac{x_n - v_n t}{c - v_n} \\ &\approx \frac{x_n}{c} \ - \ \frac{v_n}{c} t. \end{aligned} \qquad (1.35)$$

With the help of (1.35), the echoed signal due to the n-th target with reflection coefficient f_n can be found to be

$$\begin{aligned} s_n(t) &\equiv f_n \ p[t - 2T_n(t)] \\ &= f_n \ a[t - 2T_n(t)] \ \exp\big[j\omega_c[t - 2T_n(t)]\big] \\ &\approx f_n \ a(t - 2t_n) \ \exp(-j2\omega_c t_n) \ \exp[j(\omega_c + \omega_{Dn})t], \end{aligned} \qquad (1.36)$$

where

$$t_n \equiv \frac{x_n}{c},$$

and

$$\omega_{Dn} \equiv \frac{2v_n}{c}\omega_c, \qquad (1.36a)$$

is called the *temporal Doppler shift* caused by the motion of the n-th target.

- *In deriving (1.36), we used*

$$a(t - 2t_n + \frac{2v_n}{c}t) \approx a(t - 2t_n),$$

  which is a valid approximation provided that $a(t)$ is a slowly fluctuating signal as compared to the carrier $\exp(j\omega_c t)$ [9]; that is, $\omega_0 \ll \omega_c$. The implication of this approximation is that all the temporal frequency components of $P(\omega)$, $\omega \in [\omega_c - \omega_0, \omega_c + \omega_0]$, are approximately shifted by the same amount, that is, the Doppler shift shown in (1.36a). The exact Doppler shift for a given temporal frequency is

$$\omega_{Dn}(\omega) \equiv \frac{2v_n}{c}\omega,$$

  which is approximately equal to the right side of (1.36a) provided that $\omega_0 \ll \omega_c$. This constraint is satisfied in certain radar imaging problems. However, the constraint is not true in high-powered low-frequency pulsed radar as well as medical and sonar imaging problems.

- *The first line of (1.36) is the same as the component of the n-th stationary target on the left side of the system model (1.4) with x_n replaced with $x_n - v_n t$; that is,*

$$s_n(t) = f_n \ p[t - \frac{2(x_n - v_n t)}{c}].$$

The total received signal has the following form:

$$s(t) = \sum_{n=1}^{M} f_n \ a(t - 2t_n) \ \exp(-j2\omega_c t_n) \ \exp[j(\omega_c + \omega_{Dn})t]. \qquad (1.37)$$

Note that t_n and ω_{Dn} carry information regarding the target's range, x_n, and the target's speed, v_n, respectively. Our objective is to retrieve the target's parameters, that is, (t_n, ω_{Dn}), from the measurements of $s(t)$.

Inversion

Classical radar and sonar target detection and parameter estimation methods, for example, for air traffic control, are based on the inversion of the system model in (1.37) [9]. For the inversion, we take the temporal Fourier transform of both sides of (1.33); this yields

$$S(\omega) = \sum_{n=1}^{M} f_n \, A(\omega - \omega_n) \, \exp[-j2(\omega - \omega_{Dn})t_n], \qquad (1.38)$$

with

$$\omega_n \equiv \omega_c + \omega_{Dn}. \qquad (1.38a)$$

We can observe from (1.38) that the signature of the n-th target is centered around ω_n. This is shown in Figure 1.17 for a single target.

Suppose there exists only one target in the scene, for example, the n-th one. Thus, we have from (1.38)

$$S(\omega) = f_n \, A(\omega - \omega_n) \, \exp[-j2(\omega - \omega_{Dn})t_n].$$

Moreover, assume v_n and, consequently, ω_n are known. We define the *target function with speed v_n* in the spatial frequency domain via

$$F(k_x, v_n) \equiv \frac{S(\omega)}{A(\omega - \omega_n)}$$

$$= f_n \, \exp(j2\omega_{Dn}t_n) \, \exp(-jk_x x_n),$$

for $|\omega - \omega_n| \leq \omega_0$, with $k_x \equiv \frac{2\omega}{c}$.

The magnitude of the inverse spatial Fourier transform of the above is

$$|f(x, v_n)| = f_n \, 2K_0 \, \left| \frac{\sin[K_0(x - x_n)]}{K_0(x - x_n)} \right|.$$

This reconstructed target function is invariant of ω_n as well as the phase function $\exp(j2\omega_{Dn}t_n)$. Note the similarity of this reconstruction to (1.14).

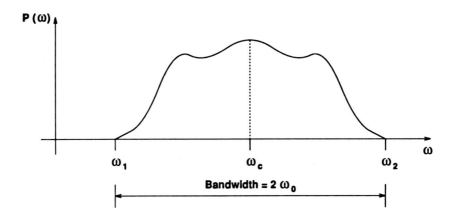

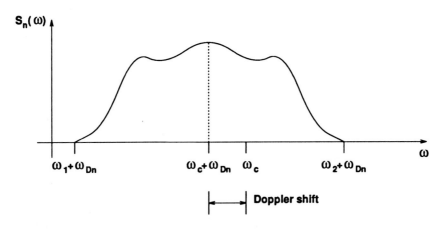

Figure 1.17 Fourier domain echo signature of a moving target.

Suppose there is more than one target with speed v_n in the scene, for example, two targets located at x_n and x_i that have a common speed v_n (i.e., a common Doppler shift ω_{Dn} and carrier ω_n too). In this case, we get

$$\begin{aligned} S(\omega) =& f_n \ A(\omega - \omega_n) \ \exp[-j2(\omega - \omega_{Dn})t_n] \\ &+ f_i \ A(\omega - \omega_n) \ \exp[-j2(\omega - \omega_{Dn})t_i] \\ =& A(\omega - \omega_n) \\ &\times \left[f_n \ \exp[-j2(\omega - \omega_{Dn})t_n] + f_i \ \exp[-j2(\omega - \omega_{Dn})t_i] \right]. \end{aligned}$$

The reconstructed target function with speed v_n becomes

$$|f(x, v_n)| \approx f_n \ 2K_0 \ |\frac{\sin[K_0(x - x_n)]}{K_0(x - x_n)}| + f_i \ 2K_0 \ |\frac{\sin[K_0(x - x_i)]}{K_0(x - x_i)}|,$$

provided that $|x_n - x_i| > \Delta_x = \frac{\pi c}{2\omega_0}$.

- The practical inversion in the k_x domain is via the following matched filtering:

$$F(k_x, v_n) = S(\omega) \ A^*(\omega - \omega_n).$$

Let us now consider the original problem involving moving targets with varying and unknown speeds. We can perform the above-mentioned inversion for a set of values v to construct a *two-dimensional* target function of (x, v). This is done via

$$F(k_x, v) = S(\omega) \ A^*[\omega - \omega(v)],$$

where the carrier $\omega(v)$ is defined by

$$\omega(v) \equiv \omega_c + \underbrace{\frac{2v}{c}\omega_c}_{Doppler\ shift}$$

The matched filtering operation in the time domain becomes

$$f(x, v) = s(t) \ * \ [p^*(-t) \ \exp(\frac{2v}{c}\omega_c t)].$$

The resultant reconstructed image, that is, $|f(x,v)|$ or $|f(x,v)|^2$, is called the *ambiguity function* [9].

Constraint and Resolution

The above-mentioned procedure has one flaw. If the support band of $A(\omega)$ is $[-\omega_0, \omega_0]$, then the targets' signatures are separable provided that

$$|\omega_{Dn} - \omega_{Dm}| > 2\omega_0,$$

for all $m \neq n$. Figure 1.18 shows two scenarios where this constraint is satisfied (top) and is violated (bottom). Using (1.38a), the above constraint can be expressed via the following:

$$\frac{2|v_m - v_n|}{c} \, \omega_c > 2\omega_0,$$

or

$$|v_m - v_n| > \frac{\omega_0 \, c}{\omega_c}.$$

Thus, the target resolution in the v domain is

$$\Delta_v \equiv \frac{\omega_0 c}{\omega_c}.$$

Thus, the *speed resolution* improves as $2\omega_0$, that is, the bandwidth of the transmitted pulse, is reduced. However, we showed in the echo imaging problem that the range resolution in the x domain deteriorates as ω_0 decreases since

$$\Delta_x = \frac{\pi c}{2\omega_0}.$$

This problem is known as the radar ambiguity problem: one cannot improve the range resolution and speed resolution independently; there is always a trade-off. (A similar ambiguity arises if one attempts to isolate each $a(t - 2t_n)$ in the time domain and retrieve the phase function $\exp[j(\omega_c + \omega_{Dn})t]$ from it; see (1.37).)

Similar approximations and ambiguities are encountered with other two-dimensional *time-frequency* methods, for example, Wigner-Ville and short-time windowed Fourier transform for range-speed imaging. The time-temporal frequency ambiguity problem has been studied extensively [9].

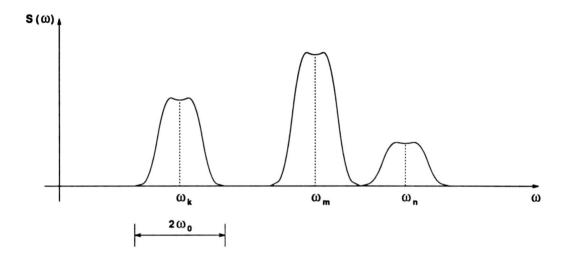

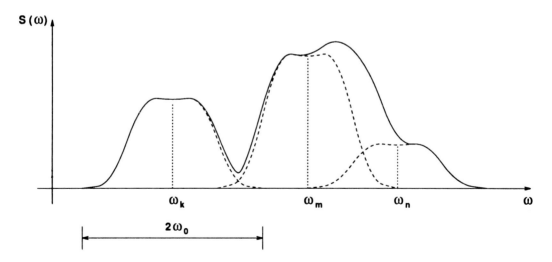

Figure 1.18 Fourier domain echo signatures of three moving targets for two different bandwidths of the transmitted signal.

The design of *perfect* $a(t)$'s (codes) to reduce the ambiguity problem is still an active area of research. In the next section, we examine one of these signals which, under certain constraints, results in independent resolution in the range and Doppler (speed) domains. Next, we examine a signaling scheme for range-speed imaging that does not suffer from the above-mentioned time/temporal frequency ambiguities.

1.9 TIME-FREQUENCY DIVERSITY (FM-CW) SIGNALING

The task in one-dimensional range-Doppler (or range-speed) imaging is the accurate retrieval of a target's location and speed. The range resolution requires a sharp rectangular pulse or a chirp pulse in the time domain that translates into a wide support band in the temporal frequency domain. On the other hand, the Doppler resolution requires a sharp pulse spectrum that is equivalent to a long duration pulse in the time domain. As we showed earlier, this is not feasible using a **single** pulse.

We now introduce a signal that is composed of **several** (repeated) *sharp* bursts over *long* intervals in both time and frequency domains. For this reason, we refer to this form of transmission as *time-frequency diversity* signaling. The repetition of a pulse over a long time duration is an approximation to a periodic signal that possesses a discrete spectral distribution. The discrete spectral support provides good Doppler resolution. Moreover, by choosing the pulse to have a large bandwidth, for example, an FM chirp or a sharp rectangular pulse, one can achieve good range resolution.

This form of signaling is a general version of linear and triangular FM-CW (FM: Frequency Modulation for high range resolution; CW: Continuous Wave, or long time duration, for high Doppler resolution) radar signaling [11]-[14]. The classical inverse method for imaging with triangular FM-CW signaling is based on an *analog* mixing of the echoed signals with the transmitted signal (dechirping) followed by a spectral analysis [12]. Barrick [11] suggested a digital signal processing of the dechirped signal that does not require the transmitted signal to be a triangular FM and can handle multiple targets.

These methods are based on certain approximations for modeling the dechirped signal (e.g., see [11]). These approximations are based on the following assumptions that are valid in certain radar problems:

i. The round-trip delay for a target in the irradiated scene is much smaller than the pulse repetition interval. Based on this assumption, a portion of the dechirped signal that contains high frequency information is assumed to be filtered and, thus, can be neglected in the formulation of the inverse problem.

ii. The transmitted signal's baseband bandwidth is much smaller than its carrier frequency. Based on this assumption, the user can approximate a moving target's Doppler shift to be a *constant* over the bandwidth of the transmitted signal.

We will examine an inverse method for FM-CW signaling that is not based on the above assumptions. The development of this FM-CW inversion is similar to one of the methods suggested by Barrick that involves the one-dimensional Fourier analysis of the entire recorded data but *without dechirping*. Moreover, the system model and inversion does not approximate a moving target's Doppler shift to be a constant over the bandwidth of the transmitted signal and does not put any restrictions on the target's range. This makes FM-CW signaling a viable range-speed inverse method in medical imaging, sonar imaging and long-range radar imaging.

The process of imaging from the echoed signals involves a *partitioning* of the spectrum of the echoed signal. This is in contrast with the well-known two-dimensional time-frequency methods, for example, ambiguity function, Wigner-Ville distribution, and short-time windowed Fourier transform [9].

Signal Model

Consider the transmitted signal in its quadrature representation form

$$p(t) = a(t) \ \exp(j\omega_c t).$$

Our objective is to search for a baseband signal $a(t)$ that provides us with resolution in the range and temporal Doppler domains that are invariant of each other. For this purpose, we need a spectral distribution for $a(t)$ that has a large bandwidth (for range resolution) and yet it is composed of *distinct spectral lines* (for temporal Doppler resolution). Furthermore, the extent of the bandwidth should be invariant of the sharpness of the spectral lines. (How the target scene is imaged using this type of signaling will be addressed.)

A candidate to design the above-mentioned baseband signal is the following:

$$a(t) \equiv \sum_{\ell=0}^{K-1} a_1(t - \ell t_2), \tag{1.39}$$

where $a_1(t)$ is a baseband signal with a *large* bandwidth, and t_2 is called the *pulse repetition interval* (pri); $\frac{1}{t_2}$ is called the *pulse repetition frequency* (prf) (see Figure 1.19). For instance, suppose $a_1(t)$ is a rectangular pulse function

$$a_1(t) \equiv \begin{cases} 1, & \text{if } t \in [0, t_1]; \\ 0, & \text{otherwise}, \end{cases}$$

that could be tapered by a window function, for example, Hamming, to reduce its side lobes in the frequency domain. For this case, the bandwidth of $a(t)$ may be increased by choosing t_1 to be as small as possible. This, as we mentioned earlier, has the disadvantage of reducing the overall transmitted energy that has implications on the output signal-to-noise power ratio.

This can be rectified by choosing $a_1(t)$ to be a baseband chirp signal

$$a_1(t) \equiv \begin{cases} \exp(j\alpha t^2), & \text{if } t \in [0, t_1]; \\ 0, & \text{otherwise}, \end{cases}$$

where α, the chirp rate, is a chosen constant. A chirp signal is a linearly modulated FM signal. A simple example of a nonlinearly modulated FM signal is the tone-modulated FM, that is,

$$a_1(t) \equiv \begin{cases} \exp[j \, \eta \, \sin(\frac{2\pi t}{t_2})\,], & \text{if } t \in [0, t_1]; \\ 0, & \text{otherwise}, \end{cases}$$

where η, the modulation index, is a chosen constant. The hardware required to generate an FM signal is more elaborate than a gating system that produces a rectangular signal.

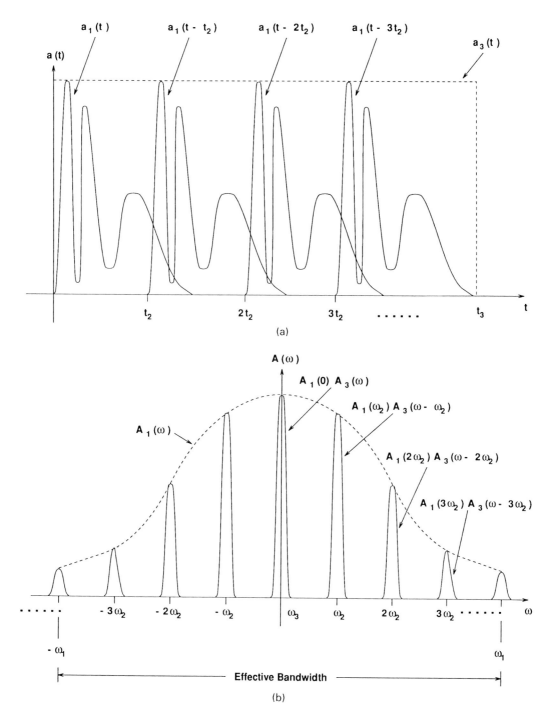

Figure 1.19 A baseband periodic FM-CW signal. (a) Temporal distribution. (b) Spectral distribution.

- *FM-CW radar signaling becomes pulsed radar signaling if the echoed signal for the pulse $a_1(t-\ell t_2)$ arrives prior to the transmission of the next pulse, that is, $a_1[t-(\ell+1)t_2]$. Thus, pulsed radar imaging may be viewed as a special case of FM-CW radar imaging (though the two imaging methods use different principles and signal processing algorithms for image formation).*

Clearly, $a(t)$ is a finite duration pulse in the interval $[0, t_3]$, where

$$t_3 \equiv (K-1)t_2 + t_1.$$

$a(t)$ is composed of K pulses with duration t_1 that are repeated every t_2 seconds in the time interval $[0, t_3]$. For reasons that will become obvious in our later discussion, we require the following constraints:

$$t_1 \ll t_2 \ll t_3,$$

when $a_1(t)$ is a rectangular pulse. (Note that there are several pulses in the time interval $[0, t_3]$, not just three.) When $a_1(t)$ is a baseband FM pulse with a large bandwidth, it is sufficient to have the following:

$$t_2 \ll t_3;$$

that is, we may use overlapping chirp pulses that fully utilize the bandwidth provided by the transducer/antenna electronic circuitry.

We can rewrite $a(t)$ as follows:

$$a(t) = a_3(t) \sum_{\ell=-\infty}^{\infty} a_1(t - \ell t_2), \qquad (1.40)$$

where

$$a_3(t) \equiv \begin{cases} 1, & \text{if } t \in [0, t_3]; \\ 0, & \text{otherwise.} \end{cases}$$

($a_3(t)$ does not have to be a rectangular pulse function; it can be tapered with, for example, a Hamming window.) The temporal Fourier transform of both sides of (1.40) yields (see Figure 1.19; in the following equation, $*$ denotes convolution in the ω domain and constants are suppressed)

$$A(\omega) = A_3(\omega) \ast \sum_{\ell=-\infty}^{\infty} A_1(\ell\omega_2)\, \delta(\omega - \ell\omega_2)$$

$$= \sum_{\ell=-\infty}^{\infty} A_1(\ell\omega_2)\, A_3(\omega - \ell\omega_2),$$

(1.41)

with

$$A_1(\omega) \equiv \mathcal{F}_{(t)}\big[a_1(t)\big],$$

[e.g., when $a_1(t)$ is a rectangular pulse, $A_1(\omega) = t_1 \mathrm{sinc}(\frac{\omega t_1}{2})\, \exp(-j\frac{\omega t_1}{2})$] that has a support band approximately within $[-\omega_1, \omega_1]$, and

$$A_3(\omega) = t_3 \mathrm{sinc}(\frac{\omega t_3}{2})\, \exp(-j\frac{\omega t_3}{2}),$$

that has a support band approximately within $[-\omega_3, \omega_3]$, where

$$\omega_1 \equiv \begin{cases} \dfrac{2\pi}{t_1} & \text{for a rectangular pulse} \\[2mm] \alpha t_1 + \dfrac{2\pi}{t_1} & \text{for a chirp pulse,} \\[2mm] \dfrac{2\pi\eta}{t_2} & \text{for a tone-modulated FM pulse,} \end{cases}$$

$$\omega_2 \equiv \frac{2\pi}{t_2}$$

$$\omega_3 \equiv \frac{2\pi}{t_3}$$

Consider the ℓ-th component of the sum in (1.41), that is, the following frequency-dependent signal:

$$A_1(\ell\omega_2)\, A_3(\omega - \ell\omega_2).$$

We observe from this component and (1.41) that $A(\omega)$ is composed of repeated versions of $A_3(\omega)$ that are centered at the harmonics of ω_2 and weighted by the value of $A_1(\omega)$ at those harmonics. Thus, provided that

$\omega_1 \gg \omega_3$, then the bandwidth of $A(\omega)$ is dictated by the bandwidth of $A_1(\omega)$, that is, $[-\omega_1, \omega_1]$ that depends on (α, t_1). Furthermore, by increasing t_3, which has no effect on the extent of the bandwidth $[-\omega_1, \omega_1]$, we can make $A_3(\omega - \ell\omega_2)$ to approximate a delta function (line spectrum) at $\omega = \ell\omega_2$, where $\ell\omega_2 \in [-\omega_1, \omega_1]$.

Single Harmonic (Narrow-Band) Model

Thus far, we have shown that the baseband signal in (1.39) provides a line spectrum that its bandwidth (which is dictated by t_1) is invariant of its sharpness (which is controlled by t_3). Next, we turn our attention to the problem of target imaging in this echo imaging problem. For this purpose, we first examine how the information on a target's speed and range is embedded in the FM-CW echoed signal.

The transmitted FM-CW signal can be expressed as a *linear* combination of the harmonics at $\omega = \omega_c + \ell\omega_2$; that is,

$$p(t) = \sum_{\ell} p_\ell(t),$$

where

$$p_\ell(t) \equiv A_1(\ell\omega_2) \, \exp[j(\omega_c + \ell\omega_2)t],$$

for $t \in [0, t_3]$. If the target region is illuminated with $p_\ell(t)$, the resultant echoed signal is

$$sp_\ell(t) \equiv \sum_{n=1}^{M} f_n \, p_\ell[t - \frac{2(x_n - v_n t)}{c}]$$

$$= A_1(\ell\omega_2) \sum_{n=1}^{M} f_n \, \exp\left[j(\omega_c + \ell\omega_2)[t - \frac{2(x_n - v_n t)}{c}]\right],$$

that can be rewritten as follows:

$$sp_\ell(t) = A_1(\ell\omega_2) \sum_{n=1}^{M} f_n \, \underbrace{\exp[-j\frac{2(\omega_c + \ell\omega_2)}{c} x_n]}_{Range-dependent}$$

$$\times \underbrace{\exp[j(\omega_c + \ell\omega_2)(1 + \frac{2v_n}{c})t]}_{Speed-dependent}.$$

The temporal Fourier transform of the above echoed signal is

$$SP_\ell(\omega) = A_1(\ell\omega_2) \sum_{n=1}^{M} f_n \, \exp[-j\frac{2(\omega_c + \ell\omega_2)}{c}x_n]$$

$$\times \; A_3[\omega - (\omega_c + \ell\omega_2)(1 + \frac{2v_n}{c})].$$

With $t_3 = \infty$ (*continuous-wave* assumption), that is, $A_3(\omega) = \delta(\omega)$, the above model becomes

$$SP_\ell(\omega) = A_1(\ell\omega_2) \sum_{n=1}^{M} f_n \, \exp[-j\frac{2(\omega_c + \ell\omega_2)}{c}x_n]$$

$$\times \; \delta[\omega - (\omega_c + \ell\omega_2)(1 + \frac{2v_n}{c})].$$

This signal can be rewritten as follows:

$$SP_\ell(\omega) = A_1(\ell\omega_2) \sum_{n=1}^{M} f_n \, \underbrace{\exp(-jk_{x\ell}\,x_n)}_{Range-dependent} \; \underbrace{\delta[\omega - \omega_\ell(v_n)]}_{Speed-dependent} \,,$$

where

$$\omega_\ell(v_n) \equiv (\omega_c + \ell\omega_2)(1 + \frac{2v_n}{c})$$

$$= \underbrace{(\omega_c + \ell\omega_2)}_{Carrier} + \underbrace{\frac{2v_n}{c}(\omega_c + \ell\omega_2)}_{Doppler\ shift},$$

and

$$k_{x\ell} \equiv \frac{2(\omega_c + \ell\omega_2)}{c}.$$

Note that $SP_\ell(\omega)$ contains a familiar phase function that carries information on a target's range, that is, $\exp(-jk_{x\ell}x_n)$. We encountered the same phase function in echo imaging of static targets. The difference now is in the fact that this information resides at $\omega_\ell(v_n)$, which is a Doppler-shifted version of the carrier of the ℓ-th harmonic.

Inversion

The total echoed signal, $s(t)$, is the **sum** of the echoed signals due to the harmonics of the FM-CW signal; that is,

$$s(t) = \sum_{\ell} sp_{\ell}(t).$$

This linear relationship translates into the following sum in the temporal frequency domain:

$$S(\omega) = \sum_{\ell} SP_{\ell}(\omega).$$

Figure 1.20 shows an example of the Fourier spectra for the FM-CW echoed signal from three targets. One target is stationary; one target has a negative speed; and the last target has a positive speed.

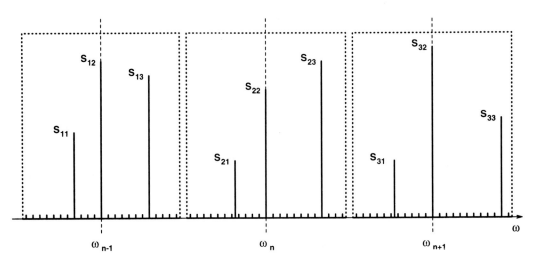

Figure 1.20 Fourier domain FM-CW echo signature.

The temporal Doppler shift introduced by the n-th target at the ℓ-th harmonic of $p(t)$ that is located at $\omega = \omega_c + \ell\omega_2$ is [see (1.36a) with ω_c replaced with $\omega_c + \ell\omega_2$]

$$\omega_{Dn\ell} \equiv \frac{2v_n}{c}(\omega_c + \ell\omega_2). \qquad (1.42)$$

Note that this Doppler shift is not the same for all the harmonics. As we showed earlier, this component appears in the distribution of $S(\omega)$ at $\omega_\ell(v_n)$. Furthermore, this Doppler-shifted component would not overlap with the Doppler-shifted components of the other harmonics provided that

$$|\omega_{Dn\ell}| < \frac{\omega_2}{2}. \qquad (1.43)$$

With (1.43) satisfied, one can retrieve the echoed signal due to each harmonic of the FM-CW signal, that is, $sp_\ell(t)$ or $SP_\ell(\omega)$. This is achieved via passing the baseband echoed signal through a bank of bandpass filters. These filters are centered around the baseband harmonics $\ell\omega_2$ and their bandwidth is equal to ω_2. Thus, the support band of the ℓ-th bandpass filter is

$$[\ell\omega_2 - \frac{\omega_2}{2}, \ell\omega_2 + \frac{\omega_2}{2}].$$

The bandpass filtering operation can be performed either in the time domain via convolving $s_b(t) = s(t)\exp(-j\omega_c t)$ with the impulse responses of the above-mentioned bandpass filters, or in the temporal frequency domain via *partitioning* $S_b(\omega)$ into regions with length ω_2 centered around the harmonics of the FM-CW signal.

This partitioning operation is shown in Figure 1.21 for the FM-CW echo signature example that was given in Figure 1.20. The resultant is a *two-dimensional* database in the FM-CW harmonic and Doppler frequency domain, that is, (ω_ℓ, ω_D).

Now we are ready to formulate the inverse problem. Suppose we denote the reflectivity function for the targets with speed v by $f(x, v)$ and its spatial Fourier transform with respect to x by $F(k_x, v)$. If (1.43) is true, then the components of $SP_\ell(\omega)$ at

$$\omega_\ell(v) = (\omega_c + \ell\omega_2) + \frac{2v}{c}(\omega_c + \ell\omega_2), \qquad (1.44)$$

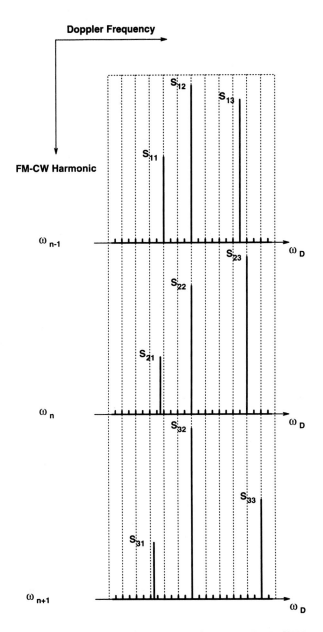

Figure 1.21 Partitioned Fourier domain FM-CW echo signature.

$\ell = 0, \pm 1, \pm 2, \ldots$, are exclusively due to targets that move with speed v. Thus, these components can be extracted from $SP_\ell(\omega)$ to reconstruct $F(k_{x\ell}, v)$. The theoretical inverse equation for this imaging problem is

$$
\begin{aligned}
F(k_{x\ell}, v) &= \frac{SP_\ell[\omega_\ell(v)]}{A_1(\ell\omega_2)} \\
&= \frac{S[\omega_\ell(v)]}{A_1(\ell\omega_2)},
\end{aligned}
\tag{1.45}
$$

where

$$
k_{x\ell} \equiv \frac{2(\omega_c + \ell\omega_2)}{c}.
\tag{1.46}
$$

- *In (1.45), we used the fact that the total received signal is the sum of the echoed signals due to all harmonics of the FM-CW signal; that is,*

$$
S(\omega) = \sum_\ell SP_\ell(\omega).
$$

Moreover, it is assumed that the target's signatures at two different harmonics of the FM-CW signal do not overlap with each other in the temporal frequency domain. The conditions for this will be discussed in the next section.

The practical matched-filtered version of the inverse equation that is not sensitive to additive noise is

$$
\begin{aligned}
F(k_{x\ell}, v) &= SP_\ell[\omega_\ell(v)] \ A_1^*(\ell\omega_2) \\
&= S[\omega_\ell(v)] \ A_1^*(\ell\omega_2),
\end{aligned}
\tag{1.47}
$$

where $*$ denotes complex conjugation.

For a fixed v, the above inversion provides samples of $F(k_x, v)$ at evenly spaced points in the k_x domain, that is, $k_{x\ell}, \ell = 0, \pm 1, \pm 2, \ldots$. The inverse discrete Fourier transform of this database with respect to ℓ yields a sampled distribution of $f(x, v)$, that is, the desired range-speed target function.

Figure 1.22a shows the partitioned FM-CW echo signature in the $(\omega_\ell, \omega_{D\ell})$ domain for a sonar range-speed imaging problem. There are 64 harmonics for the FM-CW signal in the band [5,10] KHz. The CW coherent processing time is $t_3 = .8192$ second. The imaging scene contains four targets with $(x_1, v_1) = (4.8, 0)$, $(x_2, v_2) = (2.4, -1.46)$, $(x_3, v_3) = (8.4, -1.46)$, and $(x_4, v_4) = (4.8, 1.95)$; units are (meter,meters/second). Figure 1.22b shows the transformed (interpolated) version of this FM-CW echo signature in the (ω_ℓ, v) domain where

$$\omega_{D\ell} = \frac{2v}{c}\omega_\ell;$$

that is,

$$v \equiv .5c\frac{\omega_{D\ell}}{\omega_\ell}.$$

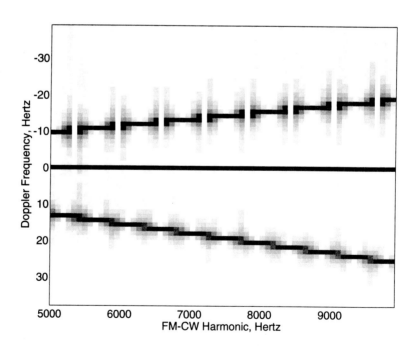

Figure 1.22a Partitioned periodic FM-CW echo signature.

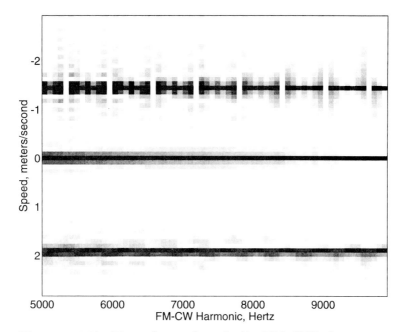

Figure 1.22b Transformed periodic FM-CW signature.

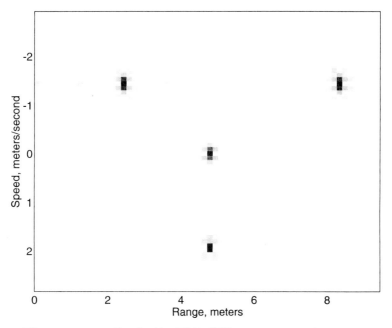

Figure 1.22c Periodic FM-CW reconstruction.

The one-dimensional inverse discrete Fourier transform of the FM-CW echo signature in the (ω_ℓ, v) domain with respect to the FM-CW harmonic, that is, ω_ℓ, is the desired target image $f(x, v)$ that is shown in Figure 1.22c.

Constraints

Suppose the target region is within a known interval $[X_1 - X_0, X_1 + X_0]$. It can be seen from (1.44) and (1.46) that the sample spacing in the k_x domain resulting from the inverse equation (1.45) or (1.47) is $\frac{2\omega_2}{c}$. Thus, the inverted data in the k_x domain would not be aliased provided that

$$\frac{4X_0}{c} \le t_2. \qquad (1.48)$$

(1.48) states that the pulse repetition interval (pri) for the short pulses $a_1(t)$ in the transmission interval $[0, t_3]$ should be greater than the arrival time difference between the echoes coming from the nearest point in the target region, that is, $x = X_1 - X_0$, and the farthest point in the target region, that is, $x = X_1 + X_0$.

Let v_{max} be the largest absolute target speed. The largest Doppler shift is caused by this speed at the largest harmonic in $p(t)$ that is $\omega_c + \omega_1$ [see (1.42)]. Thus, to satisfy (1.43) to prevent overlapping of the Doppler-shifted components of a harmonic from the other Doppler components, we should have

$$\frac{2v_{max}}{c}(\omega_c + \omega_1) < \frac{\omega_2}{2},$$

which yields the following constraint:

$$v_{max} < \frac{c\,\omega_2}{4(\omega_c + \omega_1)}. \qquad (1.49)$$

Time t_3, which determines resolution in the Doppler velocity domain, is limited by the time of arrival of the first echo from the target scene; that is,

$$t_3 \le \frac{2(X_1 - X_0)}{c}. \qquad (1.50)$$

As we mentioned earlier, it is possible to remove this restriction by using a separate transducer (radar antenna) to receive the incoming echoed signals, that is, a quasi-monostatic imaging system.

Resolution

The range resolution for time-frequency diversity signaling is dictated by the overall bandwidth of $a(t)$, that is,

$$\Delta_x \equiv \frac{2\pi c}{2\omega_1}. \tag{1.51}$$

The resolution in the Doppler velocity domain is determined by the sharpness of $A_3(\omega)$ in the frequency domain. Furthermore, the lowest harmonic in $p(t)$, that is, $\omega_c - \omega_1$, results in the smallest Doppler shift for a given target. Hence, if Δ_v is the Doppler velocity resolution, we have the following:

$$\frac{2\Delta_v}{c}(\omega_c - \omega_1) = \omega_3,$$

which yields

$$\Delta_v = \frac{c\,\omega_3}{2(\omega_c - \omega_1)}. \tag{1.52}$$

Signal Processing Considerations

Based on (1.29), the discrete Fourier transform of the baseband measured echoed signal, that is, $s_b(n\Delta_t)$, provides the samples of $S_b(\omega)$ at discrete frequencies separated by

$$\Delta_\omega = \frac{2\pi}{N\Delta_t}.$$

For a given integer ℓ, such that $\ell\omega_2 \in [-\omega_1, \omega_1]$ [i.e., within the effective bandwidth of $S_b(\omega)$], the samples of $S_b(n\Delta_\omega)$ that fall within the following band (partition) in the frequency domain:

$$[\ell\omega_2 - \frac{\omega_2}{2}\ ,\ \ell\omega_2 + \frac{\omega_2}{2}],$$

are used to interpolate $S_b[\omega_\ell(v)]$ at discrete values of v separated by [see (1.44)]

$$\delta_v \equiv \frac{c\,\Delta_\omega}{2(\omega_c - \omega_1)}.$$

This sample spacing corresponds to the spacing of the available data in the partition of the lowest harmonic in $p(t)$. In this fashion, all partitions end up with the v domain data that have a common sample spacing. Moreover, the use of the sample spacing in the lowest partition prevents aliasing in the interpolation process.

Aperiodic FM-CW Signaling

Recall the spectral distribution of the baseband signal for FM-CW periodic signaling as shown in (1.41), that is,

$$A(\omega) = A_3(\omega) \; * \; \sum_{\ell=-\infty}^{\infty} A_1(\ell\omega_2)\,\delta(\omega - \ell\omega_2)$$

$$= \sum_{\ell=-\infty}^{\infty} A_1(\ell\omega_2)\,A_3(\omega - \ell\omega_2),$$

is composed of *evenly spaced* spectral lines. This is due to the fact that $a(t)$ is a periodic signal with period t_2.

It can be shown that the autocorrelation (or the matched-filtered signal) of $a(t)$, that is,

$$\int_0^{t_3} a(t)\,a^*(t - \tau)\,dt,$$

exhibits sharp peaks every t_2 seconds. This is an undesirable feature of periodic FM-CW signaling for the following two reasons:

i. In certain radar and sonar reconnaissance applications, it is not desirable for the user to transmit a periodic signal. This is due to the fact that the target that is being imaged or a third party may exploit the properties of periodic FM-CW signals, that is, the sharp peaks that appear every t_2 seconds in its autocorrelation, to identify and locate the transmitter.

ii. Due to the physical closeness of the transmitter and receiver circuitries of a quasi-monostatic system, there is always some leakage of the transmitted signals into the receiver structure [13]. Moreover, it is difficult to completely isolate the transmitter and receiver antennas of a quasi-monostatic system such that there is no coupling between the two antennas. In this case, due to the simultaneous transmission and reception of FM-CW signaling, the transmitter leakage into the receiver is added with the incoming echoed signals. Due to the periodicity of the transmitted FM-CW signal, the leaked signal would show strong peaks every t_2 seconds at the output of the receiver's matched filter. This output could have catastrophic results in the imaging process. This factor has been one of the major drawbacks of using FM-CW signaling in practice. A Reflector Power Canceller (RPC), which has been suggested to null the reflection of the transmitted signal into the receiver circuitry for monostatic systems [13], may also be used to reduce transmitter/receiver leakage for quasi-monostatic systems.

Figure 1.23a shows a periodic FM-CW signal in the time domain. The autocorrelation of this signal is shown in Figure 1.23b. Note that the autocorrelation exhibits a peak every t_2 seconds. (This signal was intentionally generated to contain circular aliasing since in many practical imaging problems the FM-CW transmission time is not limited to $[0, t_3]$; the coherent processing of the echoed signals is limited to an interval with length t_3.) Figure 1.23c is the real part of the Fourier transform of the periodic FM-CW signal that is composed of evenly spaced spectral lines.

Signal Model: In this section, we examine an aperiodic FM-CW signaling scheme for high resolution range and Doppler (speed) imaging. The key property of the periodic signaling used in our imaging problem is its discrete spectral distribution (for Doppler resolution) over a large bandwidth (for range resolution). One may also achieve large-bandwidth spectral lines via *aperiodic* FM-CW signaling. The Fourier transform of the baseband signal for the general aperiodic signaling is

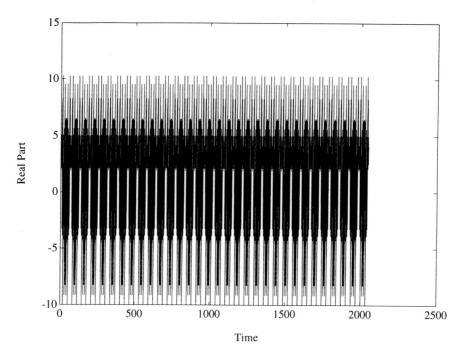

Figure 1.23a Periodic FM-CW signal.

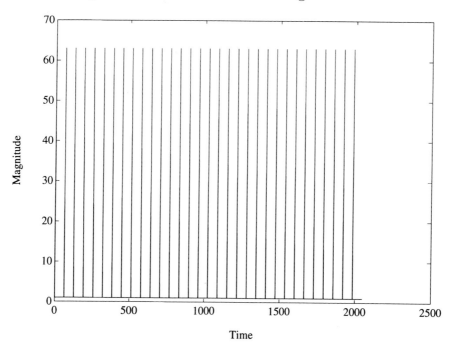

Figure 1.23b autocorrelation of periodic FM-CW signal.

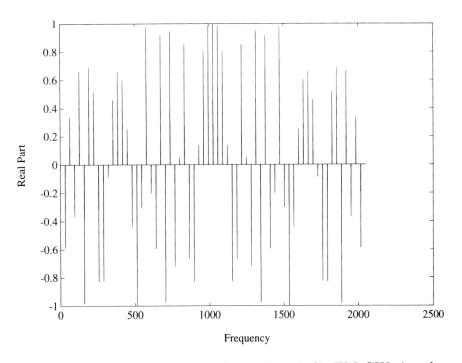

Figure 1.23c Fourier transform of periodic FM-CW signal.

$$A(\omega) = A_3(\omega) \ * \ \sum_{\ell=-\infty}^{\infty} A_\ell \ \delta(\omega - \Omega_\ell)$$

$$= \sum_{\ell=-\infty}^{\infty} A_\ell \ A_3(\omega - \Omega_\ell),$$

where Ω_ℓ's, that is, the location of the spectral lines, are *unevenly spaced* in the frequency domain. We can write Ω_ℓ as a general *nonlinear* function of ℓ, for example,

$$\Omega_\ell \equiv \Psi(\ell),$$

where $\Psi(\cdot)$ is a function chosen by the user.

This form of unevenly spaced discrete spectral distribution in the *frequency* domain is analogous to a form of *time* domain message transformation in communication theory, called *Pulse Position Modulation* (PPM), that is used for information transfer [2],[8]. Clearly, the periodic FM-CW signaling is a special case of aperiodic FM-CW signaling with

$$\Psi(\ell) \equiv \ell\omega_2.$$

Figure 1.24a shows an aperiodic FM-CW signal in the time domain. The autocorrelation of this signal is shown in Figure 1.24b. Note that this autocorrelation resembles the autocorrelation of a white process. This clearly makes its detection difficult, and the receiver's matched filter can reject a significant portion of the coupling that may exist between the transmitter and receiver antennas. Figure 1.24c is the real part of the Fourier transform of the aperiodic FM-CW signal that is composed of unevenly spaced spectral lines.

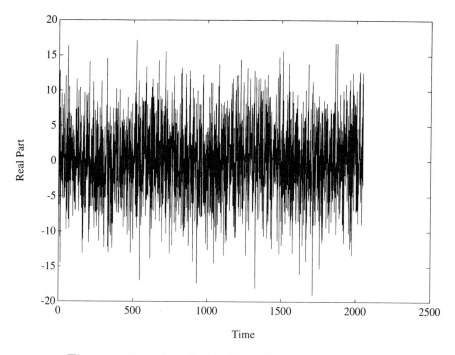

Figure 1.24a Aperiodic FM-CW signal.

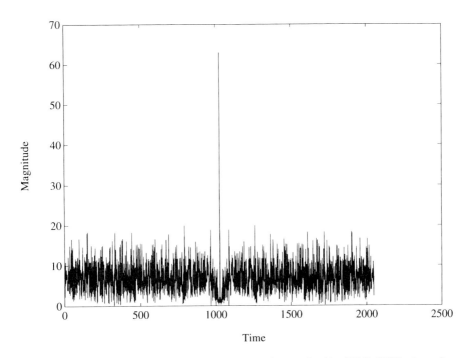

Figure 1.24b autocorrelation of aperiodic FM-CW signal.

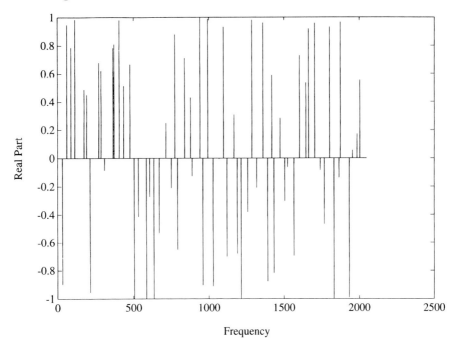

Figure 1.24c Fourier transform of aperiodic FM-CW signal.

- In practice, the signal leaked from the transmitter to the receiver channel has a dynamic range that is larger than that of echoed signals. Thus, the matched filtering that rejects the transmitter/receiver leakage should be performed in **analog** form, that is, prior to sampling and quantization of the receiver channel. In this case, the dynamic range of the quantizer can be set based on the strength of echoed signals and not the leaked signal. This would reduce quantization errors in the acquired data.

- One may also use an RPC, similar to the one suggested by Stove [13], at the output of the analog matched filter to further reduce the transmitter-receiver leakage side lobes. The reference signal for this RPC should be the autocorrelation of the aperiodic FM-CW signal.

Aperiodic FM-CW Waveform Synthesis: The above aperiodic FM-CW signal was generated by using uniformly distributed random variables to jitter the location of the spectral lines of a periodic FM-CW signal. In practice, this can be achieved by a programmable digital waveform generator that feeds the aperiodic FM-CW signal to the transmitter via a digital to analog (D/A) converter.

The type of probability distribution used in jittering the harmonics plays a key role in the sharpness of the baseband signal's autocorrelation. To show this, consider the expression for the baseband signal in the time domain, that is,

$$a(t) = \sum_{\ell} A_\ell \, \exp(j\Omega_\ell t),$$

for $t \in [0, t_3]$. We are interested in the following autocorrelation:

$$r_a(\tau) \equiv E\left[\int_0^{t_3} a(t) \, a^*(t - \tau) \, dt \right],$$

where $E[\cdot]$ represents the expectation operator in the probability space of the jitter random variables. Using the harmonic expansion for $a(t)$ in the expression for autocorrelation and after some rearrangements, we obtain

$$r_a(\tau) = \int_0^{t_3} \sum_m \sum_n A_m \, A_n \, E\left[\exp(j\Omega_m t) \, \exp[-j\Omega_n(t - \tau)] \right] dt.$$

Let

$$\Omega_m = m\omega_2 + \epsilon_m,$$

where ϵ_m's are jitter random variables. Moreover, suppose the jitter random variables are independent and identically distributed with probability density function $G(\omega)$. The characteristic function (or inverse Fourier transform) for this pdf is $g(t)$; that is,

$$E\Big[\exp(j\epsilon_m t) \Big] = g(t).$$

To simplify the expression for $r_a(t)$, we first consider the double sum in the autocorrelation function; that is,

$$\Lambda(t,\tau) \equiv \sum_m \sum_n A_m A_n^* E\Big[\exp(j\Omega_m t) \, \exp[-j\Omega_n(t - \tau)] \Big].$$

Since the jitter random variables are independent, we have

$$\Lambda(t,\tau) = \sum_m \sum_n A_m A_n^* E\Big[\exp(j\Omega_m t) \Big] E\Big[\exp[-j\Omega_n(t - \tau)] \Big]$$

$$+ \sum_m |A_m|^2 E\Big[\exp(j\Omega_m \tau) \Big]$$

$$- \sum_m |A_m|^2 E\Big[\exp(j\Omega_m t) \Big] E\Big[\exp[-j\Omega_m(t - \tau)] \Big].$$

Using the fact that

$$E\Big[\exp(j\Omega_m t) \Big] = g(t) \, \exp(jm\omega_2 t),$$

in the expression for Λ yields

$$\Lambda(t,\tau) = g(t)g^*(t - \tau) \sum_m \sum_n A_m A_n^* \exp(jm\omega_2 t) \exp[-jn\omega_2(t - \tau)]$$

$$+ g(\tau) \sum_m |A_m|^2 \, \exp(jm\omega_2 \tau)$$

$$- g(t) \, g^*(t - \tau) \sum_m |A_m|^2 \, \exp(jm\omega_2 \tau).$$

We define the periodic (nonjittered) basis pulse as follows:

$$a_0(t) \equiv \sum_{\ell} A_\ell \, \exp(j\ell w_2 t),$$

where ℓw_2's are the evenly spaced (nonjittered) harmonics and

$$A_1(\ell w_2) = A_\ell).$$

The autocorrelation of the periodic basis pulse is

$$r_{a_0}(\tau) \equiv \int_0^{t_3} a_0(t) \, a_0^*(t - \tau) \, dt$$

$$= t_3 \sum_m |A_m|^2 \, \exp(jm w_2 \tau).$$

Using these in the Λ expression yields

$$\Lambda(t,\tau) = g(t) \, g^*(t-\tau) \, a_0(t) \, a_0^*(t-\tau) + g(\tau) \, \frac{r_{a_0}(\tau)}{t_3} - g(t) \, g^*(t-\tau) \, \frac{r_{a_0}(\tau)}{t_3}.$$

We have

$$r_a(\tau) = \int_0^{t_3} \Lambda(t,\tau) \, dt.$$

We define the following signal:

$$b(t) \equiv a_0(t) \, g(t),$$

and its autocorrelation

$$r_b(\tau) \equiv \int_0^{t_3} b(t) \, b^*(t - \tau) \, dt.$$

Using these in the expression for $r_a(t)$ yields

$$r_a(\tau) = r_b(\tau) + r_{a_0}(\tau) \, g(\tau) - \frac{r_{a_0}(\tau)}{t_3} r_g(\tau),$$

where

$$r_g(\tau) \equiv \int_0^{t_3} g(t)\, g^*(t - \tau)\, dt.$$

Based on this relationship, one may design various jitter distributions, $G(\omega)$, and periodic basis function, $a_0(t)$, that yield the desired property for the baseband signal, that is, $a(t)$ is approximately a white process and, thus

$$r_a(\tau) \approx \delta(\tau).$$

From the expression for $r_a(\tau)$, one cannot easily solve for the best $g(t)$ and $a_0(t)$ in this design problem. However, one can observe from this expression that an $a_0(t)$ that resembles a white process and a $g(t)$ that has the most compact support would force $r_a(\tau)$ to possess a peak at $\tau = 0$. One way to meet those conditions is by having the jitter distribution be uniform and for $a_0(t)$ to have a flat magnitude spectrum; that is,

$$G(\omega) \equiv \begin{cases} \frac{1}{\omega_2}, & \text{if } \omega \in [\frac{-\omega_2}{2}, \frac{\omega_2}{2}], \\ 0, & \text{otherwise;} \end{cases}$$

and

$$|A_\ell| = 1.$$

The user may experiment on various sets of jittered data and select the one that most resembles a white process.

This design disregards an important issue associated with FM-CW signaling. One of the advantages of FM-CW signaling over pulsed signaling has been its ability to transmit a *constant low power* signal over a long time period (i.e., $[0, t_3]$). As a result, low power FM-CW signaling can provide the same energy that high-power pulsed signaling yields over a short period. At the same time, due to the low-power of FM-CW signaling, the user is less vulnerable to being identified.

The instantaneous power of $a(t)$ is

$$\Lambda(t, 0) = \int_0^{t_3} a(t)\, a^*(t)\, dt$$

$$= |b(t)|^2 + \frac{r_{a_0}(0)}{t_3} \left[g(0) - |g(t)|^2 \right].$$

Thus, the power level of an aperiodic FM-CW signal is not necessarily a constant.

The information content of a large-bandwidth signal, for example, an FM-CW signal, is mainly in its phase and not its amplitude. Thus, the problem with time-varying power of an aperiodic FM-CW may be resolved by selecting the transmitted baseband signal to be the amplitude-equalized version of $a(t)$; that is,

$$a_e(t) \equiv \frac{a(t)}{|a(t)|},$$

for $a(t) \neq 0$, and one otherwise. (In the digital signal processing involved in generating $a(t)$, we never encountered a case where $a(t) = 0$.)

The next concern is whether $A_e(\omega)$ is composed of discrete spectral lines that are useful for Doppler resolution. We also require these spectral lines to have equal amplitudes such that the periodic basis is a white process. As we mentioned earlier, the information content of an FM-CW signal is mainly in its phase. Thus, the amplitude equalization in the time domain should not alter the spectral form of the signal significantly. This is demonstrated in Figure 1.25a. This figure shows the magnitude of $A_e(\omega)$ that is composed of spectral lines at the original aperiodic FM-CW harmonics, that is, Ω_ℓ 's. This distribution also contains a lower power signal at the other frequency components.

One may improve on this outcome by an *iterative correction* of the designed aperiodic signal. The procedure is based on the fact that we require the signal to have a constant amplitude in the time domain and be composed of constant-amplitude discrete spectral lines in the frequency domain. To achieve these two objectives, one may impose the above-mentioned constraints iteratively to achieve a *better* solution.

Computing $a_e(t)$ via amplitude equalization of $a(t)$ is the first step of the iteration. We define $a^{(0)}(t) = a(t)$ to be the original solution at the start of the iteration (i.e., the zero-th iteration), and $a^{(1)}(t) = a_e(t)$ to be the solution in the first step of the iteration; that is,

$$a^{(1)}(t) \equiv \frac{a^{(0)}(t)}{|a^{(0)}(t)|}.$$

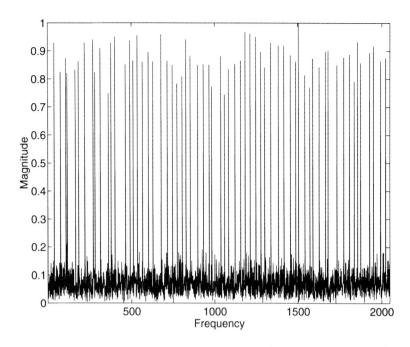

Figure 1.25a Aperiodic FM-CW synthesis: First iteration.

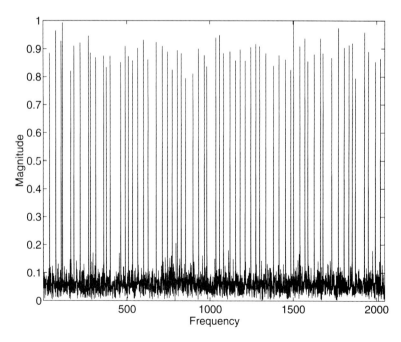

Figure 1.25b Aperiodic FM-CW synthesis: 201-st iteration.

In the second step of the iteration, we impose the constraint that the signal in the frequency domain is composed of white discrete spectral lines at Ω_ℓ's; that is,

$$A^{(2)}(\omega) \equiv \begin{cases} \frac{A^{(1)}(\omega)}{|A^{(1)}(\omega)|}, & \text{if } \omega = \Omega_\ell, \; \ell = 0, \pm 1, \pm 2, \ldots; \\ 0, & \text{otherwise.} \end{cases}$$

To generalize the iterative algorithm, the amplitude equalization in the time domain is imposed at the odd steps of the iteration; that is,

$$a^{(2n+1)}(t) \equiv \frac{a^{(2n)}(t)}{|a^{(2n)}(t)|}.$$

While at the even steps of the iteration, the signal components at frequencies other than the aperiodic FM-CW harmonics are filtered out and the rest go through amplitude equalization; that is,

$$A^{(2n)}(\omega) \equiv \begin{cases} \frac{A^{(2n-1)}(\omega)}{|A^{(2n-1)}(\omega)|}, & \text{if } \omega = \Omega_\ell, \; \ell = 0, \pm 1, \pm 2, \ldots; \\ 0, & \text{otherwise.} \end{cases}$$

There are no guarantees that this iterative method would converge to a perfect and clean aperiodic FM-CW signal with a constant amplitude in the time domain as well as the frequency domain. Figure 1.25b shows the magnitude distribution for the designed aperiodic FM-CW signal at the 201-st iteration of the algorithm.

Without using this procedure, the aperiodic FM-CW signal, which comes out of the radar antenna, may contain a similar level of noise that is due to side lobes of $A_3(\omega)$, quantization errors of the D/A converter, and phase fluctuations of the local oscillator and the antenna. Thus, the user should not expect to illuminate the target scene with a *clean* FM-CW signal. The error coming from the iterative correction method would also add to the fading and phase errors in a coherent imaging problem. The *synthesis* of a proper aperiodic FM-CW with amplitude equalization, that is, one that contains tolerable fading and phase error levels, does not have a simple analytical solution. The user may generate a set of these signals and select the one that best satisfies his desired criteria.

Inversion: The inversion for aperiodic FM-CW signaling is identical to what was shown earlier for periodic FM-CW signaling. In this case, the inversion at one of the unevenly spaced harmonics of the aperiodic signal becomes

$$F(k_{x\ell}, v) = S[\Omega_\ell(v)] \ A_\ell^*,$$

where

$$\Omega_\ell(v) = (\omega_c + \Omega_\ell) + \frac{2v}{c}(\omega_c + \Omega_\ell),$$

and

$$k_{x\ell} \equiv \frac{2(\omega_c + \Omega_\ell)}{c},$$

for $\ell = 0, \pm 1, \pm 2, \ldots$.

The resultant database for $F(\cdot)$ in the k_x domain can be shown to be unevenly spaced. There are a number of algorithms for reconstruction (interpolation) from unevenly spaced sampled data. We will discuss one of those algorithms in Chapter 2.

Consider the sonar range-speed imaging problem that was studied via periodic FM-CW signaling in Figures 1.22a-1.22c. Figure 1.26a shows aperiodic FM-CW echo signature for the same imaging problem. The two-dimensional transformed version of this database is shown in Figure 1.26b. Figure 1.26c is the reconstructed target image from aperiodic FM-CW echo data.

Constraints: We denote the maximum and minimum values of the spectral separation lines by Ω_Δ and Ω_δ, respectively; that is,

$$\Omega_\delta \leq \Omega_\ell - \Omega_{\ell-1} \leq \Omega_\Delta,$$

for the available ℓ. Based on the sampling constraints for unevenly spaced data shown in Chapter 2, the inverted data in the k_x domain would not be aliased provided that

$$\frac{4X_0}{c} \leq \frac{2\pi}{\Omega_\Delta},$$

where $2X_0$ is the extent of the target region in the spatial x domain. This constraint is analogous to (1.48) for periodic signaling.

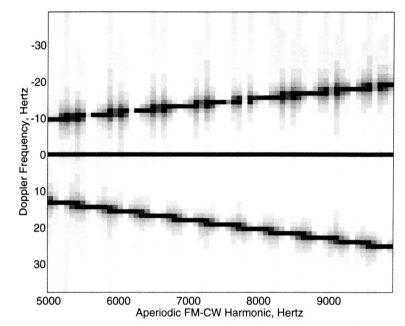

Figure 1.26a Partitioned aperiodic FM-CW echo signature.

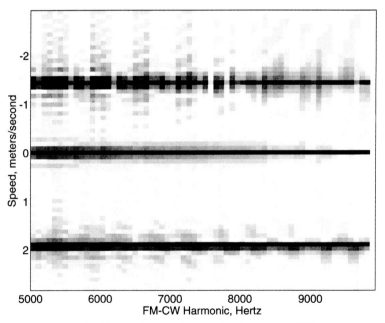

Figure 1.26b Transformed aperiodic FM-CW signature.

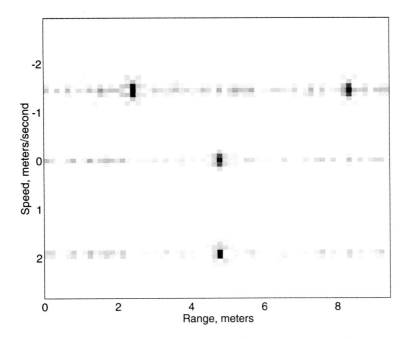

Figure 1.26c Aperiodic FM-CW reconstruction.

The Doppler separation constraint shown in (1.43) for periodic signaling becomes the following for aperiodic signaling:

$$\frac{\Omega_{\ell-1} - \Omega_\ell}{2} \; < \; \omega_{Dn\ell} \; < \; \frac{\Omega_{\ell+1} - \Omega_\ell}{2},$$

for the available ℓ. Let v_{max} be the largest absolute target speed. Then, to prevent overlapping of the Doppler shifted components of a harmonic from the other Doppler components, we should have

$$v_{max} \; < \; \frac{c\,\Omega_\delta}{4(\omega_c + \omega_1)}.$$

This constraint is analogous to (1.49) for periodic signaling.

Autonomous Vehicle Radar/Sonar

One of the applications of FM-CW signaling is in developing imaging schemes for an autonomous vehicle to extract information about its surrounding medium. These systems have been used in automobiles for Intelligent Cruise Control (ICC) and Obstacle Warning Radars (OWR) [14]. Mobile robots equipped with radar/sonar systems have also been used for imaging ocean floors and hostile environments.

The generalized system model and inverse problem that is associated with an autonomous vehicle vision system is a multidimensional one. Some of these systems can be formulated in terms of phased array imaging and synthetic aperture array imaging via FM-CW signaling, which will be discussed in Chapters 3 and 4.

We now examine a simple scenario for FM-CW imaging by an autonomous vehicle that converts the system model and inverse problem into a one-dimensional range-speed imaging system. For this, we consider a vehicle moving with speed v along the x axis on the line $z = 0$ (reference ground level) as shown in Figure 1.27.

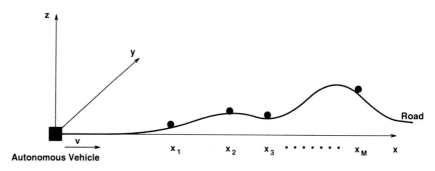

Figure 1.27 System geometry for autonomous vehicle radar.

In this imaging geometry, x is the range domain; z is the altitude domain. The third domain in the three-dimensional space y, called the cross-range domain, is not involved in our current discussion and will be brought to the picture in the next chapters. Currently, we are assuming that the vehicle and the targets in its scene are on the plane $y = 0$.

Our objective is to image variations of the road's altitude and other obstacles along the path of the vehicle. The vehicle is equipped with a quasi-monostatic transmitter/receiver (transceiver) that radiates the medium in front of the vehicle with an FM-CW signal.

We first examine the problem for the ℓ-th harmonic of the FM-CW signal, that is,

$$p_\ell(t) = A_\ell \, \exp(j\omega_\ell t),$$

where Ω_ℓ is the baseband jittered frequency of the harmonic, and $\omega_\ell = \omega_c + \Omega_\ell$. Suppose the vehicle is at $x = 0$ at $t = 0$ and maintains its altitude at $z = 0$ during the FM-CW signaling time period of $[0, t_3]$. The echoed signal due to the ℓ-th harmonic is

$$sp_\ell(t) \equiv \sum_{n=1}^{M} f_n \, p_\ell \Big[t - \frac{2\sqrt{(x_n - v_n t + vt)^2 + z_n^2}}{c} \Big]$$

$$= A_\ell \sum_{n=1}^{M} f_n \, \exp \Big[j\omega_\ell \big[t - \frac{2\sqrt{(x_n - v_n t + vt)^2 + z_n^2}}{c} \big] \Big],$$

where z_n is the altitude of the n-th target.

- For a **continuous** target model, for example, a road, the summation over the targets, that is, $\sum_{n=1}^{M}$, is replaced with an integral over x. For that model, the continuous target function $f(x)$ depends on the reflectivity distribution in space and the road's curvature. Certain parts of the road may not be visible to the vehicle's transceiver (blocked by other targets) or may have zero curvature. Such portions of the road would not have any contribution in the echo signature and would not appear in the reconstructed image.

There are various approximation-based methods to solve the inverse problem for the above system model. One method utilizes the following approximation:

$$\sqrt{(x_n - v_n t + vt)^2 + z_n^2} \approx r_n - (v_n - v)\cos\theta_n t,$$

where

$$r_n \equiv \sqrt{x_n^2 + z_n^2}$$

is called the *slant range*, and

$$\theta_n \equiv \arctan\left(\frac{z_n}{x_n}\right)$$

is the *slant angle*. Moreover, we define

$$\tilde{v}_n \equiv (v_n - v)\cos\theta_n$$

to be the relative speed in the slant range domain.

In this case, the system model becomes

$$sp_\ell(t) \approx A_\ell \sum_{n=1}^{M} f_n \underbrace{\exp[-j\frac{2\omega_\ell}{c}r_n]}_{Slant\ range\ dependent}\ \underbrace{\exp[j\omega_\ell(1 + \frac{2\tilde{v}_n}{c})t]}_{Slant\ speed\ dependent}.$$

This model is similar to the one we developed earlier with $z_n = 0$, and has a similar inverse equation. The resultant reconstructed image shows the n-th target at range r_n and speed $\tilde{v}_n$. If this target were motionless, then $v_n = 0$ and, thus, $\tilde{v}_n = -v\cos\theta_n$. In this case, one could determine the target's range and altitude, that is, (x_n, z_n), from $(r_n, \tilde{v}_n)$.

Note that the above system model assumes that the Doppler shift introduced due to the relative speed difference between the vehicle and the n-th target is *time-invariant*. This observation, which is a consequence of the approximation used to derive the system model, turns out to be invalid. A better approximation that is based on the following:

$$\sqrt{(x_n - vt)^2 + z_n^2} \approx r_n - (v_n - v)\cos\theta_n t + \frac{(v_n - v)^2 t^2}{2X_1},$$

where X_1 is the range for the target's center-of-mass, exhibits this fact. The additional term, that is, $\frac{(v_n - v)^2 t^2}{2X_1}$, adds a chirp signal to the earlier approximated system model. This chirp introduces a *time-varying* Doppler shift in the echoed signal. The effect of this chirp can be compensated for in the inversion provided that v_n is known. In Chapter 5, we will examine a similar imaging system that involves obstacles (targets) moving with unknown velocities and methods to estimate their unknown velocities.

There also exists an approximation-free inversion that utilizes the following mathematical identity:

$$\mathcal{F}_{(t)}\left[\exp\left[j\omega_\ell[t - \frac{2\sqrt{(x_n - v_n t + vt)^2 + z_n^2}}{c}]\right]\right] =$$
$$\frac{1}{\sqrt{4k_\ell^2 - k_u^2}}\exp\left[jk_u x_n + j\sqrt{4k_\ell^2 - k_u^2}\, z_n\right],$$

where

$$k_\ell \equiv \frac{\omega_\ell}{c}$$
$$k_u \equiv \frac{\omega - \omega_\ell}{v - v_n}.$$

This Fourier decomposition will be examined extensively and used in formulating inverse methods for various imaging systems.

A special case of the above system model that involves moving targets can be used for OWR applications. The objective in these problems is to identify a moving target, for example, the n-th target, that is traveling straight (head-on) toward the vehicle and could crash with it. This corresponds to the case when the altitude of the vehicle and the n-th target are the same, that is, $z_n = 0$. (We already assumed that the vehicle and the targets are on the plane $y = 0$.)

The contribution of this target in the echoed signal at the ℓ-th harmonic is

$$f_n \; p_\ell[t - \frac{2(x_n - v_n t + vt)}{c}] = A_\ell \; f_n \; \exp\left[j\omega_\ell[t - \frac{2(x_n - v_n t + vt)}{c}]\right]$$

$$= A_\ell \; f_n \; \underbrace{\exp[-j2k_\ell x_n]}_{Range\ dependent} \; \underbrace{\exp[j\omega_\ell(1 + \frac{2(v_n - v)}{c})t]}_{Speed\ dependent}.$$

Thus, a head-on target introduces a *constant* or *time-invariant* Doppler shift, while the signature of a target that is not on a crash course with the vehicle (i.e., $y_n \neq 0$ or $z_n \neq 0$) possesses a *time-varying* Doppler shift. This criterion can be used to identify targets that may collide with the vehicle.

1.10 ONE-DIMENSIONAL TRANSMISSION IMAGING

System Model

Next, we examine the one-dimensional version of an imaging problem that revolutionized medical imaging in 1970s. Consider a transmitter located at $x = 0$ and a receiver device positioned at $x = R$ in the spatial x domain. This corresponds to what we referred to as a *bistatic* imaging system. N homogenous media reside between the transmitter and receiver, that is, the region $(0, R)$ in the x domain (see Figure 1.28); the n-th homogeneous medium extended in the region (x_n, x_{n+1}), where

$$\sum_{n=1}^{N} x_{n+1} - x_n = R,$$

with $x_1 = 0$ and $x_{N+1} = R$.

We denote the speed of wave propagation and the wave attenuation coefficient in the n-th medium by $c_n > 0$ and $\epsilon_n < 0$, respectively. Suppose the transmitter emits a pulsed signal $p(t)$. Under certain constraints (no reflection and diffraction effects), the signal recorded by the receiver can be modeled to be the following attenuated and delayed version of the transmitted signal:

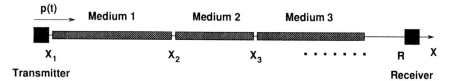

Figure 1.28 System geometry for transmission imaging.

$$s(t) = \exp[\underbrace{\sum_{n=1}^{N} (x_{n+1} - x_n)\, \epsilon_n}_{attenuation}]\; p[t - \underbrace{\sum_{n=1}^{N} \frac{x_{n+1} - x_n}{c_n}}_{time\ delay}]; \qquad (1.53)$$

that is, the time delay associated with the wave propagation through the n-th medium is

$$\frac{x_{n+1} - x_n}{c_n},$$

which depends on the c_n of that medium, and the wave attenuation in the n-th medium is

$$\exp[(x_{n+1} - x_n)\, \epsilon_n],$$

which depends on the ϵ_n of that medium.

Next, we convert this discrete model to a continuous one by letting

$$N \rightarrow \infty$$
$$x_{n+1} - x_n \rightarrow dx$$
$$c_n \rightarrow c(x)$$
$$\epsilon_n \rightarrow \epsilon(x)$$

Thus, the received signal becomes

$$s(t) = \underbrace{\exp[\int_0^R \epsilon(x) \, dx]}_{attenuation} \; p[t - \underbrace{\int_0^R \frac{1}{c(x)} \, dx}_{time\ delay}]. \tag{1.54}$$

- *The amplitude of $s(t)$ carries information only on the attenuation function $\epsilon(x)$, while the time delay between $s(t)$ and $p(t)$ is a function of the speed function $c(x)$.*

Inversion

Taking the temporal Fourier transform of both sides of the system model in (1.54) gives

$$S(\omega) = \exp[\int_0^R \epsilon(x) \, dx] \; P(\omega) \; \exp[-j\omega \int_0^R \frac{1}{c(x)} \, dx]$$
$$= \underbrace{P(\omega)}_{input\ dependent} \; \underbrace{\exp\left[\int_0^R \epsilon(x) - j\omega \frac{1}{c(x)} \, dx\right]}_{target\ dependent}. \tag{1.55}$$

We denote the *complex* target function by

$$f(x) \equiv \begin{cases} \epsilon(x) - j\omega \frac{1}{c(x)}, & \text{if } 0 < x < R; \\ 0, & \text{otherwise.} \end{cases} \tag{1.56}$$

- *A more accurate analysis of wave propagation through an attenuating medium would result in an attenuation function that varies, for example, linearly with ω. In this case, $\epsilon(x)$ should be replaced with $\omega\,\epsilon(x)$ in the expression for the complex target function.*

Using (1.56) in the system model (1.55) for $S(\omega)$ yields

$$
\begin{aligned}
S(\omega) &= P(\omega)\,\exp\Big[\int_{-\infty}^{\infty} f(x)\,dx\Big] \\
&= P(\omega)\,\exp[F(0)],
\end{aligned}
\tag{1.57}
$$

where $F(0)$ is the dc value of $f(x)$. Thus, we have the following inverse equation:

$$
F(0) = \ln\Big[\frac{S(\omega)}{P(\omega)}\Big].
$$

We observe that, unlike echo imaging, varying ω does not provide us with additional information about $F(k_x)$. In this case, it appears that there is no use in transmitting a wide-band pulsed signal in transmission imaging. Clearly, the inversion equation is not sufficient for reconstructing $f(x)$. The merits of this principle will become evident in the analysis of two-dimensional transmission imaging systems that are based on the geometrical optics approximation (Chapter 7).

Before closing this section, we establish notations and terminologies that will be used in those imaging systems. We rewrite (1.54) as follows:

$$
s(t) = e^{\gamma}\,p(t - \tau),
$$

where

$$
\gamma \equiv \int_0^R \epsilon(x)\,dx
$$

$$
\tau \equiv \int_0^R \frac{1}{c(x)}\,dx
$$

The transmission-mode imaging systems that are based on geometrical optics approximation record these two parameters without performing a Fourier transform on $s(t)$. The receiver records γ, called ***attenuation***, via an energy detector. The parameter τ, called *time-of-flight*, is recorded via a peak detector at the output of the matched filter.

We redefine the complex target function via its real and imaginary parts as follows:

$$f(x) \equiv f_r(x) + j f_i(x),$$

where

$$f_r(x) \equiv \begin{cases} \epsilon(x), & \text{if } 0 < x < R; \\ 0, & \text{otherwise} \end{cases}$$

and

$$f_i(x) \equiv \begin{cases} \frac{1}{c(x)}, & \text{if } 0 < x < R; \\ 0, & \text{otherwise} \end{cases}$$

Thus, we have the attenuation to be dependent on the real part of the target function, that is,

$$\gamma = \int_{-\infty}^{\infty} f_r(x) \, dx$$
$$= F_r(0).$$

Moreover, the time-of-flight depends only on the imaginary part of the target function, that is,

$$\tau = \int_{-\infty}^{\infty} f_i(x) \, dx$$
$$= F_i(0).$$

The complex representation relating the recorded parameters to the complex target function is

$$\gamma + j\tau = \int_{-\infty}^{\infty} f(x) \, dx$$
$$= F(0).$$

1.11 AMPLITUDE-MODULATED AND PHASE-MODULATED SIGNALS

We next consider a signal $s(u)$ in the spatial u domain and its spatial Fourier transform that has the following form:

$$S(k_u) \equiv \exp[j\phi(k_u)],$$

where $\phi(k_u)$ is a general (nonlinear) real signal. This signal is called a Phase-Modulated (PM) wave. The instantaneous frequency of the PM wave is defined via

$$U(k_u) \equiv \frac{d\phi(k_u)}{dk_u}.$$

Note that $U(k_u)$ has the same units as u. An Amplitude-Modulated Phase-Modulated (AM-PM) signal is defined by

$$S(k_u) \equiv A(k_u) \exp[j\phi(k_u)],$$

where $A(k_u)$ is called the AM component.

Example 1: Sinusoidal Signal: When $\phi(k_u)$ is a linear function of k_u, for example,

$$S(k_u) = \exp(j k_u y_0),$$

where y_0 is a constant, then $U(k_u) = y_0$. Note that in this example $S(k_u)$ is a complex sinusoid with a constant instantaneous frequency y_0. The inverse spatial Fourier transform of $S(k_u)$ is

$$s(u) = \delta(u + y_0).$$

Example 2: Chirp Signal: The following PM wave

$$S(k_u) = \exp[j(k - \frac{k_u^2}{2k}) x_0 + j k_u y_0], \tag{1.58}$$

where k and (x_0, y_0) are constants, is called a chirp signal or a Gaussian phase function that has the following instantaneous frequency function:

$$\begin{aligned} U(k_u) &= \frac{d}{dk_u}[(k - \frac{k_u^2}{2k}) x_0 + k_u y_0] \\ &= -\frac{k_u}{k} x_0 + y_0. \end{aligned} \tag{1.59}$$

The inverse Fourier transform of the chirp signal in (1.58) is another chirp signal in the u domain [7]:

$$s(u) = \exp\left[\, jkx_0 + jk\frac{(u+y_0)^2}{2x_0}\,\right]. \tag{1.60}$$

Example 3: Spherical Signal: We next consider the PM wave defined by

$$S(k_u) = \exp(j\sqrt{k^2 - k_u^2}\, x_0 + jk_u y_0), \tag{1.61}$$

with the instantaneous frequency

$$\begin{aligned} U(k_u) &= \frac{d}{dk_u}(\sqrt{k^2 - k_u^2}\, x_0 + k_u y_0) \\ &= -\frac{k_u}{\sqrt{k^2 - k_u^2}}\, x_0 + y_0. \end{aligned} \tag{1.62}$$

The inverse spatial Fourier transform of the signal in (1.61) multiplied by the amplitude function $\frac{1}{\sqrt{k^2 - k_u^2}}$ can be shown to be a *spherical* phase function [4]:

$$s(u) = \exp\left[\, jk\sqrt{x_0^2 + (u+y_0)^2}\,\right]. \tag{1.63}$$

(Section 2.4 will provide a more detailed analysis of this class of signals.) This signal will be encountered extensively in our discussion of array imaging systems.

The PM waves in Examples 2 and 3 are closely related. In fact, the two PM waves would be equal to each other provided that the following approximation (based on retention of the first two terms of the Taylor series expansion) holds:

$$\begin{aligned} \sqrt{k^2 - k_u^2} &= k\sqrt{1 - (\frac{k_u}{k})^2} \\ &= k\left[1 - \frac{1}{2}(\frac{k_u}{k})^2 + \cdots\right] \\ &\approx k - \frac{k_u^2}{2k}. \end{aligned} \tag{1.64}$$

(1.64) is a valid approximation provided that

$$\left(\frac{k_u}{k}\right)^2 \ll 1. \tag{1.65}$$

The u domain signals in (1.60) and (1.63) would also become identical if the following is true:

$$
\begin{aligned}
\sqrt{x_0^2 + (u + y_0)^2} &= x_0 \sqrt{1 + \left(\frac{u + y_0}{x_0}\right)^2} \\
&= x_0 \left[1 + \frac{1}{2}\left(\frac{u + y_0}{x_0}\right)^2 + \ldots \right] \\
&\approx x_0 + \frac{1}{2}\frac{(u + y_0)^2}{x_0},
\end{aligned} \tag{1.66}
$$

which is a valid approximation when

$$\left(\frac{u + y_0}{x_0}\right)^2 \ll 1. \tag{1.67}$$

In our discussion on Fourier array imaging, we refer to (1.64) or (1.66) as the Fresnel approximation [7]. The distinct feature of our approach in array imaging systems is that we would not need to use the Fresnel or other type of approximations to analyze the spherical phase function described in Example 3.

Another approximation to the spherical phase function is used in array processing problems that is discussed next. Denote

$$r_0 \equiv \sqrt{x_0^2 + y_0^2}$$

$$\phi_0 \equiv \arctan\left(\frac{y_0}{x_0}\right).$$

(r_0, ϕ_0) are called the *polar* coordinates for (x_0, y_0); r_0 is called the *range*, and ϕ_0 is referred to as the *angle* with respect to the broadside. We perform the following Taylor series expansion and approximation around r_0 on the left side of (1.66):

$$\sqrt{x_0^2 + (u + y_0)^2} = r_0 \sqrt{1 + \frac{2uy_0 + u^2}{r_0}}$$

$$\approx r_0 + \frac{y_0}{r_0} u$$

$$= r_0 + \sin \phi_0 u.$$

Using this approximation for the spherical wave in (1.63), we obtain

$$s(u) \approx \exp(jkr_0 + jk \sin \phi_0 u),$$

and, thus

$$S(k_u) \approx \exp(jkr_0) \, \delta(k_u - k \sin \phi_0).$$

This is known as the *plane wave* approximation for a spherical wave. This approximation is the basis of the classical passive array processing and beamforming methods for target detection and parameter estimation.

1.12 SPATIAL DOPPLER PHENOMENON

The discussion in this section establishes principles and provides the basic tools for analyzing resolution in Fourier array imaging systems. Let $S(k_u)$ be a general PM signal as defined in the previous section. We define the following signal:

$$r(u) \equiv s(u) \, i(u) = \begin{cases} s(u), & \text{if } u \in [-L, L]; \\ 0, & \text{otherwise,} \end{cases}$$

where $i(u)$ is the indicator (rectangular) function defined in Section 1.1. We refer to $[-L, L]$ as the observation/measurement *aperture*. From the Fourier transform convolution property, we have

$$R(k_u) = S(k_u) \; * \; I(k_u)$$

$$= \exp[j \phi(k_u)] \; * \; I(k_u)$$

where $*$ denotes convolution in the k_u domain. Note that the right side of the above equation represents a lowpass filtering operation. This filtering results in the suppression of the components of the PM wave at k_u values where the instantaneous frequency of the PM wave falls outside the interval $[-L, L]$, that is, the band support of the filter $i(u)$; that is,

$$R(k_u) \approx \begin{cases} S(k_u), & \text{if } |U(k_u)| < L; \\ 0, & \text{otherwise.} \end{cases} \qquad (1.68)$$

Now suppose $S(k_u)$ is an AM-PM signal. Moreover, it is assumed that the effective support band for $a(u)$ is much smaller than the support band of $i(u)$ (the indicator function), that is, $[-L, L]$. In this case, the expression shown in (1.68) is still valid for the filtered AM-PM signal.

Example 1: Sinusoidal Signal: We consider the complex sinusoidal signal

$$S(k_u) = \exp(j k_u y_0).$$

After filtering, this sinusoid will not be suppressed for all k_u values if its instantaneous frequency, that is, y_0, falls in the interval $[-L, L]$. Otherwise, $R(k_u)$ is zero for all k_u. Thus, we have

$$R(k_u) = \begin{cases} S(k_u), & \text{if } |y_0| < L; \\ 0, & \text{otherwise} \end{cases}$$

Example 2: Spherical Signal: We consider the PM signal defined in (1.61), that is,

$$S(k_u) = \exp(j \sqrt{k^2 - k_u^2} \, x_0 + j k_u y_0).$$

The region in the k_u domain where this PM wave is not suppressed after filtering is determined from the following inequality:

$$|U(k_u)| = \left| -\frac{k_u}{\sqrt{k^2 - k_u^2}} \, x_0 + y_0 \right| < L. \qquad (1.69)$$

This yields the following band:

$$k \sin \theta_1 < k_u < k \sin \theta_2, \qquad (1.70)$$

where

$$\theta_1 \equiv \arctan(\frac{y_0 - L}{x_0})$$

$$\theta_2 \equiv \arctan(\frac{y_0 + L}{x_0}).$$

(1.71)

Figure 1.29 shows the real part of the spherical wave function $s(u)$ defined in (1.63) for $k = \pi$ radians/meter and: a) $(x_0, y_0) = (1000, 0)$ meters; b) $(x_0, y_0) = (1000, 200)$ meters. Figure 1.30a and 1.30b show the real parts of $S(k_u)$ defined in (1.61) (i.e., the spatial Fourier transform of the signal in Figure 1.29) and its filtered version $R(k_u)$ when $L = 100$ meters. For $(x_0, y_0) = (1000, 0)$ meters, the solution of (1.70) yields $k_u \in [-.31, .31]$ radians/meter (see Figure 1.30a). For $(x_0, y_0) = (1000, 200)$ meters, (1.70) gives $k_u \in [.31, .9]$ radians/meter (see Figure 1.30b).

Figure 1.31a provides a graphical representation of the phenomenon dictated by (1.70)-(1.71). Suppose (x_0, y_0) identify the coordinates of a point target in the two-dimensional spatial domain (x, y), and the window (aperture) function $i(u)$ is a line segment on the line $x = 0$ extended from $u = -L$ to $u = L$. In this case, (θ_1, θ_2) are the angles of the lines connecting the target at (x_0, y_0) to the two extreme ends of the aperture line segment on $x = 0$. We call this the *spatial Doppler phenomenon* for reasons that will become obvious in later discussion. Figure 1.31a shows this for a target with $y_0 = $ (broadside target) where

$$\theta_0 \equiv \theta_2 = -\theta_1$$

corresponding to the numerical result shown in Figure 1.30a, and a target with $y_0 \neq 0$ (off-broadside target) corresponding to the numerical result shown in Figure 1.30b.

- *The signature (or contribution) of a target is approximately centered around $k \sin \phi_0$ in the k_u domain where*

$$\phi_0 \equiv \arctan(\frac{y_0}{x_0}),$$

*is the polar angle of the target in the spatial (x, y) domain. We refer to $k \sin \phi_0$ as the **spatial Doppler shift** for the target at (x_0, y_0).*

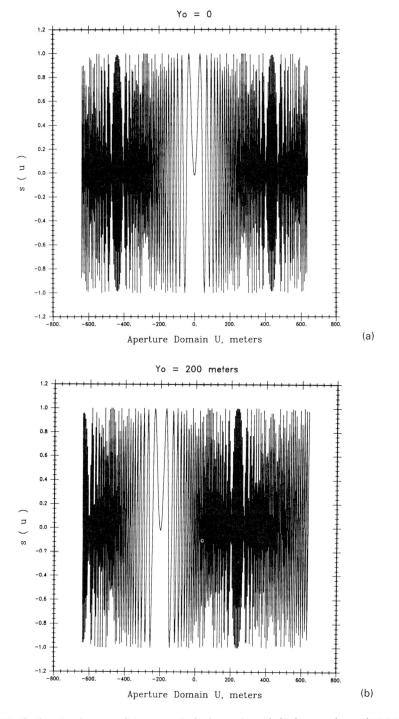

Figure 1.29 Spherical signal in spatial domain. (a) $(x_0, y_0) = (1000, 0)$ meters. (b) $(x_0, y_0) = (1000, 200)$ meters.

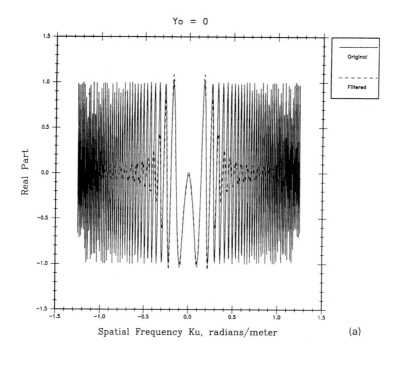

(a)

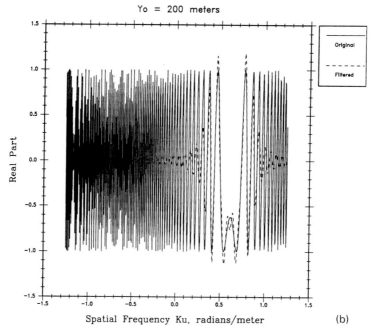

(b)

Figure 1.30 Spherical signal in spatial frequency domain. (a) $(x_0, y_0) = (1000, 0)$ meters. (b) $(x_0, y_0) = (1000, 200)$ meters.

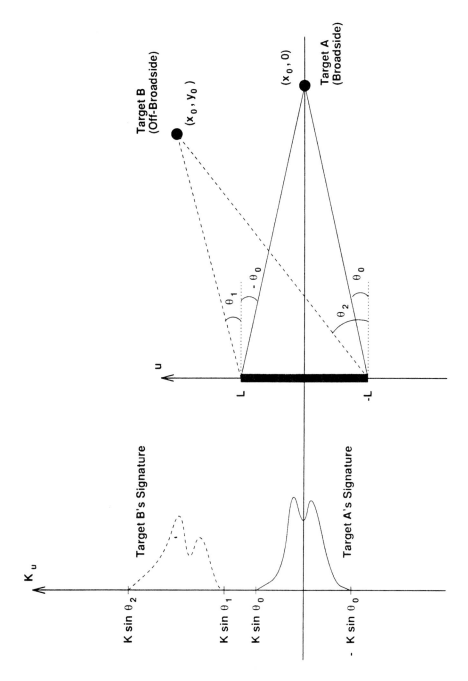

Figure 1.31a Spatial Doppler (Fourier) phenomenon.

113

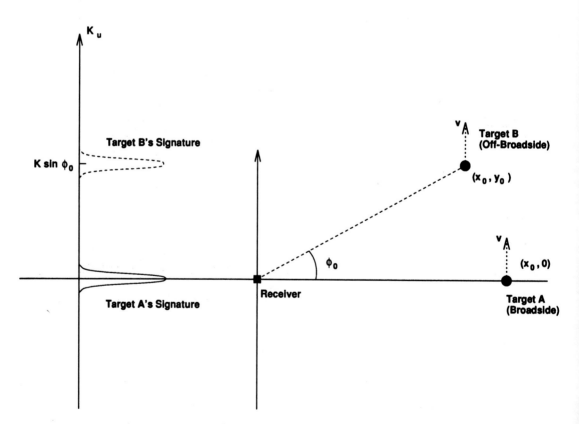

Figure 1.31b Temporal Doppler (Fourier) phenomenon.

Why Spatial Doppler

Why do we use the term **spatial** *Doppler?* This becomes obvious by examining temporal Doppler phenomenon in the two-dimensional spatial domain and relating its information content to the information conveyed by a spherical wave on an aperture. This is discussed next.

Consider the geometry shown in Figure 1.31b. A target located at (x_0, y_0) in the two-dimensional spatial domain is moving with speed v parallel to the y axis. Suppose this target emits a signal $p(t)$. For simplicity of discussion, we assume that $p(t)$ is a monotone CW signal, for example, $p(t) = \exp(j\omega t)$. (The general analysis for a multi-frequency CW signal is similar to the one we showed for FM-CW signaling.) A receiver (observer) is located at the origin, that is, $(x, y) = (0, 0)$.

The *time-dependent* target's radial distance from the receiver at the origin is

$$r(t) \equiv \sqrt{x_0^2 + (y_0 - vt)^2}.$$

Under certain conditions that we encounter in some of our imaging problems, namely $|vt| \ll r_0$, the time-dependent range may be approximated via the following (note that $\frac{y_0}{r_0} = \sin \phi_0$):

$$r(t) \approx r_0 - v \sin \phi_0 t.$$

- *This is a classical approximation that is used for system modeling in range-Doppler imaging problems that are examined in Section 3.5 (Air Traffic Control/Surveillance Radar) and Section 4.9 (Temporal Doppler-Based SAR). We will discuss more accurate system models for multi-dimensional imaging of moving targets in Chapters 3-6.*

In this case, based on the principles we developed in Section 1.8 with $v \ll c$, the signal recorded by this receiver becomes

$$s(t) \equiv p\left[t - \frac{r(t)}{c}\right]$$

$$\approx p\left[t - \frac{r_0 - v \sin \phi_0\, t}{c}\right]$$

$$= \exp\left[j\omega(t - \frac{r_0 - v \sin \phi_0\, t}{c})\right]$$

$$= \exp(-jkr_0)\, \exp\left[j(\omega + \omega_D)t\right],$$

where the temporal Doppler frequency shift is

$$\omega_D \equiv \frac{v \sin \phi_0}{c} \omega = kv \sin \phi_0,$$

and $k = \frac{\omega}{c}$ is the wavenumber.

This result indicates that for a given target speed along the y axis, the temporal Doppler shift observed by the receiver depends on the target's angle with respect to the broadside, that is, ϕ_0. For a broadside target, the temporal Doppler shift is zero. These are shown in Figure 1.31b in a transformed version of the temporal Doppler frequency that is defined via

$$k_u \equiv \frac{\omega_D}{v}$$
$$= k \sin \phi_0.$$

Now consider the case when the target is stationary while a set of receivers located at $(0, u)$, $u \in [-L, L]$, in the spatial domain record the monotone signal transmitted by the target (see Figure 1.31a). The recorded signal at the receiver located at $(0, u)$ is

$$s(u, t) \equiv p\Big[t - \frac{\sqrt{x_0^2 + (y_0 - u)^2}}{c}\Big]$$
$$= \exp\Big[j\omega(t - \frac{\sqrt{x_0^2 + (y_0 - u)^2}}{c})\Big]$$
$$= \exp\Big[-jk\sqrt{x_0^2 + (y_0 - u)^2}\Big] \, \exp(j\omega t).$$

• *In this model, we have neglected a slowly fluctuating amplitude function that does not play an important role in our analysis. We will provide a more detailed analysis on properties of propagating waves in Chapters 2 and 3.*

After baseband conversion, the received signal becomes

$$s(u, t) \, \exp(-j\omega t) = \exp\Big[-jk\sqrt{x_0^2 + (y_0 - u)^2}\Big],$$

which is a spherical signal. Based on the results of (1.70)-(1.71) and Figure 1.31a, the spatial Fourier transform of this signal with respect to u is also centered at

$$k_u \equiv k \sin \phi_0,$$

which we called the target signature's **spatial** Doppler shift.

This spatial Doppler shift is identical to the temporal Doppler shift for a moving target. However, this target information is now generated by varying the spatial coordinates of the receiver, that is, $u \in [-L, L]$.

- *Spatial Doppler/Fourier shift is a **position-induced** phenomenon that is generated via varying a stationary receiver's position with respect to a stationary target's coordinates. However, **temporal Doppler shift** is a **motion-induced** phenomenon that is resulted from the relative difference between the target's speed and the receiver's speed.*

We will revisit the class of spherical signals and spatial Doppler phenomenon in Chapter 2. This principle is the basis of Fourier array imaging methods that are developed throughout this book.

Cross-Range Imaging from the Filtered Signal

Let $s(u)$ be the spherical wave function shown in (1.63). From (1.61), (1.68), and (1.70), we can write

$$R(k_u) \approx \begin{cases} \exp(j \sqrt{k^2 - k_u^2} \, x_0 + j k_u y_0), & \text{if } k \sin \theta_1 < k_u < k \sin \theta_2; \\ 0, & \text{otherwise.} \end{cases} \tag{1.72}$$

We define the following signal:

$$F(k_u) \equiv R(k_u) \, \exp(-j \sqrt{k^2 - k_u^2} \, x_0). \tag{1.73}$$

We call this signal the spatial Fourier transform of the *cross-range* target function. (The reason for using this terminology will become obvious later.) Substituting (1.72) in (1.73) yields

$$F(k_u) \approx \begin{cases} \exp(j k_u y_0), & \text{if } k \sin \theta_1 < k_u < k \sin \theta_2; \\ 0, & \text{otherwise.} \end{cases} \tag{1.74}$$

It is clear from (1.74) that $f(u)$ is a bandpass signal of the form

$$f(u) \approx 2K_0 \underbrace{\frac{\sin[K_0(u + y_0)]}{K_0(u + y_0)}}_{sinc\ pattern} \underbrace{\exp[j K_c(u + y_0)]}_{sinusoidal\ carrier}, \qquad (1.75)$$

where

$$
\begin{aligned}
K_0 &\equiv \frac{k\ \sin\theta_2 - k\ \sin\theta_1}{2} \\
K_c &\equiv \frac{k\ \sin\theta_2 + k\ \sin\theta_1}{2}
\end{aligned}
\qquad (1.76)
$$

($2K_0$: bandwidth; K_c: carrier spatial frequency).

- *Let $r_0 \equiv \sqrt{x_0^2 + y_0^2}$ (target's range) and $\phi_0 \equiv \arctan(\frac{y_0}{x_0})$ (target's angle with respect to the broadside). Provided that $L \ll r_0$, we can rewrite (1.76) as follows:*

$$
\begin{aligned}
K_0 &\approx k\ \frac{L}{r_0}\ \cos\phi_0^2 \\
K_c &\approx k\ \sin\phi_0.
\end{aligned}
$$

We have

$$|f(u)| \approx 2K_0\ |\frac{\sin[K_0(u + y_0)]}{K_0(u + y_0)}|. \qquad (1.77)$$

Thus, $|f(u)|$ is the magnitude of a sinc pattern positioned at $u = -y_0$. Moreover, the support region of this sinc pattern is approximately equal to the extent of its first lobe in the u domain, that is,

$$\Delta y_0 \equiv \frac{\pi}{K_0}. \qquad (1.78)$$

We call Δy_0 the *cross-range resolution* for the single target located at $u = -y_0$, and $|f(u)|$ the reconstructed cross-range image. ($y = -u$ is called the cross-range domain.)

- *Δy_0 decreases as K_0 increases. Thus, the cross-range resolution improves as [see (1.71) and (1.76)]:*

i. k, *the wavenumber, increases;*

ii. L, *the aperture length in the* u *domain, increases;*

iii. $r_0 \equiv \sqrt{x_0^2 + y_0^2}$, *target's range, decreases;*

iv. $\phi_0 \equiv \arctan(\frac{y_0}{x_0})$, *target's angle with respect to the broadside, decreases.*

Example 2, continued: Figure 1.32 shows the magnitude (solid line) and real part (dashed line) of $F(k_u)$ for the two cases ($y_0 = 0$ and $y_0 = 200$ meters) cited earlier. Note that the support band (i.e., $[k \sin \theta_1, k \sin \theta_2]$) and the frequency of $F(k_u)$ within its support band (i.e., y_0) are distinguishable. This will not be the case with the multiple targets case examined next.

Multiple Targets

Now suppose $S(k_u)$ is a linear combination of the type of signal shown in (1.61), that is,

$$S(k_u) = \sum_n S_n(k_u), \qquad (1.79)$$

with

$$S_n(k_u) \equiv f_n \, \exp(j\sqrt{k^2 - k_u^2} \, x_0 + j k_u y_n),$$

where the sum over n could be finite or infinite. (Note that x_0 is fixed in (1.79); it is assumed that $y_n < y_{n+1}$ for all n). We refer to (1.79) as the multiple targets case. From (1.63), the inverse Fourier transform of (1.79) with respect to k_u can be found to be

$$s(u) = \sum_n s_n(u),$$

with

$$s_n(u) \equiv f_n \, \exp\left[jk\sqrt{x_0^2 + (u + y_n)^2} \, \right].$$

Note that $s(u)$ is a linear combination (weighted sum) of spherical waves.

The measured signal is $s(u)$ within a finite aperture; that is,

$$r(u) \equiv s(u) \, i(u) = \begin{cases} s(u), & \text{if } u \in [-L, L]; \\ 0, & \text{otherwise,} \end{cases}$$

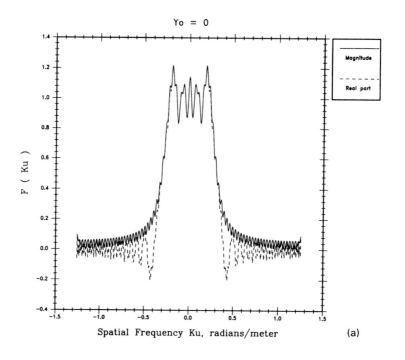

(a)

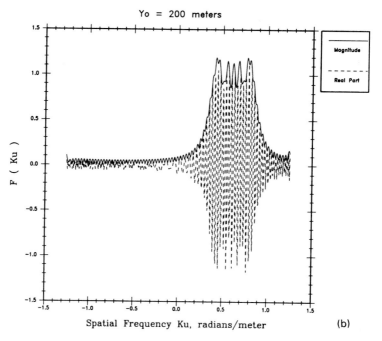

(b)

Figure 1.32 Target reconstruction in k_u domain. (a) $(x_0, y_0) = (1000, 0)$ meters. (b) $(x_0, y_0) = (1000, 200)$ meters.

where $i(u)$ is the indicator (rectangular) function. For the multiple target case, we have

$$r(u) = \sum_n s_n(u) \, i(u) = \begin{cases} \sum_n s_n(u), & \text{if } u \in [-L, L]; \\ 0, & \text{otherwise.} \end{cases}$$

The spatial Fourier transform of the measured signal is

$$R(k_u) = \sum_n R_n(k_u),$$

with

$$R_n(k_u) \equiv S_n(k_u) \ * \ I(k_u),$$

where $*$ denotes convolution in the k_u domain.

The target function in the spatial frequency domain is defined via

$$F(k_u) \equiv R(k_u) \, \exp(-j\sqrt{k^2 - k_u^2} \, x_0),$$

or

$$F'(k_u) = \sum_n R_n(k_u) \, \exp(-j\sqrt{k^2 - k_u^2} \, x_0)$$

$$= \sum_n F_n(k_u),$$

where

$$F_n(k_u) \approx \begin{cases} f_n \, \exp(jk_u y_n), & \text{if } k \, \sin\theta_{1n} \ < \ k_u \ < \ k \, \sin\theta_{2n}; \\ 0, & \text{otherwise,} \end{cases}$$

with

$$\theta_{1n} \equiv \arctan(\frac{y_n - L}{x_0})$$

$$\theta_{2n} \equiv \arctan(\frac{y_n + L}{x_0}).$$

Using the linearity property of the Fourier transform and the steps that led to (1.75), we can show that

$$f(u) \approx \sum_n f_n(u)$$

$$\approx \sum_n f_n \, 2K_{0n} \, \frac{\sin[K_{0n}(u + y_n)]}{K_{0n}(u + y_n)} \, \exp[j K_{cn}(u + y_n)]$$

(1.80)

(the function $f_n(u)$ on the first line of (1.80) is different from the scalar f_n on the second line of this equation), where

$$K_{0n} \equiv \frac{k \, \sin \theta_{2n} - k \, \sin \theta_{1n}}{2}$$

$$K_{cn} \equiv \frac{k \, \sin \theta_{2n} + k \, \sin \theta_{1n}}{2}$$

($2K_{0n}$: bandwidth; K_{cn}: carrier spatial frequency).

Moreover, if the support region of each sinc pattern does not overlap with the other sinc patterns, that is,

$$y_n + \Delta y_n \; < \; y_{n+1} - \Delta y_{n+1},$$

for all n, then each sinc pattern and, consequently, each target is resolvable or distinguishable, and we can write

$$|f(u)| \approx \sum_n |f_n(u)|$$

$$\approx \sum_n f_n \, 2K_{0n} \, \left| \frac{\sin[K_{0n}(u + y_n)]}{K_{0n}(u + y_n)} \right|.$$

(1.81)

- *The resolution of each target in the u domain depends on its coordinates since*

$$\Delta y_n = \frac{\pi}{K_{0n}},$$

(1.82)

and K_{0n} depends on y_n.

Example 2, continued: We consider the signal cited in Example 1 with multiple targets at $y_1 = 200$ meters, $y_2 = 0$ meters and $y_3 = -100$ meters with varying amplitudes. Figures 1.33 and 1.34 show the real parts of $R(k_u)$ and $F(k_u)$, respectively (with $L = 100$ meters). Note that the *signature* (contribution) of each target is not distinguishable anymore in the k_u domain. However, our objective is to identify targets in the spatial domain. In this case, *no matter how the targets' signatures may overlap with each other in the k_u domain, our ability to resolve targets in the spatial domain improves as the support band of each target signature, that is, $2K_{0n}$, widens* (via increasing L or k). This is in contrast with the plane wave approximation-based processing used in passive array processing and beamforming; these will be examined in Chapter 3. Figure 1.35 shows the magnitude (solid line) and real part (dashed line) of $f(u)$ for $L = 100$ meters (resolution = 10.5 meters approximately for all targets), and $L = 50$ meters (resolution = 21 meters).

- *It can be seen from (1.80) that each sinc pattern has its own carrier frequency (i.e., K_{cn}). However, the imaging problem of identifying targets in the cross-range domain is based on $|f(u)|$ shown in (1.81) that is independent of the carrier frequencies.*

PROJECTS

1. Develop a forward FFT program for nonnegative time signals and spatial signals that are centered around the origin. Make sure that the center element of the resultant frequency domain array corresponds to the origin in the temporal/spatial frequency domain. This will simplify your future processing of the frequency domain data.

   Develop an inverse FFT program by modifying the call to the forward FFT program. This program should provide the option of yielding nonnegative sequences for time signals and sequences centered around the origin for spatial signals. Some of the spatial signals that we will encounter may also reside in the nonnegative spatial domain (e.g., in the echo imaging problem).

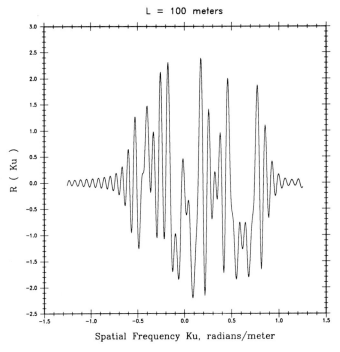

Figure 1.33 Target signature in k_u domain.

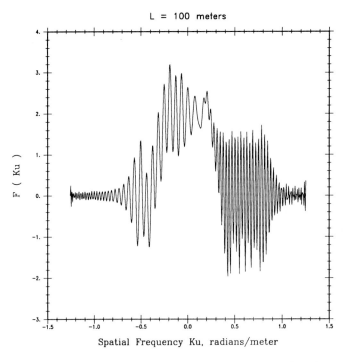

Figure 1.34 Target reconstruction in k_u domain.

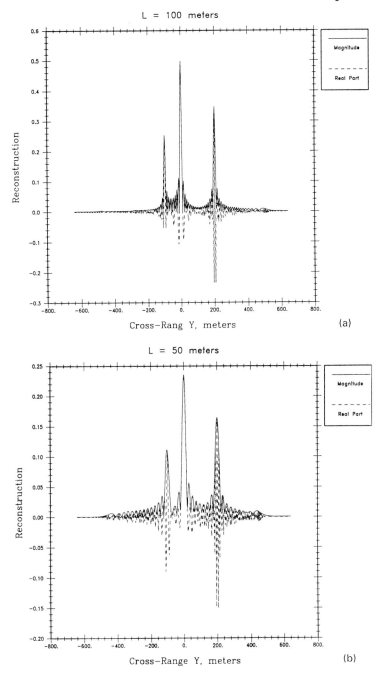

Figure 1.35 Target reconstruction in u domain. (a) $L = 100$ meters.
(b) $L = 50$ meters.

Use the FFT program to find the Fourier transforms of rectangular, triangular, sinusoidal, and chirp signals. For a chirp signal, for example,

$$s(t) = \exp[j(\omega_c t + \alpha t^2)],$$

the instantaneous frequency is

$$\frac{d}{dt}[\omega_c t + \alpha t^2] = \omega_c + 2\alpha t.$$

Thus, make sure that the sample spacing in the time domain satisfies

$$\frac{2\pi}{\Delta_t} < 2\eta(\omega_c + 2\alpha t_0),$$

where η is a constant that is between one and two (based on Carson's rule [2]; choose, for example, $\eta = 1.5$), and t_0 is the maximum value that $|t|$ attains in the time interval in which the chirp signal is simulated.

2. Use the linear transformation on the signals examined in Project 1 and observe its effect in the FFT of the signals.

3. Use the following nonlinear transformation

$$t = at' + bt'^2,$$

on the signals examined in Project 1 and observe its effect in the FFT of the signals.

4. Simulate a bandpass signal by amplitude modulating a complex sinusoidal carrier, for example, $\exp(j\omega_c t)$, with a rectangular pulse. Perform bandpass to lowpass conversion on this signal and obtain the FFT of the resultant baseband signal.

5. Repeat Project 4 with a complex chirp carrier $\exp[j(\omega_c t + \alpha t^2)]$. Use $\exp(-j\omega_c t)$ for the coherent detection (i.e., the local oscillator used for mixing).

6. Derive (1.5) from (1.4), and (1.12) from (1.10)-(1.11).

7. Develop an echo imaging program to simulate and reconstruct multiple targets. Use the signals used in Projects 4 and 5 for the pulsed signal $p(t)$. Vary the parameters of the system and observe the effect in the resolution.

   Corrupt the observed signal $s(t)$ with an additive white noise. Reconstruct the target function defined via

   $$F(k_x) \equiv \frac{S(\omega)}{P(\omega)},$$

   and

   $$F(k_x) \equiv S(\omega) \, P^*(\omega).$$

   Examine the sensitivity of these two inverse equations to the additive noise.

8. Repeat Project 7 for an environment with multiple moving targets. Reconstruct the ambiguity function $|f(x,v)|$ for the target scene. Compare the ambiguity functions for rectangular and chirp signaling.

9. Repeat Project 8 using FM-CW signaling and its corresponding inversion.

10. Simulate the spherical wave and its two approximations, that is, the chirp and plane wave signals. Obtain their FFTs and compare.

11. Simulate a spherical wave and observe the spatial Doppler phenomenon as in Example 2, Section 1.12. First use a single target and then multiple targets. Vary the parameters of the system and observe their effects on the cross-range resolution.

REFERENCES

1. R. N. Bracewell, *The Fourier Transform and its Applications*, 2nd edition, New York: McGraw-Hill, 1978.

2. B. Carlson, *Communication Systems*, New York: McGraw-Hill, 1986.

3. B. Friedman, *Principles and Techniques of Applied Mathematics*, New York: Wiley, 1956.

4. P. M. Morse and H. Feshbach, *Methods of Theoretical Physics*, New York: McGraw Hill, Parts 1 and 2, 1953.

5. A. Naylor and G. Sell, *Linear Operator Theory in Engineering and Science*, New York: Springer-Verlag, 1982.

6. A. V. Oppenheim and A. S. Wilsky, *Signals and Systems*, Englewood Cliffs, NJ: Prentice Hall, 1983.

7. A. Papoulis, *Systems and Transforms with Applications in Optics*, New York: McGraw-Hill, 1968.

8. H. E. Rowe, *Signals and Noise in Communication Systems*, New York: Van Nostrand, 1965.

9. H. L. Van Trees, *Detection, Estimation, and Modulation Theory*, New York: Wiley, Part III, Chapter 9, 1971.

10. J. Klauder, *et al.*, "The theory and design of chirp radars," *The Bell System Technical Journal*, vol. XXXIX, no. 4, pp. 745-808, July 1960.

11. D. E. Barrick, "FM/CW radar signal and digital processing," NOAA Technical Report ERL 283-WPL 26, July 1973.

12. H. D. Griffiths, "New ideas in FM radar," *Electronics and Communication Engineering Journal*, vol. 2, no. 5, pp. 185-194, October 1990.

13. A. G. Stove, "Linear FMCW radar techniques," *IEE Proceedings-F*, vol. 139, no. 5, pp. 343-350, October 1992.

14. A. G. Stove, "Obstacle detection radar for cars," *Electronics and Communication Engineering Journal*, vol. 3, no. 5, pp. 232-240, October 1991.

15. M. I. Skolnik, *Introduction to Radar Systems*, New York: McGraw-Hill, 1980.

Chapter 2
TWO-DIMENSIONAL SIGNALS

Fourier array imaging involves processing of multidimensional signals of space and time, for example, $f(x, y)$ and $s(u, t)$. We now examine the properties of two-dimensional signals relevant to array imaging problems. Of particular interest is the Fourier decomposition of a two-dimensional impulse response, called the Green's function, that is discussed in Section 2.3. This Fourier decomposition, which we will also refer to as *spatial Doppler processing*, is the key for formulating inversion in array imaging systems. References [2],[4], and [7] provide more detailed analyses of two-dimensional signals and systems.

2.1 TWO-DIMENSIONAL SIGNALS

Let x and y be two dependent or independent variables. Any mapping $f(\cdot, \cdot)$ of the domain defined by (x, y) is called a two-dimensional signal or function, and is denoted by $f(x, y)$.

Examples:

1. Disk function with radius R:

$$f(x, y) = \begin{cases} 1 & \sqrt{x^2 + y^2} \leq R \\ 0 & \text{otherwise.} \end{cases}$$

A disk function and its Fourier transform, which will be discussed in the next section, are shown in Figure 2.1.

2. Rectangular function:

$$f(x, y) = \begin{cases} 1 & |x| \leq a \text{ and } |y| \leq b \\ 0 & \text{otherwise.} \end{cases}$$

A two-dimensional rectangular pulse function and its Fourier transform are shown in Figure 2.2.

Disk Function

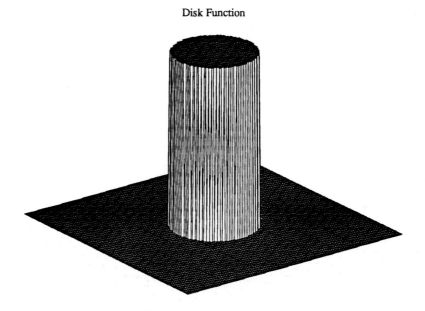

Fourier Transform of Disk Function

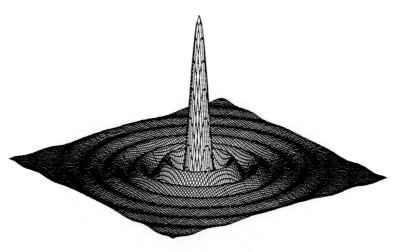

Figure 2.1 Disk function and its Fourier transform.

Two-Dimensional Rectangular Pulse

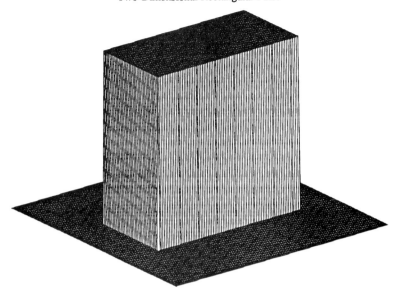

Fourier Transform of Two-Dimensional Rectangular Pulse

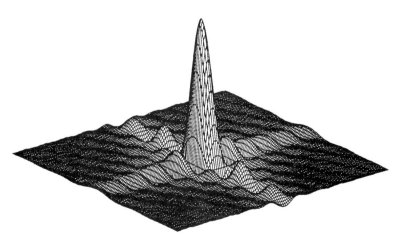

Figure 2.2 Two-dimensional rectangular pulse function and its Fourier transform.

3. Delta sheet:

$$f(x, y) = \delta(x)$$

or

$$f(x, y) = \delta(y)$$

4. Two-dimensional delta function:

$$f(x, y) = \delta(x)\,\delta(y)$$
$$= \delta(x, y)$$

5. Diverging cylindrical/spherical phase function with wavenumber k:

$$f(x, y) = \frac{\exp(jk\sqrt{x^2 + y^2})}{\sqrt{x^2 + y^2}}$$
$$\equiv \frac{\exp(jkr)}{r},$$

where $r \equiv \sqrt{x^2 + y^2}$. This function is composed of a sinusoidal phase function, that is, $\exp(jkr)$, and a decaying amplitude function, that is, $\frac{1}{r}$. This functional form is similar to the one-dimensional sinc function. The function $\frac{\exp(jkr)}{r}$ or another form of it,

$$f(x, y) = \frac{\exp(jkr)}{\sqrt{r}},$$

is closely related to a signal called *Green's Function* that will be examined in our discussion on Fourier properties of propagating waves (Section 2.4).

An example of Green's function and its Fourier transform are shown in Figures 2.3 and 2.4. Green's function and its Fourier transform are *radially symmetric* functions that will be defined later. Figures 2.3 and 2.4 show the real parts of the functions in the radial as well as two-dimensional spatial and spatial frequency domains.

Green s Function

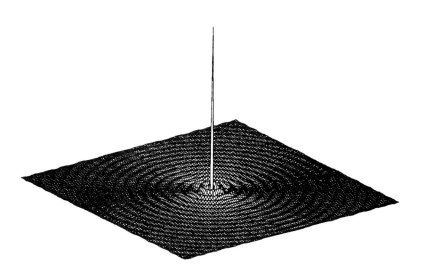

Radial Distribution of Green s Function

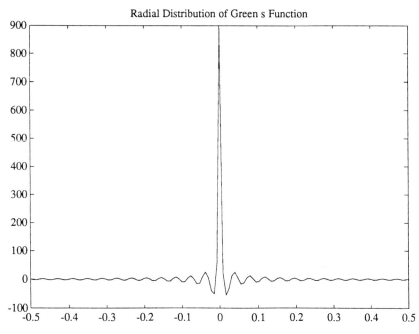

Figure 2.3 Green's function in the spatial domain.

Fourier Transform of Green s Function

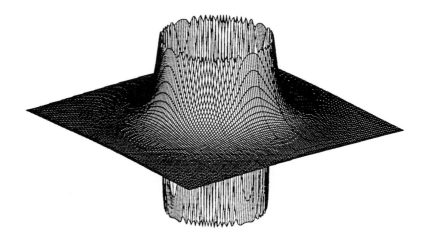

x10⁻⁴   Radial Distribution of Fourier Transform of Green s Function

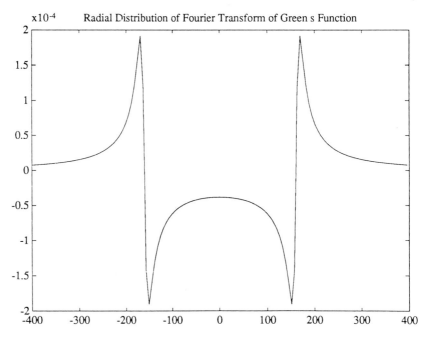

Figure 2.4 Green's function in the spatial frequency domain.

Separable Functions: The function $f(x, y)$ is separable if it can be written as

$$f(x, y) = f_1(x) \; f_2(y).$$

Signals in examples (2,3,4) are separable.

Polar Function Mapping

A two-dimensional function $f(x, y)$ may also be represented by the polar transformation of the domain (x, y)

$$f_p(\theta, r) \equiv f(x, y)$$

where

$$\theta \equiv \arctan(\frac{y}{x})$$

$$r \equiv \sqrt{x^2 + y^2}.$$

(Note that $f(x, y) \neq f_p(x, y)$.) For instance, if $f(x, y)$ is the disk function, then

$$f_p(\theta, r) = \begin{cases} 1 & r \le |R| \\ 0 & \text{otherwise.} \end{cases}$$

Note that this function is invariant of θ.

Radially Symmetric Functions: A two-dimensional function $f(x, y)$ is said to be radially symmetric (or circularly symmetric) if $f(x, y)$ depends only on $r = \sqrt{x^2 + y^2}$ and, thus, is invariant of $\theta = \arctan(\frac{y}{x})$. Signals described in examples (1,5) are radially symmetric; see Figures 2.3 and 2.4.

2.2 TWO-DIMENSIONAL FOURIER TRANSFORM

The two-dimensional Fourier transform of a signal $f(x, y)$ is defined via

$$F(k_x, k_y) = \int_{-\infty}^{\infty} \int_{-\infty}^{\infty} f(x, y) \; \exp[-j(k_x x + k_y y)] \; dx dy$$

$$= \mathcal{F}_{(x,y)}[f(x, y)],$$

where (k_x, k_y) represent the radian spatial frequency domain for (x, y). The inverse Fourier transform of $F(k_x, k_y)$ with respect to (k_x, k_y) is defined via

$$f(x, y) = \frac{1}{(2\pi)^2} \int_{-\infty}^{\infty} \int_{-\infty}^{\infty} F(k_x, k_y) \, \exp[j(k_x x + k_y y)] dk_x dk_y$$

$$= \mathcal{F}_{(k_x, k_y)}^{-1} [F(k_x, k_y)].$$

If $f(x, y)$ is a separable two-dimensional signal, that is,

$$f(x, y) = f_1(x) \, f_2(y)$$

then its two-dimensional Fourier transform becomes

$$F(k_x, k_y) = F_1(k_x) \, F_2(k_y),$$

which is also a separable two-dimensional signal.

Example 1: Separable rectangular function:

$$f(x, y) = \begin{cases} 1 & \text{for } x \le a \text{ and } y \le b \\ 0 & \text{otherwise} \end{cases}$$

$$= \text{rect}(\frac{x}{2a}) \, \text{rect}(\frac{y}{2b}),$$

where

$$\text{rect}(\alpha) = \begin{cases} 1 & |\alpha| \le 0.5 \\ 0 & \text{otherwise}. \end{cases}$$

Then, we have the following in the spatial frequency domain:

$$F(k_x, k_y) = 2a \, \frac{\sin(k_x a)}{k_x a} \, 2b \, \frac{\sin(k_y b)}{k_y b}$$

$$= 4ab \, \text{sinc}(k_x a) \, \text{sinc}(k_y b).$$

(Recall that $\sin(\alpha)/\alpha = \text{sinc}(\alpha)$.) An example is shown in Figure 2.2.

Example 2: Nonseparable disk function:

$$f(x,y) = \begin{cases} 1 & \sqrt{x^2 + y^2} \leq R \\ 0 & \text{otherwise.} \end{cases}$$

It can be shown that [4],[7]

$$F(k_x, k_y) = R^2 \frac{J_1(R\sqrt{k_x^2 + k_y^2})}{R\sqrt{k_x^2 + k_y^2}},$$

where J_1 is the Bessel function of the first kind, first order. $\frac{J_1(x)}{x}$ is called the Airy pattern with

$$\lim_{x \to 0} \frac{J_1(x)}{x} = \frac{1}{2}.$$

An example is shown in Figure 2.1.

Vector Representation of Fourier Transform

We define the following spatial vector:

$$\mathbf{r} \equiv \begin{bmatrix} x \\ y \end{bmatrix},$$

and spatial frequency vector:

$$\mathbf{k_r} \equiv \begin{bmatrix} k_x \\ k_y \end{bmatrix}.$$

Using these vectors, we can write

$$f(x,y) = f(\mathbf{r})$$
$$F(k_x, k_y) = F(\mathbf{k_r}).$$

The two-dimensional Fourier transform can be rewritten as follows:

$$F(\mathbf{k_r}) = \int_{\mathbf{r}} f(\mathbf{r}) \exp(-j\mathbf{k_r}^T \mathbf{r}) \, d\mathbf{r}.$$

Moreover, for the inverse two-dimensional Fourier transform we have

$$f(\mathbf{r}) = \frac{1}{(2\pi)^2} \int_{\mathbf{k_r}} F(\mathbf{k_r}) \, \exp(j\mathbf{k_r}^T \, \mathbf{r}) \, d\mathbf{k_r}.$$

Polar Representation of Fourier Transform

Earlier, we defined

$$f_p(\theta, r) = f(x, y)$$

to be the polar function mapping of the spatial signal $f(x, y)$, where

$$\theta = \arctan(\frac{y}{x})$$
$$r = \sqrt{x^2 + y^2}.$$

The polar function mapping of $F(k_x, k_y)$ in the spatial frequency may be defined via

$$F_p(\phi, \rho) \equiv F(k_x, k_y)$$

where

$$\phi \equiv \arctan(\frac{k_y}{k_x})$$
$$\rho \equiv \sqrt{k_x^2 + k_y^2}.$$

*Note that $F_p(\cdot, \cdot)$ is **not** the Fourier transform of $f_p(\cdot, \cdot)$.*

Using the polar mapping functions, the forward Fourier transform integral, that is,

$$F(k_x, k_y) = \int_{-\infty}^{\infty} \int_{-\infty}^{\infty} f(x, y) \, \exp[-j(k_x x + k_y y)] \, dx dy,$$

may be rewritten as follows:

$$F_p(\phi, \rho) = \int_0^{\infty} \int_0^{2\pi} r \, f_p(\theta, r) \, \exp[-j\rho r \cos(\theta - \phi)] \, d\theta \, dr.$$

Moreover, the inverse Fourier transform integral becomes

$$f_p(\theta, r) = \frac{1}{(2\pi)^2} \int_0^\infty \int_0^{2\pi} \rho \, F_p(\phi, \rho) \, \exp[j\rho r \cos(\theta - \phi)] \, d\phi \, d\rho.$$

Radially symmetric functions: Suppose $f(x, y)$ is a radially symmetric signal; that is,

$$f_p(\theta, r) \equiv f_p(r),$$

is invariant of θ. In this case, the forward Fourier transform integral becomes

$$F_p(\phi, \rho) = \int_0^\infty r \, f_p(r) \underbrace{\left[\int_0^{2\pi} \exp[-j\rho r \cos(\theta - \phi)] \, d\theta \right]}_{Hankel\ function} dr$$

$$= \int_0^\infty r \, f_p(r) \, H_0(\rho r) \, dr$$

$$\equiv F_p(\rho),$$

where $H_0(\cdot)$ is the Hankel function of the zero-th order.

- *The signal $F_p(\phi, \rho)$ is invariant of ϕ. Thus, $F(k_x, k_y)$, which depends only on $\rho = \sqrt{k_x^2 + k_y^2}$, is also a radially symmetric signal when $f(x, y)$ is a radially symmetric function. For instance, both the disk function and its two-dimensional Fourier transform are radially symmetric functions.*

Using the above procedure, the inverse Fourier transform for a radially symmetric function can be rewritten as follows:

$$f_p(r) = \frac{1}{(2\pi)^2} \int_0^\infty \rho \, F_p(\rho) \, H_0^*(\rho r) \, d\rho,$$

where H_0^* is the complex conjugate of H_0.

Marginal Fourier Transforms

The marginal (one-dimensional) Fourier transform of $f(x, y)$ with respect to x is defined by

$$F_x(k_x, y) \equiv \mathcal{F}_{(x)}[f(x, y)]$$
$$= \int_{-\infty}^{\infty} f(x, y) \; \exp(-jk_x x) \; dx.$$

Also, the marginal (one-dimensional) Fourier transform of $f(x, y)$ with respect to y is

$$F_y(x, k_y) \equiv \mathcal{F}_{(y)}[f(x, y)]$$
$$= \int_{-\infty}^{\infty} f(x, y) \; \exp(-jk_y y) \; dy.$$

Note that
$$F(k_x, k_y) = \mathcal{F}_{(y)}[F_x(k_x, y)]$$
$$= \mathcal{F}_{(x)}[F_y(x, k_y)].$$

Projection of a Two-Dimensional Signal

Projection of $f(x, y)$ along the x axis is defined via

$$F_x(0, y) = F_x(k_x, y)|_{k_x = 0}$$
$$= \int_{-\infty}^{\infty} f(x, y) \; \exp(-jk_x x) \; dx|_{k_x = 0}$$
$$= \int_{-\infty}^{\infty} f(x, y) \; dx,$$

and its Fourier transform with respect to y is

$$\mathcal{F}_{(y)}[F_x(0, y)] = \mathcal{F}_{(y)}[F_x(k_x, y)]|_{k_x = o}$$
$$= F(0, k_y).$$

Figure 2.5 shows the projection of a two-dimensional signal $f(x, y)$ along the x axis and its Fourier transform.

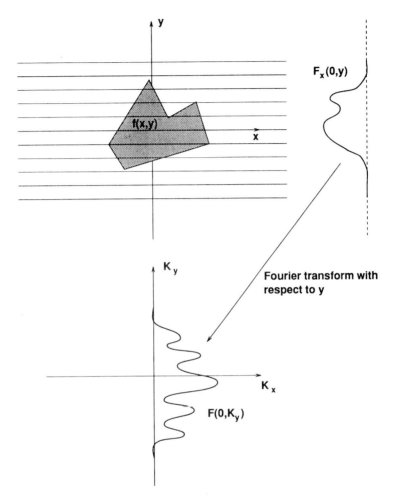

Figure 2.5 Projection along the x-axis and its Fourier transform.

Similarly, the projection of $f(x, y)$ along the y-axis is defined to be the following:

$$F_y(x, 0) = F_y(x, k_y)|_{k_y=0}$$

$$= \int_{-\infty}^{\infty} f(x, y) \, dy.$$

The spatial Fourier transform of this projection with respect to x is

$$\mathcal{F}_{(x)}[F_y(x,0)] = F(k_x,0).$$

Projections of a two-dimensional signal and their Fourier properties will be further studied in later sections of this chapter. These principles form the basis for image formation in computer assisted tomography systems that will be discussed in Chapter 7.

Example 3: For the two-dimensional rectangular function, that is,

$$f(x,y) = \begin{cases} 1 & |x| \le a \ \& \ |y| \le b \\ 0 & \text{otherwise}, \end{cases}$$

we have

$$F_x(0,y) = \int_{-\infty}^{\infty} f(x,y)\ dx = \begin{cases} 2a & |y| \le b \\ 0 & |y| > b, \end{cases}$$

and

$$\mathcal{F}_{(y)}[F_x(0,y)] = 2a\ 2b\ \text{sinc}(bk_y) = 4ab\ \text{sinc}(bk_y).$$

But we showed earlier that

$$F(k_x,k_y) = 4ab\ \text{sinc}(ak_x)\ \text{sinc}(bk_y),$$

that also yields

$$F(0,k_y) = 4ab\ \text{sinc}(bk_y).$$

Similarly, we have

$$F_y(x,0) = \int_{-\infty}^{\infty} f(x,y)dy = \begin{cases} 2b & |x| \le a \\ 0 & |x| > a\ , \end{cases}$$

that gives

$$\mathcal{F}_{(x)}[F_y(x,0)] = 2b\ 2a\ \text{sinc}(ak_x) = 4ab\ \text{sinc}(ak_x) = F(k_x,0)$$

Example 4: Consider the two-dimensional delta function, that is,

$$f(x, y) = \delta(x - x_0, y - y_0) = \delta(x - x_0)\,\delta(y - y_0).$$

Recall that

$$\mathcal{F}_{(x)}[\delta(x - x_0)] = \exp(-jk_x x_0)$$
$$\mathcal{F}_{(y)}[\delta(y - y_0)] = \exp(-jk_y y_0).$$

Thus, we have

$$F(k_x, k_y) = \exp[-j(k_x x_0 + k_y y_0)].$$

Computing the projection functions and their Fourier transforms, we get

$$F_x(0, y) = \int_{-\infty}^{\infty} f(x, y)\,dx = \int_{-\infty}^{\infty} \delta(x - x_0)\,\delta(y - y_0)\,dx = \delta(y - y_0)$$

$$F_y(0, x) = \int_{-\infty}^{\infty} f(x, y)\,dy = \int_{-\infty}^{\infty} \delta(x - x_0)\,\delta(y - y_o)\,dy = \delta(x - x_0)$$

Thus, we have

$$\mathcal{F}_{(y)}[F_x(0, y)] = \mathcal{F}_{(y)}[\delta(y - y_0)] = \exp(-jk_y y_0) = F(0, k_y)$$

and

$$\mathcal{F}_{(x)}[F_y(0, x)] = \mathcal{F}_{(x)}[\delta(x - x_0)] = \exp(-jk_x x_0) = F(k_x, 0)$$

2.3 TWO-DIMENSIONAL LINEAR SHIFT-INVARIANT SYSTEMS

Let $f(\cdot, \cdot)$ be a mapping of (x, y). A two-dimensional system is a structure that transforms $f(x, y)$ to another mapping of the (x, y) domain, for example, $g(x, y)$. In this case, $g(x, y)$ is called the response of $f(x, y)$.

Linear Systems

Let $g_1(x, y)$ and $g_2(x, y)$ be the responses of $f_1(x, y)$ and $f_2(x, y)$ respectively. This two-dimensional system is said to be linear if its response to the input

$$a_1 f_1(x, y) + a_2 f_2(x, y)$$

is the output

$$a_1 g_1(x, y) + a_2 g_2(x, y)$$

for all constant values of (a_1, a_2) and all input functions (f_1, f_2).

Shift-Invariant Systems

Let $g(x, y)$ be the response of $f(x, y)$. The two-dimensional system is said to be shift invariant if its response to the input

$$f(x - x_0, y - y_0)$$

is the output

$$g(x - x_0, y - y_0)$$

for all constants (x_0, y_0) and all input functions $f(\cdot, \cdot)$.

Linear Shift-Invariant (LSI) Systems

These systems have both of the above properties, that is, linearity and shift-invariance. Impulse response for an LSI system, call it $h(x, y)$, is defined to be the response of the system to the input $\delta(x, y)$.

A two-dimensional LSI system is causal if its impulse response has the following property:

$$h(x, y) = 0 \quad for \ x < 0 \ or \ y < 0$$

We will not be concerned with the processing of causal spatial domain systems in our applications. In fact, all imaging systems are noncausal.

The Input/Output (also denoted with I/O) relationship in the spatial (x, y) domain for a two-dimensional LSI system is governed by the following two-dimensional convolution:

$$g(x, y) = \int_{-\infty}^{\infty} \int_{-\infty}^{\infty} f(a, b) \, h(x - a, y - b) \, da \, db$$

or equivalently,

$$g(x, y) = \int_{-\infty}^{\infty} \int_{-\infty}^{\infty} f(x - a, y - b) \, h(a, b) \, da \, db$$

that is identified via

$$g(x, y) = f(x, y) * *h(x, y)$$

where ** denotes the two-dimensional convolution operator.

A two-dimensional LSI system is said to be separable if

$$h(x, y) = h_1(x) \, h_2(y)$$

In this case
$$g(x, y) = [f(x, y) * h_1(x)] * h_2(y)$$
$$= [f(x, y) * h_2(y)] * h_1(x).$$

A two-dimensional system is said to be stable if for a bounded input, the system output is also bounded (BIBO stability). It can be shown that a system is BIBO stable if its impulse response is absolutely integrable; that is,

$$\int_{-\infty}^{\infty} \int_{-\infty}^{\infty} |h(x, y)| \, dx dy \ < \infty$$

Example: The impulse response of the shift operator is defined via

$$h(x, y) = \delta(x - x_0, y - y_0)$$

This is a BIBO system since

$$\int_{-\infty}^{\infty} \int_{-\infty}^{\infty} |h(x, y)| dx dy = 1 \ < \infty$$

This is a separable system since

$$h(x, y) = \delta(x - x_0) \, \delta(y - y_0)$$

The output of this system for an input $f(x, y)$ is

$$g(x, y) = f(x, y) * *\delta(x - x_0, y - y_0) = f(x - x_0, y - y_0)$$

Using the convolution property of the Fourier transform, it can be shown that if the following I/O relationship holds in the spatial (x, y) domain for an LSI system:

$$g(x, y) = f(x, y) * *h(x, y),$$

then the following I/O relationship exists in the spatial frequency domain (k_x, k_y) for that LSI system:

$$G(k_x, k_y) = H(k_x, k_y) \ F(k_x, k_y),$$

where

$$H(k_x, k_y) = \mathcal{F}_{(x,y)}[h(x, y)],$$

is called the *transfer function* of the two-dimensional LSI system.

Duality

In general, convolution in the spatial domain is equivalent to multiplication in the spatial frequency domain. Similarly, multiplication in the spatial domain is equivalent to convolution in the spatial frequency domain. Thus, if

$$g(x, y) = f(x, y) \ h(x, y),$$

then

$$G(k_x, k_y) = F(k_x, k_y) * * H(k_x, k_y)$$

$$= \frac{1}{(2\pi)^2} \int_{-\infty}^{\infty} \int_{-\infty}^{\infty} F(\alpha, \beta) \ H(k_x - \alpha, k_y - \beta) \ d\alpha \ d\beta$$

$$= \frac{1}{(2\pi)^2} \int_{-\infty}^{\infty} \int_{-\infty}^{\infty} F(k_x - \alpha, k_y - \beta) \ H(\alpha, \beta) \ d\alpha \ d\beta.$$

Differentiation

If

$$g(x, y) = \frac{\partial}{\partial x} f(x, y)$$

then

$$G(k_x, k_y) = j k_x \, F(k_x, k_y).$$

In general, if

$$g(x, y) = \frac{\partial^m}{\partial x^m} f(x, y)$$

then

$$G(k_x, k_y) = (j k_x)^m \cdot F(k_x, k_y).$$

Similarly, if

$$g(x, y) = \frac{\partial^n}{\partial y^n} f(x, y)$$

then

$$G(k_x, k_y) = (j k_y)^n \, F(k_x, k_y).$$

Differentiation can be viewed as processing a signal through an LSI system. For the m-th partial derivative of the function with respect to x, the LSI system's transfer function is

$$H(k_x, k_y) = (j k_x)^m$$

and for the n-th partial derivative of the function with respect to y, the LSI system's transfer function is

$$H(k_x, k_y) = (j k_y)^n.$$

2.4 FOURIER PROPERTIES OF PROPAGATING WAVES

We examined the Fourier properties of a spherical wave across a finite aperture in Chapter 1. The discussion in this section provides a system theory approach to analyze the multidimensional temporal frequency and spatial frequency distribution of a propagating wave. This study is intended to help the reader gain additional insight on the Fourier properties of the radiation *source* as well as the *scattered* waves generated by the target under study in an array imaging problem.

Reference [5] provides a thorough discussion on the spatial and spatial Fourier properties of propagating waves as well as their physical significance. Our treatment of these concepts in this section is from a linear shift-invariant system theory point of view.

Green's Function (Impulse Response) [5]

Consider the two-dimensional LSI system whose impulse response, $h(x, y)$, satisfies the following differential equation:

$$\frac{\partial^2}{\partial x^2} h(x, y) + \frac{\partial^2}{\partial y^2} h(x, y) + k^2 \, h(x, y) = -\underbrace{\delta(x, y)}_{Impulse\ Input} \,, \qquad (2.1)$$

where k (wavenumber) is a constant. Equation (2.1) can be rewritten as a linear operator on $h(x, y)$ as follows:

$$\underbrace{\left[\frac{\partial^2}{\partial x^2} + \frac{\partial^2}{\partial y^2} + k^2 \right]}_{Linear\ Operator} h(x, y) = -\delta(x, y).$$

Recall that $\frac{\partial^2}{\partial x^2} + \frac{\partial^2}{\partial y^2} \equiv \nabla^2$ is called the Laplacian operator. The differential equation (2.1) is commonly written in the following form:

$$[\nabla^2 + k^2] \, h(x, y) = -\delta(x, y). \qquad (2.2)$$

Taking the two-dimensional Fourier transform of both sides of (2.1), we get

$$[-k_x^2 - k_y^2 + k^2] \, H(k_x, k_y) = -1$$

or equivalently

$$H(k_x, k_y) = \frac{1}{k_x^2 + k_y^2 - k^2}. \qquad (2.3)$$

The locus of the poles of $H(k_x, k_y)$, which is found by solving the following characteristic equation:

$$k_x^2 + k_y^2 - k^2 = 0,$$

is the circle of radius k centered at the origin of the (k_x, k_y) domain. Figure 2.6 shows the magnitude distribution of $H(k_x, k_y)$. The dark circle of radius k is the locus of the poles of $H(k_x, k_y)$. A Green's function and its Fourier transform were shown earlier in Figures 2.3 and 2.4.

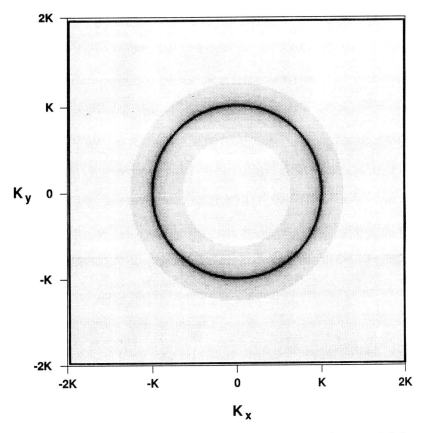

Figure 2.6 Green's function and its poles in the spatial frequency domain.

A similar principle also exists for the three-dimensional spatial domain (x, y, z), that is,

$$[\nabla^2 + k^2]\, h(x, y, z) = -\delta(x, y, z)$$

that in the three-dimensional spatial frequency domain becomes

$$H(k_x, k_y, k_z) = \frac{1}{k_x^2 + k_y^2 + k_z^2 - k^2}$$

where the three-dimensional Laplacian operator is defined as follows:

$$\nabla^2 \equiv \frac{\partial^2}{\partial x^2} + \frac{\partial^2}{\partial y^2} + \frac{\partial^2}{\partial z^2}$$

The locus of the poles of $H(k_x, k_y, k_z)$, which is found by solving the following characteristic equation:

$$k_x^2 + k_y^2 + k_z^2 - k^2 = 0,$$

is the sphere of radius k centered at the origin of the (k_x, k_y, k_z) domain.

The impulse response $h(\cdot)$ is known as the free space Green's function. This signal is the radiation pattern of an *ideal point source* that emits a wave at temporal frequency ω in a homogeneous medium with propagation speed c, and $k = \frac{\omega}{c}$ is called the wavenumber. For two-dimensional geometries, the Green's function is

$$h(x, y) = j\pi H_0(k\sqrt{x^2 + y^2}) = j\pi H_0(kr), \qquad (2.4)$$

where $H_0(\cdot)$ is the Hankel function of the first kind, zero-th order, and $r = \sqrt{x^2 + y^2}$. It can be shown that

$$\lim_{kr \to \infty} H_0(kr) \approx \underbrace{\sqrt{\frac{2}{\pi kr}}}_{amplitude\ function}\ e^{-j\frac{\pi}{4}}\ \underbrace{\exp(jkr)}_{phase\ function} \qquad (2.5)$$

The asymptotic expression shown in (2.5) is a valid approximation for the Green's function when $r \gg \lambda \equiv \frac{2\pi}{k}$ (wavelength).

The Green's function in the three-dimensional spatial domain is

$$h(x,y,z) = \frac{\exp(jkr)}{r} = \underbrace{\frac{1}{r}}_{amplitude\ function} \underbrace{\exp(jkr)}_{phase\ function}, \qquad (2.6)$$

where $r = \sqrt{x^2 + y^2 + z^2}$.

- *In array imaging problems, the distances are sufficiently large such that the phase functions of the two-dimensional and three-dimensional Green's functions both behave as* $\exp(jkr)$*. Moreover, their* **amplitude** *functions vary very slowly with respect to their* **phase** *functions and do not play an important role in the imaging problem. From this point on, we use the cylindrical phase function*

$$\exp(jk\sqrt{x^2 + y^2}),$$

and the spherical phase function

$$\exp(jk\sqrt{x^2 + y^2 + z^2}),$$

to identify the Green's functions. We also use the same spatial Fourier decomposition, which is discussed next, to represent the two Green's functions.

Fourier Decomposition of the Nontransient Impulse Response

From the inverse Fourier transform equation, we have

$$h(x,y) = \frac{1}{(2\pi)^2} \int_{k_x} \int_{k_y} H(k_x, k_y) \exp[j(k_x x + k_y y)]\, dk_x\, dk_y$$

$$= \frac{1}{(2\pi)^2} \int_{k_x} \int_{k_y} \frac{1}{k_x^2 + k_y^2 - k^2} \exp[j(k_x x + k_y y)]\, dk_x\, dk_y$$

$$= \frac{1}{(2\pi)^2} \int_{k_x} \int_{k_y} \frac{1}{(k_x - k_1)(k_x - k_2)} \exp[j(k_x x + k_y y)]\, dk_x\, dk_y$$

$$(2.7)$$

where

$$k_1 \equiv \sqrt{k^2 - k_y^2}$$

$$k_2 \equiv -\sqrt{k^2 - k_y^2}$$

The decomposition in (2.7) represents both nontransient (nonevanescent) and transient (evanescent) components of the impulse response. However, we are concerned with array imaging systems where the transmitting and receiving elements are far enough from the target to be imaged such that one may neglect the transient response in the impulse response. In this case, (2.7) may be rewritten as follows with the help of the residue theorem:

$$h(x, y) = \begin{cases} \frac{j}{2\pi} \int_{-k}^{k} \left[\frac{1}{(k_x - k_2)} \exp[j(k_x x + k_y y)] \right]_{k_x = k_1} dk_y, & \text{if } x > 0; \\ \frac{j}{2\pi} \int_{-k}^{k} \left[\frac{1}{(k_x - k_1)} \exp[j(k_x x + k_y y)] \right]_{k_x = k_2} dk_y, & \text{if } x < 0; \end{cases}$$

that yields

$$h(x, y) = \begin{cases} \frac{j}{2\pi} \int_{-k}^{k} \frac{1}{2\sqrt{k^2 - k_y^2}} \exp[j(\sqrt{k^2 - k_y^2}\, x + k_y y)]\, dk_y, & \text{if } x > 0; \\ \frac{j}{2\pi} \int_{-k}^{k} \frac{-1}{2\sqrt{k^2 - k_y^2}} \exp[-j(\sqrt{k^2 - k_y^2}\, x + k_y y)]\, dk_y, & \text{if } x < 0; \end{cases}$$

$$(2.8)$$

We now proceed with the impulse response on the positive side of the x axis. From (2.8), we can write

$$h(x, y) = \frac{j}{4\pi} \int_{-k}^{k} \frac{\exp(j\sqrt{k^2 - k_y^2}\, x)}{\sqrt{k^2 - k_y^2}} \exp(jk_y y)\, dk_y, \qquad (2.9)$$

which is in the form of an inverse Fourier integral; that is,

$$h(x, y) = \frac{j}{2} \mathcal{F}_{(k_y)}^{-1} \left[\frac{\exp(j\sqrt{k^2 - k_y^2}\, x)}{\sqrt{k^2 - k_y^2}} \right] \qquad (2.10)$$

Angular Spectrum (Polar Representation)

We define the following transformation from k_y to θ:

$$\theta = \arctan\left(\frac{k_y}{\sqrt{k^2 - k_y^2}}\right),$$

that has the following inverse

$$k_y = k \sin \theta.$$

Note that for a fixed k_y or θ, the signal

$$\exp[j\sqrt{k^2 - k_y^2}\, x + j k_y y] = \exp(jk\cos\theta x + jk\sin\theta y)$$

represents a plane wave propagating at angle θ. Making a variable transformation from k_y to θ in (2.9) yields

$$h(x,y) = \frac{j}{2} \int_{-\pi/2}^{\pi/2} \exp(jk\cos\theta x + jk\sin\theta y)\ d\theta. \qquad (2.11)$$

- *The significance of (2.11) is in the fact that the diverging spherical signal/wave represented by $h(x,y) = \exp(jk\sqrt{x^2 + y^2})$ can be expressed as an infinite coherent sum (integral) of plane waves propagating in all directions ($\theta \in [-\pi/2, \pi/2]$). This is known as* **angular spectral decomposition** *of $h(x,y)$.*

Figure 2.7 shows geometrical representations of spherical and plane waves in the spatial (x, y) domain.

Spatio-Temporal Propagating Waves

Consider the two-dimensional LSI system whose impulse response is the Green's function that is identified by the differential equation in (2.1). Suppose the signal $f(x, y)$ (force function) is applied to this system. The resultant output is denoted by $s(x, y)$ and satisfies the following differential equation:

$$\left[\frac{\partial^2}{\partial x^2} + \frac{\partial^2}{\partial y^2} + k^2\right] s(x, y) = -f(x, y).$$

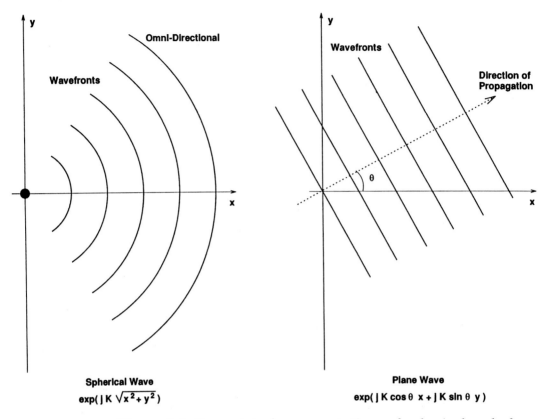

Figure 2.7 Geometrical representations of spherical and plane waves.

From the convolution theorem, we have

$$s(x, y) = f(x, y) \ast\ast h(x, y),$$

where $\ast\ast$ denotes two-dimensional convolution in the spatial (x, y) domain. Moreover, we have the following in the spatial frequency domain:

$$
\begin{aligned}
S(k_x, k_y) &= F(k_x, k_y)\, H(k_x, k_y) \\
&= \frac{F(k_x, k_y)}{k_x^2 + k_y^2 - k^2}.
\end{aligned}
$$

We are interested in finding the **nontransient** component of the output $s(x, y)$ on the positive side of the x axis. Suppose $f(x, y)$ is a bounded and space-limited signal. In this case, its spatial Fourier transform, that is, $F(k_x, k_y)$, does not possess any poles in the spatial frequency domain. Thus, based on the steps used in (2.8)-(2.10) to find the nontransient component of the impulse response, we have the following for the nontransient component of $s(x, y)$:

$$
\begin{aligned}
s(x, y) &= \frac{j}{4\pi} \int_{-k}^{k} \frac{F(\sqrt{k^2 - k_y^2}, k_y) \, \exp(j \sqrt{k^2 - k_y^2} \, x)}{\sqrt{k^2 - k_y^2}} \, \exp(j k_y y) \, dk_y \\
&= \frac{j}{2} \, \mathcal{F}_{(k_y)}^{-1} \left[\frac{F(\sqrt{k^2 - k_y^2}, k_y) \, \exp(j \sqrt{k^2 - k_y^2} \, x)}{\sqrt{k^2 - k_y^2}} \right].
\end{aligned}
$$

Note that the response $s(x, y)$ is also a function of ω. We make this fact explicit by rewriting the response as $s(x, y, \omega)$, that is, a signal that depends on the spatial domain (x, y) and the temporal frequency domain ω. Taking the inverse Fourier transform of $s(x, y, \omega)$ with respect to ω yields a signal in the (x, y, t) domain. For notational simplicity, we identify this new signal with $s(x, y, t)$; that is, (in the following, the constants are suppressed)

$$
\begin{aligned}
s(x, y, t) &\equiv \mathcal{F}_{(\omega)}^{-1} \Big[s(x, y, \omega) \Big] \\
&= \int_{\omega} \int_{k_y} \frac{F(\sqrt{k^2 - k_y^2}, k_y) \, \exp(j \sqrt{k^2 - k_y^2} \, x)}{\sqrt{k^2 - k_y^2}} \\
&\qquad \times \, \exp(j k_y y + j \omega t) \, dk_y \, d\omega \\
&= \mathcal{F}_{(\omega, k_y)}^{-1} \left[\frac{F(\sqrt{k^2 - k_y^2}, k_y) \, \exp(j \sqrt{k^2 - k_y^2} \, x)}{\sqrt{k^2 - k_y^2}} \right].
\end{aligned}
$$

$s(x, y, t)$ represents a **spatio-temporal** propagating wave.

- $s(x, y, t)$, *which is a three-dimensional signal, has a* **two-dimensional** *Fourier decomposition. This is due to the fact that the spectral distribution of $s(x, y, t)$ in the k_x domain resides only on the delta surface defined by*

$$k_x \equiv \sqrt{k^2 - k_y^2}.$$

Thus, we may also express $s(x, y, t)$ via the following three-dimensional inverse Fourier transform:

$$s(x, y, t) = \mathcal{F}^{-1}_{(\omega, k_x, k_y)} \left[\frac{F(k_x, k_y)\, \delta(k_x - \sqrt{k^2 - k_y^2})}{\sqrt{k^2 - k_y^2}} \right].$$

From the inverse temporal Fourier transform of the differential equation that governs $s(x, y, \omega)$, one can show that the spatio-temporal signal $s(x, y, t)$ satisfies the following differential equation:

$$\left[\frac{\partial^2}{\partial x^2} + \frac{\partial^2}{\partial y^2} - \frac{1}{c^2} \frac{\partial^2}{\partial t^2} \right] s(x, y, t) = -f(x, y),$$

that is known as the homogeneous *Helmholtz wave equation* [5].

2.5 COORDINATE TRANSFORMATION

Define the following general transformation of the (x, y) domain:

$$\begin{bmatrix} x' \\ y' \end{bmatrix} \equiv \begin{bmatrix} g_1(x, y) \\ g_2(x, y) \end{bmatrix}$$

The Jacobian of the transformation is

$$J(x, y) \equiv \left| \frac{\partial(x', y')}{\partial(x, y)} \right| = \begin{vmatrix} \frac{\partial g_1}{\partial x} & \frac{\partial g_1}{\partial y} \\ \frac{\partial g_2}{\partial x} & \frac{\partial g_2}{\partial y} \end{vmatrix}$$

$$= \left| \frac{\partial g_1}{\partial x} \frac{\partial g_2}{\partial y} - \frac{\partial g_1}{\partial y} \frac{\partial g_2}{\partial x} \right|,$$

where $|\cdot|$ denotes the absolute value of the determinant of the partial derivatives matrix.

Any integral in (x',y') domain can be represented in terms of an integral in the (x,y) domain via [3]

$$\int_{x'}\int_{y'} s'(x',y')\,dy'\,dx' = \int_x\int_y s(x,y)\ \underbrace{|\frac{\partial(x',y')}{\partial(x,y)}|}_{J(x,y)}\,dy\,dx$$

where

$$s'(x',y') = s(x,y).$$

Similarly

$$\int_x\int_y s(x,y)\,dy\,dx = \int_{x'}\int_{y'} s'(x',y')\ \underbrace{|\frac{\partial(x,y)}{\partial(x',y')}|}_{J'(x',y')\equiv\frac{1}{J(x,y)}}\,dy'\,dx'$$

Suppose

$$s(x,y) = \delta(x,y)$$

Using the properties of the delta function and the above integrals, one can show that [3]

$$\delta(x,y) = J(x,y)\,\delta(x',y')$$
$$\delta(x',y') = J'(x',y')\,\delta(x',y')$$

Consider a signal $f(x,y)$ and denote its mapping into the (x',y') domain by $f'(x',y')$; that is,

$$f(x,y) = f'(x',y').$$

Note that in general, $f'(x',y') \neq f(x',y')$ *and* $f(x,y) \neq f'(x,y)$. Now consider the two-dimensional Fourier transform of $f'(x',y')$ with respect to (x',y'):

$$F'(k_{x'},k_{y'}) = \int_{x'}\int_{y'} f'(x',y')\ \exp[-j(k_{x'}x' + k_{y'}y')]\,dy'\,dx'$$

Performing variable transformations from (x', y') to (x, y) in the above integral, we get

$$F'(k_{x'}, k_{y'}) = \int_x \int_y f(x, y) \, \exp[-jk_{x'}g_1(x, y) - jk_{y'}g_2(x, y))] J(x, y) \, dy dx$$

(2.12)

Next, we use (2.12) to establish a relationship between $F(k_x, k_y)$ and $F'(k_{x'}, k_{y'})$ for certain classes of transformations.

Shift (Translation) Transformation

This transformation is depicted in Figure 2.8 with

$$\begin{bmatrix} x' \\ y' \end{bmatrix} = \begin{bmatrix} x \\ y \end{bmatrix} - \begin{bmatrix} x_0 \\ y_0 \end{bmatrix}.$$

The Jacobian of the transformation is

$$J(x, y) = \begin{vmatrix} 1 & 0 \\ 0 & 1 \end{vmatrix} = 1.$$

In this case, (2.12) becomes

$$F'(k_{x'}, k_{y'}) = \int_x \int_y f(x, y) \, \exp[-jk_{x'}(x - x_0) - jk_{y'}(y - y_0)] \, dy dx$$

$$= \exp[j(k_{x'}x_0 + k_{y'}y_0)] \underbrace{\int_x \int_y f(x, y) \exp[-j(k_{x'}x + k_{y'}y] dy dx}_{F(k_{x'}, k_{y'})}$$

Thus, we have

$$F'(k_{x'}, k_{y'}) = \exp[j(k_{x'}x_0 + k_{y'}y_0)] \, F(k_x, k_y) \qquad (2.13)$$

where for the shift transform

$$\begin{bmatrix} k_{x'} \\ k_{y'} \end{bmatrix} = \begin{bmatrix} k_x \\ k_y \end{bmatrix}. \qquad (2.14)$$

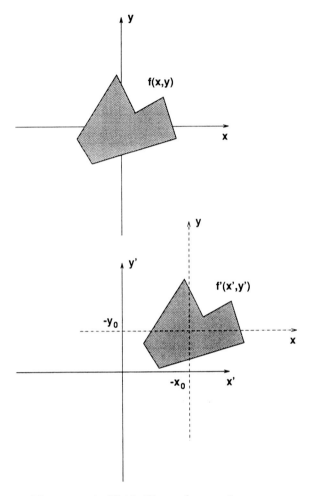

Figure 2.8 Shift Transformation.

Rotation Transformation

For this transformation, we have (see Figure 2.9)

$$\begin{bmatrix} x' \\ y' \end{bmatrix} = \underbrace{\begin{bmatrix} \cos\theta & \sin\theta \\ -\sin\theta & \cos\theta \end{bmatrix}}_{\Theta} \begin{bmatrix} x \\ y \end{bmatrix}$$

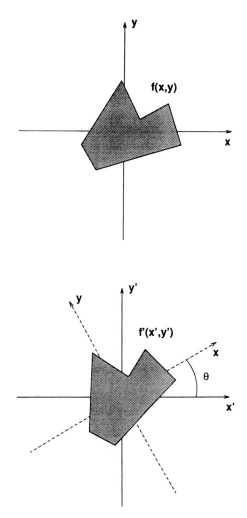

Figure 2.9 Rotation transformation.

with the following Jacobian function:

$$J(x,y) = ||\Theta|| = |\cos^2 \theta + \sin^2 \theta| = 1$$

where Θ is the rotation matrix and θ is a constant.

To relate the spatial Fourier transforms of $f(x, y)$ and $f'(x', y')$ for the rotation transformation, we proceed with the vector representation of the Fourier transform. Let

$$\mathbf{r}' \equiv \Theta \, \mathbf{r}$$

Thus, (2.12) becomes

$$F'(\mathbf{k_{r'}}) = \int_{\mathbf{r'}} f'(\mathbf{r'}) \, \exp[-j\mathbf{k}_{\mathbf{r'}}^T \, \mathbf{r'}] \, d\mathbf{r'}$$

$$= \int_{\mathbf{r}} f(\mathbf{r}) \, \exp[-j\mathbf{k}_{\mathbf{r'}}^T \, \Theta \, \mathbf{r}] \, d\mathbf{r}.$$

We denote the spatial frequency domain that appears in the above exponent by the following:

$$\mathbf{k}_{\mathbf{r}}^T \equiv \mathbf{k}_{\mathbf{r'}}^T \, \Theta.$$

Using this in the above Fourier integral, we obtain

$$F'(\mathbf{k_{r'}}) = \int_{\mathbf{r}} f(\mathbf{r}) \, \exp[-j\mathbf{k}_{\mathbf{r}}^T \, \mathbf{r}] \, d\mathbf{r}$$

$$= F(\mathbf{k_r}).$$

Moreover, from the transpose of the both sides of

$$\mathbf{k}_{\mathbf{r}}^T = \mathbf{k}_{\mathbf{r'}}^T \, \Theta$$

we can write

$$\mathbf{k_r} = \Theta^T \, \mathbf{k_{r'}}.$$

One of the properties of the rotation matrix is that its inverse and transpose are equal to each other; that is,

$$\Theta^T = \Theta^{-1}.$$

Thus, we have

$$\mathbf{k_{r'}} = \Theta \, \mathbf{k_r}.$$

This implies that the Fourier transform of the θ-rotated transformation of a two-dimensional signal is the θ-rotated transformation of the Fourier transform of the original signal; that is,

$$F'(k_{x'}, k_{y'}) = F(k_x, k_y), \qquad (2.15)$$

where

$$\begin{bmatrix} k_{x'} \\ k_{y'} \end{bmatrix} = \begin{bmatrix} \cos\theta & \sin\theta \\ -\sin\theta & \cos\theta \end{bmatrix} \begin{bmatrix} k_x \\ k_y \end{bmatrix}. \qquad (2.16)$$

Suppose $F_p(\cdot)$ and $F_p'(\cdot)$ are the polar mapping functions in the spatial frequency domain for $F(\cdot)$ and $F'(\cdot)$. Then, from (2.15)-(2.16), we have

$$F_p'(\phi - \theta, \rho) = F_p(\phi, \rho).$$

(Note that in the above discussion θ is the rotation angle. In Sections 2.1 and 2.2 where we introduced polar function mapping, we used (θ, r) to identify the polar spatial domain.)

Scale Transformation

This transformation, shown via an example in Figure 2.10, is defined by

$$\begin{bmatrix} x' \\ y' \end{bmatrix} = \begin{bmatrix} ax \\ by \end{bmatrix}$$

with

$$J(x, y) = |ab|$$

where a, b are constants. Then, for this transformation (2.12) can be rewritten as follows:

$$F'(k_{x'}, k_{y'}) = |ab| \; F(k_x, k_y), \qquad (2.17)$$

where

$$\begin{bmatrix} k_{x'} \\ k_{y'} \end{bmatrix} = \begin{bmatrix} \frac{k_x}{a} \\ \frac{k_y}{b} \end{bmatrix} \qquad (2.18)$$

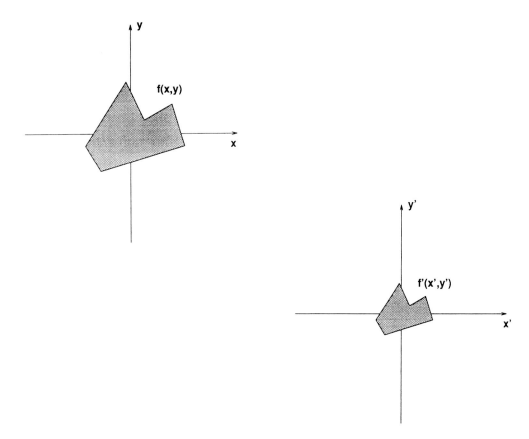

Figure 2.10 Scale transformation.

General Linear Transformations

A generalized linear mapping of the spatial domain can be identified via

$$\mathbf{r}' \equiv \underline{A}\,\mathbf{r} - \mathbf{r}_0$$

Equivalently, we have

$$\mathbf{r}' = \begin{bmatrix} x' \\ y' \end{bmatrix} = \underbrace{\begin{bmatrix} a & b \\ c & d \end{bmatrix}}_{\underline{A}} \begin{bmatrix} x \\ y \end{bmatrix} - \underbrace{\begin{bmatrix} x_0 \\ y_0 \end{bmatrix}}_{\mathbf{r_0}}.$$

The Jacobian of this transformation is

$$J(x,y) = ||\underline{A}|| = |det(\underline{A})|$$

Thus, we have from (2.12)

$$F'(\mathbf{k_{r'}}) = \int_{x'}\int_{y'} f'(\mathbf{r'}) \, \exp[-j\mathbf{k_{r'}^T} \, \mathbf{r'}] \, d\mathbf{r'}$$

$$= \int_x\int_y f(\mathbf{r}) \, \exp[-j\mathbf{k_{r'}^T} \, (\underline{A} \, \mathbf{r} - \mathbf{r_0})] \, |det(\underline{A})| \, d\mathbf{r}$$

$$= |ad - bc| \, \exp[j\mathbf{k_{r'}^T} \, \mathbf{r_0}] \int_x\int_y f(\mathbf{r}) \, \exp[-j\mathbf{k_{r'}^T} \, \underline{A} \, \mathbf{r}] \, d\mathbf{r}$$

$$= |ad - bc| \, \exp[j\mathbf{k_{r'}^T} \, \mathbf{r_0}] \, F(\mathbf{k_r}),$$

(2.19)

where

$$\mathbf{k_r^T} = \mathbf{k_{r'}^T} \, \underline{A},$$

or

$$\mathbf{k_r} = \underline{A}^T \, \mathbf{k_{r'}},$$

which yields

$$\mathbf{k_{r'}} = (\underline{A}^T)^{-1} \, \mathbf{k_r}.$$

(2.20)

Example, Fourier Slice Theorem: We showed that

$$F_x(k_x,y) = \int_{-\infty}^{\infty} f(x,y) \, \exp(-jk_x x) \, dx.$$

Setting $k_x = 0$ in the above yields

$$F_x(0,y) = \int_{-\infty}^{\infty} f(x,y) \, dx.$$

Recall that this was the projection of $f(x,y)$ along the x axis. Moreover, we showed that

$$\mathcal{F}_{(y)}[F_x(0,y)] = F(0,k_y).$$

Similarly, we have

$$\mathcal{F}_{(x)}[F_y(x,0)] = F(k_x,0).$$

Consider the rotation transformation $\mathbf{r'} = \Theta \, \mathbf{r}$, and let $f'(x',y') = f(x,y)$ (see Figure 2.11).

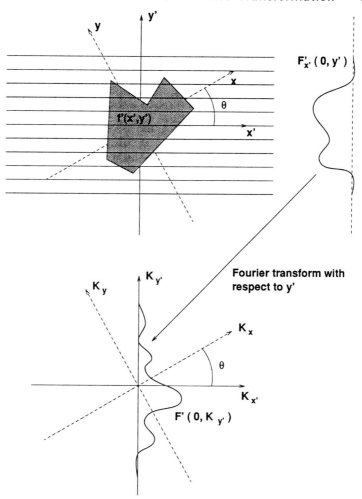

Figure 2.11 Projection along the x'-axis and its Fourier transform.

For the projection along the x' axis and its Fourier transform, we have

$$F'_{x'}(0, y') = \int_{-\infty}^{\infty} f'(x', y')\ dx'$$

and

$$\mathcal{F}_{(y')}[F'_{x'}(0, y')] = F'(0, k_{y'}).$$

However, from the properties of the rotational transformation (2.19)-(2.20), we have

$$F'(k_{x'}, k_{y'}) = F(k_x, k_y)$$

with

$$\mathbf{k_{r'}} = \Theta \, \mathbf{k_r},$$

or

$$\mathbf{k_r} = \Theta^{-1} \, \mathbf{k_{r'}}.$$

Hence

$$\mathcal{F}_{(y')}[F'_{x'}(0, y')] = F\left(\Theta^{-1} \begin{bmatrix} 0 \\ k_{y'} \end{bmatrix} \right) = F(-k_{y'} \sin\theta, k_{y'} \cos\theta).$$

Similarly

$$\mathcal{F}_{(x')}[F'_{y'}(x', 0)] = F\left(\Theta^{-1} \begin{bmatrix} k_{x'} \\ 0 \end{bmatrix} \right) = F(k_{x'} \cos\theta, k_{x'} \sin\theta).$$

In general, the locus of the Fourier transform of the projection of $f(x, y)$ in any direction, for example, x', lies on the line orthogonal to its spatial frequency axis (see Figure 2.11). Consider an imaging system where the measurements provide the line integrals of $f(x, y)$ in the (θ, y') domain. In this case, $F(k_x, k_y)$ could be uniquely identified by these measurements.

- *This principle is the basis of image formation in the transmission-mode imaging with nondiffracting radiation sources (see Computer-Assisted Tomography, CAT, in [2],[10],[11] and Chapter 7). The database obtained from the Fourier transform of the measurements in the (θ, y') domain [i.e., the data in the $(\theta, k_{y'})$ domain] is called **polar**. We will encounter this form of database in certain reflection-mode (echo) imaging systems.*

The transformation of information in a spatial domain signal $f(x, y)$ into its projections in the (θ, y') domain is called the *Radon transform* of that function. One should not assume that all imaging system yield the Radon transform of the target function.

2.6 TWO-DIMENSIONAL SAMPLING

In this section, we consider generalized (nonlinear) sampling in the spatial frequency domain. This is an issue associated with array imaging systems where the available data (measurements of the imaging system) could be translated to the spatial frequency samples of the desired object function. A brief review, however, is given first of uniform rectangular sampling in the spatial domain due to the reader's familiarity with the subject and to provide basic notation.

Rectangular Sampling in the Spatial Domain

Let $f(x, y)$ be a two-dimensional signal. Its rectangular δ-sampled signal is defined by

$$f_s(x, y) = f(x, y) \sum_{m=-\infty}^{\infty} \sum_{n=-\infty}^{\infty} \delta(x - m\Delta_x, y - n\Delta_y)$$

$$= \sum_{m=-\infty}^{\infty} \sum_{n=-\infty}^{\infty} f(x, y) \, \delta(x - m\Delta_x, y - n\Delta_y),$$

where Δ_x and Δ_y are chosen constants denoting the sample spacings in the x and y domain respectively.

Equivalently, we can write

$$f_s(x, y) = \sum_{m} \sum_{n} f_{mn} \, \delta(x - m\Delta_x, y - n\Delta_y)$$

where $f_{mn} \equiv f(m\Delta_x, n\Delta_y)$.

Using the following Poisson sum formula:

$$\sum_{m=-\infty}^{\infty} \delta(x - m\Delta_x) = \frac{1}{\Delta_x} \sum_{m=-\infty}^{\infty} \exp(j\frac{2\pi m x}{\Delta_x})$$

$$\sum_{n=-\infty}^{\infty} \delta(y - n\Delta_y) = \frac{1}{\Delta_y} \sum_{n=-\infty}^{\infty} \exp(j\frac{2\pi n y}{\Delta_y})$$

we can write

$$f_s(x,y) = \frac{1}{\Delta_x \Delta_y} \sum_m \sum_n f(x,y) \quad \underbrace{\exp[j2\pi(\frac{m}{\Delta_x}x + \frac{n}{\Delta_y}y)]}_{linear\ phase\ function\ of\ x\ \&\ y}$$

The two-dimensional Fourier transform of the above is

$$F_s(k_x,k_y) = \frac{k_{x0}k_{y0}}{(2\pi)^2} \sum_{m=-\infty}^{\infty} \sum_{n=-\infty}^{\infty} F(k_x - mk_{x0}, k_y - nk_{y0})$$

where

$$k_{x0} = \frac{2\pi}{\Delta_x} \quad \text{and} \quad k_{y0} = \frac{2\pi}{\Delta_y}.$$

Thus, provided that $F(k_x, k_y)$ has a finite support in the spatial frequency domain, for example,

$$F(k_x, k_y) = 0 \quad \text{for } |k_x| \geq \frac{k_{x0}}{2} \ \& \ |k_y| \geq \frac{k_{y0}}{2} \ ,$$

then $f(x,y)$ can be recovered from $f_s(x,y)$ via lowpass filtering.

Rectangular Sampling in the Spatial Frequency Domain

Uniform rectangular sampling in the frequency domain can be represented via

$$F_\delta(k_x, k_y) = \sum_m \sum_n F(k_x, k_y)\, \delta(k_x - m\Delta_{k_x})\, \delta(k_y - n\Delta_{k_y})$$

$$= \sum_m \sum_n F_{mn}\, \delta(k_x - m\Delta_{k_x}, k_y - n\Delta_{k_y})$$

where Δ_{k_x} and Δ_{k_y} are constants and $F_{mn} = F(m\Delta_{k_x}, n\Delta_{k_y})$. Then, it can be shown that

$$f_\delta(x,y) = \frac{1}{\Delta_{k_x} \Delta_{k_y}} \sum_m \sum_n f(x - mX_s, y - nY_s)$$

where

$$X_s \equiv \frac{2\pi}{\Delta k_x} \quad \text{and} \quad Y_s \equiv \frac{2\pi}{\Delta k_y}.$$

We consider the class of signals $f(x, y)$ with a finite support defined as follows:

$$f(x, y) = 0 \qquad \text{for} \quad \sqrt{x^2 + y^2} \geq X_0.$$

We call this support the Disk of radius X_0 centered at the origin denoted by $(D : X_0)$.

We can write

$$F_\delta(k_x, k_y) = F(k_x, k_y) \left[\sum_m \delta(k_x - m\Delta_{k_x}) \right] \left[\sum_n \delta(k_y - n\Delta_{k_y}) \right].$$

Using the Poisson sum formula, we can convert the delta sum into exponentials as follows:

$$F_\delta(k_x, k_y) = \frac{1}{\Delta_{k_x}\Delta_{k_y}} \sum_m \sum_n \underbrace{F(k_x, k_y) \exp[j2\pi(\frac{mk_x}{\Delta_{k_x}} + \frac{nk_y}{\Delta_{k_y}})]}_{for~a~fixed~(m,n)~=~\mathcal{F}_{(x,y)}[f(x-\frac{2\pi m}{\Delta k_x}, y-\frac{2\pi n}{\Delta k_y})]}$$

This yields

$$f_\delta(x, y) = \mathcal{F}^{-1}_{(k_x, k_y)}[F_\delta(k_x, k_y)]$$

$$= \frac{1}{\Delta_{k_x}\Delta_{k_y}} \sum_m \sum_n f(x - \frac{2\pi m}{\Delta_{k_x}}, y - \frac{2\pi n}{\Delta_{k_y}}).$$

To avoid linear aliasing, the following should be true:

$$2X_0 \leq \frac{2\pi}{\Delta k_x} \quad \text{and} \quad 2X_0 \leq \frac{2\pi}{\Delta k_y}.$$

Figures 2.12a and 2.12b, respectively, depict $f_\delta(x, y)$ when $f(x, y)$ is $\delta(x, y)$ and a two-dimensional rectangular function.

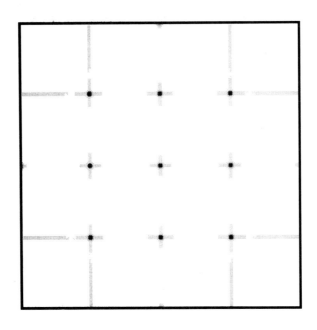

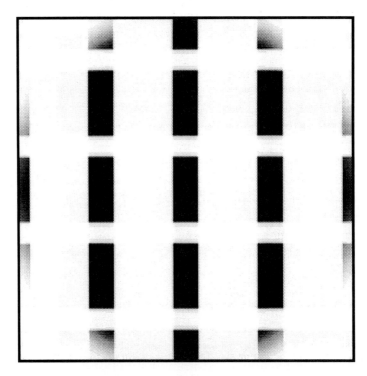

Figure 2.12 Rectangular sampling in the spatial frequency domain: Delta-sampled signal $f_\delta(x, y)$. (a) Delta function. (b) Rectangular pulse.

Generalized Sampling in the Spatial Frequency Domain

Generalized sampling in the spatial frequency domain refers to uniform sampling in a two-dimensional domain that is a *nonlinear* transformation of the (k_x, k_y) domain. Uniform rectangular sampling is a special case. Two examples will be used to facilitate the discussion of the given concepts: hexagonal sampling (generalized linear transformation), and polar sampling (a nonlinear transformation).

Define the general transformation

$$\begin{bmatrix} \alpha \\ \beta \end{bmatrix} \equiv \begin{bmatrix} T_1(k_x, k_y) \\ T_2(k_x, k_y) \end{bmatrix}.$$

In array imaging problems, (α, β) is referred to as the *measurement* domain.

Example 1: Hexagonal (linear) Sampling [8]:

$$\begin{bmatrix} \alpha \\ \beta \end{bmatrix} \equiv \begin{bmatrix} ak_x + bk_y \\ ck_x + dk_y \end{bmatrix}.$$

Note that rectangular sampling corresponds to the case of $b = c = 0$. The inverse of the hexagonal transformation is also linear, that is,

$$\begin{bmatrix} k_x \\ k_y \end{bmatrix} = \begin{bmatrix} A\alpha + B\beta \\ C\alpha + D\beta \end{bmatrix}$$

The Jacobian of the hexagonal transformation is

$$|\frac{\partial(\alpha, \beta)}{\partial(k_x, k_y)}| = |T'(k_x, k_y)| = |ad - bc|.$$

Example 2: Polar Sampling [10],[11]:

$$\alpha = \sqrt{k_x^2 + k_y^2}$$

$$\beta = \arctan(\frac{k_y}{k_x})$$

The Inverse of this transformation is

$$k_x = \alpha \cos \beta$$
$$k_y = \alpha \sin \beta$$

The Jacobian of the polar transformation is

$$|T'(k_x, k_y)| = \frac{1}{\sqrt{k_x^2 + k_y^2}}.$$

In the following discussion, we present a study on the spectral properties of the generalized two-dimensional sampled data. The study is similar to the spectral analysis of Pulse Position Modulation (PPM) given in [1],[9]. This will establish a basis for reconstructing the original signal under certain constraints.

Delta-Sampled Signal

We define

$$G(\alpha, \beta) \equiv F(k_x, k_y)$$

or, equivalently

$$G[T_1(k_x, k_y), T_2(k_x, k_y)] = F(k_x, k_y)$$

It is assumed that the imaging system provides evenly spaced samples of $G(\alpha, \beta)$ in the (α, β) measurement domain, for example, $\alpha_m = m\Delta_\alpha$ and $\beta_n = n\Delta_\beta$. Our task is to reconstruct the space-limited function $f(x, y)$ from the available samples of $F(k_x, k_y)$ at (k_{xmn}, k_{ymn}), where

$$\alpha_m = m\Delta_\alpha = T_1(k_{xmn}, k_{ymn})$$
$$\beta_n = n\Delta_\beta = T_2(k_{xmn}, k_{ymn}).$$

It can be shown [3] that if

$$\alpha_0 = T_1(k_{x0}, k_{y0})$$
$$\beta_0 = T_2(k_{x0}, k_{y0})$$

then

$$\delta(k_x - k_{x0}, k_y - k_{y0}) = |T'(k_x, k_y)| \; \delta(\alpha - \alpha_0, \beta - \beta_0). \qquad (2.21)$$

We define the delta-sampled signal via

$$F_\delta(k_x, k_y) \equiv \sum_{(m,n)} F(k_{xmn}, k_{ymn}) \; \delta(k_x - k_{xmn}, k_y - k_{ymn})$$

$$= F(k_x, k_y) \sum_{(m,n)} \delta(k_x - k_{xmn}, k_y - k_{ymn}).$$

Using (2.21), we can rewrite F_δ as follows:

$$F_\delta(k_x, k_y) = F(k_x, k_y) \; |T'(k_x, k_y)|$$
$$\times \sum_m \sum_n \delta[T_1(k_x, k_y) - m\Delta_\alpha, T_2(k_x, k_y) - n\Delta_\beta].$$

Recall the Poisson sum formula:

$$\sum_m \delta[T_1(k_x, k_y) - m\Delta_\alpha] = \frac{1}{\Delta_\alpha} \sum_m \exp[j\frac{2\pi m}{\Delta_\alpha} T_1(k_x, k_y)]$$

and

$$\sum_n \delta[T_2(k_x, k_y) - n\Delta_\beta] = \frac{1}{\Delta_\beta} \sum_n \exp[j\frac{2\pi n}{\Delta_\beta} T_2(k_x, k_y)].$$

Using the Poisson sum formula, we obtain for F_δ

$$F_\delta(k_x, k_y) = \frac{1}{\Delta_\alpha \Delta_\beta} F(k_x, k_y) \; |T'(k_x, k_y)|$$
$$\times \sum_m \sum_n \exp[j\frac{2\pi m}{\Delta_\alpha} T_1(k_x, k_y) + j\frac{2\pi n}{\Delta_\beta} T_2(k_x, k_y)].$$

Jacobian Modified Response

Define the Jacobian Modified Response as follows:

$$R(k_x, k_y) \equiv \frac{F_\delta(k_x, k_y)}{|T'(k_x, k_y)|}$$

$$= \underbrace{\frac{1}{\Delta_\alpha \Delta_\beta} F(k_x, k_y)}_{amplitude\ function}$$

$$\times \underbrace{\sum_m \sum_n \exp[j \frac{2\pi m}{\Delta_\alpha} T_1(k_x, k_y) + j \frac{2\pi n}{\Delta_\beta} T_2(k_x, k_y)]}_{two\ dimensional\ phase\ modulated\ signal}$$

- *The sampling constraints and reconstruction algorithm are based on separating the zero-th harmonic, that is, $(m, n) = (0, 0)$, component from the AM-PM components in the above sum [10]. The AM-PM components are referred to as **nonlinear aliasing**. This is due to the fact that the harmonics that cause aliasing are nonlinear functions of (k_x, k_y). This is in contrast with the rectangular sampling where aliasing is due to **linear** phase functions of the spatial frequency domain. This is also true for the general linear (hexagonal) sampling as shown in the next example.*

Example 1, continued: For the hexagonal sampling, we get

$$R(k_x, k_y) = \frac{F(k_x, k_y)}{\Delta_\alpha \Delta_\beta |ad - bc|}$$

$$\times \sum_m \sum_n \exp[j \frac{2\pi m}{\Delta_\alpha}(ak_x + bk_y) + j \frac{2\pi n}{\Delta_\beta}(ck_x + dk_y)]$$

$$= \frac{F(k_x, k_y)}{\Delta_\alpha \Delta_\beta |ad - bc|}$$

$$\times \underbrace{\sum_m \sum_n \exp[j 2\pi (\frac{ma}{\Delta_\alpha} + \frac{nc}{\Delta_\beta}) k_x + j 2\pi (\frac{mb}{\Delta_\alpha} + \frac{nd}{\Delta_\beta}) k_y]}_{= \mathcal{F}_{(x,y)}[\delta(x - \frac{2\pi ma}{\Delta_\alpha} - \frac{2\pi nc}{\Delta_\beta}, y - \frac{2\pi mb}{\Delta_\alpha} - \frac{2\pi nd}{\Delta_\beta})]}$$

Note the presence of the *linear* phase functions of (k_x, k_y) on the right side of the above equation. For $(m,n) \neq (0,0)$, these are the *linear* aliasing components. The inverse spatial Fourier transform of the above yields

$$r(x,y) = \frac{1}{\Delta_\alpha \Delta_\beta} \sum_{(m,n)} f(x - \frac{2\pi m a}{\Delta_\alpha} - \frac{2\pi n c}{\Delta_\beta}, y - \frac{2\pi m b}{\Delta_\alpha} - \frac{2\pi n d}{\Delta_\beta}).$$

Figures 2.13a and 2.13b are the distributions of the Jacobian modified response, $r(x,y)$, for a hexagonal sampling case when $f(x,y)$ is $\delta(x,y)$ and a two-dimensional rectangular function, respectively.

- For the hexagonal sampling, the delta-sampled signal $f_\delta(x,y)$ is related to $r(x,y)$ via a constant. This is due to the fact that the Jacobian function for the hexagonal sampling is a constant.

Sampling Constraints

An important issue in Fourier array imaging is the selection of the sampling spacing in the measurement domain (α, β) to avoid nonlinear aliasing. For this, the instantaneous frequency of the two-dimensional PM wave

$$\exp[j\frac{2\pi m}{\Delta_\alpha}T_1(k_x, k_y) + j\frac{2\pi n}{\Delta_\beta}T_2(k_x, k_y)]$$

should satisfy the following constraint [10]:

$$\underbrace{2\pi|\frac{m}{\Delta_\alpha}\nabla T_1(k_x, k_y) + \frac{n}{\Delta_\beta}\nabla T_2(k_x, k_y)|}_{instantaneous\ frequency\ for\ the\ PM\ wave} \geq 2X_0$$

for all available (k_x, k_y) and (m,n), where ∇ is the gradient operator in the (k_x, k_y) domain. The constraint can be rewritten as follows:

$$2\pi \Big[[\frac{m}{\Delta_\alpha}\frac{\partial T_1(k_x, k_y)}{\partial k_x} + \frac{n}{\Delta_\beta}\frac{\partial T_2(k_x, k_y)}{\partial k_x}]^2$$
$$+ [\frac{m}{\Delta_\alpha}\frac{\partial T_1(k_x, k_y)}{\partial k_y} + \frac{n}{\Delta_\beta}\frac{\partial T_2(k_x, k_y)}{\partial k_y}]^2 \Big]^{1/2} \geq 2X_0.$$

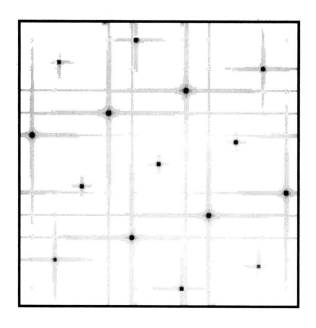

Figure 2.13 Hexagonal sampling in the spatial frequency domain: Jacobian modified response. (a) Delta function. (b) Rectangular pulse.

Example 1, continued: For the hexagonal sampling case, we get

$$2\pi\sqrt{(\frac{ma}{\Delta_\alpha} + \frac{nc}{\Delta_\beta})^2 + (\frac{mb}{\Delta_\alpha} + \frac{nd}{\Delta_\beta})^2} \geq 2X_0 \quad \forall (m,n) \neq 0$$

to avoid nonlinear aliasing. This results in the following constraints:

$$
\begin{aligned}
2\pi \left| \, |\frac{a}{\Delta_\alpha}| - |\frac{c}{\Delta_\beta}| \, \right| \geq 2X_0 \\
2\pi \left| \, |\frac{b}{\Delta_\alpha}| - |\frac{d}{\Delta_\beta}| \, \right| \geq 2X_0
\end{aligned}
\tag{2.22}
$$

The constraints in (2.22) can be shown to be sufficient but not necessary for rejecting aliasing.

Example 2, continued: For the case of polar sampling, it is sufficient to satisfy the constraints only for $(m,n) = (1,0)$ and $(m,n) = (0,1)$ to find $(\Delta_\alpha, \Delta_\beta)$ (see [10]):

$$(m,n) = (1,0) \quad \longrightarrow \quad \Delta_\alpha \leq \frac{\pi}{X_0}$$

$$(m,n) = (0,1) \quad \longrightarrow \quad \Delta_\beta \leq \frac{\pi}{X_0\sqrt{k_x^2 + k_y^2}}$$

Note that Δ_β is a function of (k_x, k_y). Thus, choose the maximum available value for $\sqrt{k_x^2 + k_y^2}$, call it α_0, in the constraint. This yields

$$\Delta_\beta \leq \frac{\pi}{\alpha_0 X_0}.$$

Figures 2.14a and 2.14b are the distributions of the Jacobian modified response, $r(x,y)$, for a polar sampling case when $f(x,y)$ is $\delta(x,y)$ and a two-dimensional rectangular function, respectively. Figure 2.14c shows the delta-sampled signal $f_\delta(x,y)$ for the case shown in Figure 2.14b. *Note that for the polar sampling the Jacobian function is not a constant.*

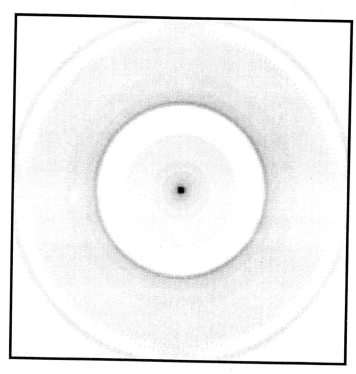

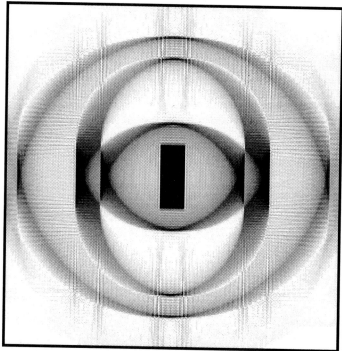

Figure 2.14 Polar sampling in the spatial frequency domain: Jacobian modified response. (a) Delta function. (b) Rectangular pulse.

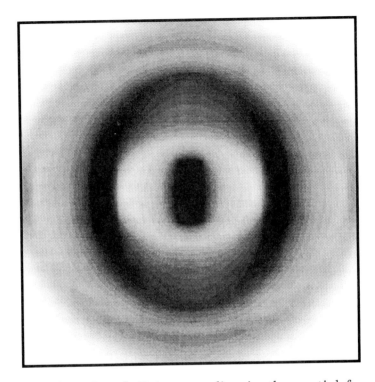

Figure 2.14 (*continued*) Polar sampling in the spatial frequency
domain: Delta-sampled signal for a rectangular pulse.

Using the above-mentioned constraints for polar sampling, it can
be shown that for the Fourier slice data the number of projections
required for alias-free reconstruction should be greater than $\frac{\pi}{2}$ times
the number of line integrals per projection [10].

2.7 RECONSTRUCTION

We now examine the problem of reconstructing the object function
$f(x, y)$ from the knowledge of the Jacobian modified response $R(k_x, k_y)$.
This corresponds to the final step in obtaining the desired image in
Fourier array imaging systems.

The object is modeled to be space-limited within the disk of radius X_0 in the spatial domain. The indicator function for this disk is

$$i(x, y) = \begin{cases} 1 & \sqrt{x^2 + y^2} \leq X_0 \\ 0 & \text{otherwise,} \end{cases}$$

and

$$I(k_x, k_y) = \qquad X_0^2 \underbrace{\frac{J_1(\sqrt{k_x^2 + k_y^2}\, X_0)}{\sqrt{k_x^2 + k_y^2}\, X_0}}$$

Airy Pattern (two dimensional interpolating function)

We showed that under certain sampling constraints, we have

$$r(x, y) = \frac{1}{\Delta_\alpha \Delta_\beta} f(x, y) \qquad \text{for} \quad \sqrt{x^2 + y^2} < X_0$$

Thus, we can write

$$F(k_x, k_y) = \Delta_\alpha \Delta_\beta \left[R(k_x, k_y) * {}* I(k_x, k_y) \right]$$

in the spatial frequency domain, and

$$f(x, y) = \Delta_\alpha \Delta_\beta\, r(x, y)\, i(x, y)$$

in the spatial domain.

Spatial Frequency Domain Reconstruction

Using the expression for the Jacobian modified response in the above filtering operations yields

$$F(k_x, k_y) = \sum_{(m,n)} \frac{\Delta_\alpha \Delta_\beta F(k_x, k_y)}{|T'(k_x, k_y)|} \delta(k_x - k_{xmn}, k_y - k_{ymn}) * {}* I(k_x, k_y)$$

$$= \Delta_\alpha \Delta_\beta \sum_{(m,n)} \frac{F(k_{xmn}, k_{ymn})}{|T'(k_{xmn}, k_{ymn})|}\, I(k_x - k_{xmn}, k_y - k_{ymn})$$

For reconstruction, the above sum is evaluated on a uniform grid in the (k_x, k_y) plane, for example, $(k_{xi}, k_{yj}) = (i\Delta k_x, j\Delta k_y) = (\frac{i\pi}{X_0}, \frac{j\pi}{X_0})$. Then, the inverse two-dimensional DFT of $F(k_{xi}, k_{yj})$ results in the spatial domain image.

Spatial Domain Reconstruction

We have

$$f(x,y) = \begin{cases} \Delta_\alpha \Delta_\beta \ r(x,y) & \sqrt{x^2 + y^2} \le X_0 \\ 0 & \text{otherwise.} \end{cases}$$

Thus, within the disk of radius X_0, we can compute

$$f(x,y) = \Delta_\alpha \Delta_\beta \int\int R(k_x, k_y) \ \exp(jk_x x + jk_y y) \ dk_x dk_y$$
$$= \Delta_\alpha \Delta_\beta \int\int \sum_{(m,n)} \frac{F(k_{xmn}, k_{ymn})}{|T'(k_{xmn}, k_{ymn})|} \ \delta(k_x - k_{xmn}, k_y - k_{ymn})$$
$$\exp(jk_x x + jk_y y) \ dk_x dk_y$$
$$= \Delta_\alpha \Delta_\beta \sum_{(m,n)} \frac{F(k_{xmn}, k_{ymn})}{|T'(k_{xmn}, k_{ymn})|} \ \exp(jk_{xmn}x + jk_{ymn}y)$$

For reconstruction, the above sum is evaluated on a uniform grid on the (x,y) plane, for example, $(x_i, y_j) = (i\Delta_x, j\Delta_y)$. This is computationally intensive due to the complex exponential term.

Point Spread Function

In a practical array imaging problem, the spatial frequency domain data available for $F(k_x, k_y)$ resides within a finite band in the (k_x, k_y) domain. This is due to the fact that the measurements in a practical imaging system are discrete and finite. We now examine the implications of this limitation in the information conveyed by a reconstructed image in an imaging system.

In Chapter 1, we encountered and discussed a similar problem in one-dimensional echo imaging. We showed that the *bandpass* data obtained for $F(k_x)$ from the measurements convey *edge* information about the desired image when the *magnitude* of the bandpass data is used for display purposes. We called the resultant image the *point spread function* of the imaging system.

Now we consider the same problem in the two-dimensional spatial frequency domain. Suppose the samples of $F(k_x, k_y)$ are available in a two-dimensional rectangular region centered at (K_{xc}, K_{yc}) and lengths $2K_{x0}$ and $2K_{y0}$, respectively, in the k_x and k_y axes. The indicator function for this support region is:

$$H(k_x, k_y) \equiv \begin{cases} 1 & |k_x - K_{xc}| \leq K_{x0} \text{ and } |k_y - K_{yc}| \leq K_{y0} \\ 0 & \text{otherwise.} \end{cases}$$

In the spatial domain, this signal is

$$h(x, y) = 4K_{x0}K_{y0} \frac{\sin(K_{x0}x)}{K_{x0}x} \exp(K_{xc}x) \frac{\sin(K_{y0}y)}{K_{y0}y} \exp(K_{yc}y).$$

Thus, the information extracted from the measurements can be represented via the following bandpass filtered version of the target function:

$$G(k_x, k_y) \equiv F(k_x, k_y) \, H(k_x, k_y).$$

To examine the effects of this bandpass filtering, we consider a target function that is a unit delta function at (x_n, y_n) in the spatial domain, that is,

$$f(x, y) = \delta(x - x_n, y - y_n).$$

The spatial Fourier transform of the target function is

$$F(k_x, k_y) = \exp[-j(k_x x_n + k_y y_n)].$$

Moreover, the actual signal obtained in the imaging system becomes

$$G(k_x, k_y) = \exp[-j(k_x x_n + k_y y_n)] \, H(k_x, k_y).$$

This translates into the following signal in the spatial domain:

$$g(x, y) = h(x - x_n, y - y_n)$$

$$= 4K_{x0}K_{y0} \frac{\sin[K_{x0}(x - x_n)]}{K_{x0}(x - x_n)} \exp[jK_{xc}(x - x_n)]$$

$$\times \frac{\sin[K_{y0}(y - y_n)]}{K_{y0}(y - y_n)} \exp[jK_{yc}(y - y_n)].$$

Finally, the magnitude function for this signal is

$$|g(x, y)| = 4K_{x0}K_{y0} \left|\frac{\sin[K_{x0}(x - x_n)]}{K_{x0}(x - x_n)}\right| \left|\frac{\sin[K_{y0}(y - y_n)]}{K_{y0}(y - y_n)}\right|.$$

This result indicates that the reconstruction introduces a linear phase function in the (x, y) domain image that is transparent in its magnitude. Furthermore, this magnitude image that is extracted from bandpass data conveys location information regarding the reconstructed target.

We call this magnitude function the two-dimensional *point spread function* (similar to the *impulse response*) of the imaging system. Clearly, when the target function is composed of several delta functions with varying magnitude, e.g,

$$f(x, y) = \sum_n f_n \, \delta(x - x_n, y - y_n),$$

then

$$|g(x, y)| \approx \sum_n f_n \, |h(x - x_n, y - y_n)|$$

$$= 4K_{x0}K_{y0} \sum_n f_n \left|\frac{\sin[K_{x0}(x - x_n)]}{K_{x0}(x - x_n)}\right| \left|\frac{\sin[K_{y0}(y - y_n)]}{K_{y0}(y - y_n)}\right|,$$

provided that the point spread functions of the individual targets do not (approximately) overlap with each other. The *resolution* in the spatial domain is dictated by the main lobe of the sinc functions; that is,

$$\Delta_x \equiv \frac{\pi}{K_{x0}}$$

$$\Delta_y \equiv \frac{\pi}{K_{y0}}.$$

Before closing this section, we should point out the following practical issues:

i. The target function encountered in array imaging systems is not simply composed of delta functions. In this case, the bandpass data provide edge information about the target function.

ii. In certain imaging systems, the rectangular support region is in a rotated version of the (k_x, k_y) domain, for example, $(k_{x'}, k_{y'})$. In this case, the resolution equations are valid for the rotated version of the spatial domain, that is, (x', y').

iii. The support region for the available data in the (k_x, k_y) domain is not always rectangular. In this case, the point spread function is not *exactly* a two-dimensional sinc pattern. However, if $2K_{x0}$ and $2K_{y0}$, respectively, are the *approximate* supports of $H(k_x, k_y)$ along the k_x and k_y axes, then the above-mentioned resolution equations still hold.

iv. In Section 1.12, we discussed cross-range imaging of multiple targets from their spatial Doppler signatures. We showed that each target had a distinct support band and, consequently, point spread function that depend on the target's spatial coordinates. In two-dimensional array imaging problems, we will also encounter scenarios where each target's signature in the measured data varies with the target's coordinates. In this case, if $H_n(k_x, k_y)$ is the indicator function of the n-th target's support band, then the reconstructed image becomes

$$|g(x, y)| \approx \sum_n f_n \, |h_n(x - x_n, y - y_n)|.$$

This implies that the reconstructed image possesses a *shift-varying* point spread function.

PROJECTS

1. Simulate the two-dimensional signals examined in Section 1.2. Obtain their two-dimensional FFTs. Check the projection property for the two-dimensional rectangular function.

2. Simulate the Green's function

$$H(k_x, k_y) = \frac{1}{k_x^2 + k_y^2 - k^2},$$

in the (k_x, k_y) domain. Associate a small imaginary part with the wavenumber k (e.g., one percent of its real part) such that your simulated data would not become one over zero (infinity) in the real (k_x, k_y) domain. Obtain the inverse two-dimensional FFT of the Green's function, that is, $h(x, y)$. Check the amplitude behavior and zero-crossings (phase behavior) of $h(x, 0)$ as k is varied. Using this data, obtain a relationship between the zero-crossing and k. Show that the phase function of $h(x, 0)$ is $\exp(jkx)$.

3. Simulate shifted, rotated, and scaled versions of a two-dimensional spatial domain rectangular signal in the (k_x, k_y) domain using equations (2.13)-(2.14), (2.15)-(2.16), and (2.17)-(2.18), respectively. Obtain the inverse two-dimensional FFTs of the simulated data.

4. Simulate rectangular, hexagonal, and polar sampled data of a two-dimensional spatial domain rectangular signal in a *lowpass* region in the (k_x, k_y) domain. Use a reconstruction algorithm to interpolate the samples of the signal on a uniform grid centered around the lowpass region of the available samples in the (k_x, k_y) domain. Obtain the inverse two-dimensional FFT of the uniform grid data.

If you use the reconstruction algorithm described in Section 2.6, multiply the interpolating kernel $I(k_x, k_y)$ with a two-dimensional Hamming window, with an extent equal to the first, for example, three side lobes of the $I(\cdot)$ kernel, to reduce your computational time. Select the size of the interpolating window, that is, $i(x, y)$, to be, for example, four times larger than X_0. This will enable you to observe some of the nonlinear harmonics of the signal in the (x, y) domain (that is how Figures 2.12-2.14 were generated). Repeat the interpolation without incorporating the Jacobian function; this gives you the distribution of the delta sampled signal within your interpolating window in the spatial domain.

5. Repeat Project 4 with rectangular and hexagonal sampled data in a *bandpass* region in the (k_x, k_y) domain. Choose the sampled data to be bandpass only in the k_x domain, bandpass only in the k_y domain, and bandpass in both the k_x and k_y domains. The uniform grid should be selected to be centered around the bandpass region of the available data.

REFERENCES

1. B. Carlson, *Communication Systems,* New York: McGraw-Hill, 1986.

2. D. E. Dudgeon and R.M. Mersereau, *Multidimensional Digital Signal Processing,* Englewood Cliffs, NJ: Prentice Hall, 1984.

3. B. Friedman, *Principles and Techniques of Applied Mathematics,* New York: Wiley, 1956.

4. J. Goodman, *Introduction to Fourier Optics,* New York: McGraw-Hill, 1968.

5. P. M. Morse and H. Feshbach, *Methods of Theoretical Physics,* New York: McGraw-Hill, Parts 1 and 2, 1953.

6. A. Naylor and G. Sell, *Linear Operator Theory in Engineering and Science,* New York: Springer-Verlag, 1982.

7. A. Papoulis, *Systems and Transforms with Applications in Optics,* New York: McGraw-Hill, 1968.

8. D. Peterson and D. Middleton, "Sampling and reconstruction of wave-number limited functions in N-dimensional Euclidean spaces," *Inform. Contr.,* vol. 5, p. 279, 1962.

9. H. E. Rowe, *Signals and Noise in Communication Systems,* New York: Van Nostrand, 1965.

10 M. Soumekh, "Band-limited interpolation from unevenly spaced sampled data," *IEEE Transactions on Acoustics, Speech, and Signal Processing,* vol. ASSP-36, no. 1, pp. 110-122, January 1988.

11 H. Stark, J. Woods, I. Paul, and R. Hingerani, "Direct Fourier reconstruction in computer tomography," *IEEE Transactions on Acoustics, Speech, and Signal Processing,* vol. 29, pp 237-245, 1981.

Chapter 3

PHASED ARRAY IMAGING

3.1 PHASED ARRAYS

Active arrays are transmitting/receiving instruments that are widely used in imaging problems of remote sensing (radar, sonar, and geophysical exploration), nondestructive testing, diagnostic medicine, and artificial (e.g., robot) vision to extract information about the shape and location of objects embedded in a medium [1]-[3],[5],[7]-[8]. For this purpose, the medium under study is exposed to various radiation patterns induced by an array. The resultant echoed signals are then processed in inverse equations developed based on the wave/object interaction system model.

An array is made up of more primitive or basic components called *elements* or *transducers*. A transducer is capable of both transmitting energy into a medium and recording (receiving) the energy dissipated by the targets in a medium; such a device is also referred to as a *transceiver* in certain texts. When an element transmits energy into a medium, the distribution of the resultant energy in the spatial domain is called the element's *radiation pattern* in the transmit mode. An element's radiation pattern in the receive mode is the manner by which it combines and records the energy being dissipated from the various points in the spatial domain. An element is assumed to be a *reversible* linear system. Thus, its transmit mode and receive mode radiation patterns are identified by the same equation; we will examine this in Section 3.2

When a set of these elements is used for transmission/reception, the resultant device is called an *array*. The reason we need to use several elements in an imaging problem is related to a measure of the performance of the imaging system that is called *resolution*; this will be discussed later in this chapter. When the elements are arranged along a line, the resultant is called a *linear* array. Linear arrays possess the simplest hardware for construction and calibration. We are mainly concerned with linear arrays in this book. However, we will also examine certain *circular* array imaging problems.

If we illuminate a medium by turning on (or energizing) all the elements of an array, then the medium experiences the *sum* of the array elements' radiation patterns; that is, an array represents a *linear* system. The resultant energy distribution in the spatial domain is called *one* of the array's radiation patterns. Other radiation patterns of the array may be generated via associating a *complex* weight (i.e., both amplitude and phase) with the radiation pattern of each element on the array; these will be discussed in Sections 3.3 and 3.4. In general, any linear combination of the elements' radiation patterns results in a radiation pattern of the array. Thus, the array's radiation patterns belong to the linear signal subspace defined by the elements' radiation patterns. The same principle holds for the receive mode of the array.

The term *phased* array refers to the fact that the linear signal subspace of a physical array is generated, and exploited for imaging purposes, via varying the relative time *delay* of the transmitted pulsed signal and the resultant received echoed signal among the array's elements. These time delays are equivalent to *phase* functions in the temporal frequency domain, as we will see later in this chapter. Figure 3.1 provides a graphical representation of the transmit and receive modes of a phased array.

We discuss two phased array imaging methods. One method is based on the principle of beam *steering/scanning* in the angular domain and beam *focusing* in the range domain. Based on an approximation, the angular steering and range focusing, respectively, can be achieved via generating linear and quadratic phase functions across the phased array's aperture [3],[8]. This analog focusing method is widely used in ultrasonic medical imaging via instruments called *B-scanners*. The origin of this imaging methodology can be traced back to target detection and parameter estimation with air traffic control/surveillance radar. These as well as computer-assisted discrete focusing, that is, *generalized beamforming*, will be examined.

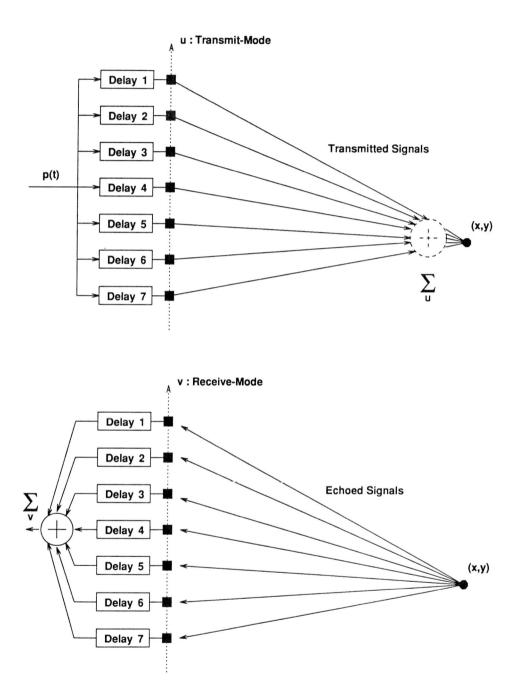

Figure 3.1 Transmit and receiver modes of a phased array.

The other phased array imaging method utilizes beam-steered data obtained via linearly varying the relative phase among the elements of an array, also known as phased array scan data; quadratic phasing is not utilized for range focusing. The system model and inversion for this method, which are based on the spatial Doppler phenomenon, incorporate the radiation pattern of the array's elements.

This approximation-free inversion for phased array data utilizes the Fourier decomposition of an element's radiation pattern. This inversion can be viewed as a *wavefront* reconstruction-based method for phased array data that performs imaging (focusing) via multi-dimensional digital signal processing algorithms in a computer instead of using conventional analog focusing methods in space that are based on approximations.

We will also use these principles to develop an inversion method for spatial-velocity imaging of targets using phased arrays that illuminate the target scene with an FM-CW signal. The spatial Fourier-based system model and inversion for phased array data indicates that one may increase the array's aperture and the frequency of the impinging wave to improve resolution in the cross-range and the cross-range speed domains. Meanwhile, increasing these two imaging system parameters, that is, the array's aperture and the frequency of the impinging wave, results in the breakdown of the assumptions and approximations that are used in the conventional analog focusing methods in space.

We begin with an analysis of the radiation pattern for an element and its Fourier properties.

3.2 AN ELEMENT'S RADIATION PATTERN

Ideal (Point) Transmitting/Receiving Element

An ideal or point radiating source is a device that has no dimension (like a black hole) and radiates energy to its surrounding medium. The transmitted energy can be time-dependent. From this point on, we call this energy distribution, that varies with time and space, a time-spatial *signal* (or function).

Suppose an ideal source is positioned at the origin in the spatial domain and radiates a time-dependent signal $p(t)$. The time-spatial signal observed at a given point in the spatial domain, for example, (x, y), is

$$h_0(x, y, t) \equiv \frac{1}{\sqrt{x^2 + y^2}} \, p\left[t - \frac{\sqrt{x^2 + y^2}}{c}\right], \tag{3.1}$$

where c is the propagation speed in the medium.

- *The two-dimensional spatial signal in (3.1) contains certain approxima-tions that we discussed in Chapter 2 (Green's function).*

The amplitude function $1/\sqrt{x^2 + y^2}$ represents the wave *dispersion* (not attenuation) in the medium; we are not concerned with the physical origin of this amplitude function that does not play an important role in analysis of coherent array imaging systems. The delay term $\sqrt{x^2 + y^2}/c$ associated with $p(\cdot)$ represents the one-way time delay for the wave prop-agation from the source to (x, y); this delay is the critical component for our analysis. Note that the two-dimensional system model in (3.1) is similar to the one-dimensional echo model we examined in Chapter 1 except for the amplitude function.

Suppose we move the ideal source to another location, for example, $(0, a)$, in the spatial domain. This simply translates to a shift in the y domain. In this case, the signal experienced at (x, y) becomes

$$h_0(x, y - a, t) \equiv \frac{1}{\sqrt{x^2 + (y - a)^2}} \, p\left[t - \frac{\sqrt{x^2 + (y - a)^2}}{c}\right]. \tag{3.2}$$

Taking the temporal Fourier transform of both sides of (3.2) with respect to t yields [for notational simplicity, we use $h_0(\cdot)$ to identify the temporal Fourier transform of $h_0(\cdot)$; $k \equiv \frac{\omega}{c}$ is the wavenumber]

$$h_0(x, y - a, \omega) = \frac{1}{\sqrt{x^2 + (y - a)^2}} \, P(\omega) \, \exp\left[-j\omega \frac{\sqrt{x^2 + (y - a)^2}}{c}\right]$$

$$= P(\omega) \, \frac{\exp[-jk\sqrt{x^2 + (y - a)^2}]}{\sqrt{x^2 + (y - a)^2}}. \tag{3.3}$$

Equation (3.3) is called the *radiation pattern* of an ideal element at the temporal frequency ω in its transmit mode. The receive mode radiation pattern for the element has the same functional form. This can be shown via (3.2) and (3.3) by having a radiating source at (x, y) and a receiver that records radiation at $(0, a)$.

Nonideal Transmitting/Receiving Element

In practice, we deal with nonideal elements that have nonzero dimensions. We consider one that is located at the origin. We can model this nonideal element as being made up of an infinite number of differential ideal elements located at $(0, a)$, $a \in [-L_e, L_e]$, that are simultaneously energized; $2L_e$ is the size of the nonideal element. We denote the intensity of the signal transmitted by the differential ideal source at $(0, a)$ by $i(a)$; clearly $i(a) = 0$ for $|a| > L_e$. The intensity signal $i(a)$ is a known function that is specified by the manufacturer of the element. For most transducers, it is assumed that $i(a) = 1$ (or any other constant) for $|a| \le L_e$.

Thus, for a given temporal frequency ω, the nonideal element's radiation pattern at (x, y) is

$$
\begin{aligned}
h(x, y, \omega) &\equiv \int_{-L_e}^{L_e} i(a)\, h_0(x, y - a, \omega)\, da \\
&= P(\omega) \int_{-L_e}^{L_e} i(a)\, \frac{\exp[-jk\sqrt{x^2 + (y - a)^2}]}{\sqrt{x^2 + (y - a)^2}}\, da \\
&= P(\omega) \int_{-\infty}^{\infty} i(a)\, \frac{\exp[-jk\sqrt{x^2 + (y - a)^2}]}{\sqrt{x^2 + (y - a)^2}}\, da \\
&= i(y) \, * \, h_0(x, y, \omega),
\end{aligned}
\tag{3.4}
$$

where $*$ denotes convolution in the y domain. In the following discussion, we use $P(\omega) = 1$ for notational simplicity.

- *When $i(y) = \delta(y)$, then $h(x, y, \omega) = h_0(x, y, \omega)$, that is, the transmitting element is an ideal point source.*

The radiation pattern for an ideal point source located at $(x, y - a)$ has the following Fourier decomposition (see Chapter 2):

$$h_0(x, y - a, \omega) = \frac{\exp[-jk\sqrt{x^2 + (y-a)^2}]}{\sqrt{x^2 + (y-a)^2}}$$

$$= \int_{-k}^{k} \frac{1}{\sqrt{k^2 - k_u^2}} \exp[-j\sqrt{k^2 - k_u^2}\, x - jk_u(y-a)]\, dk_u.$$

(3.5)

[In writing (3.4)-(3.5), it is assumed that the Green's functions for two-dimensional and three-dimensional imaging geometries are the same.] Substituting (3.5) in (3.4) yields

$$h(x, y, \omega) = \int_{-\infty}^{\infty} i(a) \int_{-k}^{k} \frac{1}{\sqrt{k^2 - k_u^2}}$$

$$\times \exp[-j\sqrt{k^2 - k_u^2}\, x - jk_u(y-a)]\, dk_u\, da$$

$$= \int_{-k}^{k} \frac{1}{\sqrt{k^2 - k_u^2}} \underbrace{\left[\int_{-\infty}^{\infty} i(a)\, \exp(jk_u\, a)\, da \right]}_{Fourier\ integral}$$

$$\times \exp(-j\sqrt{k^2 - k_u^2}\, x - jk_u y)\, dk_u$$

$$= \int_{-k}^{k} \frac{1}{\sqrt{k^2 - k_u^2}}\, I(k_u)\, \exp(-j\sqrt{k^2 - k_u^2}\, x - jk_u y)\, dk_u,$$

(3.6)

where $I(\cdot)$ is the Fourier transform of $i(\cdot)$.

We can rewrite (3.6) as follows:

$$h(x, y, \omega) = \int_{-k}^{k} H(k_u, \omega)\, \exp(-j\sqrt{k^2 - k_u^2}\, x - jk_u y)\, dk_u, \qquad (3.7)$$

where

$$H(k_u, \omega) = \frac{1}{\sqrt{k^2 - k_u^2}}\, I(k_u).$$

- *When $i(y) = \delta(y)$ (ideal point source case), then $I(k_u) = 1$ and $H(k_u, \omega) = \frac{1}{\sqrt{k^2 - k_u^2}}$.*

- *The significance of (3.7) is that the radiation pattern of an element, irrespective of being ideal or nonideal, can be expressed as a* **linear combination** *(the integral in k_u) of* **plane waves** *in the spatial domain, that is,* **linear phase functions** *of (x, y).*

For most transducer elements used in practice, it is assumed that the amplitude and phase functions are uniform across the aperture. This implies that $i(a)$ is a rectangular pulse; that is, $i(a) = 1$ for $|a| \leq L_e$. In this case, we have

$$H(k_u, \omega) = \frac{1}{\sqrt{k^2 - k_u^2}} \, 2L_e \frac{\sin L_e k_u}{L_e k_u}.$$

- *The support band for $H(k_u, \omega)$ in the k_u domain is approximately equal to the first side-lobe (main-lobe) of the sinc function, that is, $\frac{\pi}{L_e}$. Clearly, this bandwidth increases as L_e decreases. When $L_e = 0$, that is, for an ideal point source, the spectrum of the sinc function is flat. This radiation pattern is referred to as* **omni-directional**, *that is, the plane waves on the right side of (3.7) that make up the radiation pattern have a common amplitude (equal energy) and phase (synchronized) in the polar domain; this is shown next.*

Polar Representation: Making a variable transformation from k_u to φ, where

$$k_u = k \sin \varphi,$$

in the integral of (3.7), one obtains the plane wave decomposition in the *polar* domain

$$
\begin{aligned}
h(x, y, \omega) &= \int_{-\pi/2}^{\pi/2} H_p(\varphi, \omega) \, \exp[-jk \cos \varphi x - jk \sin \varphi y] \, d\varphi \\
&= \int_{-\pi/2}^{\pi/2} H_p(\varphi, \omega) \, \exp[-jkr \cos(\varphi - \theta)] \, d\varphi,
\end{aligned}
\tag{3.8}
$$

where

$$
\begin{aligned}
H_p(\varphi, \omega) &\equiv k \cos \varphi \, H(k_u, \omega) \\
&= \sqrt{k^2 - k_u^2} \, H(k_u, \omega),
\end{aligned}
$$

and

$$r \equiv \sqrt{x^2 + y^2}$$

$$\theta \equiv \arctan(\frac{y}{x}).$$

We define

$$g(\theta, \omega) \equiv \exp(j2kr \cos \theta).$$

Thus, we can rewrite (3.8) as follows:

$$h(x, y, \omega) = \int_{-\pi/2}^{\pi/2} H_p(\varphi, \omega) \; g(\theta - \varphi, \omega)d\varphi$$

$$= H_p(\theta, \omega) \; * \; g(\theta, \omega),$$

where $*$ denotes convolution in the θ domain.

Let $\tilde{H}_p(\xi, \omega)$ be the Fourier transform of $H_p(\theta, \omega)$; thus, ξ represents the Fourier domain for θ. Using the filtering properties of PM signals that was discussed in Chapter 1, one can show that $\tilde{H}_p$ has a finite support in the ξ domain that is

$$\xi \in [-kL_e, kL_e].$$

For an omni-directional radiation pattern (i.e., $L_e = 0$), we have

$$H_p(\theta, \omega) = 1, \quad \text{and} \quad \tilde{H}_p(\xi, \omega) = \delta(\xi).$$

- *With $\theta = [-\pi, \pi]$, ξ takes on only integer values, and $\tilde{H}_p$ represents the Fourier coefficients for the periodic signal H_p.*

Provided that $L_e \ll \sqrt{x^2 + y^2}$, (3.7) can be rewritten as follows:

$$h(x, y, \omega) \approx a(x, y) \; \exp(-jk\sqrt{x^2 + y^2}), \qquad (3.9)$$

where $a(x, y)$ is a slowly fluctuating amplitude function.

The models in (3.7)-(3.9) will be exploited in the spatial Doppler-based method discussed later in this chapter. Before doing that, we examine some of the classical approximation-based inverse methods used in array imaging problems of diagnostic medicine and radar.

3.3 DYNAMIC FOCUSING

The objective in dynamic imaging is to image a target region via focusing the transmit and receive radiation patterns of an array at each single point of the imaging area. A method that achieves radial and angular focusing via utilizing an approximation is described in this section.

Consider the general phased array imaging system shown in Figure 3.1. A linear array is located on the line $x = 0$ in the spatial (x, y) domain; the array is centered at the origin and its length is equal to $2L$. In the transmit mode, the array's elements are identified by the spatial coordinates $(0, u)$, $u \in [-L, L]$. In the receive mode, the array's elements are identified by the spatial coordinates $(0, v)$, $v \in [-L, L]$. Both u and v take on discrete evenly spaced values in the interval $[-L, L]$.

We denote the polar coordinates for (x, y) by (r, θ); that is,

$$r \equiv \sqrt{x^2 + y^2}$$

$$\theta \equiv \arctan(\frac{y}{x}).$$

Also, we denote the time required for the pulsed signal to travel from the element at $(0, u)$ to the point (x, y) in the spatial domain by

$$T(x, y - u) \equiv \frac{\sqrt{x^2 + (y - u)^2}}{c}. \tag{3.10}$$

We use the Taylor series expansion around r on the right side of (3.10) and retain only the first two terms; that is,

$$T(x, y - u) = \frac{r}{c} \left[1 + \frac{-2yu + u^2}{2r^2} + \dots \right]$$

$$\approx \frac{r}{c} - \frac{y}{r} \frac{u}{c} + \frac{u^2}{2rc} \tag{3.11}$$

$$= \frac{r}{c} - \frac{u \sin \theta}{c} + \frac{u^2}{2rc}.$$

The condition for the validity of the approximation in (3.11) was given in Section 1.5.

The time function

$$\tau(u,r,\theta) \equiv \frac{u\sin\theta}{c} - \frac{u^2}{2rc} \tag{3.12}$$

is the time difference between the propagation from the center element at $(0,0)$ to (x,y) and the propagation from the element at $(0,u)$ to (x,y); that is,

$$\tau(u,r,\theta) \approx T(x,y) - T(x,y-u)$$
$$= \frac{r}{c} - T(x,y-u),$$

or

$$\tau(u,r,\theta) + T(x,y-u) \approx \frac{r}{c}.$$

Thus, the transmitted signals from all the elements at $u \in [-L,L]$ reach (x,y) at the same time if the time delay in (3.12) is associated with their time of propagation. In other words, the element at $(0,u)$ should transmit the following signal:

$$p\,[\,t\,-\,\tau(u,r,\theta)\,].$$

The signal that reaches (x,y) due to this transmission is (the amplitude function $\frac{1}{r}$ that is due to dispersion is suppressed in Sections 3.3-3.5)

$$p\,\left[\,t-\tau(u,r,\theta)-T(x,y-u)\,\right] \approx p(t-\frac{r}{c}),$$

which is invariant of u.

The total signal experienced at (x,y) is the sum of all the transmitted signals over the available discrete u values; that is,

$$\tilde{s}_{xy}(r,\theta,t) \equiv \int_{-L}^{L} p\,\left[\,t-\tau(u,r,\theta)-T(x,y-u)\,\right]\,du$$
$$\approx \int_{-L}^{L} p(t-\frac{r}{c})\,du$$
$$= 2L\,p(t-\frac{r}{c}).$$

We can observe from the above equation that all the transmitted pulses are added constructively (coherently) at (x, y).

- *In the above formulation, we used continuous u instead of discrete u and suppressed amplitude functions. The consequences of having a finite number of discrete elements will be discussed.*

The same time delay procedure is used in the receive mode to retrieve the echoed signal due to the reflector at (x, y). In this case, the received signal becomes

$$s_{xy}(r, \theta, t) \equiv \int_{-L}^{L} \tilde{s}_{xy}\left[r, \theta, t - \tau(v, r, \theta) - T(x, y - v)\right] dv \tag{3.13}$$
$$\approx 4L^2 \; p(t - \frac{2r}{c}),$$

The integral over v represents the electronic addition of the output of all the receivers; $\tau(v, r, \theta) + T(x, y - v) \approx \frac{r}{c}$ was used in deriving (3.13). The signal in (3.13) has the following temporal Fourier transform:

$$S_{xy}(r, \theta, \omega) \approx 4L^2 \; P(\omega) \; \exp(-j2kr). \tag{3.13a}$$

To summarize the transmit mode and receive mode focusing that led to (3.13), we write

$$s_{xy}(r, \theta, t) = \int_u \int_v du \; dv$$
$$\times p\left[t - \tau(u, r, \theta) - T(x, y - u) - \tau(v, r, \theta) - T(x, y - v)\right]$$
$$\approx 4L^2 \; p(t - \frac{2r}{c}).$$

- *One can observe from (3.12) that, based on the approximation in (3.11), the **angular steering** and **range focusing**, respectively, can be achieved via generating **linear** and **quadratic phase functions** across the phased array's aperture [3],[8]. By rapidly varying this phase distribution via electronic means, the steered-focused beam can be swept through the medium under study, thus producing the medium's reflectivity index along a set of radial lines.*

One should not anticipate that the contribution of the echoed signals from the spatial points in the target region that are not at the focal point, that is, (x, y), is zero. In fact, the echoed signal from an arbitrary point reflector from the target region, for example, (X, Y) when the beam is focused at (x, y) with polar coordinates (r, θ), is

$$
s_{XY}(r, \theta, t) = \int_u \int_v du\ dv
$$
$$
\times p\big[t - \tau(u, r, \theta) - T(X, Y - u) - \tau(v, r, \theta) - T(X, Y - v)\big]
$$

The *total* echoed signal from the target region when the beam is focused at polar coordinates (r, θ) is

$$
s(r, \theta, t) \equiv \int_X \int_Y f(X, Y)\ s_{XY}(r, \theta, t)\ dX dY,
$$

where $f(X, Y)$ is the *reflectivity function* of the target area. The dynamic focusing algorithm performs well provided that the total echoed signal $s(r, \theta, t)$ is dominated by the echoed signal from the focal point (x, y); that is,

$$
s(r, \theta, t) \approx \text{constant } f(x, y)\ s_{xy}(r, \theta, t).
$$

- *The image that is anticipated to be produced via dynamic focusing is the target's reflectivity function. This two-dimensional signal represents the spatial distribution of certain properties, for example, density or index of refraction, of the target under study.*

Figure 3.2 shows the data acquisition system for dynamic focusing. In this system, the output of the receiver's electronic adder is fed to an energy detector, that is, an incoherent processor. The measured datum for a given focusing point (r, θ) is

$$
\int_t |s(r, \theta, t)|^2\ dt \approx \int_t \text{constant } |f(x, y)\ s_{xy}(r, \theta, t)|^2\ dt
$$
$$
= \text{constant } |f(x, y)|^2.
$$

(In certain phased array imaging systems, the time integral is performed over $|s(r, \theta, t)|$.)

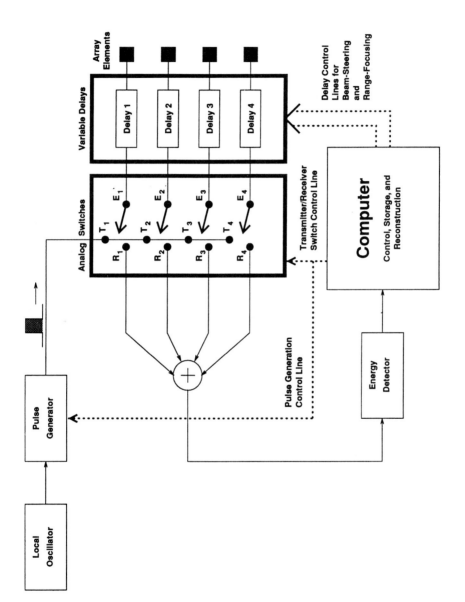

Figure 3.2 Data acquisition system for dynamic focusing.

Thus, this imaging system does not perform coherent processing on the incoming echoed signals. In this case, the phase function $\exp(-j2kr)$ that carries radial information is lost due to the incoherent processing. Recall that in the one-dimensional echo imaging example we examined in Chapter 1, this phase function was the information used for determining the targets' range values.

- *The dynamic focusing system does not perform the temporal Fourier transform shown in (3.13a); that transform is presented for our analytical discussion.*

An incoherent processor has the advantages of being less costly and possessing simpler electronic circuitry than a coherent processor. The main drawback of an incoherent processor will become evident in the discussion of radial beamwidth.

Angular Beamwidth

Equation (3.13) indicates that the transmitted signals are coherently (constructively) added at (r, θ). However, for the success of this procedure, we also require that the illuminated signal's energy at other spatial points be very small. For instance, the output of the receiver's electronic adder due to the signal echoed from a unit reflector at the polar coordinates (r, ψ) $(\psi \neq \theta)$ is

$$s_{xy}(r, \theta, t) \equiv \int_u \int_v du \, dv$$
$$\times p\big[t - \tau(u, r, \theta) - T(x, y - u) - \tau(v, r, \theta) - T(x, y - v)\big]$$
$$\approx \int_u \int_v p\Big[t - \frac{2r}{c} - \frac{(\sin\theta - \sin\psi)\, u}{c} - \frac{(\sin\theta - \sin\psi)\, v}{c}\Big] du\, dv$$

The temporal Fourier transform of this signal is

$$S_{xy}(r, \theta, \omega) \approx P(\omega)\, \exp(-j2kr) \int_{-L}^{L} \exp\big[-jk(\sin\theta - \sin\psi)\, u\big]\, du$$
$$\times \int_{-L}^{L} \exp\big[-jk(\sin\theta - \sin\psi)\, v\big]\, dv.$$

The two *separable* integrals over the transmit domain, u, and the receive domain, v, both represent the Fourier transform of a rectangular pulse extended in $[-L, L]$ (i.e., the aperture function) at the spatial frequency $k(\sin\theta - \sin\psi)$. Thus, we can write

$$S_{xy}(r, \theta, \omega) = P(\omega) \, \exp(-j2kr) \, 4L^2 \, \text{sinc}^2[kL(\sin\theta - \sin\psi)] \quad (3.13b)$$

that should contain much smaller energy than the signal in (3.13a); the energy ratio between these two signals is the sinc-squared function.

Thus, *the ability to resolve targets in the angular domain depends on the extent of the side lobes of the sinc-squared pattern in (3.13b), that is,* $\text{sinc}^2[kL(\sin\theta - \sin\psi)]$. If we assume that the main lobe of the sinc pattern contains most of it energy, then the two targets at (r, θ) and (r, ψ) are resolvable from each other if

$$k|\sin\theta - \sin\psi| \; > \; \frac{2\pi}{2L},$$

(some texts associate a number between one to two with right side of this constraint), or

$$|\sin\theta - \sin\psi| \; > \; \frac{\lambda}{2L},$$

where $\lambda \equiv \frac{2\pi}{k}$ is the wavelength. We call this the resolution or beamwidth in the angular domain. When the beam angle θ is small (e.g., less than 30 degrees) and

$$\Delta_\theta \equiv |\theta - \psi| \ll 1,$$

then the angular beamwidth can be rewritten as follows:

$$\Delta_\theta \; > \; \frac{\lambda}{2L}.$$

For a general value of steer angle θ and $|\theta - \psi| \ll \theta$, the angular beamwidth becomes

$$\Delta_\theta \; > \; \frac{\lambda}{2L \cos\theta}.$$

Thus, the angular resolution deteriorates when $|\theta|$ increases.

Radial Beamwidth

To examine the extent of the focused beam in the radial domain, we consider the output of the receiver's electronic adder due to the signal echoed from a unit reflector at the polar coordinates (ρ, θ) close to the focal point $(\rho \neq r; \Delta_r \equiv r - \rho; |\Delta_r| \ll r)$; that is

$$
\begin{aligned}
s_{xy}(r, \theta, t) &\equiv \int_u \int_v du \; dv \\
&\quad \times p\big[t - \tau(u, r, \theta) - T(x, y - u) - \tau(v, r, \theta) - T(x, y - v)\big] \\
&\approx \int_u \int_v p\Big[t - \frac{2\rho}{c} - (\frac{1}{\rho} - \frac{1}{r})\frac{u^2}{2c} - (\frac{1}{\rho} - \frac{1}{r})\frac{v^2}{2c} \Big] du \; dv \\
&\approx \int_u \int_v p\Big[t - \frac{2\rho}{c} - \frac{\Delta_r u^2}{2cr^2} - \frac{\Delta_r v^2}{2cr^2} \Big] du \; dv.
\end{aligned}
$$

The temporal Fourier transform of this signal is

$$
\begin{aligned}
S_{xy}(r, \theta, \omega) &\approx P(\omega) \; \exp(-j2k\rho) \int_{-L}^{L} \exp\Big[-j\frac{k\Delta_r u^2}{2r^2}\Big] du \\
&\qquad \times \int_{-L}^{L} \exp\Big[-j\frac{k\Delta_r v^2}{2r^2}\Big] dv.
\end{aligned}
$$

The two separable integrals over the transmit domain, u, and the receive domain, v, both represent integrals of chirp signals over the finite region $[-L, L]$. The value of this form of integral goes to zero in an oscillatory fashion as L approaches infinity. It is difficult to obtain a closed-form solution for this integral when L is finite. The use of Cornu spirals has been suggested for this analysis [8].

For the problem of finding the focused beam's radial dispersion, we are interested in the minimum value of Δ_r, call it radial beamwidth, that makes the chirp signal integral yield a value much smaller than $2L$ (i.e., the value of the integral when $\rho = r$). A crude yet simple way to satisfy this constraint is to have the chirp signal possess at least its first cycle in $[-L, L]$; thus, the integration over the first cycle and part of the next cycle that are extended in $[-L, L]$ yields a relatively small number. This condition results in the following radial beamwidth:

$$\Delta_r \approx \frac{2r^2 \lambda}{L^2}.$$

- *We showed in Chapter 1 that the resolution in the **coherent** one-dimensional echo imaging system was*

$$\frac{\pi c}{\omega_0},$$

  where $[-\omega_0, \omega_0]$ is the baseband bandwidth of the transmitted signal. This resolution could be attained in dynamic focusing via the coherent processing of the output of the receiver's electronic adder instead of introducing the quadratic phase function across the phased array's aperture. The use of a coherent processor would increase the complexity and the cost of the imaging system.

Resolution

Resolution is a measure of the ability of the user to resolve targets in the spatial domain (x, y) from a reconstructed image. For dynamic focusing, the resolution in the polar domain (r, θ) is governed by $(\Delta_r, \Delta_\theta)$.

We denote the resolution in the range and cross-range domains by Δ_x and Δ_y, respectively. Most dynamic imaging systems operate within a small interval in the angular domain; this is due to the rapid breakdown of the approximation in (3.11) for large θ values. In this case, we can write

$$x = r \, \cos \theta \approx r$$

$$y = r \, \sin \theta \approx r \, \theta.$$

Thus, the resolution in the (x, y) domain is

$$\Delta_x \approx \Delta_r = \frac{2r^2 \lambda}{L^2}$$

$$\Delta_y \approx r \, \Delta_\theta = \frac{r \lambda}{2L}.$$

- *The **coherent spatial Doppler-based** phased array imaging that is discussed in Section 3.6 yields the same cross-range resolution shown in the above, that is, $\frac{r\lambda}{2L}$, and the coherent range resolution, i.e, $\frac{\pi c}{\omega_0}$. However, the spatial Doppler-based method is not constrained and affected by the **system model approximation errors** introduced by the approximation in (3.11).*

In radar problems, the cross-range resolution is commonly rewritten as

$$\Delta_y \approx \frac{r\lambda}{D},$$

where $D \equiv 2L$ is the diameter of the radar antenna. Δ_y is referred to as the *Rayleigh resolution*.

- *In remote sensing problems of radar r is on the order of kilometers and D is on the order of meters. Thus, one should anticipate a poor cross-range resolution in radar imaging using physical arrays/antennas. In Chapter 4, we will examine an array imaging method that synthesizes a large aperture antenna via varying the relative coordinates of the radar and target.*

Constraint for Validity

The approximation in (3.11) would not result in large phase errors in (3.13) or (3.13a) provided that

$$k\frac{u^2 - 2uy}{r} \ll 1.$$

Using the fact that the maximum value that $|u|$ attains is L and $y = r\sin\theta$, the above constraint becomes

$$k(\frac{L^2}{r} + 2L\sin\theta) \ll 1.$$

From this constraint, one can observe that the approximation-based range-focused beam-steered echo imaging (dynamic focusing) method fails as:

i. *The range of the imaging point is decreased. This prevents imaging areas close to the array.*

ii. *The scan angle is increased. This prohibits imaging wide sectors within the object under study.*

iii. *The array's aperture size is increased to improve the range/cross-range resolution.*

iv. *The wavelength is decreased to improve the range/cross-range resolution.*

Example: To demonstrate the inaccuracies associated with dynamic focusing, we examine the range-focused beam-steered radiation patterns for a phased array echo imaging system. In this imaging problem, the length of the phased array is 32 mm; that is, $[-L, L] = [-16, 16]$ mm. The sample spacing in the aperture domain is equal to .5 mm; that is, there are 64 elements on the array. The target area is 128 mm X 128 mm. The distance of the center of the array from the center of the target area is 90 mm. The wavenumber of the center frequency of the transmitted signal is 2π radians/mm. The range of wavenumbers used is $[2\pi.823, 2\pi1.177]$ radians/mm. The (coherent) resolution at the center of the reconstructed image, that is, $(x, y) = (90, 0)$ mm, is approximately 1.5 mm in both x and y domains. The array is on the left side of the images shown.

Figure 3.3a shows the radiation pattern for a beam steered at the angle zero without the quadratic phase function for range-focusing (this is also known as range-focused at infinity). Figure 3.3b is the radiation pattern for a beam steered at the angle zero that is range-focused (range 90 mm) at the center of the object area, that is, $(x, y) = (90, 0)$ mm. Figure 3.3c depicts the radiation pattern for a beam steered at angle 38.7° and range-focused at infinity. Figure 3.3d is the beam-steered (angle 38.7°) and range-focused (range 64 mm) radiation pattern at the point with coordinates $(x, y) = (50, 40)$ mm in the spatial domain. As stated earlier, Figures 3.3a and 3.3c (range infinity) correspond to removing quadratic phase terms used for range focusing.

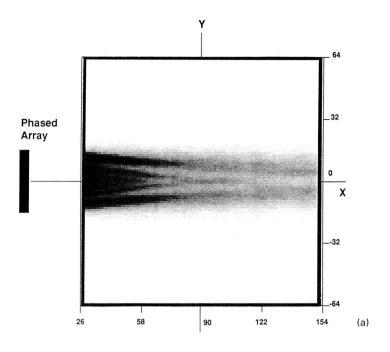

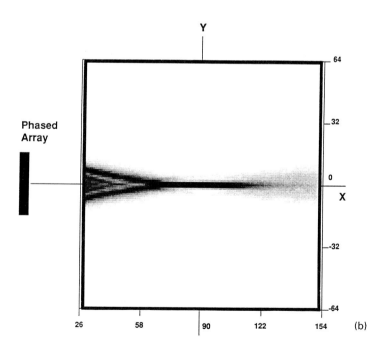

Figure 3.3 Radiation patterns of a phased array. (a) Beam
steered at the angle zero (range infinity). (b)
Beam focused at $(x, y) = (90, 0)$ mm.

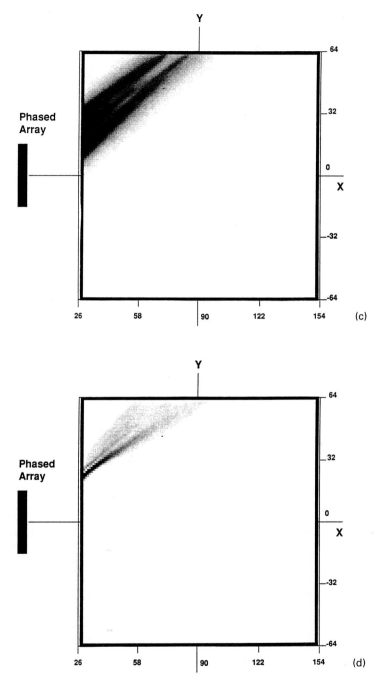

Figure 3.3 (*continued*) (c) Beam steered at the angle 38.7°
(range infinity). (d) Beam focused at $(x, y) =$
$(50, 40)$ mm.

208

- *The inversion that will be introduced in Section 3.6 for phased array scan data does not utilize an approximation in representing the array's radiation patterns. The reconstructed images obtained via this inversion do not exhibit degradations at the edges of wide-angle sectors of the scan, a problem that is associated with the approximation-based inversion of dynamic focusing. Furthermore, the inversion procedure does not require the quadratic phase function to focus in the range domain.*

Approximation-Free Focusing

One may circumvent the approximation associated with (3.11) using the following delay function:

$$\tau(u, r, \theta) = T(x, y) - T(x, y - u).$$

This delay function ensures that the transmitted pulses from the elements of the array arrive at (x, y) at exactly the same time and, thus, are added coherently (constructively). However, there are still no guarantees that the transmitted signals at the other (nonfocused) spatial points are combined such that the total signal experienced at those points is negligible (as compared with the signal at the focal point). For instance, in the examples cited in the previous section, the result of approximation-free focusing is almost identical to the angular-range focusing for broadside targets. The approximation-free focusing shows only a slight improvement for off-broadside targets.

3.4 GENERALIZED BEAMFORMING

The focusing approach discussed in the previous section utilized a sum of the delayed versions of an array in the transmit and receive modes to manipulate the linear signal subspace spanned by the array's radiation patterns. A more generalized method to tap into the array's signal subspace is based on a *weighted* sum of the delayed version of the array's radiation patterns. This is known as array beamforming. Next, we discuss the governing equations for the transmit mode of a beamformer; the receive mode beamformer can be constructed via replacing u with v in the following. (As we mentioned earlier, the integrals over the u and v, that is, the transmit and receive domains, are separable and, thus, the analysis of one does not depend on the other.)

For a generalized beamformer, the total transmitted signal at (x, y) becomes

$$\tilde{s}_{xy}(r, \theta, t) \equiv \int_u w(u, r, \theta) \; p[t - \tau(u, r, \theta) - T(x, y - u)] \; du, \qquad (3.14)$$

where $w(u, r, \theta)$ is the **weight** function; (r, θ) are the polar coordinates of (x, y). *Note that now the signal illuminated by the transmitter at $(0, u)$ possesses a user-prescribed amplitude, i.e, $w(u, r, \theta)$, and time (phase) delay, that is, $\tau(u, r, \theta)$.*

The classical array beamforming problem is how to select $w(u, r, \theta)$ to improve the performance of dynamic focusing at (x, y) in the spatial domain. For this purpose, consider the temporal Fourier transform of both sides of (3.14), that is,

$$\tilde{S}_{xy}(r, \theta, \omega) = P(\omega) \int_u w(u, r, \theta) \; \exp\left[-j\omega\left[\tau(u, r, \theta) + T(x, y - u)\right]\right] \; du.$$
$$(3.15)$$

Using (3.11) and (3.12) in (3.15) yields

$$\tilde{S}_{xy}(r, \theta, \omega) \approx P(\omega) \; \exp(-jkr) \int_u w(u, r, \theta) \; du \qquad (3.16)$$
$$= P(\omega) \; \exp(-jkr) \; W(0, r, \theta),$$

where $W(k_u, r, \theta)$ is the spatial Fourier transform of $w(u, r, \theta)$ with respect to u. *Note that due to the finite aperture of the array, $w(u, r, \theta) = 0$ for $|u| > L$.*

Equation (3.16) indicates that the transmitted signals are coherently (constructively) added at (r, θ). However, for the success of this procedure, we also require that the illuminated signal's energy at other spatial points be very small. For instance, at the polar coordinates (r, ψ) $(\psi \neq \theta)$ the transmitted signal is

$$\tilde{S}_{xy}(r, \theta, \omega) \approx P(\omega) \exp(-jkr) \int_u w(u, r, \theta) \exp\left[-jk(\sin\theta - \sin\psi)u\right] du$$
$$= P(\omega) \; \exp(-jkr) \; W\left[k(\sin\theta - \sin\psi), r, \theta\right].$$

When the receive mode radiation pattern is incorporated, the overall radiation pattern becomes

$$S_{xy}(r, \theta, \omega) \approx P(\omega) \, \exp(-j2kr) \, W^2 \big[k(\sin\theta - \sin\psi), r, \theta \big]. \qquad (3.17)$$

- *The case of $w(u, r, \theta) = 1$ for $|u| \leq L$, and zero otherwise, corresponds to the scenario we discussed in the previous section for dynamic focusing where no weighting function was introduced across the aperture. In this case, $W(k_u, r, \theta)$ is a sinc function and (3.17) becomes identical to (3.13b).*

Thus, as long as the side lobes of $W(k_u, r, \theta)$ are small in the k_u domain, the focusing algorithm performs well. For this criterion, the sampled $w(u, r, \theta)$ in the aperture domain should be selected accordingly.

- *This problem is equivalent to and, thus, can be framed as the design of **optimal digital filters**. This issue has been examined extensively [1].*

- *Introducing a weight (window) function across the aperture **does not** improve angular beamwidth that is still given by*

$$\Delta_\theta \; > \; \frac{\lambda}{2L\cos\theta}.$$

*The weight function simply dampens the **side lobes** of $W(k_u, r, \theta)$.*

3.5 AIR TRAFFIC CONTROL/SURVEILLANCE RADAR

Next, we examine a radar imaging system utilized for civilian air traffic control and military air surveillance [5]. The objective in this problem is to identify moving targets within a region in the air close to the user (radar station), and estimate the moving targets' locations and speeds. For this purpose the target is illuminated with a microwave source and resultant echoed waves are measured for the imaging phase. *Sonar* refers to a similar system in water that utilizes acoustic waves to irradiate the target. Similar principles have also been utilized in medical imaging to determine the blood flow speed. In the following, we restrict our discussion to the analysis of two-dimensional imaging scenarios; the generalization of this concept to the three-dimensional geometries is straightforward.

Electronically Scanning Array

One of the imaging modalities for moving target location and speed estimation is based on utilization of physical arrays. This system, which requires an elaborate electronic control in both transmit and receive modes, is mainly used in military surveillance applications. For this purpose, a phased (or a generalized beamformer) array can be used to illuminate and focus at a *finite* number of angles, for example, $\theta = \theta_1, \theta_2, \theta_3, \ldots$, in the desired air region in a repetitive manner and record the resultant echoed signals (see Figure 3.4). Based on the approximation in (3.11), the angular focusing is achieved via associating the following delay with the element at $(0, u)$:

$$\tau(u, \theta) \equiv \frac{u \sin \theta}{c}.$$

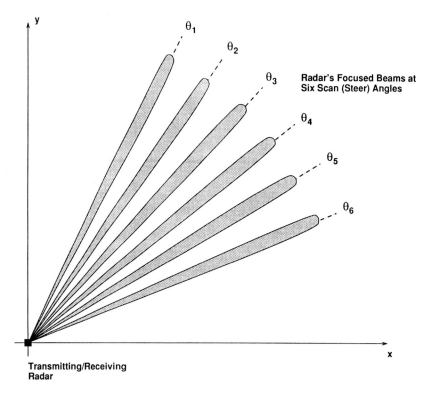

Figure 3.4 Focused beams for an air traffic control/surveillance radar.

- *Commercial radar systems do not utilize the incoherent range focusing used in dynamic focusing. In long-range problems of radar imaging, the quadratic phasing for range focusing is ineffective due to the rapid failure of the approximation that is associated with its principle. Radar systems perform a coherent processing on the temporal echoed data for range estimation that is similar to the coherent processing shown in the one-dimensional echo imaging example in Chapter 1.*

The focusing in the angular domain is referred to as *electronic* scanning. This is due to the fact that angular sectors within the air region are focused by electronically varying the phase and weight of the array elements. Provided that the scanning repetition rate is high, this system provides almost *real time* data about the target region that is changing with time at the finite angularly focused regions in the spatial domain.

To demonstrate the information contents of the echoed signal and processing techniques used to retrieve them, we consider the beam focused at a fixed angle, for example, θ. Suppose a target with polar coordinates (r, θ) falls within the focused beam. This target is moving with speed v in the direction that makes angle ϕ with respect to the line that connects the target to the radar (see Figure 3.5a); this line is called the radar's *broadside* beam. In this case, the target's speed along the radar's broadside beam is $v \cos \phi$.

Recall our discussion in Chapter 1 regarding the temporal Doppler phenomenon caused due to moving targets. For the temporal Doppler phenomenon in the two-dimensional spatial domain, we approximated the time-dependent target's range by the following:

$$r - v \cos \phi \, t.$$

Using this approximation and an analysis similar to the one performed in Chapter 1, we can show that the echoed signal for the imaging system shown in Figure 3.5a is a time-delayed and temporal Doppler-shifted version of the transmitted signal; that is,

$$s_{xy}(\theta, t) \approx f_p(r, \theta) \, p\left[t - \frac{2(r - v \cos \phi \, t)}{c}\right]$$

$$\approx f_p(r, \theta) \, a(t - \frac{2r}{c}) \, \exp(-j\omega_c \frac{2r}{c}) \, \exp[j(\omega_c + \omega_D)t], \tag{3.18}$$

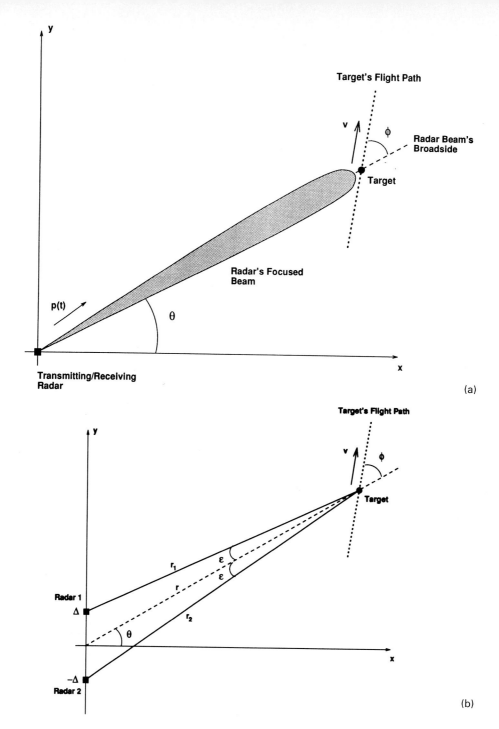

Figure 3.5 Imaging system geometry for air traffic control and surveillance radar. (a) Monostatic radar. (b) Stereo (bistatic) radars.

where

$$f_p(r, \theta) \equiv f(x, y)$$

is the target region's reflectivity function in the polar domain, and

$$\omega_D \equiv \frac{2v \cos \phi}{c} \omega_c \qquad (3.19)$$

is the temporal Doppler shift caused by the target's motion.

Based on the system model in (3.8)-(3.9), for a given scan angle θ, the inverse problem is now translated into a one-dimensional range-speed imaging system. Using the inversion described in Chapter 1 for the system model in (3.18), one can estimate the target's range, r, and the target's speed along the radar beam's broadside, $v \cos \phi$.

The processing used to identify Doppler shifts in the echoed signal and, consequently, to detect and/or imaging moving targets, is called *Moving Target Indication* (MTI) or *Moving Target Doppler* (MTD) [5]. A similar processing, called *Airborne Moving Target Indication* (AMTI), utilizes a radar mounted on an aircraft for data collection. One of the first tasks of the MTI processor is to filter out the components of the echoed signal that are due to stationary targets, for example, clouds, and are not Doppler shifted. This operation is called *clutter* rejection or filtering.

As we showed in Chapter 1, the inversion of the system model in (3.18) suffers from the time/temporal frequency ambiguity problem. Moreover, the rapid scanning of the phased array limits the period of time that the phased array can maintain its focused beam in a given angular direction. Due to this fact, FM-CW signaling, which requires a relatively long illumination time (i.e., t_3), may not be a viable option in this range-speed imaging problem.

We will reformulate phased array spatial-velocity imaging in Section 3.10. We will also formulate air traffic control and surveillance radar imaging problems in the framework of what we call blind-velocity inverse synthetic aperture radar imaging in Chapter 5. The problem encountered in AMTI will also be framed as blind-velocity synthetic aperture radar imaging in Chapter 5.

Stereo and Bistatic Radar

The radar imaging system shown in Figure 3.5a provides the target's range r and the target's speed along the radar's broadside beam $v \cos \phi$. To obtain the target's *velocity*, one may use the stereo radar system shown in Figure 3.5b. This system is analogous to a radar system known as *monopulse* radar [5]. In a stereo radar system, two radars that are located at $(0, \Delta)$ and $(0, -\Delta)$, where $\Delta \ll r$ and r is the target's range, are used to illuminate the target scene and/or record the resultant echoed signals.

For the time being, suppose the two radars simultaneously illuminate the target scene, and each radar receives only the echoed signals due to its own transmission (i.e., there are no bistatic measurements). To prevent measurements of bistatic echoed signals, Radar 1 and Radar 2 may transmit, respectively, pulsed signals $p_1(t)$ and $p_2(t)$ that are orthogonal to each other; that is,

$$\int_t p_1(t) \, p_2^*(t) \, dt = 0.$$

Consequently, the matched filter for each radar system rejects (filters out) the echoed signals that are due to transmission by the other radar.

The received signals by Radar 1 and Radar 2, respectively, are

$$s_{1xy}(\theta, t) \approx f_p(r, \theta) \, p_1 \left[t - \frac{2(r_1 - v_1 t)}{c} \right]$$

$$s_{2xy}(\theta, t) \approx f_p(r, \theta) \, p_2 \left[t - \frac{2(r_2 - v_2 t)}{c} \right],$$

where the range values are

$$r_1 \equiv \sqrt{r^2 + \Delta^2 - 2r\Delta \sin \theta}$$

$$r_2 \equiv \sqrt{r^2 + \Delta^2 + 2r\Delta \sin \theta},$$

and the speed values are

$$v_1 \equiv v \cos(\phi + \epsilon)$$

$$v_2 \equiv v \cos(\phi - \epsilon),$$

with

$$\epsilon \approx \frac{\Delta \cos \theta}{R_1}.$$

In this case, the speeds (v_1, v_2) can be estimated by the two radar systems from the measured Doppler shifts in s_{1xy} and s_{2xy}. Then, from the knowledge of (v_1, v_2) one can estimate (v, ϕ). The range value r is estimated from the measurements of r_1 and r_2 via the two measured echoed signals.

There are also stereo radar systems that utilize only one radar, for example, Radar 1, for transmission and both radars for reception of resultant echoed signals. Thus, the measurements made by Radar 1 are monostatic, that is, s_{1xy} that was shown earlier, while Radar 2 makes bistatic measurements. For this case, the signal recorded by Radar 2 is (*bistatic radar* equation)

$$s_{12xy}(\theta, t) \approx f_p(r, \theta) \; p_1 \left[t - \frac{r_1 + r_2 - (v_1 + v_2) \, t}{c} \right].$$

The speeds obtained from the Doppler shifts of the data measured by Radar 1 and Radar 2, respectively, are

$$v_1 = v \cos(\phi + \epsilon)$$

$$v_{12} \equiv \frac{v_1 + v_2}{2} \approx v \cos \phi.$$

These speeds can then be used to solve for (v, ϕ).

Mechanically Rotating Antenna

Due to cost constraints, civilian air traffic control radar systems are not phased arrays. The radar antennas used in these applications have a fixed radiation pattern that is angularly focused at broadside. To scan the desired air region, these antennas are continuously rotated along a fixed axis, and perform transmission/reception to produce the radiation patterns shown in Figure 3.4 (see also Figure 3.12). The speed of rotation is much smaller than the speed of wave propagation (light). In this case, one may assume that the radar practically stops in its rotational motion, illuminates the target area, makes its corresponding reception, and then moves to its next rotational position.

Based on the approximation in (3.11), the system model and inversion for this radar problem are identical to the one shown in (3.18) and its corresponding inversion.

3.6 ELECTRONICALLY SCANNING LINEAR ARRAYS

We next consider a phased array imaging system that illuminates the target area with the array's angularly steered radiation patterns and coherently processes the resultant spatio-temporal echoed signals. The resultant database in this imaging problem is identical to the one acquired by an air surveillance radar (Section 3.5). However, we now remove the assumption that the angularly steered beams are focused; that was a consequence of the approximation in (3.11) that will not be used in the inversion described in this section. The approximation-free inversion for this system is based on the spatial Fourier (Doppler) decomposition for an element's radiation pattern that was presented in Section 3.2.

System Model and Inversion

We consider array imaging in the two-dimensional spatial domain using one-dimensional beam-steering with a linear array. Three-dimensional imaging with two-dimensional beam-steering of a planar array can be formulated in a similar fashion. Consider the imaging system geometry shown in Figure 3.1. Let us first review the imaging system geometry. A linear array is located on the line $x = 0$; the array is centered at the origin and its length is equal to $2L$. In the transmit mode, the array's elements are identified by the spatial coordinates $(0, u)$, $u \in [-L, L]$. In the receive mode, the array's elements are identified by the spatial coordinates $(0, v)$, $v \in [-L, L]$. Both u and v take on discrete evenly spaced values in the interval $[-L, L]$. We begin our formulation by assuming continuous measurements in the (u, v) domain for an infinitely extended linear array. The effects of finite aperture and discrete sampling on the array will be examined later.

To steer the array's beam in the transmit mode at a given direction, for example, angle θ with respect to the broadside, all elements of the array illuminate the test object simultaneously with delayed versions of a known pulse function $p(t)$. The delay associated with an element of the array located at $(0, u)$ is

$$\tau(u, \theta) \equiv \frac{u \sin \theta}{c}, \tag{3.40}$$

where c is the speed of propagation; thus, this element transmits the temporal signal $p[t - \tau(u, \theta)]$. The time required for the pulsed signal to travel from the element at $(0, u)$ to the point (x, y) in the spatial domain was shown in (3.28) to be

$$T(x, y - u) = \frac{\sqrt{x^2 + (y - u)^2}}{c}.$$

Thus, the transmitted signal at (x, y) due to illumination of the element at $(0, u)$ is $p[t - \tau(u, \theta) - T(x, y - u)]$. Then, the total transmitted signal at (x, y) is

$$\int_u a(x, y - u)\, p[t - \tau(u, \theta) - T(x, y - u)]\, du, \tag{3.21}$$

where $a(x, y - u)$ is the spatial amplitude associated with the radiation pattern of an element (see Section 3.2).

In the receive mode, it takes $T(x, y - v)$ units of time for the echoed signals from (x, y) to reach a receiving element at $(0, v)$. Moreover, the same time delays are also used in the receive mode to reinforce the echoed signals that are traveling at angle θ with respect to the broadside. The total echoed signal recorded due to a unit reflector at (x, y) is the sum (integral) of the echoed signals detected at all the receiving elements; that is,

$$s_{xy}(\theta, t) \equiv \int_u \int_v a(x, y - u)\, a(x, y - v)$$
$$\times p\big[t - \tau(u, \theta) - T(x, y - u) - \tau(v, \theta) - T(x, y - v)\big]\, dv\, du. \tag{3.22}$$

Taking the Fourier transform of both sides of (3.22) with respect to time yields

$$
S_{xy}(\theta, \omega) = \int_u \int_v a(x, y - u) \, a(x, y - v) \, P(\omega)
$$

$$
\times \exp\left[-j\omega[\tau(u, \theta) + T(x, y - u) + \tau(v, \theta) + T(x, y - v)]\right] dv du
$$

$$
= P(\omega) \int_u \int_v h(x, y - u, \omega) \, h(x, y - v, \omega)
$$

$$
\times \exp(-jk\sin\theta u) \, \exp(-jk\sin\theta v) \, dv \, du,
$$

$$(3.23)$$

where ω denotes the radian temporal frequency domain, $k \equiv \frac{\omega}{c}$ is the wavenumber, $P(\omega)$ is the temporal Fourier transform of $p(t)$, and

$$
h(x, y - u, \omega) \equiv a(x, y - u) \, \exp[-jk\sqrt{x^2 + (y - u)^2}]. \qquad (3.24)
$$

In Section 3.2, we mentioned that $h(x, y - u, \omega)$ is called an element's radiation pattern at frequency ω. Moreover, we have from (3.7) the following spatial Fourier decomposition:

$$
h(x, y - u, \omega) = \int_{-k}^{k} H(k_u, \omega) \, \exp[-j\sqrt{k^2 - k_u^2} \, x - jk_u(y - u)] \, dk_u.
$$

$$(3.25a)$$

We may also write

$$
h(x, y - v, \omega) = \int_{-k}^{k} H(k_v, \omega) \, \exp[-j\sqrt{k^2 - k_v^2} \, x - jk_v(y - v)] \, dk_v.
$$

$$(3.25b)$$

Substituting (3.25a),(3.25b) in (3.23), and after some rearrangements, one obtains the following:

$$
S_{xy}(\theta, \omega) = P(\omega) \int_{-k}^{k} \int_{-k}^{k} dk_u \, dk_v \, H(k_u, \omega) \, H(k_v, \omega)
$$

$$
\times \exp[-j(\sqrt{k^2 - k_u^2} + \sqrt{k^2 - k_v^2})x - j(k_u + k_v)y]
$$

$$
\times \int_u \exp[j(k_u - k\sin\theta)u] \, du \int_v \exp[j(k_v - k\sin\theta)v] \, dv.
$$

$$(3.26)$$

At the present time, we assume that the phased array is infinitely extended and, thus, the integrals in the (u, v) domain are for $u \in (-\infty, \infty)$ and $v \in (-\infty, \infty)$; we will examine finite aperture effects in the next section. Thus, we have

$$\int_u \exp[j(k_u - k \sin \theta)u] \, du = \delta(k_u - k \sin \theta)$$

$$\int_v \exp[j(k_v - k \sin \theta)v] \, dv = \delta(k_v - k \sin \theta). \tag{3.27}$$

(The right side of (3.27) should have the factor 2π multiplying the delta functions. This constant factor is removed for notational simplicity.) Substituting (3.27) in (3.26) yields

$$
\begin{aligned}
S_{xy}(\theta, \omega) =& P(\omega) \int_{-k}^{k} \int_{-k}^{k} H(k_u, \omega)H(k_v, \omega)\delta(k_u - k \sin \theta)\delta(k_v - k \sin \theta) \\
& \times \exp[-j(\sqrt{k^2 - k_u^2} + \sqrt{k^2 - k_v^2})x - j(k_u + k_v)y] \, dk_u \, dk_v \\
=& P(\omega) \, H^2(k \sin \theta, \omega) \, \exp(-j2k \cos \theta \, x - j2k \sin \theta \, y)
\end{aligned}
\tag{3.28}
$$

Suppose $f(x, y)$ is the reflectivity function for the test object. Hence, the temporal Fourier transform of the total echoed signals from all reflectors in the spatial domain can be found from (3.28) to be

$$
\begin{aligned}
S(\theta, \omega) \equiv& \int_x \int_y f(x, y) \, S_{xy}(\theta, \omega) \, dx \, dy \\
=& P(\omega) \, H^2(k \sin \theta, \omega) \\
& \times \underbrace{\int_x \int_y f(x, y) \, \exp(-j2k \cos \theta \, x - j2k \sin \theta \, y) \, dx \, dy}_{Two \ dimensional \ Fourier \ integral}
\end{aligned}
\tag{3.29}
$$

The double integral in the (x, y) domain on the right side of (3.29) is in the form of a two-dimensional Fourier transform. Thus, we have from (3.29) the following:

$$S(\theta, \omega) = P(\omega) \, H^2(k \sin \theta, \omega) \, F(2k \cos \theta, 2k \sin \theta). \tag{3.30}$$

Finally, we can write the following inverse equation from (3.30):

$$F(2k \cos \theta, 2k \sin \theta) = \frac{S(\theta, \omega)}{P(\omega) \, H^2(k \sin \theta, \omega)}, \qquad (3.31)$$

for (θ, ω) values where $P(\omega) \, H(k \sin \theta, \omega) \neq 0$. *Note that the mapping from the measurement domain (θ, ω) to the image's spatial frequency domain is polar* (see Figure 3.6).

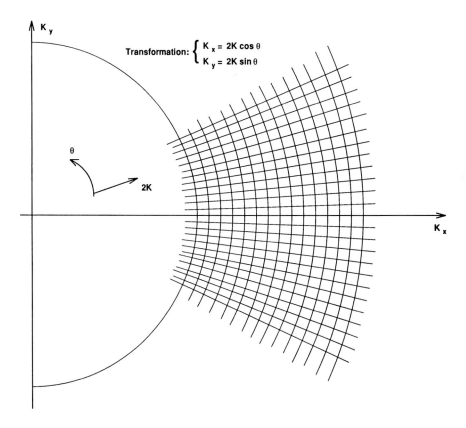

Figure 3.6 Mapping of the measurement domain $(\theta, 2k)$ into the target's spatial frequency domain (k_x, k_y) in array imaging with beam-steered data.

- *In practice, the deconvolution in (3.31) is performed via the following matched-filtering operation (* denotes complex conjugation):*

$$F(2k \cos \theta, 2k \sin \theta) = S(\theta, \omega) \left[P(\omega) \, H^2(k \sin \theta, \omega) \right]^*.$$

In summary, the inverse method utilized the Fourier decomposition of the radiation pattern for an element of the array. *This decomposition enabled us to convert* **nonlinear** *phase functions of the spatial (x, y) domain and transmit/receive (u, v) domains into linear phase functions.* Then, the integrals in the (x, y) and (u, v) domains were analyzed via Fourier transformation resulting in a one-to-one relationship between the data in the (θ, ω) (measurement) domain and (k_x, k_y) (image's spatial frequency) domain.

Thus, the inversion that we developed for imaging with phased array beam-steered data is based on a **spatial Fourier processing on aperture data**. For this processing, the *linear phase delay* across the aperture combined with the simultaneous excitation of the elements in the transmit mode (i.e., the physical addition of their phased delayed radiation patterns in the target scene) is simply a **physical/hardware discrete spatial Fourier transformer** in the transmit aperture domain, that is, u. A hardware discrete spatial Fourier transformation is performed in the receive aperture domain, that is, v, via a linear delay function across the aperture and a hardware adder.

3.7 RESOLUTION, RECONSTRUCTION, AND SAMPLING CONSTRAINTS

Next, we examine the sampling constraints and resolution for phased array beam-steered imaging systems. Figure 3.7 shows the data acquisition system for array imaging with beam-steered data. The pulsed signal, that is, $p(t)$, is approximately a bandpass signal with its power concentrated within a known band, for example, $[\omega_1, \omega_2]$. Equivalently, the available wavenumbers of the phased array's radiation pattern are within a bandpass region identified via $k \in [k_1, k_2] \equiv [\omega_1/c, \omega_2/c]$.

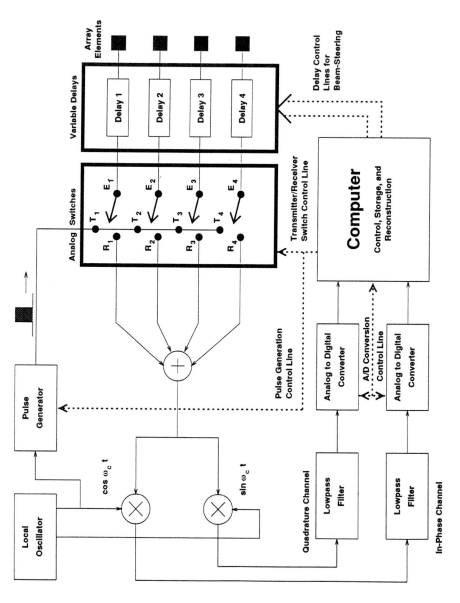

Figure 3.7 Data acquisition system for array imaging with beam-steered data.

For a given scan angle θ, the signal at the output of the phased array, that is, $s(\theta, t)$, is mixed with $\cos \omega_c t$ and $\sin \omega_c t$ on the two branches of a quadrature detector where $\omega_c \equiv (\omega_2 + \omega_1)/2$ is the center frequency of the pulsed signal.

The resultant signal is a lowpass signal within the band $[-\omega_0, \omega_0]$ where $\omega_0 \equiv (\omega_2 - \omega_1)/2$. This signal is sampled at or above the required Nyquist rate, that is, $\Delta_t \leq \frac{\pi}{\omega_0}$. The sampled signal is then zero-padded, if required (this will be discussed), to extend the time length of the sample sequence to T_0, where T_0 is a constant that will be determined later. Next, the discrete Fourier transform of the resultant sequence is computed to obtain the samples of $S(\omega, \theta)$ at evenly spaced values of ω; the sample spacing in the ω domain is $\Delta_\omega \equiv \frac{2\pi}{T_0}$ and, thus, the sample spacing in the wavenumber domain is $\Delta_k \equiv \frac{2\pi}{cT_0}$.

Suppose the spacing of the elements on the phase array is Δ_u. The scan angles are chosen within an interval $[-\theta_0, \theta_0]$ with spacing Δ_θ. $(\Delta_\theta, \Delta_u, \Delta_k)$ are the *input* parameters of the imaging system. We also define the *output* parameter of the imaging system to be the resolution in the (x, y) domain. In this section, we develop principles to determine the input parameters of a phased array scan imaging system for an error-free reconstruction. We also examine the relationship between the resolution in the reconstructed image, that is, the output parameter, to the bandwidth of the pulsed signal and the aperture length.

Finite Aperture Effects

Considering the fact that the extent of the aperture is limited to the region $[-L, L]$, (3.27) should be rewritten as follows:

$$\int_u \exp[j(k_u - k \sin \theta)u] \, du = 2L \frac{\sin L(k_u - k \sin \theta)}{L(k_u - k \sin \theta)}$$
$$\int_v \exp[j(k_v - k \sin \theta)v] \, dv = 2L \frac{\sin L(k_v - k \sin \theta)}{L(k_v - k \sin \theta)} \quad (3.32)$$

Substituting (3.32) in (3.26) yields

$$S_{xy}(\theta, \omega) = P(\omega)$$

$$\times \int_{-k}^{k} H(k_u, \omega) \, \exp(-j\sqrt{k^2 - k_u^2} \, x - jk_u y) \, 2L \frac{\sin L(k_u - k\sin\theta)}{L(k_u - k\sin\theta)} \, dk_u$$

$$\times \int_{-k}^{k} H(k_v, \omega) \, \exp(-j\sqrt{k^2 - k_v^2} \, x - jk_v y) \, 2L \frac{\sin L(k_v - k\sin\theta)}{L(k_v - k\sin\theta)} \, dk_v$$

$$(3.33)$$

The integral in the k_u domain on the right side of (3.33) is in the form of a convolution integral of $H(k_u, \omega) \, \exp(-j\sqrt{k^2 - k_u^2} \, x - jk_u y)$ with the aperture transfer function $2L \frac{\sin L k_u}{L k_u}$ (sinc function), which is a lowpass filter, evaluated at $k_u = k\sin\theta$; that is,

$$I(k\sin\theta) \equiv \int_{-k}^{k} H(k_u, \omega) \, \exp(-j\sqrt{k^2 - k_u^2} \, x - jk_u y)$$

$$(3.34)$$

$$\times \, 2L \frac{\sin L(k_u - k\sin\theta)}{L(k_u - k\sin\theta)} \, dk_u.$$

This lowpass filtering operation does not have a significant effect on $H(k_u, \omega)$ which in most practical problems is a slowly fluctuating function. For example, for a flat transducer element with size $2L_e$, one can show that $H(k_u, \omega) \propto \frac{\sin L_e k_u}{L_e k_u}$ (see Section 3.2) which is a slowly fluctuating signal with respect to the aperture sinc function since $L_e << L$. Thus, (3.34) can be rewritten as follows:

$$I(k\sin\theta) \approx H(k\sin\theta, \omega) \int_{-k}^{k} \exp(-j\sqrt{k^2 - k_u^2} \, x - jk_u y)$$

$$(3.35)$$

$$\times \, 2L \frac{\sin L(k_u - k\sin\theta)}{L(k_u - k\sin\theta)} dk_u$$

However, the phase modulated (PM) function on the right side of (3.35), that is,

$$\exp(-j\sqrt{k^2 - k_u^2} \, x - jk_u y),$$

for certain values of (x, y), could become a highly fluctuating signal with respect to the lowpass filter function. The convolution of this PM function with the lowpass filter approximately results in the suppression (filtering) of the components of the PM wave at the values of $k_u = k \sin \theta$ where the instantaneous frequency of the PM wave falls outside the interval $[-L, L]$.

The instantaneous frequency of the PM function in the k_u domain is found via

$$\frac{\partial}{\partial k_u} \left[\sqrt{k^2 - k_u^2} \, x + k_u y \right] = \frac{-k_u}{\sqrt{k^2 - k_u^2}} \, x + y. \qquad (3.36)$$

Hence, the range of $k_u = k \sin \theta$ values where the PM wave is not suppressed is found from the following inequalities:

$$-L \leq \frac{-k_u}{\sqrt{k^2 - k_u^2}} \, x + y = -\tan \theta \, x + y \leq L. \qquad (3.37)$$

Solving for the range of values of θ from (3.37), we obtain the following band for the θ values where $I(k \sin \theta)$ is not suppressed to zero:

$$\Omega(x, y) \equiv \left[\arctan(\frac{y - L}{x}), \arctan(\frac{y + L}{x}) \right]. \qquad (3.38)$$

Note that this band is a function of the unit reflector coordinates, that is, (x, y). We refer to this as the spatial Doppler phenomenon for array imaging with beam-steered data. This is shown in Figure 3.8 for a broadside target and an off-broadside target. Finally, we can rewrite (3.35) as follows:

$$I(k \sin \theta) \approx H(k \sin \theta, \omega) \, \exp(-jk \cos \theta \, x - jk \sin \theta \, y), \qquad (3.39)$$

for $\theta \in \Omega(x, y)$, and zero otherwise. A similar analysis can also be performed for the effects of finite aperture in the receiver domain, that is, v. In this case, (3.26) becomes equal to what is shown in (3.28), that is,

$$S_{xy}(\theta, \omega) = P(\omega) \, H^2(k \sin \theta, \omega) \, \exp(-j2k \cos \theta \, x - j2k \sin \theta \, y),$$

for $\theta \in \Omega(x, y)$, and zero otherwise.

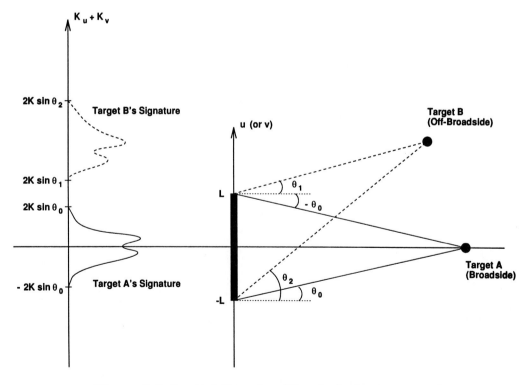

Figure 3.8 Spatial Doppler (Fourier) phenomenon in array
imaging with beam-steered data.

Resolution

The implication of (3.38)-(3.39), as viewed from the inverse equation in (3.31), is that the contribution of the scan data in forming/imaging a scatterer at (x, y) is limited to the spatial frequency band $(k_x, k_y) = (2k \cos \theta, 2k \sin \theta)$ with $\theta \in \Omega(x, y)$ and $\omega \in [\omega_1, \omega_2]$. This band, which does not have a specific shape, in effect dictates the resolution of the reconstructed image at (x, y). The spatial frequency coverages for a broadside and an off-broadside targets are shown in Figure 3.9. This clearly results in a shift-varying resolution in the reconstructed image. The variations of the bandwidth and resolution with respect to (x, y) are also referred to as shift-varying *point spread function* in echo imaging systems.

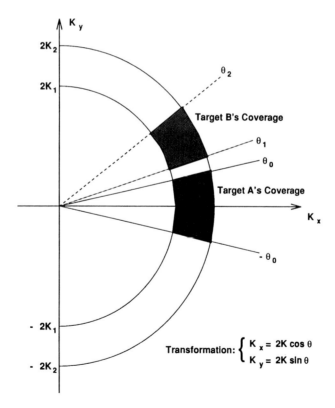

Figure 3.9 Spatial frequency coverage for a single target in array imaging with beam-steered data.

For a reflector at (x, y) identified by its polar coordinates (r, ϕ), the following principles govern its resolution in the reconstructed image (see the discussion on point spread function in Chapter 2). When the spatial domain is rotated by ϕ with respect to the center of the phased array, the resolution in the resultant rotated geometry, call it (x', y'), can be found from (3.38) to be

$$\Delta_{x'} \equiv 2\pi \frac{1}{2(k_2 - k_1)}$$

$$\Delta_{y'} \equiv 2\pi \frac{r}{4kL \cos \phi}. \tag{3.40}$$

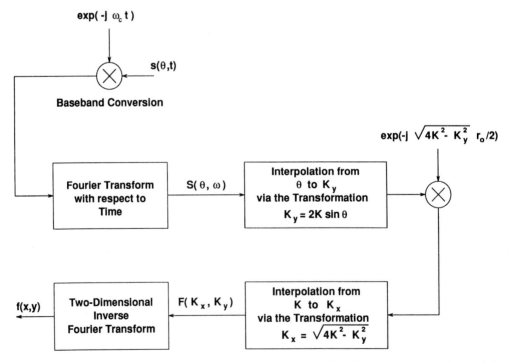

Figure 3.10 Reconstruction algorithm for array imaging with beam-steered data.

Input Parameters Selection and Reconstruction

Figure 3.10 outlines the reconstruction algorithm for array imaging with beam-steered data. The spatial frequency coverage dictated by the inverse equation is based on a polar transformation from (k_x, k_y) to $(2k, \theta)$. For the purpose of reconstruction and visual display, the data in the polar domain should be interpolated on a uniform grid in the (k_x, k_y) domain. Then, the two-dimensional inverse discrete spatial Fourier transform of the data interpolated on the uniform grid is computed. The resultant spatial domain image is complex bandpass information (though this data set is treated as baseband data by the two-dimensional DFT operator) due to the fact that the pulsed signal $p(t)$ is a bandpass signal. Thus, similar to other echo imaging systems, the magnitude of this image is displayed for visualization.

Suppose we are interested in imaging an area with depth r_0 within the scan sector $[-\theta_0, \theta_0]$. Thus, the imaging area's extent in the x and y domains are, respectively, r_0 and $2r_0 \sin \theta_0$. Hence, the sample spacing on the uniform grid in the (k_x, k_y) domain should satisfy

$$\Delta_{k_x} \leq \frac{2\pi}{r_0}, \tag{3.41}$$

$$\Delta_{k_y} \leq \frac{2\pi}{2r_0 \sin \theta_0}. \tag{3.42}$$

$I(k_u = k \sin \theta)$ [see (3.34),(3.35)] is a lowpass function with its support band within $[-L, L]$ in the spatial domain. Moreover, the right side of (3.33) contains the product of $I(k_u = k \sin \theta)$ and $I(k_v = k \sin \theta)$. Thus, the support band of $S_{xy}(\theta, \omega)$ [see (3.33)] or, equivalently, the support band of $S(\theta, \omega)$ in the spatial Fourier counterpart of $k \sin \theta$ is $[-2L, 2L]$. This property has consequences in the image interpolation and measurement domain sampling as described next.

In the interpolation phase, for a fixed ω, the sampled signal $S(\theta, \omega)$, that is band-limited to $[-2L, 2L]$ in the spatial Fourier domain counterpart of $k \sin \theta$, is interpolated at evenly spaced k_y values separated by Δ_{k_y}. This is achieved via the nonuniform interpolation with the corresponding Jacobian function for the transformation $k_y = 2k \sin \theta$ (see

Section 2.5 or [6]). This transforms the polar data of $(2k, \theta)$ into $(2k, k_y)$ domain.

To avoid nonlinear aliasing in transformation from θ to k_y, we once again consider the fact that $S(\theta, \omega)$ is band-limited to $[-2L, 2L]$ in the spatial Fourier domain counterpart of $k \sin \theta$. In this case, based on the nonlinear (nonuniform) sampling principles developed in Section 2.5, one can show that the sample spacing in the scan domain θ should satisfy the following constraint to avoid nonlinear aliasing:

$$\Delta_\theta \leq \frac{2\pi}{4Lk_2} = \frac{\lambda_2}{4L}. \tag{3.43}$$

Next, the x domain data is centered to $[-r_0/2, r_0/2]$ by multiplying the $(2k, k_y)$ domain data with the phase function

$$\exp\left[-j\sqrt{4k^2 - k_y^2}\, r_0/2\right].$$

Then, for a fixed k_y, the data in the k (or ω) domain is interpolated into the k_x domain with a sinc function with bandwidth $[-r_0/2, r_0/2]$. The nonuniform interpolation algorithm with the appropriate Jacobian function for the transformation $k_x = \sqrt{4k^2 - k_y^2}$ is also used for this task. To avoid nonlinear aliasing in this phase, the following constraint should be satisfied:

$$\Delta_k \leq \frac{2\pi}{2r_0} \cos\theta_0.$$

Thus, the duration of the zero-padded time sequence should satisfy

$$T_0 \geq \frac{1}{\cos\theta_0} \frac{2r_0}{c}. \tag{3.44}$$

Finally, we consider the effects of sampling on the aperture. In this case, the integrals over u and v in (3.32) are sums over discrete values of u and v with sample spacing $\Delta_u = \Delta_v$. This implies that the right side of (3.32) is a *periodic* sinc function of k_u or k_v. Thus, we have to set the sampling on the aperture to avoid *circular* convolution aliasing in (3.33).

Using the fact that the support band of $S_{xy}(\theta, \omega)$ is $\Omega(x, y)$ [see (3.38)] and the fact that $L \gg \Delta_u$ in most practical problems, one can avoid circular convolution aliasing provided that the following is satisfied:

$$\frac{2\pi}{\Delta_u} \geq 2k_2 \ \sin\left[\arctan(\frac{L + |y|}{x})\right],$$

or

$$\Delta_u \leq \frac{\pi}{k_2 \ \sin\left[\arctan(\frac{L+|y|}{x})\right]}. \tag{3.45}$$

Clearly, Δ_u should be determined based on the worst scenario in (3.45). This corresponds to the case of $x = 0$. In this case,

$$\Delta_u \leq \frac{\pi}{k_2} = \frac{\lambda_2}{2};$$

that is, the sample spacing on the aperture should be less than half of the wavelength of the highest frequency of the pulsed signal.

3.8 ELECTRONICALLY SCANNING CIRCULAR ARRAYS

This section is a reformulation of the principles developed in Section 3.6 for circular phased arrays. Figure 3.11 shows the imaging system geometry for the transmit and receive modes of a circular phased array. The circular array is located on the circle of radius R. In the transmit mode, the array's elements are identified by the spatial coordinates $(R \cos \alpha, R \sin \alpha)$, $\alpha \in [-\alpha_0, \alpha_0]$. In the receive mode, the array's elements are identified by the spatial coordinates $(R \cos \beta, R \sin \beta)$, $\beta \in [-\alpha_0, \alpha_0]$. Both α and β take on discrete evenly spaced values in the interval $[-\alpha_0, \alpha_0]$. We present our analysis for continuous measurements in the (α, β) domain with $\alpha_0 = \frac{\pi}{2}$. Due to the complexity of notation, we will not examine the effects of finite aperture and discrete sampling on a circular array.

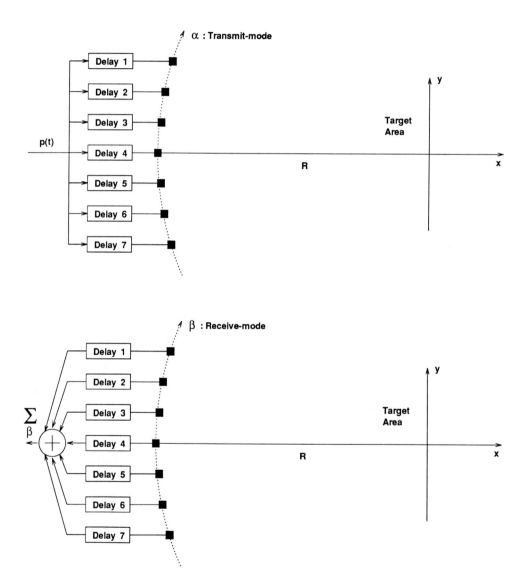

Figure 3.11 Transmit and receive modes of a circular phased array.

Once again, we exploit the array's radiation pattern signal subspace by generating a linear phase delay across the circular aperture. The delay associated with a transmitting element of the array located at $(R\cos\alpha, R\sin\alpha)$ is

$$\tau(\alpha, \xi) \equiv \frac{\xi\alpha}{c}, \tag{3.46}$$

where ξ is a variable controlled by the user. (ξ, t) is the new measurement domain; ξ replaces the steer angle θ. The time required for the pulsed signal to travel from the element at $(R\cos\alpha, R\sin\alpha)$ to the point (x, y) in the spatial domain is

$$T(x - R\cos\alpha, y - R\sin\alpha) = \frac{\sqrt{(x - R\cos\alpha)^2 + (y - R\sin\alpha)^2}}{c}.$$

Thus, the transmitted signal at (x, y) due to illumination of the element at $(R\cos\alpha, R\sin\alpha)$ is

$$p[t - \tau(\alpha, \xi) - T(x - R\cos\alpha, y - R\sin\alpha)].$$

Then, the total transmitted signal at (x, y) is

$$\int_\alpha a(x - R\cos\alpha, y - R\sin\alpha)\, p[t - \tau(\alpha, \xi) - T(x - R\cos\alpha, y - R\sin\alpha)]\, d\alpha. \tag{3.47}$$

In the receive mode, it takes $T(x - R\cos\beta, y - R\sin\beta)]$ units of time for the echoed signals from (x, y) to reach a receiving element at $(R\cos\beta, R\sin\beta)$. Moreover, the delay introduced to the incoming echoed signals by this receiving element is $\tau(\beta, \xi)$. Thus, the total recorded echoed signal due to a unit reflector at (x, y) becomes

$$s_{xy}(\xi, t) \equiv \int_\alpha \int_\beta a(x - R\cos\alpha, y - R\sin\alpha)\, a(x - R\cos\beta, y - R\sin\beta)$$
$$\times p[t - \tau(\alpha, \xi) - T(x - R\cos\alpha, y - R\sin\alpha)$$
$$- \tau(\beta, \xi) - T(x - R\cos\beta, y - R\sin\beta)]d\alpha d\beta. \tag{3.48}$$

The temporal Fourier transform of both sides of (3.48) yields

$$S_{xy}(\xi, \omega) = \int_\alpha \int_\beta a(x - R\cos\alpha, y - R\sin\alpha)\ a(x - R\cos\beta, y - R\sin\beta)$$
$$\times\ P(\omega)\exp\left[-j\omega[\tau(\alpha, \xi) - T(x - R\cos\alpha, y - R\sin\alpha)\right.$$
$$\left. -\ \tau(\beta, \xi) - T(x - R\cos\beta, y - R\sin\beta)]\right] d\alpha d\beta$$
$$=P(\omega)\int_\alpha\int_\beta d\alpha\ d\beta \exp(-jk\xi\alpha)\ \exp(-jk\xi\beta)$$
$$\times\ h(x - R\cos\alpha, y - R\sin\alpha)\ h(x - R\cos\beta, y - R\sin\beta)$$
$$\tag{3.49}$$

where

$$h(x - R\cos\alpha, y - R\sin\alpha, \omega) \equiv a(x - R\cos\alpha, y - R\sin\alpha)$$
$$\times\exp[-jk\sqrt{(x - R\cos\alpha)^2 + (y - R\sin\alpha)^2}],$$

is an element's radiation pattern at frequency ω (see Section 3.2). The plane wave decomposition of this radiation pattern at the transmit and receive modes can be found from (3.8) to be

$$h(x - R\cos\alpha, y - R\sin\alpha, \omega)$$
$$= \int_{-\pi/2}^{\pi/2} H_p(\varphi_\alpha, \omega)\ \exp[-jkr\cos(\varphi_\alpha - \theta)]\ \exp[jkR\cos(\varphi_\alpha - \alpha)]\ d\varphi_\alpha$$
$$h(x - R\cos\beta, y - R\sin\beta, \omega)$$
$$= \int_{-\pi/2}^{\pi/2} H_p(\varphi_\beta, \omega)\ \exp[-jkr\cos(\varphi_\beta - \theta)]\ \exp[jkR\cos(\varphi_\beta - \beta)]\ d\varphi_\beta$$
$$\tag{3.50}$$

where (r, θ) are the polar coordinates for (x, y) (θ is not used to identify the scan angle anymore).

Substituting (3.50) in (3.49), and after some rearrangements, one obtains the following:

$$
\begin{aligned}
S_{xy}(\xi,\omega) =& P(\omega) \int_{-\pi/2}^{\pi/2} \int_{-\pi/2}^{\pi/2} d\varphi_\alpha \, d\varphi_\beta \; H_p(\varphi_\alpha,\omega) \, H_p(\varphi_\beta,\omega) \\
& \times \, \exp\left[-jkr[\cos(\varphi_\alpha - \theta) + \cos(\varphi_\beta - \theta)]\right] \\
& \times \int_\alpha \exp[jkR\cos(\varphi_\alpha - \alpha)] \; \exp(-jk\xi\alpha) \, d\alpha \\
& \times \int_\beta \exp[jkR\cos(\varphi_\beta - \beta)] \; \exp(-jk\xi\beta) \, d\beta.
\end{aligned}
\tag{3.51}
$$

The above two integrals in the (α,β) domain are the Hankel function integrals (similar to the Fourier spectrum of a tone-modulated PM signal), and can be shown to be (with $\alpha_0 = \frac{\pi}{2}$)

$$
\begin{aligned}
\int_\alpha \exp[jkR\cos(\varphi_\alpha - \alpha)] \; \exp(-jk\xi\alpha) \, d\alpha =& H_{k\xi}(kR) \; \exp(jk\xi\varphi_\alpha) \\
\int_\beta \exp[jkR\cos(\varphi_\beta - \beta)] \; \exp(-jk\xi\beta) \, d\beta =& H_{k\xi}(kR) \; \exp(jk\xi\varphi_\beta)
\end{aligned}
\tag{3.52}
$$

where $H_{k\xi}(\cdot)$ is the Hankel function of the first kind, $k\xi$ order. Substituting (3.52) in (3.51) yields

$$
\begin{aligned}
S_{xy}(\xi,\omega) =& P(\omega) \int_{-\pi/2}^{\pi/2} \int_{-\pi/2}^{\pi/2} d\varphi_\alpha \, d\varphi_\beta \; H_p(\varphi_\alpha,\omega) \, H_p(\varphi_\beta,\omega) \\
& \times \, \exp\left[-jkr[\cos(\varphi_\alpha - \theta) + \cos(\varphi_\beta - \theta)]\right] \\
& \times \, H_{k\xi}(kR) \; \exp(jk\xi\varphi_\alpha) \, H_{k\xi}(kR) \; \exp(jk\xi\varphi_\beta)
\end{aligned}
\tag{3.53}
$$

$H_p(\cdot)$ is commonly a slowly fluctuating amplitude function. Due to this fact, we can assume that it is a constant function, for example, one.

In this case, (3.53) becomes

$$S_{xy}(\xi,\omega) = P(\omega) \, H^2_{k\xi}(kR)$$
$$\times \int_{-\pi/2}^{\pi/2} \exp[-jkr\cos(\varphi_\alpha - \theta)] \, \exp(jk\xi\varphi_\alpha) \, d\varphi_\alpha$$
$$\times \int_{-\pi/2}^{\pi/2} \exp[-jkr\cos(\varphi_\beta - \theta)] \, \exp(jk\xi\varphi_\beta) \, d\varphi_\beta$$
$$= P(\omega) \, H^2_{k\xi}(kR) \; H^2_{k\xi}(kr) \, \exp(j2k\xi\theta)$$

(3.54)

With $r \gg \lambda$, the fluctuations (information contents) of the Hankel function $H_{k\xi}(kr)$ are mainly in its phase component. Thus, we can write the following approximation (within an amplitude function):

$$H^2_{k\xi}(kr) \approx H_{2k\xi}(2kr).$$

(3.55)

Using (3.55) in (3.54) yields

$$S_{xy}(\xi,\omega) = P(\omega) \, H^2_{k\xi}(kR) \; H_{2k\xi}(2kr) \, \exp(j2k\xi\theta).$$

(3.56)

The temporal Fourier transform of the total echoed signals from all reflectors in the spatial domain can be found from (3.56) to be

$$S(\xi,\omega) \equiv \int_x\!\int_y f(x,y) \, S_{xy}(\xi,\omega) \, dx \, dy$$
$$= P(\omega) \, H^2_{k\xi}(kR) \int_x\!\int_y f(x,y) \, H_{2k\xi}(2kr) \, \exp(j2k\xi\theta) \, dx \, dy.$$

(3.57)

We define

$$S_0(\xi,\omega) \equiv \frac{S(\xi,\omega)}{P(\omega) \, H^2_{k\xi}(kR)}$$
$$= \int_x\!\int_y f(x,y) \, H_{2k\xi}(2kr) \, \exp(j2k\xi\theta) \, dx \, dy.$$

(3.58)

From the Hankel integral equation, we have

$$\int_\varphi \exp[j2kr\cos(\varphi - \theta)] \ \exp(-j2k\xi\varphi) \ d\varphi = H_{2k\xi}(2kr) \ \exp(j2k\xi\theta).$$
(3.59)

Taking the inverse Fourier transform of both sides of (3.58) with respect to ξ, and with the help of (3.59), one obtains

$$
\begin{aligned}
s_0(\varphi, \omega) &= \int_x \int_y f(x,y) \ \exp[j2kr\cos(\varphi - \theta)] \ dx \ dy \\
&= \int_x \int_y f(x,y) \ \exp(j2k\cos\varphi x + j2k\sin\varphi y) \ dx \ dy \qquad (3.60) \\
&= F(2k\cos\varphi, 2k\sin\varphi).
\end{aligned}
$$

Equation (3.60) provides the following inverse equation:

$$F(2k\cos\varphi, 2k\sin\varphi) = \mathcal{F}_{(\xi)}^{-1}\left[\frac{S(\xi,\omega)}{P(\omega) \ H_{k\xi}^2(kR)} \right], \qquad (3.61)$$

where φ is the Fourier counterpart for ξ. *Note that the coverage dictated by the inverse equation (3.61) for circular phased arrays is also polar.*

3.9 MECHANICALLY ROTATING ELEMENT

We next consider echo imaging using the database obtained via mechanically rotating an element. This imaging system does not utilize phasing of the elements of an array. This subject is discussed in this chapter due to its relevance to phased array imaging.

In Section 3.5 (Air Traffic Control/Surveillance Radar), we addressed this problem within the framework of the approximation in (3.8)-(3.9), which assumed the antenna beam is *focused* in a given angular orientation of the rotating element. This simplified model converted the inverse problem into a one-dimensional range-speed imaging system. We now utilize the spatial Doppler principle to solve this inverse problem without the need for (3.11).

System Model

As we mentioned in Section 3.5, the element used in this echo imaging problem has a fixed radiation pattern that is angularly focused at broadside (see Figure 3.12). To scan the desired imaging region, these antennas are continuously rotated along a fixed axis, and perform transmission/reception (see Figure 3.4). The speed of rotation is much smaller than the speed of wave propagation. Thus, one may assume that the element practically stops in its rotational motion, illuminates the target area, makes its corresponding reception, and then moves to its next rotational position.

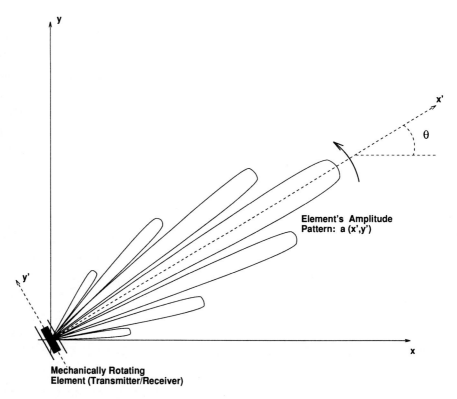

Figure 3.12 Echo imaging system geometry with a mechanically rotating element.

Suppose the element is positioned at the origin in the spatial (x, y) domain. The spatial amplitude associated with this element when it is facing the broadside (i.e., the line $y = 0$) is $a(x, y)$. When the element is rotated by the angle θ (or, equivalently, if the spatial (x, y) domain is rotated by θ), the new radiation pattern's spatial amplitude function becomes $a(x', y')$, where

$$\begin{bmatrix} x' \\ y' \end{bmatrix} \equiv \begin{bmatrix} \cos\theta & \sin\theta \\ -\sin\theta & \cos\theta \end{bmatrix} \begin{bmatrix} x \\ y \end{bmatrix}. \tag{3.62}$$

If $p(t)$ is the transmitted pulse signal by the element, the time-dependent radiation pattern experienced at (x, y) is

$$a(x', y')\, p(t - \frac{\sqrt{x^2 + y^2}}{c}),$$

with (x', y') as defined in (3.62). (Note that $\sqrt{x'^2 + y'^2} = \sqrt{x^2 + y^2}$.) The element possesses the same radiation pattern at its receive mode. Thus, the echoed signal received due to a unit reflector at (x, y) is

$$s_{xy}(\theta, t) \equiv a^2(x', y')\, p(t - \frac{2\sqrt{x^2 + y^2}}{c}).$$

The temporal Fourier transform of this signal is

$$S_{xy}(\theta, \omega) = P(\omega)\ \underbrace{a^2(x', y')\ \exp(-j2k\sqrt{x^2 + y^2})}_{\textit{Transmit/receive radiation pattern}}. \tag{3.63}$$

Let $H_p(\varphi, \omega)$ be the polar domain plane wave decomposition for the broadside amplitude pattern $a^2(x, y)$ at frequency 2ω; that is, [see (3.8)]

$$a^2(x, y)\ \exp(-j2k\sqrt{x^2 + y^2}) = \int_{-\pi/2}^{\pi/2} H_p(\varphi, \omega)\ \exp[-j2kr\cos(\varphi - \phi)]\, d\varphi,$$

$$\tag{3.64}$$

where (r, ϕ) represent the polar transformation for (x, y):

$$r \equiv \sqrt{x^2 + y^2}$$

$$\phi \equiv \arctan(\frac{y}{x}).$$

Using the rotational transformation property of the Fourier transform, one can show that the polar domain plane wave decomposition for the beam that is rotated by the angle θ is

$$a^2(x', y') \; \exp(-j2k\sqrt{x^2 + y^2}) =$$
$$\int_{-\pi/2}^{\pi/2} H_p(\theta - \varphi, \omega) \; \exp[-j2kr\cos(\varphi - \phi)] \; d\varphi. \tag{3.65}$$

- *For the broadside beam in (3.64), $H_p(\varphi, \omega)$ has most of its energy around $\varphi = 0$ [i.e., $H(k_u, \omega)$ is a lowpass signal in the k_u domain]. However, for the rotated beam in (3.65), $H_p(\theta - \varphi, \omega)$ has its energy centered around $\varphi = \theta$.*

- *The classical approximation used in air traffic control and diagnostic medicine echo imaging using a mechanically rotating element assumes that*

$$H_p(\theta - \varphi, \omega) \approx \delta(\theta - \varphi),$$

*that is to say the beam is **focused** at the angle θ.*

The temporal Fourier transform of the total received signal from a target region with reflectivity distribution $f(x, y)$ is found from the following:

$$S(\theta, \omega) \equiv \int_x \int_y f(x, y) \; S_{xy}(\theta, \omega) \; dx \; dy. \tag{3.66}$$

Using (3.63) and (3.65) in (3.66) yields

$$
S(\theta,\omega) = P(\omega) \int_{-\pi/2}^{\pi/2} H_p(\theta - \varphi, \omega)
$$
$$
\times \underbrace{\left[\int_x \int_y f(x,y)\ \exp[-j2kr\cos(\varphi - \phi)]\ dx dy \right]}_{Two\ dimensional\ Fourier\ integral}\ d\varphi \qquad (3.67)
$$
$$
= P(\omega) \int_{-\pi/2}^{\pi/2} H_p(\theta - \varphi, \omega)\ F(2k\cos\varphi, 2k\sin\varphi)\ d\varphi.
$$

(Note that $2kr\cos(\varphi - \phi) = 2k\cos\varphi\, r\cos\phi + 2k\sin\varphi\, r\sin\phi = 2k\cos\varphi\, x + 2k\sin\varphi\, y$, that is, a linear function of (x,y). This makes the integral over (x,y) a two-dimensional Fourier integral.)

Inversion

We denote the polar mapping of $F(2k\cos\varphi, 2k\sin\varphi)$ by $F_p(\varphi, 2k)$. Thus, the system model in (3.67) can be rewritten as follows:

$$
S(\theta,\omega) = P(\omega) \int_{-\pi/2}^{\pi/2} H_p(\theta - \varphi, \omega)\ F_p(\varphi, 2k)\ d\varphi \qquad (3.68)
$$
$$
= P(\omega)\ H_p(\theta, \omega)\ *\ F_p(\theta, 2k),
$$

where $*$ denotes convolution in the θ domain.

We denote the Fourier transform domain for θ by ξ. Taking the Fourier transform of both sides of (3.68) with respect to θ yields

$$
\tilde{S}(\xi,\omega) = P(\omega)\ \tilde{H}_p(\xi,\omega)\ \tilde{F}_p(\xi, 2k), \qquad (3.69)
$$

with

$$
\tilde{S}(\xi,\omega) \equiv \mathcal{F}_{(\theta)}\big[\ S(\theta,\omega)\ \big],
$$
$$
\tilde{H}_p(\xi,\omega) \equiv \mathcal{F}_{(\theta)}\big[\ H_p(\theta,\omega)\ \big],
$$
$$
\tilde{F}_p(\xi, 2k) \equiv \mathcal{F}_{(\theta)}\big[\ F_p(\theta, 2k)\ \big].
$$

- *With $\theta \in [-\pi, \pi]$, ξ takes on only integer values, and $\tilde{S}$, $\tilde{H}_p$ and $\tilde{F}_p$ represent the Fourier coefficients for the periodic signals S, H_p and F_p, respectively.*

From (3.69), we obtain the following inversion in the (ξ, ω) domain:

$$\tilde{F}_p(\xi, 2k) = \frac{\tilde{S}(\xi, \omega)}{P(\omega)\,\tilde{H}_p(\xi, \omega)},$$

or equivalently

$$F(2k\cos\theta, 2k\sin\theta) = \mathcal{F}_{(\xi)}^{-1}\left[\frac{\tilde{S}(\xi, \omega)}{P(\omega)\,\tilde{H}_p(\xi, \omega)}\right]. \qquad (3.70)$$

The spatial frequency coverage dictated by the inverse equation (3.70) is polar.

Resolution

Using the results of Section 3.2, one can show that $\tilde{H}_p$ has a finite support in the ξ domain that is

$$\xi \in [-2kL_e, 2kL_e],$$

where $2L_e$ is the rotating element's aperture size. This translates to the following angular resolution for a target at the polar coordinates (r, ϕ):

$$\Delta_\phi \equiv \frac{\lambda}{2L_e},$$

which is the classical Rayleigh resolution. For an omni-directional radiation pattern (i.e., $L_e = 0$), where

$$H_p(\theta, \omega) = 1,$$

the angular resolution is infinity; that is, one cannot resolve targets in the angular domain.

The radial resolution for this coherent echo imaging system is dictated by the baseband bandwidth of $p(t)$, that is,

$$\Delta_r = \frac{\pi c}{\omega_0}.$$

3.10 SPATIAL-VELOCITY IMAGING WITH FM-CW SIGNALING

One of the areas of interest in diagnostic medicine echo imaging is to obtain the rate of blood flow through an artery and assess the contraction pressure of the heart's muscles. These can be retrieved by imaging the velocity distribution as well as the location of the reflectors in the target scene. Phased array imaging of moving targets also has applications in radar and sonar imaging problems. We examined a similar problem in the case of air traffic control radar/sonar where the objective was to image and determine the velocity of discrete and isolated moving targets in a homogeneous medium (air or water).

The simplest spatial-velocity imaging system involves a focused beam in the one-dimensional spatial domain for range-speed imaging, (x, v_x) that was discussed in Chapter 1. In multi-dimensional imaging systems, the spatial-velocity imaging involves retrieving target information in, for example, (x, y, v_x, v_y) domain or (x, y, z, v_x, v_y, v_z) domain. For instance, in air traffic control radar systems, a scanning beam, that is assumed to be focused, is used for range and radial-speed imaging in various angular directions. This scheme is not a *true* multi-dimensional phased array spatial-velocity imaging method.

Intuitively, one may anticipate that if the information on the location of targets in the cross-range can be retrieved from the aperture data of an array, then some information on the target's cross-range speed distribution is also contained within the aperture data. In fact, we show that *if the conventional approximations are not used to model the beam-steered radiation patterns of an array as focused beams, then the target's velocity distribution as well as its spatial distribution can be obtained from the aperture data with FM-CW signaling.*

This should not be surprising. As we discussed in Section 3.5, a *monopulse* radar, that possesses a single transmitting antenna and two separate receiving antennas, can be used for estimating a target's velocity provided that its beams could be approximated to be truly focused in space. The elements of an array provide a similar, yet far more complicated and more informative, type of database as the two receivers of a monopulse radar do for velocity imaging of a nonrigid target.

System Model and Inversion

We examine this inverse problem for an electronically scanning linear phased array imaging system. We assume a scenario where every other element of the linear array is a transmitter; the remaining ones are receiving elements (see Figure 3.13). In this case, we can illuminate the target region with a long duration FM-CW signal and record the resultant echoed signals. As we will show later in this section, FM-CW transmission and reception within the array's aperture provides us with good resolution in both the spatial domain and the velocity domain.

In practice, the speed of a reflector in the target scene is much smaller than the wave propagation speed. Due to this fact, we can model the target motion to be a linear function of time during the FM-CW coherent processing time; that is, a reflector velocity is a constant during the data acquisition period. The spatially dependent velocity distribution for the target region is denoted by $[\psi(x,y), v_o(x,y)]$; v_o and ψ are, respectively, the speed of the reflector at (x,y) and the direction of its motion. Note that the target is a nonrigid structure and, thus, (v_o, ψ) vary with (x,y).

- *We now use v_o and ψ to identify a reflector's speed and angular direction of motion, respectively. v will be used to identify the receive mode of a phase array, and (r, ϕ) are the polar coordinates for (x, y).*

We first analyze the problem for a single harmonic of the FM-CW signal. The ℓ-th harmonic of the FM-CW signal is

$$A_\ell \, \exp(j\omega_\ell t).$$

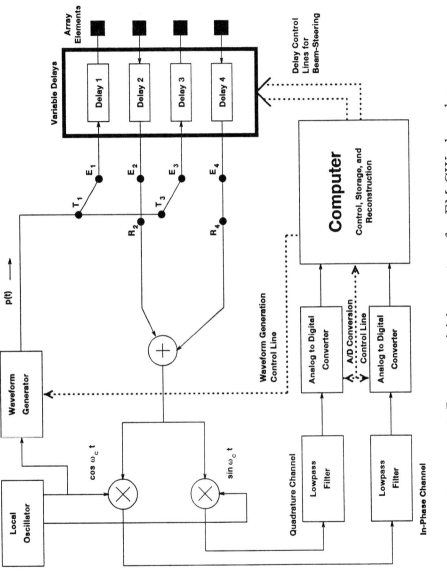

Figure 3.13 Data acquisition system for FM-CW phased array imaging.

247

Thus, the signal transmitted by the transmitter at $(0, u)$ at this harmonic and scan angle θ is

$$A_\ell \ \exp[j\omega_\ell(t - \frac{u \sin \theta}{c})],$$

where $\frac{u \sin \theta}{c}$ is the time delay associated with the transmitting element at $(0, u)$ at scan angle θ.

In practice, $v_o(x, y) \ll c$. Thus, the (x, y)-dependent phase function of the signal that reaches the reflector at (x, y) is [9, Chapter 13]

$$\exp\left[j\omega_\ell[t - \frac{u \sin \theta}{c} - \frac{\sqrt{(x + v_o \cos \psi \ t)^2 + (y + v_o \sin \psi \ t - u)^2}}{c}]\right], \quad (3.71)$$

where $(x + v_o \cos \psi t, y + v_o \sin \psi t)$ are the target's coordinates at time t.

We first examine the above system model via the classical approximations used in bistatic (monopulse) radar, as described in Section 3.5 and Figure 3.5b, and later on was carried into diagnostic medicine echo imaging of nonrigid moving targets. For this, the following second order Taylor series approximation is used:

$$\sqrt{(x + v_o \cos \psi \ t)^2 + (y + v_o \sin \psi \ t - u)^2} \approx$$
$$\sqrt{x^2 + (y - u)^2} + v_o \cos(\psi - \phi) \ t - \frac{u v_o \sin \phi \ t}{r} + \frac{v_o^2 t^2}{2r}.$$

There are three time-dependent terms in the above approximation. The first term, $v_o \cos(\psi - \phi) \ t$, represents a constant Doppler shift in the signal model in (3.71) that depends on the reflector's location and angular direction of motion. The second term, $-\frac{u v_o \sin \phi \ t}{r}$, also corresponds to a constant Doppler shift; however, it depends on the transmitter location u. The third term, $\frac{v_o^2 t^2}{2r}$, is a chirp signal that complicates the analysis of the signal model in (3.71) for the purpose of inversion.

One can obtain a similar analysis for the signal that is being recorded by a receiving element at $(0, v)$ using the following approximation:

$$\sqrt{(x + v_o \cos \psi \ t)^2 + (y + v_o \sin \psi \ t - v)^2} \approx$$
$$\sqrt{x^2 + (y - v)^2} + v_o \cos(\psi - \phi) \ t - \frac{v v_o \sin \phi \ t}{r} + \frac{v_o^2 t^2}{2r}.$$

Thus, for a transmitting element that is located at $(0, u)$ and a receiving element that is at $(0, v)$, the measured temporal Doppler shift at the ℓ-th harmonic of the FM-CW signal, that is, $\omega_\ell \equiv \omega_c + \Omega_\ell$, is

$$\omega_D(x, y) \approx \frac{v_o(x, y)\, \eta(x, y)}{c} \omega_\ell, \tag{3.72}$$

where

$$\eta(x, y) \equiv 2\cos(\psi - \phi) - \frac{(u + v)\sin\psi(x, y)}{r} + \frac{v_o t}{r}. \tag{3.73}$$

Based on the Doppler model in (3.72), the following approximations may be made to obtain a computationally manageable inversion. Provided that $|u| \le L$ and $|v| \le L$ are sufficiently small (much smaller than the target's range) such that the right side of (3.73) is invariant of (u, v), that is,

$$\eta(x, y) \approx 2\cos(\psi - \phi),$$

then the temporal Doppler shift in (3.72) also becomes *invariant* of the transmitter/receiver position. This approximation allows the user to image the target region in the spatial domain for all reflectors that possess a common $v_o \cos(\psi - \phi)$ (temporal Doppler shift). The resultant is a three-dimensional reflectivity function, $f[x, y, v_o \cos(\psi - \phi)]$.

- *This procedure does not provide the user with the* **velocity** *distribution since the three-dimensional reflectivity function $f[x, y, v_o \cos(\psi - \phi)]$ depends on $v_o \cos(\psi - \phi)$. One may use another set of measurements, made simultaneously with another phased array from another view angle, that is,* **stereo** *measurements, to construct a four-dimensional reflectivity function that depends on (x, y, v_o, ψ). The resultant reconstructed image carries information on a target's velocity vector as well as its location in the imaging scene. This imaging scheme is similar to the stereo radar system shown in Figure 3.5b for estimating a moving target's velocity.*

Next, we examine the imaging problem via the spherical wave decomposition without requiring the above-mentioned approximations that assume that the aperture length, that is, $2L$, is much smaller than the target's range. The use of a larger aperture not only improves the cross-range resolution but also generates a database analogous to the one acquired via two distant stereo monopulse radars for velocity imaging. In fact, a closer and more accurate examination of the system model in this imaging problem via the spatial Doppler phenomenon would indicate that a single phased array is sufficient for obtaining the four-dimensional spatial-velocity image of the target scene.

The total transmitted signal experienced at the reflector is the sum of the radiation patterns of the array's elements, that is, all $u \in [-L, L]$. Using the spherical wave decomposition for the phase function in (3.71) and the steps used in Section 3.6, the total signal at the reflector at (x, y) becomes

$$A_\ell \; H(k_\ell \sin\theta, \omega_\ell) \; \underbrace{\exp[-j(k_\ell \cos\theta x + k_\ell \sin\theta y)]}_{Coordinates\ information}$$

$$\times \; \exp(j\omega_\ell t) \; \underbrace{\exp[jk_\ell v_o \cos(\theta - \psi)t]}_{Doppler\ information},$$

where $k_\ell = \frac{\omega_\ell}{c}$.

An identical analysis can be performed for the receive mode of the phased array. The total recorded signal due to the moving reflector at (x, y) is

$$A_\ell \; H^2(k_\ell \sin\theta, \omega_\ell) \; \underbrace{\exp[-j(2k_\ell \cos\theta x + 2k_\ell \sin\theta y)]}_{Coordinates\ information}$$

$$\times \; \exp(j\omega_\ell t) \; \underbrace{\exp[j2k_\ell v_o \cos(\theta - \psi)t]}_{Doppler\ information}. \tag{3.74}$$

The linear phase function of (x, y) in (3.74), that is,

$$\exp[-j(2k_\ell \cos\theta x + 2k_\ell \sin\theta y)],$$

provides spatial frequency domain polar data for imaging the target function in the (x, y) domain that was described in Section 3.6. The other phase function in (3.74), that is,

$$\exp[j2k_\ell v_o \cos(\theta - \psi)t],$$

contains information on the temporal Doppler frequency shift in the carrier ω_ℓ that is induced by the reflector's motion. The temporal Doppler frequency shift is

$$2k_\ell v_o \cos(\theta - \psi).$$

The four-dimensional spatial-velocity imaging of a nonrigid moving target may now be accomplished using the system model in (3.74). For the imaging process, one may use the following steps:

Step 1. *For a given velocity vector (v_o, ψ), retrieve the temporal frequency Doppler data that reside on the contour $2k_\ell v_o \cos(\theta - \psi)$ in the (θ, ω_ℓ) domain.*

Step 2. *Use the inversion algorithm for phased array scan data described in Section 3.6 to image the reflectors that move with the velocity vector (v_o, ψ).*

Step 3. *Select another velocity vector and repeat Steps 1 and 2.*

The above procedure is computationally intensive. This should be anticipated since we are dealing with a four-dimensional imaging problem. In this problem, we are forced to perform the imaging for a *range* of values of (v_o, ψ) since the moving target under study is *nonrigid*.

- *The scanning, that is, varying θ, is done in a sequential function of time. Thus, a given moving reflector does not possess the same reference coordinates at all scan angles. If the θ-th scan has a delay of t_θ, then the following phase delay*

$$\exp[-j2k_\ell v_o \cos(\theta - \psi)t_\theta],$$

should be added to the system model in (3.74), and should be incorporated in the inversion algorithm. This phase compensates for the fact that the reflector's location varies as scan angle is changed.

Constraints

In the case of FM-CW phased array imaging, the sampling constraints in the aperture and time domains and processing issues that are associated with them are identical to the ones described in Section

3.7. The only additional constraints are on the spectral separation of the FM-CW harmonics; these are described next.

We denote the maximum and minimum values of the spectral separation lines for the aperiodic FM-CW signal by Ω_Δ and ω_δ, respectively; that is,

$$\Omega_\delta \leq \Omega_\ell - \Omega_{\ell-1} \leq \Omega_\Delta,$$

for the available ℓ. As we mentioned before, the Doppler information is in the following sinusoidal phase function:

$$\exp[j2k_\ell v_o \cos(\theta - \psi)t].$$

The temporal Doppler shifted components at the ℓ-th harmonic would not overlap with the temporal Doppler shifted components of the other harmonics provided that

$$2k_\ell\, v_{max} \leq \frac{\Omega_\delta}{2},$$

where v_{max} is the maximum value of $v_o(x,y)$. For the case of periodic FM-CW signaling where $\Omega_\delta = \omega_2 = \frac{2\pi}{t_2}$, the above constraint becomes

$$4v_{max}\, t_2 \leq \lambda,$$

where λ is the smallest wavelength in the illuminating FM-CW signal.

The other constraint comes from the Nyquist sampling requirement in the k_x domain that was also discussed in Section 3.7 in terms of sample spacing in the wavenumber domain, that is, k. For FM-CW phased array imaging, the largest sample spacing in the wavenumber domain, that is, k_ℓ's, is $\frac{\Omega_\Delta}{c}$. Thus, if the depth of the imaging area is r_0, then we should satisfy the following constraint (see Section 3.7):

$$\Omega_\Delta \leq \frac{2\pi c}{2r_0}.$$

For the case of periodic FM-CW signaling where $\Omega_\Delta = \omega_2 = \frac{2\pi}{t_2}$, the above constraint becomes

$$t_2 \geq \frac{2r_0}{c}.$$

Based on this constraint, one should select the pri, t_2, to be greater than the arrival time difference between the echoes from the nearest point in the target region and the farthest point in the target region. A similar constraint should also be satisfied in other echo imaging systems that utilize FM-CW signaling.

Spatial Resolution

Recall the constraint in (3.37) that dictated the cross-range resolution for phased array imaging of a static target; that is,

$$| - \tan \theta \, x + y| \ \leq \ L.$$

This yielded the following band in the θ for the scan angles that illuminate the static reflector at (x, y):

$$\Omega(x, y) \equiv \left[\arctan(\frac{y - L}{x}), \arctan(\frac{y + L}{x}) \right].$$

Using a similar analysis, one can show that a moving reflector at (x, y) is illuminated by the array's radiation pattern at scan angle θ provided that

$$| - \tan \theta (x + v_o \cos \psi t) + (y + v_o \sin \psi t)| \ \leq \ L.$$

This has interesting implications. Depending on the velocity vector of the reflector, the moving reflector's support band in the scan angle might be smaller, equal, or even greater than $\Omega(x, y)$.

At one extreme, the reflector could be completely missed by all the phased array's scanned beams. In this case, the target is not resolvable anymore. At the other extreme, the target could be in *all* of the phased array's scanned beams. For this scenario, we anticipate a resolution that is *better* than the Rayleigh resolution, that is, $\frac{r_0 \lambda}{4L}$. This corresponds to the array imaging method described in Chapter 4 where the target motion *synthesizes* the effect of an aperture that is larger than the physical array.

This fact is demonstrated in Figures 3.14a-b for a sonar imaging problem. These figures show the phased array data versus the temporal

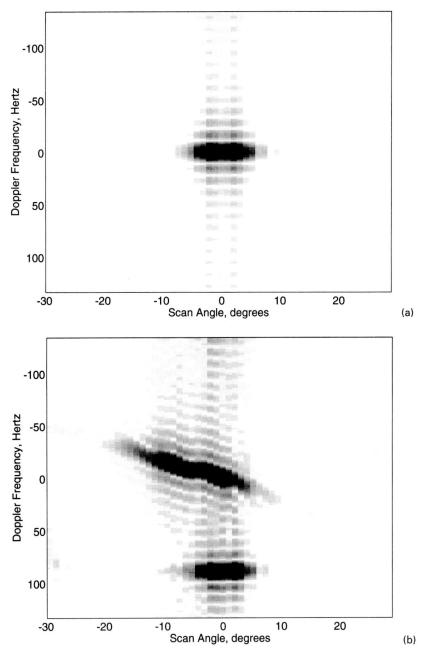

Figure 3.14 Phased array Doppler data. (a) Two stationary targets. (b) Two moving targets.

Doppler frequency and scan angle domains at a given harmonic of the illuminated FM-CW signal. The parameters of this imaging problem are as follows: the broadside range $r_0 = 200$ meters; the array aperture is $2L = 40$ meters and there are 56 elements on this aperture (28 transmitters and 28 receivers); the scan angle interval is $[-\theta_0, \theta_0] = [-30, 30]$ degrees and 56 scan angles are used in this interval; the propagation speed is $c = 1500$ meters/second; the FM-CW harmonic studied is at 1 KHz; the CW coherent processing time $t_3 = 89.3$ milliseconds and 199 time samples are taken in this period; the total data acquisition time, that is, the number of scan angles times t_3, is 5 seconds.

Two targets are used for this example. Both targets are located at (200,0) meters at the midpoint of the data acquisition interval. Figure 3.14a shows the targets' signature when the targets are not moving. As anticipated, the temporal Doppler frequency shift for both targets is equal to zero and, thus, the two signatures overlap with each other.

Next, we associate equal nonzero speed $v_o = 67.2$ meters/second with both targets. However, one target is moving parallel to the x-axis (i.e., $\psi = 0$), and the other one is moving parallel to the y-axis (i.e., $\psi = \pi/2$). Figure 3.14b is the resultant Doppler signature. Notice that the target with $\psi = 0$ does not show a significant increase in its support band in the scan angle domain as compared with the one shown in Figure 3.14a for static targets. This is due to the fact that this target's motion, that is parallel to the x-axis (range), does not synthesize a larger aperture to improve resolution in the cross-range domain. Meanwhile, the other target with $\psi = \pi/2$, that is, its motion is parallel to the cross-range domain y, does show a larger support band in the scan angle domain that yields better cross-range resolution than the static target scenario. The principles associated with cross-range resolution in synthetic aperture array imaging are discussed in Chapter 4.

One encounters a different scenario in phased array imaging of blood flow in diagnostic medicine. In these problems, the continuous blood flow produces a *regenerating* moving target scene. To simulate this case, we use $t_\theta = 0$ with the following parameters: $r_0=5$ cm; $L = 2$ cm and there are 100 elements on the array (50 transmitters and 50 receivers); $\theta_0 = 23.58$ degrees and the number of scan angles is 66; $\lambda = .1$ cm; $t_3 = 30$

milliseconds with 48 samples during the coherent processing time; the two moving targets have $v_o = 13.2$ cm/second and $\psi = 0, \pi/2$; the total data acquisition time is 2 seconds. Figure 3.15 shows the phased array Doppler data of these two targets.

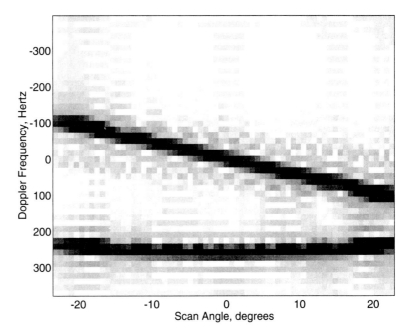

Figure 3.15 Phased array Doppler data for two regenerating moving targets (flow).

Velocity Resolution

The ability of the user to resolve Doppler cells in the frequency domain is dictated by the sharpness of the FM-CW spectral lines. This sharpness is determined by the support band of the sinc function $A_3(\omega)$ that is approximately equal to the width of its main lobe, that is, $\omega_3 = \frac{2\pi}{t_3}$. Thus, the Doppler resolution in FM-CW phased array imaging is

$$\Delta_{\omega_D} = \omega_3.$$

The temporal Doppler frequency shift for an arbitrary reflector is

$$\omega_D \equiv 2k_\ell v_o \cos(\theta - \psi).$$

Moreover, we have the following differentials:

$$\frac{\partial \omega_D}{\partial v_o} = 2k_\ell \ \cos(\psi - \theta)$$

$$\frac{\partial \omega_D}{\partial \psi} = 2k_\ell \ v_o \ \sin(\psi - \theta).$$

Thus, the resolution in the (v_o, ψ) domain is

$$\Delta_{v_o} = \frac{\Delta_{\omega_D}}{\left|\frac{\partial \omega_D}{\partial v_o}\right|} \tag{3.75}$$

$$= \frac{\omega_3}{2k_\ell \ |\cos(\psi - \theta)|},$$

and

$$\Delta_\psi = \frac{\Delta_{\omega_D}}{\left|\frac{\partial \omega_D}{\partial \psi}\right|} \tag{3.76}$$

$$= \frac{\omega_3}{2k_\ell \ v_o \ |\sin(\psi - \theta)|}.$$

Equations (3.75) and (3.76) correspond to a *shift-varying* resolution. The following observations can be made from these equations:

i. *Resolution in both speed, v_o, and direction of motion, ψ, improve when the wavelength is decreased.*

ii. *Resolution in both speed, v_o, and direction of motion, ψ, improve when the CW illumination time, t_3, is increased.*

iii. *The resolution in the v_o domain improves when $|\psi - \theta|$ approaches 0 or 2π.*

iv. *The resolution in the ψ domain deteriorates when $|\psi - \theta|$ approaches 0 or 2π.*

v. *The resolution in the ψ domain improves as v_o gets larger.*

The conclusions in items i and ii can be found in other CW signaling-based imaging systems. The results in items iii and iv relate the scan angle in phased array imaging to resolution in the velocity domain. These state that if the target direction of motion is parallel to the scan direction, then the resolution in the speed domain improves while the resolution in the angle of motion domain worsens. Similar principles govern velocity resolution in stereo (monopulse) radar where the phased array radiation pattern is approximated to be focused at each scan angle.

Another quantitative measure of resolution in the velocity domain can be constructed via considering a fixed value of (x, y) and the following ambiguity function in the (v_o, ψ) domain:

$$\Gamma(\hat{v}_o, \hat{\psi}) \equiv | \sum_\ell \int_\theta \int_t |A_\ell \ H^2(k_\ell \sin \theta, \omega_\ell)|^2$$

$$\times \ \exp\left[\ j2k_\ell[v_o \cos(\theta - \psi) - \hat{v}_o \cos(\theta - \hat{\psi})]t \ \right] \ dt \ d\theta|,$$

where the integral over t is over the period of CW signaling, that is, t_3, and the integral over θ is over the resolution scan angles, that is, $\theta \in \Omega(x, y)$, where $\Omega(x, y)$ is a function of the aperture length as described in Section 3.7 and (3.38).

Carrying out the integral over time on the right side of the ambiguity function results in the following:

$$\Gamma(\hat{v}_o, \hat{\psi}) = | \sum_\ell \int_\theta |A_\ell \ H^2(k_\ell \sin \theta, \omega_\ell)|^2$$

$$\times \ \text{sinc}\left[\ k_\ell[v_o \cos(\theta - \psi) - \hat{v}_o \cos(\theta - \hat{\psi})]t_3 \ \right] \ d\theta|.$$

Finally, it should be noted that the Doppler frequency contours for two targets, for example,

$$2k_\ell v_{o1} \cos(\theta - \psi_1),$$

and

$$2k_\ell v_{o2} \cos(\theta - \psi_2),$$

may have an intersection point (area) in the (θ, ω_ℓ) domain no matter what the velocity resolution is. The samples of the two targets at that intersection point area are not separable in the (θ, ω_ℓ) domain. In this case, some of the samples of one target leaks into the reconstructed image for the other target. This could introduce serious errors (e.g., a target spatial reconstruction may appear in several velocity values) or could result in negligible errors. This depends on the targets' relative location, velocity, aperture length, and various other parameters of the imaging system.

PROJECTS

1. Simulate the range-focused and beam-steered radiation patterns similar to the ones shown in the example of Section 3.3.

2. Repeat Project 1 using various weight functions for the aperture window as mentioned for the generalized beamformer in Section 3.4.

3. Use the coherent temporal Fourier processing (electronically scanning arrays) described in Section 3.5 to image and estimate the speeds of multiple moving targets in the polar spatial domain. This image can be converted to the target image in the rectangular spatial domain via interpolation.

4. Simulate the data acquisition system and imaging geometry for the spatial Doppler-based phased array imaging of Section 3.6. Develop the reconstruction algorithm for this system.

5. Simulate the data acquisition system and imaging geometry for the spatial-velocity imaging with FM-CW signaling described in Section 3.10. Develop the spatial reconstruction algorithm for this system for a fixed velocity vector. Develop the ambiguity function for this problem.

REFERENCES

1. D. E. Dudgeon and R. M. Mersereau, *Multidimensional Digital Signal Processing,* Englewood Cliffs, NJ: Prentice Hall, 1984.

2. R. Hoctor and S. Kassam, "The unifying role of the coarray in aperture synthesis for coherent and incoherent imaging," *Proc. IEEE,* vol. 78, pp. 735-752, April 1990.

3. A. Macovski, "Ultrasonic imaging using arrays," *Proc. IEEE,* p. 484, April 1979.

4. P. Morse and H. Feshbach, *Methods of Theoretical Physics,* New York: McGraw Hill, 1968.

5. M. I. Skolnik, *Introduction to Radar Systems,* New York: McGraw-Hill, 1980.

6. M. Soumekh, "Band-limited interpolation from unevenly spaced sampled data," *IEEE Trans. on Acoustics, Speech and Signal Processing,* vol. ASSP-36, pp. 110-122, January 1988.

7. M. Soumekh, "Array imaging with beam-steered data," *IEEE Trans. on Image Processing,* July 1992.

8. B. D. Steinberg, *Principles of Aperture and Array System Design,* New York: Wiley, 1976.

9. H. Van Tress, *Detection, Estimation and Modulation Theory,* Part III, New York: Wiley, 1971.

Chapter 4

SYNTHETIC APERTURE ARRAY IMAGING

We now examine an array imaging system that utilizes the motion of a *single* element transducer to synthesize the effect of a phased array with a size equal to the path length that the element traverses. Synthetic aperture array, also known as Synthetic Aperture Radar (SAR), has already become a viable technology in remote sensing problems of radar. A mobile element, with a dimension much smaller than a phased array's size, could also bring flexibility in data acquisition and processing for array imaging systems of diagnostic medicine and nondestructive testing. In particular, synthetic aperture array imaging may provide ways for imaging a target that cannot be studied with phased arrays due to constraints imposed by the target's anatomy. We refer to synthetic aperture array imaging as SAR imaging throughout this chapter.

4.1 SYNTHETIC APERTURE RADAR

This chapter is concerned with the inversion algorithms for and signal processing issues associated with SAR and Inverse SAR (ISAR) imaging. Due to the fact that the antenna's aperture is much smaller than the target's range in most radar imaging problems, one has to improve on the cross-range resolution by employing *synthesized* imaging geometries.

SAR is a coherent active imaging method that utilizes the motion of a radar mounted on a vehicle such as an aircraft (airborne SAR) or a satellite (spaceborne SAR) to synthesize the effect of a large aperture array [1]-[7],[9]-[10],[12]-[15]. The motion of the vehicle results in the collection of echoed signals from the target when illuminated with the radar's radiation pattern from various views. The SAR imaging (inverse) problem is to integrate these echoed signals for high-resolution imaging. In a similar fashion, ISAR exploits the motion of the target to synthesize a large aperture imaging system.

It is more convenient to first formulate and present SAR imaging in a two-dimensional spatial domain that is referred to as *ground-plane* SAR. The resulting principles and algorithms are then carried to three-dimensional SAR systems, called *slant-plane* SAR, and three-dimensional imaging using interferometric (stereo) SAR.

Our analysis starts with the study of linear array (airborne) monostatic SAR imaging with a pulsed radar. *Pulsed* SAR imaging is based on the principle of *position-induced* synthetic aperture. The data acquisition for these imaging systems is composed of a monostatic radar that illuminates the target with a single large-bandwidth pulse and records the resultant echoed signal for that transmission. This procedure is repeated as the radar-carrying vehicle changes its coordinates (aspect angle) with respect to the target to synthesize the effect of a large aperture antenna.

The corresponding system model assumes that the vehicle stops, makes a transmission and its corresponding reception, and then moves to its next coordinates on the synthetic aperture. This imaging scheme does not rely on temporal Doppler information in the echoed signal that is caused by the difference between the radar and the target velocities. The effect of the temporal Doppler shift, which cannot be determined accurately when the radar signal is a pulse with a flat large-bandwidth spectrum, is negligible in the inversion algorithm.

After developing a system model for pulsed SAR, we present three inverse methods for SAR imaging. The first method is based on the spatial Fourier (Doppler) decomposition for the Green's function examined in Section 2.3. This method does not make any approximations in the SAR system model and does not require any constraints on the relative size of the synthetic aperture for its image formation.

The second inversion is the Fresnel approximation-based method that was first introduced for *strip map-mode* SAR imaging, for example, [1],[4],[6]. This method fails rapidly as the synthetic aperture size (that determines resolution) becomes greater than the extent of the illuminated target area. Other factors, such as increasing the radar signal's temporal frequency, also result in the failure of this inversion; these will be shown.

The third inversion is the plane wave approximation-based method. The plane wave approximation-based inversion for radar detection was first suggested by Bojarski [3]. Lewis [7] speculated that Bojarski's inversion may be used to fuse the signatures of a target obtained at various view angles to *image* the target's reflectivity function, a concept similar to SAR imaging. The plane wave approximation-based inversion for SAR imaging has been extensively documented, for example, [1],[9]. It imposes less restrictions on the relative size of the synthetic aperture than the Fresnel approximation-based inversion. Due to this fact, it is used for *spotlight-mode* SAR where relatively large synthetic apertures are used for improving cross-range resolution.

After developing imaging principles for linear array monostatic SAR with a pulsed radar, we examine temporal Doppler-based SAR imaging and the use of FM-CW signaling in these problems. *Continuous wave* SAR imaging utilizes the temporal Doppler shifts in the echoed signal caused by the difference between the radar and target velocities; this results in a *motion-induced* synthetic aperture.

To achieve good resolution in range, these SAR systems continuously illuminate the target with a periodic large-bandwidth (FM) signal. The radar system used is a quasi-monostatic one to record the echoed signal while irradiating the target. The length of the coherent processing time on the echoed signal is one of the factors that determines resolution; a larger coherent processing time yields better resolution. A major drawback for the classical (Fresnel or plane wave approximation-based) inverse methods for FM-CW SAR imaging is that the radar-target relative aspect angle varies during the coherent processing time. This results in a problem known as motion through resolution cells.

We will develop an inverse method for FM-CW SAR imaging that does not suffer from motion through resolution errors. The approach is based on the spherical wave decomposition principle in terms of plane waves, that is, the spatial Doppler phenomenon. We will show that FM-CW SAR and pulsed SAR possess identical sampling constraints for and imaging information in their measurement domains. Bistatic SAR imaging is briefly discussed. The chapter closes with the analysis of spaceborne SAR imaging with pulsed and FM-CW radar signaling.

4.2 PULSED SAR SYSTEM MODEL

We begin by considering a two-dimensional imaging system encountered in the ground-plane SAR geometry (Figure 4.1a); the slant-plane geometry will be treated using the same principles in the later sections. In this case, both the radar and the target under study lie on a plane, for example, $z = 0$, in the spatial domain. We use vectors (x, y) and (k_x, k_y) to identify, respectively, the spatial and the spatial frequency domains. The x-coordinate is used to identify range (a more proper term is slant-range as we will show), and y specifies the cross-range domain.

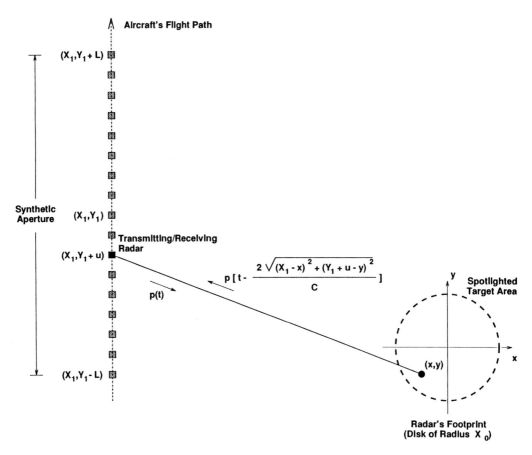

Figure 4.1a Imaging system geometry for airborne monostatic SAR imaging.

- *We will show in Section 4.6 that the above-mentioned two-dimensional geometry is the transformation of the three-dimensional **actual** range, cross-range, and altitude domain into the two-dimensional slant-range and cross-range domain; the slant-range, which is called x in our present discussion, is the square root of the sum of the squares of the actual range and altitude (see Figure 4.1b).*

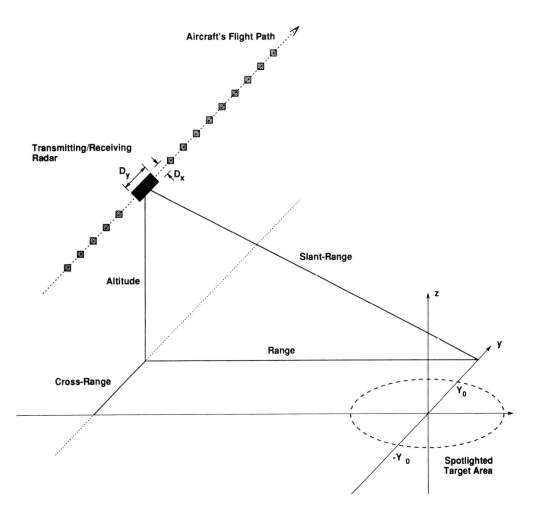

Figure 4.1b Imaging system geometry for SAR imaging in the three-dimensional spatial domain.

The transmitting/receiving radar moves along the line $x = X_1$ in the (x, y) domain. This radar makes a transmission and its corresponding reception at $(X_1, Y_1 + u)$ for $u \in [-L, +L]$ (synthesized aperture) on the (x, y) plane; X_1 (range) and Y_1 (squint-mode cross-range) are known constants; $Y_1 = 0$ corresponds to the broadside case. We denote the polar coordinates for (X_1, Y_1) by (R_1, θ_1). In Figure 4.1a, the solid square on the synthetic aperture corresponds to the position of the transmitting/receiving radar for a fixed u. The shaded squares are some of the other possible spatial coordinates for the radar along the aircraft's flight path.

- *The above-mentioned measurement scenario is unrealistic. This is due to the fact that the aircraft that carries the radar is continuously moving. Thus, in the receive mode, the radar does not have the same coordinates that it possessed in the transmit mode. However, due to the fact that the aircraft's speed is much smaller than the speed of light, one may assume that the aircraft stops, makes a transmission and its corresponding reception, and then moves to its next synthetic aperture position. Even if this is not a valid assumption in certain synthetic aperture echo imaging problems, for example, sonar, one can compensate for known motion deviations in the transmit-receive modes as shown in Section 4.5. This*

  measurement assumption for pulsed SAR imaging will not be used in FM-CW SAR imaging discussed in Section 4.10.

The target area illuminated/spotlighted by the radar (the radar's footprint) is the disk of radius X_0 centered at the origin in the spatial domain. X_0, which is defined by

$$X_0 = \frac{R_1 \lambda}{D}, \tag{4.1}$$

is a known constant; λ is the wavelength of the transmitted wave and D is the radar antenna's diameter. We mentioned in Chapter 3 that X_0, which is on the order of a kilometer, represents the resolution of the physical radar antenna without being moved to synthesize the effects of a larger aperture antenna. The physical radar antenna mounted on the vehicle could be a phased array that steers the radar's footprint electronically on the desired target area (spotlighting). When the vehicle is at the coordinates $(X_1, Y_1 + u)$, the steer angle for spotlighting is

$$\arctan(\frac{Y_1 + u}{X_1}).$$

- *In practical three-dimensional SAR systems, the physical radar antenna or the array that is mounted on the aircraft/satellite is commonly a two-dimensional rectangular planar aperture with size, for example, D_x along the slant-range direction and D_y along the cross-range direction (see Figure 4.1b). Then, D_x and D_y, respectively, determine the size of the spotlighted area in the x and y domains:*

$$X_0 = \frac{R_1 \lambda}{D_x}$$

is the spotlight extent in the x domain; and

$$Y_0 = \frac{R_1 \lambda}{D_y}$$

is the spotlight extent in the y domain. The exact expressions for (X_0, Y_0) involve the aircraft's altitude and squint angle. While one should be aware of these factors, the radar's footprint does not play a role in formulating the SAR's inverse problem; (X_0, Y_0) enter the picture when we discuss SAR system sampling constraints. Moreover, in most practical SAR systems, X_0 and Y_0 are close to each other. For notational convenience and ease of analysis, we assume that $X_0 = Y_0$ or let X_0 be the largest of the two spotlight extents. We will point out the important equations where X_0 should be replaced with Y_0.

The radar illuminates the target area with a time-dependent pulsed signal $p(t)$. The round-trip time delay of the echoed signal recorded by the radar due a point reflector at (x, y) is

$$\frac{2\sqrt{(X_1 - x)^2 + (Y_1 + u - y)^2}}{c}.$$

Thus, the total recorded echoed signal becomes (amplitude functions are suppressed)

$$s(u,t) \equiv \int \int f(x,y) \; p[t - \frac{2\sqrt{(X_1 - x)^2 + (Y_1 + u - y)^2}}{c}] \; dx dy, \quad (4.2)$$

where $f(x,y)$ is the target area's reflectivity function; the integral in the (x,y) domain is over the target region, that is, the disk of radius X_0 centered at the origin.

- *Spatial and spatial frequency domain **amplitude** functions are not critical in SAR imaging where the range is significantly greater than the object's size and synthesized aperture. Amplitude functions are suppressed throughout this chapter.*

- *The synthetic aperture domain u is generated via the motion of the aircraft in SAR (or the motion of the target in ISAR). Thus, u is equal to the constant speed of the aircraft multiplied with **time**. However, this time domain is different from the time-delay domain that is identified via t in (4.2). The length of time for the pulsed signal to make its round-trip travel between the radar and a target reflector is **much smaller** than the length of time for the aircraft to travel the spatial interval of length $2L$ that is, the size of the synthetic aperture. This is due to the fact that the wave propagation speed c is much larger than the aircraft's speed. For this reason, the synthetic aperture domain u is also called the **slow-time** domain and the time-delay domain t is referred to as the **fast-time** domain. In our discussion on FM-CW SAR imaging, the slow-time and fast-time domains will be represented by the same variable.*

Figure 4.2 is a depiction of transmitted and received time domain signals in pulsed SAR imaging for three discrete coordinates of the moving radar. The transmitted signal is shown to be a rectangular pulse amplitude modulating a sinusoidal carrier; this signal a multi-frequency bandpass signal (a sinc function centered around the carrier frequency in the temporal frequency domain).

The resultant echoed signal is a linear combination of delayed versions of the transmitted pulse [as shown in eq. (4.2)] and, thus, is a bandpass signal with its band centered around the carrier frequency. The transmitted pulsed signal could be any multi-frequency bandpass signal, for example, a chirp signal in the time domain.

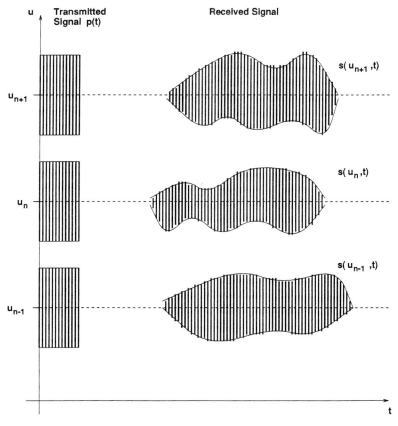

Figure 4.2 A depiction of transmitted and received signals in pulsed SAR imaging.

Taking the temporal (**fast-time**) Fourier transform of both sides of
(4.2) yields [for notational simplicity, we use $s(u, \omega)$ to represent the
temporal/fast-time Fourier transform of $s(u, t)$]

$$s(u, \omega) = P(\omega) \int \int f(x, y) \exp[-j2k\sqrt{(X_1 - x)^2 + (Y_1 + u - y)^2}] dx dy.$$
(4.3)

Developing inverse methods based on the system model in (4.3) is described next. For notational simplicity, we also denote the normalized
version of $s(u, \omega)$ by $p(\omega)$, that is, $\frac{s(u,\omega)}{P(\omega)}$ or its matched-filtered form that
is $s(u, \omega) \, P^*(\omega)$ by $s(u, \omega)$.

• *The normalized system model, that is,*

$$s(u, \omega) = \int \int f(x, y) \, \exp[-j2k\sqrt{(X_1 - x)^2 + (Y_1 + u - y)^2}] \, dx dy,$$

*is a two-dimensional **convolution** integral. This integral represents the
input/output relationship in a two-dimensional LSI system: the input to
the LSI system is the target function $f(x, y)$; the impulse response of
the LSI system is the Green's function at frequency 2ω, that is,*

$$\exp[-j2k\sqrt{x^2 + y^2}];$$

and the output measurement in the spatial domain is made at

$$(x, y) \equiv (X_1, Y_1 + u),$$

that are the coordinates of the aircraft that carries the radar antenna.

Figure 4.3 shows examples of the SAR signal $s(u, \omega)$ in the synthetic
aperture for a fixed ω. Figures 4.3a and 4.3b are for a broadside (i.e.,
$\theta_1 = 0$) and a squint-mode (i.e., $\theta_1 \neq 0$) scenario, respectively. Both
signals exhibit a chirp-type behavior in the u domain; this phenomenon
has nothing to do with the nature of the transmitted pulse signal in the
time domain t that, as we mentioned earlier, could be chosen to be a
chirp signal. It is shown in [15] that $s(u, \omega)$ satisfies a chirp differential
equation.

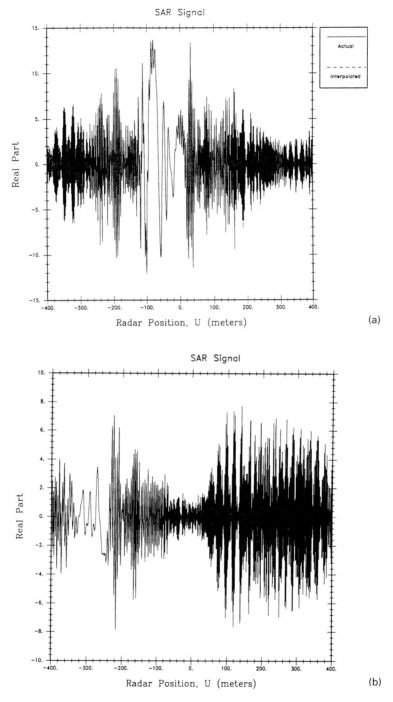

Figure 4.3 Two examples of SAR signal $s(u, \omega)$. (a) Broadside. (b) Squint-mode.

271

4.3 PULSED SAR SPATIAL DOPPLER-BASED INVERSION

The spherical wave with wavenumber $2k$ on the right side of (4.3), that is,

$$\exp[-j2k\sqrt{(X_1-x)^2+(Y_1+u-y)^2}],$$

was shown in Section 2.3 to have the following spatial Fourier (**slow-time Doppler**) decomposition in terms of plane waves (amplitude function $\frac{1}{\sqrt{4k^2-k_u^2}}$ is suppressed):

$$\int_{-2k}^{2k}\exp[j\sqrt{4k^2-k_u^2}\,(X_1-x)+jk_u(Y_1+u-y)]\,dk_u \qquad (4.4)$$

As mentioned earlier, the significance of this decomposition is in the fact that it transforms nonlinear phase functions of (x,y,u) into linear phase functions of (x,y,u).

Substituting (4.4) for the spherical wave function in the system model (4.3), and after some rearrangements, one obtains the following:

$$s(u,\omega) = \int_{-2k}^{2k}\exp(j\sqrt{4k^2-k_u^2}\,X_1+jk_uY_1)\,\exp(jk_uu)$$
$$\times\underbrace{\left[\int\int f(x,y)\exp[-j(\sqrt{4k^2-k_u^2}\,x+k_uy)]dxdy\right]}_{Two\ dimensional\ Fourier\ integral}\,dk_u$$
$$=\int_{-2k}^{2k}\exp(j\sqrt{4k^2-k_u^2}\,X_1+jk_uY_1)$$
$$\times\,F(\sqrt{4k^2-k_u^2},k_u)\,\exp(jk_uu)\,dk_u.$$
$$(4.5)$$

At the present time, we assume that the radar makes measurements for $u \in (-\infty,\infty)$; we will examine finite aperture effects in later sections. Taking the spatial (**slow-time**) Fourier transform of both sides of (4.5) with respect to u (Doppler processing) yields the following:

$$S(k_u,\omega) = \exp(j\sqrt{4k^2-k_u^2}\,X_1+jk_uY_1)\,F(\sqrt{4k^2-k_u^2},k_u). \qquad (4.6)$$

Finally, from (4.6), we can write the following inversion:

$$F(k_x, k_y) = \exp(-j\sqrt{4k^2 - k_u^2}\, X_1 - jk_u Y_1)\, S(k_u, \omega), \qquad (4.7)$$

where

$$\begin{aligned} k_x &\equiv \sqrt{4k^2 - k_u^2} \\ k_y &\equiv k_u \end{aligned} \qquad (4.8)$$

represent the contours of the available data to reconstruct $F(\cdot, \cdot)$ from the spatial Doppler data. An example of the spatial frequency coverage dictated by (4.8) is depicted in Figure 4.4. Note that this coverage is similar, though not identical, to the *polar* data coverage of a phased array that was discussed in Chapter 3.

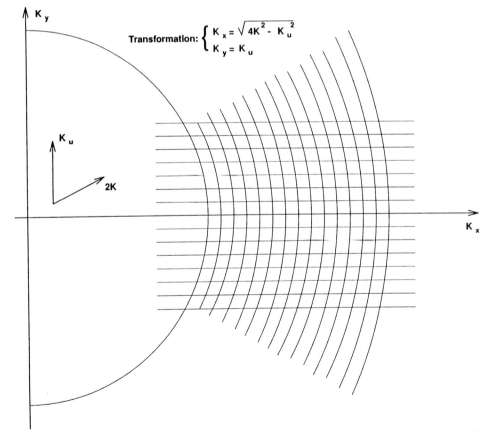

Figure 4.4 Mapping of the measurement domain $(k_u, 2k)$ into the target's spatial frequency domain (k_x, k_y) in monostatic SAR/ISAR imaging.

We observe from (4.7) that with $(X_1, Y_1) = (0, 0)$ (i.e., the origin is at the center of the synthesized aperture), the *two-dimensional fast-time and slow-time Fourier SAR data* become equal to the spatial Fourier transform of the target's reflectivity function. The role of the *linear* phase function of (k_x, k_y) in (4.7), that is, $\exp(-jk_x X_1 - jk_y Y_1)$, is simply to center the target area (i.e., the disk of radius X_0) at the origin in the spatial domain (baseband conversion). This is a practical requirement for the reconstruction algorithm (the interpolation as well as inverse discrete Fourier transformation; see the next section).

4.4 RESOLUTION, RECONSTRUCTION, AND SAMPLING CONSTRAINTS

Figure 4.5 shows the data acquisition system for monostatic active SAR imaging. The radar signal is composed of temporal frequencies or, equivalently, wavenumbers in a bandpass region identified via $k \in [k_1, k_2]$. Without loss of generality, we assume that the temporal data are processed in a fashion such that samples of $s(k_u, \omega)$ are available at evenly spaced values of $k \in [k_1, k_2]$ with sample spacing Δ_k. (Clearly, Δ_k is inversely proportional to the coherent processing of the echoed data in the time domain.) We denote the wavenumber for the center temporal frequency of the radar signal by $k_c \equiv \frac{k_2 + k_1}{2}$. Suppose the radar measurements are made for $u \in [-L, L]$ with even sample spacing of Δ_u. (Δ_u, Δ_k) are the *input* parameters of the imaging system. We also define the *output* parameters of the imaging system to be (Δ_x, Δ_y), the range and cross-range resolutions. In this section, we develop principles to determine the input parameters of a SAR problem for an error-free reconstruction as well as the resultant output parameters.

Sampling on the Synthetic Aperture

We begin by rewriting the system model (4.3) using the spatial Fourier decomposition of the spherical wave; this yields for the SAR data

$$s(u, \omega) = \int\int f(x, y) \times$$

$$\left[\int_{-2k}^{2k} \exp[j\sqrt{4k^2 - k_u^2}(X_1 - x) + jk_u(Y_1 + u - y)]dk_u \right]dxdy,$$

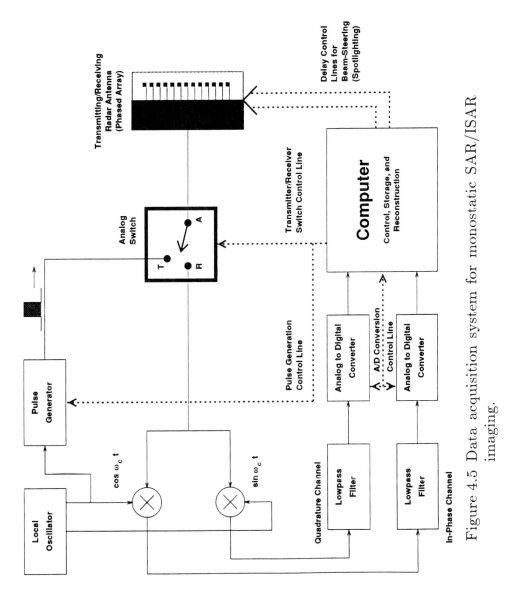

Figure 4.5 Data acquisition system for monostatic SAR/ISAR imaging.

that can be expressed as follows:

$$s(u,\omega) = \int\int f(x,y) \times$$
$$\mathcal{F}_{(k_u)}^{-1}\left[\exp[j\sqrt{4k^2 - k_u^2}\,(X_1 - x) + jk_u(Y_1 - y)] \right] dx\,dy \tag{4.9}$$

for $u \in [-L, L]$, and zero otherwise. We next perform the slow-time Doppler analysis (Fourier transform with respect to u) on $s(u,\omega)$ and take into account finite aperture effects (i.e., $L < \infty$).

By incorporating the fact that we have access only to the values of $u \in [-L, L]$, the Fourier transform with respect to u of both sides of (4.9) yields

$$S(k_u, \omega) = \int\int dx\,dy\,f(x,y) \times$$
$$\left[\exp[j\sqrt{4k^2 - k_u^2}\,(X_1 - x) + jk_u(Y_1 - y)] \, * \, 2L\frac{\sin(Lk_u)}{Lk_u} \right], \tag{4.9a}$$

where $*$ denotes convolution in the k_u domain. Note that the aperture transfer function, that is, $2L\frac{\sin(Lk_u)}{Lk_u}$ (sinc function), is a lowpass filter. Hence, the convolution of this filter with the phase modulated function $\exp[j\sqrt{4k^2 - k_u^2}\,(X_1 - x) + jk_u(Y_1 - y)]$ approximately results in the suppression (filtering) of the components of the PM wave at the values of k_u where the instantaneous frequency of the PM wave falls outside the interval $[-L, L]$.

For a point scatterer at (x, y), the instantaneous frequency of the phase modulated function in the k_u domain is found via

$$\frac{\partial}{\partial k_u}\left[\sqrt{4k^2 - k_u^2}\,(X_1 - x) + k_u(Y_1 - y)\right] = \frac{-k_u}{\sqrt{4k^2 - k_u^2}}(X_1 - x) + (Y_1 - y).$$

Hence, the range of k_u values where the PM wave is not suppressed is found from the following inequalities:

$$-L \leq \frac{-k_u}{\sqrt{4k^2 - k_u^2}}(X_1 - x) + (Y_1 - y) \leq L. \tag{4.10}$$

Solving for this interval from (4.10), one obtains the following band in the k_u domain (with $x, y, L \ll R_1$):

$$\Omega(y) \equiv [2k \sin \theta_1 - 2k \frac{L-y}{R_1} \cos^2 \theta_1, 2k \sin \theta_1 + 2k \frac{L+y}{R_1} \cos^2 \theta_1]. \quad (4.11)$$

Note that this band is a function of the point scatterer's cross-range, that is, y. We refer to this as the spatial Doppler phenomenon in SAR imaging. This is depicted in Figure 4.6 for a broadside and an off-broadside target.

The support band of the SAR signal $s(u, \omega)$ in the k_u domain, call it Ω_s, is the union of the support bands for the echoed signals from all point reflectors in the target region; hence

$$\Omega_s = \bigcup_{|y| \leq X_0} \Omega(y)$$

$$= \bigcup_{|y| \leq X_0} [2k \sin \theta_1 - 2k \frac{L-y}{R_1} \cos^2 \theta_1, 2k \sin \theta_1 + 2k \frac{L+y}{R_1} \cos^2 \theta_1]$$

$$= [2k \sin \theta_1 - 2k \frac{L+X_0}{R_1} \cos^2 \theta_1, 2k \sin \theta_1 + 2k \frac{L+X_0}{R_1} \cos^2 \theta_1].$$
$$(4.12)$$

- *It is more appropriate to use* Y_0*, the actual size of the spotlighted area in the cross-range domain, instead of* X_0 *in (4.12), that is,*

$$\Omega_s = [2k \sin \theta_1 - 2k \frac{L+Y_0}{R_1} \cos^2 \theta_1, 2k \sin \theta_1 + 2k \frac{L+Y_0}{R_1} \cos^2 \theta_1],$$

and the equations that are based on (4.12).

We observe from (4.12) that the SAR signal is a bandpass signal with its center spatial frequency at $k_u = 2k \sin \theta_1$ and bandwidth $4k \frac{L+X_0}{R_1} \cos^2 \theta_1$. Figure 4.7a shows a lowpass signal that is the spatial Fourier transform of the signal in Figure 4.3a (broadside; $2k \sin \theta_1 = 0$). Figure 4.7b shows a bandpass signal that is the spatial Fourier transform of the signal in Figure 4.3b (squint-mode; $2k \sin \theta_1 \neq 0$).

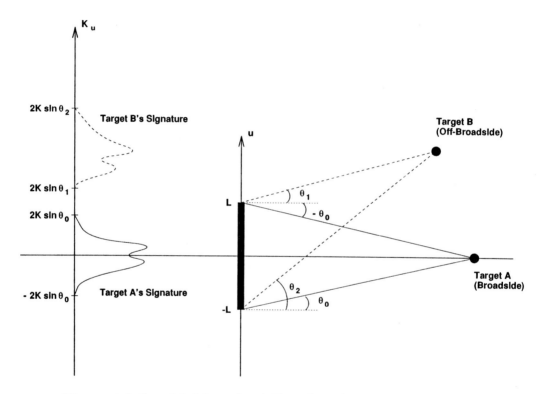

Figure 4.6 Spatial (slow-time) Doppler phenomenon in monostatic SAR/ISAR imaging.

Figure 4.8 shows the two-dimensional magnitude distribution of the SAR signal in the (k_u, ω) domain for a SAR scene composed of both a broadside target region (its signature is the vertical strip that is centered around $k_u = 0$), and a squint target region (its signature is the slanted strip that is centered around $k_u = -8\pi$ radians/meter).

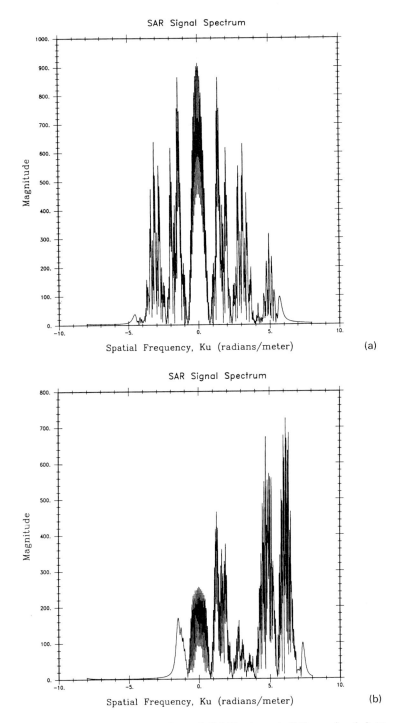

Figure 4.7 Two examples of SAR signal $S(k_u, \omega)$. (a) Broad-side. (b) Squint-mode.

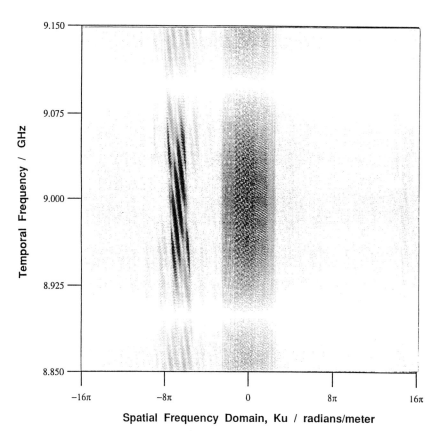

Figure 4.8 Two-dimensional magnitude distribution of SAR signal $S(k_u, \omega)$ for a SAR scene composed of both broadside and squint targets.

- *The center spatial frequency for the squint target region, i.e, $2k \sin \theta_1$, varies linearly with k (or ω). This phenomenon explains why the signature of the squint target region in Figure 4.8 is slanted. This characteristic of SAR signals will be exploited in Chapter 5 for blind-velocity SAR/ISAR imaging of moving targets.*

Based on (4.12), to sample and process the bandpass SAR signal without aliasing:

i. One should use a sample spacing in the u domain that satisfies

$$\Delta_u \leq 2\pi \frac{R_1}{4k(L + X_0)\cos^2 \theta_1};\qquad (4.13)$$

ii. The samples of the bandpass SAR signal should be multiplied by $\exp(-j2k \sin \theta_1 u)$ (bandpass to lowpass conversion) prior to the discrete Fourier transformation with respect to the discrete u's.

- *In practice, the synthetic aperture is sampled at a fixed rate for all temporal frequencies of the radar signal. Hence, the maximum value that k can attain, that is, $k = k_2$, should be used in (4.12)-(4.13) (yielding the highest required sampling rate) to determine the sample spacing across the synthetic aperture at all temporal frequencies of the radar signal.*

For the broadside case (i.e., $\theta_1 = 0$), the result shown in (4.13) is the same as the minimum sampling interval required in the plane wave approximation-based inversion to avoid nonlinear aliasing in the polar data. A disturbing feature of this sampling rate is its dependence on the length of the synthesized aperture, that is, $2L$. This clearly imposes limitations and/or introduces redundancies in the data collection by the aircraft carrying radar. We will examine a method to circumvent this problem in later sections.

There exists another constraint on the sampling rate on the synthetic aperture of a pulsed SAR system that utilizes a monostatic radar (i.e., an antenna that is used for both transmission and reception) instead of a quasi-monostatic radar. In such a scenario, the echoed signal for a given transmitted pulse should arrive prior to the transmission of the next pulse. Let t_1 be the duration of the transmitted pulse and v_R be the aircraft's speed along the cross-range domain. We denote the time interval between two successive pulses via

$$t_2 \equiv \frac{\Delta_u}{v_R};$$

t_2 is called the *pulse repetition interval* (pri); $\frac{1}{t_2}$ is called the *pulse repetition frequency* (prf). Thus, the echo from a transmitted pulse arrives prior to the next transmission provided that

$$\frac{2(R_1 + X_0)}{c} + t_1 \; < \; t_2. \qquad (4.13a)$$

Resolution

With $L, X_0 \ll R_1$, it is clear that the bandwidth of $s(u, \omega)$, that is, $4k\frac{L+X_0}{R_1}\cos^2\theta_1$, is much smaller than $2k$, which is the radius of the circular contour of the available data defined by $(k_x, k_y) = (\sqrt{4k^2 - k_u^2}, k_u)$ [see (4.8)]. Moreover, the bandwidth of the radar signal is commonly much smaller than its center frequency; that is, $k_2 - k_1 \ll k_c$. Using these facts, one can approximate (4.8) by the following:

$$k_x \approx \tan\theta_1 \left(\frac{2k}{\sin\theta_1} - k_u\right)$$
$$k_y = k_u \qquad\qquad (4.14)$$

Equation (4.14) is a linear transformation from (k_u, k) to (k_x, k_y). For this transformation, the available evenly spaced samples in the (k_u, k) domain map into *hexagonal* samples in the (k_x, k_y) domain (see Section 2.5). Suppose we denote the (k_x, k_y) domain rotated by θ_1 by $(k_{x'}, k_{y'})$. In this case, the spatial frequency coverage of the available data for a point scatterer is approximately a *rectangular* bandpass region in the $(k_{x'}, k_{y'})$ domain; the lengths of the sides of this rectangle are $\frac{4kL\cos^2\theta_1}{R_1}\frac{1}{\cos\theta_1} = \frac{4kL\cos\theta_1}{R_1}$ in the $k_{y'}$ domain [see (4.11)] and $2(k_2 - k_1)$ in the $k_{x'}$ domain.

Figure 4.9 shows the spatial frequency coverages for a broadside and an off-broadside targets. The magnitude of the image reconstructed from this form of bandpass spatial frequency coverage provides information only regarding the *surface* or *shape* of the object under study.

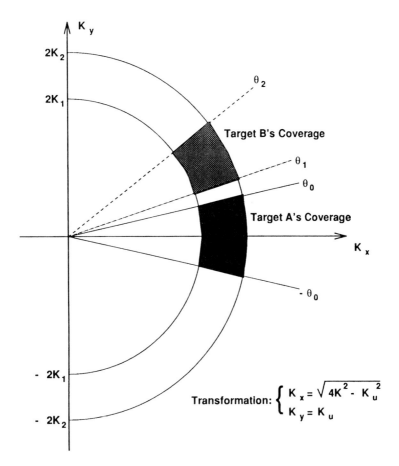

Figure 4.9 Spatial frequency coverage for a single target in monostatic SAR/ISAR imaging.

Suppose we denote the spatial domain (x, y) rotated by θ_1 by (x', y') (call them the squint range and squint cross-range domains; see Figure 4.10). In this case, the resolution of the surface reconstructed image from SAR data in the squint range domain is

$$\Delta_{x'} = \frac{2\pi}{2(k_2 - k_1)}, \qquad (4.15)$$

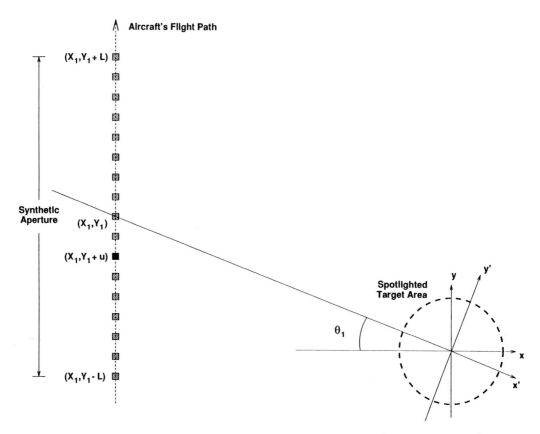

Figure 4.10 Squint-range and cross-range domains in airborne monostatic SAR imaging.

and in the squint cross-range domain is

$$\Delta_{y'} = 2\pi \frac{R_1}{4 k_c L \cos \theta_1}. \qquad (4.16)$$

For the broadside case, the result shown in (4.16) is the well-known Rayleigh resolution for imaging a target by illuminating it with a wave with wavenumber $2k$ through an aperture with length $2L$.

Zero-Padding in the Measurement Domain

The available evenly spaced samples of $S(k_u, \omega)$ map into a set of unevenly spaced samples of $F(\cdot)$ in the (k_x, k_y) domain [see (4.8) or (4.14)]. In this case, we could utilize the reconstruction and sampling principles developed in Section 2.5 for the hexagonal transformation (4.14) or (4.8). In particular, constraints in (2.22) can be used to determine Δ_{k_u} and Δ_k from X_0 and θ_1. This yields the following (for notational simplicity, it is assumed that $0 \leq \theta_1 \leq \frac{\pi}{2}$):

$$\frac{2\pi}{\Delta_{k_u}} > 2X_0 \left(1 + \tan\theta_1\right)$$

$$\frac{2\pi}{\Delta_k} > \frac{4X_0}{\cos\theta_1}$$

To translate these constraints to the parameters in the domain (u, t), we use the DFT equations of Section 1.2. This yields

$$L_0 = \frac{\pi}{\Delta_{k_u}} > X_0 \left(1 + \tan\theta_1\right)$$

$$T_0 = \frac{2\pi}{\Delta_k \, c} > \frac{4X_0}{\cos\theta_1 \, c}$$

where $[-L_0, L_0]$ is the *processed* or *zero-padded* synthetic aperture (as opposed to the actual synthetic aperture $[-L, L]$ where the measurements are made and $L \leq L_0$); and T_0 is the processed or zero padded time interval for echoed signals. The interpolation step from k_u to k_y that is required for the reconstruction algorithm (Figure 4.11) is equivalent to the zero-padding of the u domain data prior to the (discrete) spatial Fourier transformation to the k_u domain.

Reconstruction Algorithm

The reconstruction algorithm for the general squint-mode SAR imaging is shown in Figure 4.11 and is summarized next. This implementation requires three bandpass to lowpass conversions: one in the spatial domain and two in the spatial frequency domain. (There is another bandpass to lowpass conversion in the coherent processing of the temporal echoed data.) For one of these conversions, we use the fact that the available bandpass data are centered around $(k_x, k_y) = (2k_c \cos\theta_1, 2k_c \sin\theta_1)$. For a given temporal frequency of the radar signal, we perform the following operations:

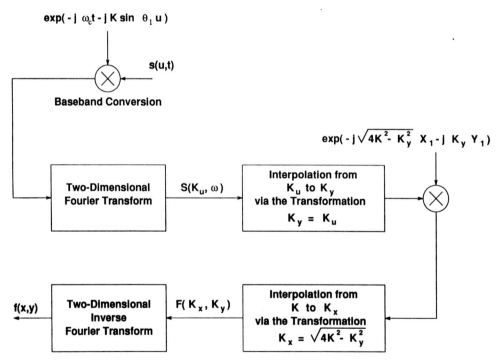

Figure 4.11 Reconstruction algorithm for monostatic SAR/ISAR imaging.

Step 1: *Multiply the data collected in the u domain by* $\exp(-j2k\sin\theta_1 u)$. This converts the bandpass synthetic aperture data in squint-mode to lowpass. This operation is essential prior to the discrete Fourier transform operation of Step 2 to avoid aliasing [see (4.12)]. The operation is unnecessary for the broadside case (i.e., $\theta_1 = 0$).

Step 2: *Take the discrete Fourier transform of the lowpass converted data in the u domain.* Note that the data obtained via this DFT operation should be assigned to the values of $k_u \in [-k_{u0} + 2k\sin\theta_1, k_{u0} + 2k\sin\theta_1]$ where $k_{u0} \equiv \frac{2\pi}{2\Delta_u}$.

Step 3: *Multiply the transformed data by* $\exp(-j\sqrt{4k^2 - k_u^2}X_1 - jk_uY_1)$. This operation shifts the origin to the center of the target region (a bandpass to lowpass conversion in the spatial domain). Any constant or amplitude function, such as the Jacobian for the UFR [11] reconstruction, could also be incorporated in this step.

Step 4: *Assign the resultant data to*

$$(k_x, k_y) = (\sqrt{4k^2 - k_u^2} - 2k_c\cos\theta_1, k_u - 2k_c\sin\theta_1).$$

This operation performs the spatial frequency data assignment as dictated by (4.8). It also shifts the bandpass spatial frequency data to the lowpass spatial frequency domain via subtracting $(2k_c\cos\theta_1, 2k_c\sin\theta_1)$ from the spatial frequencies identified in (4.8). This introduces a linear phase function in the (x, y) domain that is transparent in the final magnitude reconstruction. The shift should be the same for all temporal frequencies (that is why k_c is used.), otherwise, the reconstructed spatial domain data would exhibit undesirable compressions and expansions.

Step 5: *Interpolate the assigned unevenly spaced data on a lowpass uniform grid in the spatial frequency domain.*

Step 6: *Repeat Steps 1-5 for the available temporal frequencies of the radar signal.*

Step 7: *Take the inverse two-dimensional discrete Fourier transform of the data on the uniform grid. Obtain the magnitude of the resultant data and display.*

SAR Signal Compression

Recall the support band we found for the SAR signal $s(u,\omega)$ in the k_u domain in (4.12), that is,

$$\Omega_s = [2k\sin\theta_1 - 2k\frac{L+X_0}{R_1}\cos^2\theta_1, 2k\sin\theta_1 + 2k\frac{L+X_0}{R_1}\cos^2\theta_1].$$

This result indicated that the bandwidth of $s(u,\omega)$ in the k_u domain is $4k\frac{L+X_0}{R_1}\cos^2\theta_1$ and, thus, the following constraint [see (4.13)] for the sample spacing on the synthetic aperture should be satisfied:

$$\Delta_u \le 2\pi\frac{R_1}{4k(L+X_0)\cos^2\theta_1}.$$

As mentioned earlier, there are practical difficulties associated with the constraint (4.13) that depends on the length of the synthetic aperture, that is, $2L$. In this section, we show that the above-mentioned dependence can be removed. This also results in a significant reduction in the size of the required SAR data to be collected especially in the case of spotlight-mode SAR imaging.

We consider the echoed data from a unit-reflectivity point scatterer at the origin [see (4.3)]; that is,

$$\begin{aligned}
s_0(u,\omega) &\equiv \exp[j2k\sqrt{(X_1-0)^2+(Y_1+u-0)^2}]\\
&= \exp[j2k\sqrt{X_1^2+(Y_1+u)^2}].
\end{aligned} \tag{4.17}$$

Using (4.11), it can be shown that the support band for the signal in (4.17) is the following:

$$\Omega(0) \equiv [2k\sin\theta_1 - 2k\frac{L}{R_1}\cos^2\theta_1, 2k\sin\theta_1 + 2k\frac{L}{R_1}\cos^2\theta_1]. \tag{4.18}$$

From (4.18), it is clear that the bandwidth of the signal in (4.17) is $4k\frac{L}{R_1}\cos^2\theta_1$.

We define the *normalized* or *compressed* SAR signal, call it $s_c(u,\omega)$, by dividing the SAR signal with $s_0(u,\omega)$ [or multiplying the SAR signal with the complex conjugate of $s_0(u,\omega)$]; this yields

$$s_c(u,\omega) \equiv s(u,\omega)\ s_0^*(u,\omega)$$

$$= s(u,\omega)\ \exp[-j2k\sqrt{X_1^2 + (Y_1 + u)^2}].$$

Substituting for SAR signal, we get

$$s_c(u,\omega) = \int\int dx\ dy\ f(x,y)\ \times$$

$$\exp\left[j2k[\sqrt{(X_1 - x)^2 + (Y_1 + u - y)^2} - \sqrt{X_1^2 + (Y_1 + u)^2}]\right].$$

$$(4.19)$$

The phase of the PM wave on the right side of (4.19) has the following Taylor series expansion around $\sqrt{X_1^2 + (Y_1 + u)^2}$ (with $L, X_0 \ll R_1$):

$$\sqrt{(X_1 - x)^2 + (Y_1 + u - y)^2} - \sqrt{X_1^2 + (Y_1 + u)^2} =$$

$$\frac{.5(x^2 + y^2) - X_1 x - Y_1 y}{R_1} - \frac{y}{R_1}u + \dots$$

$$(4.20)$$

The contribution of the higher order terms on the right side of (4.20) in the bandwidth of $s_c(u,\omega)$ can be shown to be negligible. Thus, the only significant term that depends on u on the right side of (4.20) is $-\frac{y}{R_1}u$. In this case, the support band of the normalized SAR signal becomes

$$\Omega_{s_c} = \bigcup_{|y| \leq X_0} [2k\frac{y}{R_1}]$$

$$= [-2k\frac{X_0}{R_1}, 2k\frac{X_0}{R_1}].$$

$$(4.21)$$

A more accurate analysis would show that the support band of the normalized SAR signal is

$$\Omega_{s_c} = [-2k\frac{X_0}{R_1}\cos^2\theta_1, 2k\frac{X_0}{R_1}\cos^2\theta_1].$$

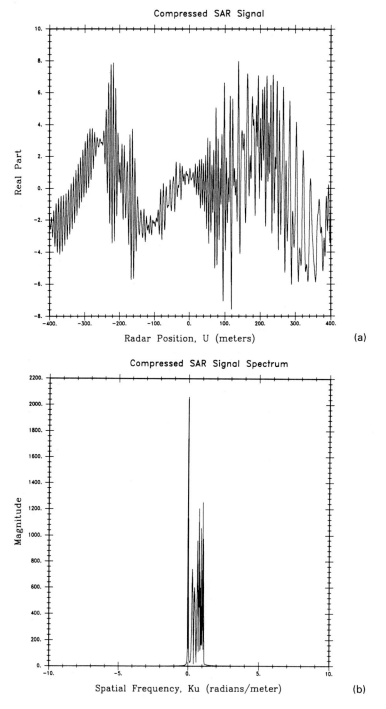

Figure 4.12 Compressed SAR signal. (a) $s_c(u, \omega)$. (b) $S_c(k_u, \omega)$.

Figure 4.12a shows the distribution of $s_c(u, \omega)$ for the squint-mode SAR signal in Figure 4.3b. Figure 4.12b shows the magnitude spectrum of the normalized SAR signal in Figure 4.12a. One can observe a reduction in the support band of this signal as compared with the bandpass signal shown in Figure 4.7b (that is the magnitude spectrum of the signal in Figure 4.3b). SAR signal compression is depicted for broadside and squint-mode cases in Figures 4.13a and 4.13b, respectively.

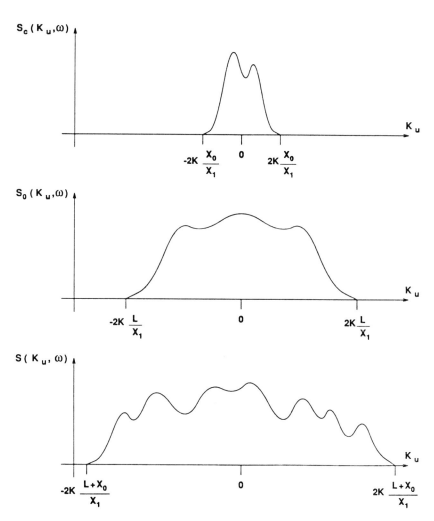

Figure 4.13a SAR signal compression: Broadside.

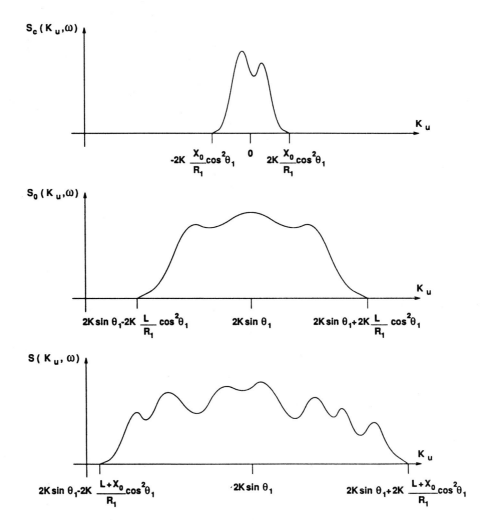

Figure 4.13b SAR signal Compression: Squint-mode.

We can observe from (4.21) that the normalized SAR signal is a *lowpass* signal with bandwidth $\pm 2k\frac{X_0}{R_1}$ in the k_u domain. Thus, the sample spacing for $s_c(u, \omega)$ in the u domain, call it Δ_{u_c}, should satisfy the following:

$$\Delta_{u_c} \leq 2\pi \frac{R_1}{4kX_0}, \qquad (4.22)$$

which is independent of L.

Substituting for X_0 from (4.1) in (4.22), one obtains

$$\Delta_{u_c} \leq \frac{D}{4}, \tag{4.23}$$

where D is the diameter of the physical radar antenna mounted on the moving vehicle. At the broadside, the ratio of the sampling rates in (4.13) [for $s(u,\omega)$] and (4.22) [for $s_c(u,\omega)$] is $\frac{L+X_0}{X_0}$, which is significant in spotlight-mode SAR imaging where $L > X_0$.

- *One may use Y_0 instead of X_0 in (4.21)-(4.22) and D_y instead of D in (4.23).*

Now suppose the SAR signal $s(u,\omega)$ is measured at $u = m\Delta_{u_c}$, where m takes on integer values in the interval $(\frac{-L}{\Delta_{u_c}}, \frac{L}{\Delta_{u_c}})$. Clearly, this measured SAR signal is undersampled and its Doppler analysis would contain aliasing errors. However, we can recover samples of the normalized SAR signal without any error via (4.19); that is,

$$s_c(m\Delta_{u_c},\omega) = s(m\Delta_{u_c},\omega) \, \exp[-j2k\sqrt{X_1^2 + (Y_1 + m\Delta_{u_c})^2}]. \tag{4.24}$$

The sequence defined in (4.24) represents unaliased samples of the normalized SAR signal. Thus, these samples can be used to interpolate $s_c(u,\omega)$ at all values of u, specifically at $u = n\Delta_u$ where n is an integer that takes on values in the interval $(\frac{-L}{\Delta_u}, \frac{L}{\Delta_u})$; that is,

$$s_c(n\Delta_u,\omega) = \sum_m s_c(m\Delta_{u_c},\omega) \, \frac{\sin[\frac{2kX_0(n\Delta_u - m\Delta_{u_c})}{R_1}]}{\frac{2kX_0(n\Delta_u - m\Delta_{u_c})}{R_1}}. \tag{4.25}$$

Finally, the oversampled sequence $s_c(n\Delta_u,\omega)$ can be converted into the unaliased samples of the SAR signal by the following:

$$s(n\Delta_u,\omega) = s_c(n\Delta_u,\omega) \, \exp[j2k\sqrt{X_1^2 + (Y_1 + n\Delta_u)^2}]. \tag{4.26}$$

Equation (4.26) represents the desired SAR data to be used in the reconstruction algorithm. The SAR signal compression algorithm is summarized in Figure 4.13c. Note that the new pulse repetition interval becomes

$$t_2 \equiv \frac{\Delta_{u_c}}{v_R}.$$

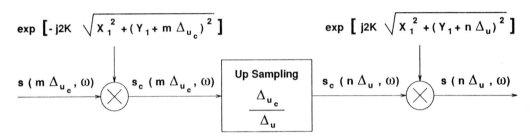

Figure 4.13c SAR signal compression algorithm.

Pulse and Frequency Diversity

We now examine two methods for selecting the transmitted radar signal that have practical implications. One is referred to as *pulse* diversity, which reduces the vulnerability of the transmitting/receiving radar to being identified and tracked, and multipath effects. The second radar signaling method, called *frequency* diversity or stepped-frequency [17] illumination, is utilized to improve the signal-to-noise power ratio at temporal frequencies away from the center frequency ω_c and remove the need for using high-speed analog to digital (A/D) converters to sample the SAR signal in the fast-time domain. One may also combine the pulse diversity and frequency diversity radar signaling schemes.

- *When SAR imaging was introduced, high-speed A/D converter technology was not advanced enough to provide an accurate coherent processing of the SAR signal. The resultant phase error was a major obstacle in achieving the high-resolution cross-range information anticipated by the theory of synthetic aperture radar.*

Using the stepped-frequency SAR signaling, Wehner [17] bypassed the fast-time sampling phase errors. This, as we will see, is achieved at the expense of a lower sampling rate in the synthetic aperture (slow-time) domain that may result in aliased data in that measurement domain.

Pulse Diversity: Suppose the temporal radar signal transmitted when the aircraft is at $(X_1, Y_1 + u)$ is $p_u(t)$, that is, it varies with u (Figure 4.14 shows an example).

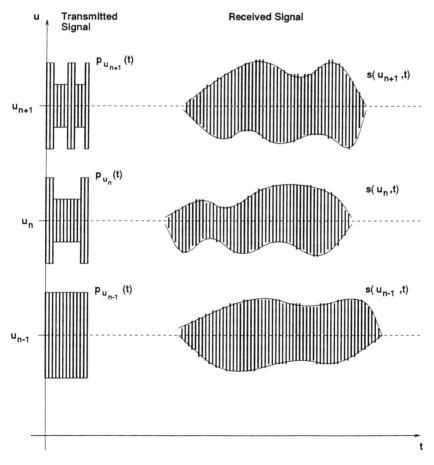

Figure 4.14 Pulse diversity in SAR imaging.

In this case, the recorded SAR signal becomes

$$s(u,t) \equiv \int \int f(x,y) \; p_u[t - \frac{2\sqrt{(X_1 - x)^2 + (Y_1 + u - y)^2}}{c}] \; dx dy.$$

The temporal Fourier transform of this signal is

$$s(u,\omega) = P_u(\omega) \int \int f(x,y) \exp[-j2k\sqrt{(X_1 - x)^2 + (Y_1 + u - y)^2}] dx dy$$

The SAR signal normalized by $P_u(\omega)$, that is,

$$\frac{s(u,\omega)}{P_u(\omega)} = \int \int f(x,y) \; \exp[-j2k\sqrt{(X_1 - x)^2 + (Y_1 + u - y)^2}] \; dx dy,$$

has the same functional form as the right side of (4.5). Thus, the inversion outlined in (4.7) is still applicable with $s(u,\omega)$ replaced with its normalized version. *In practice, the source deconvolution, that is,* $\frac{s(u,\omega)}{P_u(\omega)}$*, is performed via the matched filtering operation* $s(u,\omega) \, P_u^*(\omega)$*.*

Suppose the transmitted pulses on two different coordinates of the radar on the synthetic aperture are orthogonal to each other; that is,

$$\int_t p_{u_m}(t) \, p_{u_n}^*(t) \; dt = 0,$$

for $m \neq n$. In this case, the target that is being imaged or a third party would not be able to use the correlation between the transmitted pulses to identify and locate the radar-carrying aircraft. Moreover, the multipath signals that are due to transmission at u_m would not interfere with the echoed signals that are due to the transmission at u_n. This is due to the fact that the output of the matched filter for $p_{u_n}(t)$ rejects (filters out) the multipath signals that are delayed versions of $p_{u_m}(t)$.

To design the transmitted pulses, one may use a set of orthogonal codes for the baseband transmitted pulses, that is, $a_{u_n}(t)$'s. A simple and practical choice is based on a pseudorandom sequence generator that produces codes that are approximately orthogonal to each other.

Frequency Diversity: Consider a scenario when the radar transmits *multiple* long duration pulses (narrow-band signals) instead of a single short duration pulse in the aperture interval $u \in [u_n, u_n + \Delta_{u_c})$, where $u_n = n \Delta_{u_c}$, $n = 0, \pm1, \pm2, \ldots$ (see Figure 4.15). Furthermore, the carrier frequencies of these long pulses vary linearly with u in the interval $[\omega_1, \omega_2)$; that is,

$$\omega_c(u) = \omega_1 + \frac{\omega_2 - \omega_1}{\Delta_{u_c}} (u - u_n).$$

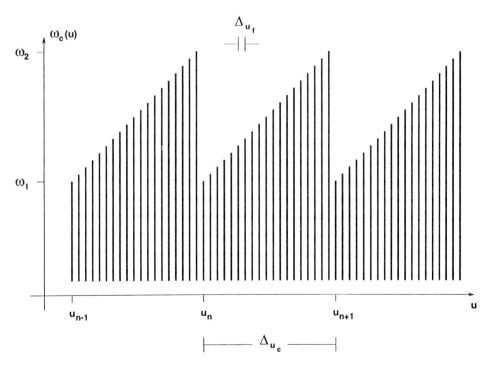

Figure 4.15 Frequency Diversity (stepped-frequency) in SAR imaging.

Note that

$$\omega_c(u_n) = \omega_1, \qquad \text{for} \ \ n = 0, \pm1, \pm2, \ldots$$

$\omega_c(u)$, $u \in [-L, L]$, is a sawtooth function of u with its transitions occurring at $u = u_n$'s.

For a given $u \in [-L, L]$, the output of the coherent receiver is simply integrated and stored via an A/D converter. Thus, this processing provides only one sample of the SAR signal $s(u, \omega)$ (which is due to the narrow-band nature of the transmitted pulses) that is

$$s[u, \omega_c(u)].$$

It is not difficult to see that this corresponds to a *hexagonal* sampling in the domain of $s(u, \omega)$. Thus, under the hexagonal sampling constraints shown in Chapter 2, one can recover $s(u, \omega)$ from the measured data.

Note that the pulse repetition frequency, that is, the number of pulses transmitted per unit of u, for this form of data collection (denoted by $\frac{1}{\Delta_{u_f}}$ in Figure 4.15) is much larger than $\frac{1}{\Delta_{u_c}}$. The frequency diversity or stepping SAR signaling enables the user to transmit high power signals for all temporal frequencies in the band $[\omega_1, \omega_2)$. Furthermore, one does not have to sample the SAR signal at the rate of $\omega_2 - \omega_1$ in the fast-time domain. The long duration of each pulse is limited by the target's range as well as the number of pulses transmitted per Δ_{u_c} in the aperture domain.

The main disadvantage of stepped-frequency radar signaling is that the radar's pulse repetition frequency should be high enough to scan the fast-temporal frequency band $[\omega_1, \omega_2)$ to obtain the desired range resolution without aliasing the synthetic aperture (slow-time) domain data. This problem becomes more critical in blind-velocity SAR/ISAR imaging. In these problems, one cannot perform SAR signal compression in the aperture domain since the target's velocity and, consequently, the normalization signal is unknown. This forces the user to sample the slow-time (synthetic aperture) data at a much higher rate that is larger than $\frac{1}{\Delta_u}$ which is also unknown (an estimate of this parameter is usually available to the user via, for example, a tracking or MTI/AMTI radar). This further limits the number of frequencies that could be stepped by the radar. In Chapter 5, we will examine this issue via real stepped-frequency data for a DC-9 aircraft.

Relation to FM-CW Signaling: Next, we show that stepped-frequency signaling is equivalent to FM-CW signaling when the synthetic aperture domain u is expressed in terms of the fast-time domain, that is, $u = v_R t$ (v_R is the aircraft's speed). In Chapter 1, we examined a radar signaling method known as FM-CW signaling that has the following form for its baseband signal:

$$a(t) = a_3(t) \sum_\ell a_1(t - \ell t_2).$$

Consider the case when $a_1(t)$ is composed of a finite number of evenly spaced rectangular pulses that are amplitude-modulating sinusoids with frequencies that are being increased (stepped) linearly:

$$a_1(t) \equiv \sum_{m=1}^{M} a_0(t - m\Delta_t) \, \exp\left[jm\Delta_\omega(t - m\Delta_t)\right];$$

$a_0(t)$ is a rectangular pulse; the number of modulated rectangular pulses is

$$M \equiv \frac{\Delta_{u_c}}{\Delta_{u_f}};$$

Δ_ω is the step frequency defined via

$$\Delta_\omega \equiv \frac{\omega_2 - \omega_1}{M};$$

and the time interval between two consecutive rectangular pulses is

$$\Delta_t \equiv \frac{\Delta_{u_f}}{v_R}.$$

In this case, the FM-CW signal becomes a stepped-frequency signal with

$$t_2 \equiv \frac{\Delta_{u_c}}{v_R}.$$

This fact will be exhibited for the DC-9's stepped-frequency ISAR data in Chapter 5.

4.5 COMPENSATION FOR DEVIATIONS IN FLIGHT PATH

In this section, we present methods for modifying the inversion formulated in the previous sections for the case when the radar's flight path deviates from the line $x = X_1$. It is assumed that the flight path's variable range and cross-range, identified via $[X_1 + X(u), Y_1 + Y(u) + u]$ with $|X(u)| \ll X_1$ and $|Y(u)| \ll Y_1$, are known or could be approximated [2],[15]. In this case, the system model becomes

$$s(u, \omega) = \int \int dx \, f(x, y) \times$$
$$\exp[j2k\sqrt{(X_1 + X(u) - x)^2 + (Y_1 + Y(u) + u - y)^2}]. \tag{4.27}$$

Using the spherical wave decomposition that resulted in (4.5) or (4.9) on the system model in (4.27), one obtains

$$s(u, \omega) = \int \int dx \, dy \, f(x, y) \times$$
$$\left[\int_{-2k}^{2k} \exp[j\sqrt{4k^2 - k_u^2}(X_1 + X(u) - x) + jk_u(Y_1 + Y(u) + u - y)]dk_u \right] \tag{4.28}$$

Provided that $|k_u - 2k\sin\theta_1| \ll 2k$, $|X(u)| \ll X_1$ and $|Y(u)| \ll Y_1$ in the integrals on the right side of (4.28), we can use the following approximation:

$$\exp[j\sqrt{4k^2 - k_u^2}\,X(u) + jk_uY(u)] \approx \exp[j2k\cos\theta_1 X(u) + j2k\sin\theta_1 Y(u)]$$

in (4.28); this yields

$$s(u, \omega) = \exp[j2k\cos\theta_1 X(u) + j2k\sin\theta_1 Y(u)] \int \int f(x, y) \times$$
$$\left[\int_{-2k}^{2k} \exp[j\sqrt{4k^2 - k_u^2}\,(X_1 - x) + jk_u(Y_1 + u - y)]\, dk_u \right] dx dy, \tag{4.29}$$

or

$$s(u,\omega)\ \exp[-j2k\cos\theta_1 X(u) - j2k\sin\theta_1 Y(u)] = \int\int f(x,y)\times$$

$$\left[\int_{-2k}^{2k}\exp[j\sqrt{4k^2 - k_u^2}\,(X_1 - x) + jk_u(Y_1 + u - y)]\,dk_u\right]\,dxdy.$$

$$(4.30)$$

Note the functions that appear on the right sides of the system models in (4.9) and (4.30) are the same. Hence, using the same principles that resulted in the inversion (4.7), one can obtain the following inversion for the system model in (4.27):

$$F(\sqrt{4k^2 - k_u^2}, k_u) = \exp(-j\sqrt{4k^2 - k_u^2}X_1 - jk_u Y_1)\ \times$$

$$\mathcal{F}_{(u)}\left[s(u,\omega)\exp[-j2k\cos\theta_1 X(u) - j2k\sin\theta_1 Y(u)]\right]$$

$$(4.31)$$

Thus, the inverse equation (4.31) modifies the recorded data for each u based on a variable range phase function, $2k\cos\theta_1 X(u)$, prior to the slow-time Doppler processing (Fourier transformation with respect to u).

Equation (4.29) indicates that the variable range phase function is *invariant* of the object parameters and appears as an *additive* phase error to the desired information. Moreover, the propagation channel may introduce other additive phase errors. In this case, the recorded signal should be expressed as follows:

$$s(u,\omega) = \exp[j\phi(u,\omega)]\int\int f(x,y)\times$$

$$\left[\int_{-2k}^{2k}\exp[j\sqrt{4k^2 - k_u^2}\,(X_1 - x) + jk_u(Y_1 + u - y)]dk_u\right]dxdy$$

$$(4.32)$$

where

$$\phi(u,\omega) \equiv 2k\cos\theta_1 X(u) + 2k\sin\theta_1 Y(u) + \phi_r(u,\omega). \qquad (4.33)$$

In this case, $\phi_r(u,\omega)$, the random portion of the phase error, is a combination of the channel's noise, the radar's random maneuvers, and the errors introduced in estimating the radar's deterministic maneuvers, that is, $X(u)$. One may develop algorithms, based on a priori statistics available on the random phase error, to recover $\phi(u,\omega)$ [2],[15].

ISAR Imaging of Maneuvering Targets

The general system model for ISAR imaging of a maneuvering target is

$$s(u,\omega) = \int\int dx\ dy\ f(x,y) \times$$
$$\exp[j2k\sqrt{(X_1 + X(u) - x)^2 + (Y_1 + Y(u) - y)^2}],$$

where $[X(u), Y(u)]$ represents the target's trajectory. This ISAR model is similar to the SAR system model in (4.27). Provided that the target's trajectory is known, one can project this data into the target's ISAR data along a straight line via the procedure shown in (4.30). The straight line, for example, the linear trajectory $[X_1 + Au, Y_1 + Bu]$, is selected to be the linear least square estimator of the target's trajectory, that is, the contour defined by $[X(u), Y(u)]$. In this case, one can use an inversion similar to (4.31) to image the maneuvering target.

An important issue in ISAR imaging of a maneuvering target is to determine the target's trajectory $[X(u), Y(u)]$. This problem, called blind-velocity ISAR imaging, is addressed in Chapter 5.

4.6 SLANT-PLANE GEOMETRY AND INTERFEROMETRIC SAR

The slant-plane data collection geometry corresponds to the three-dimensional spatial domain imaging geometries that exist in practice (see Figure 4.16). In this case, the radar is assumed to be moving along the line $x = X_1$ on the plane $z = 0$, and the target is identified via the reflectivity function $f(x, y, z)$. In this section, we show that the inversion principles developed for the two-dimensional synthetic aperture geometries can be utilized to reconstruct the *slant*-plane reflectivity function (which is defined later in this section).

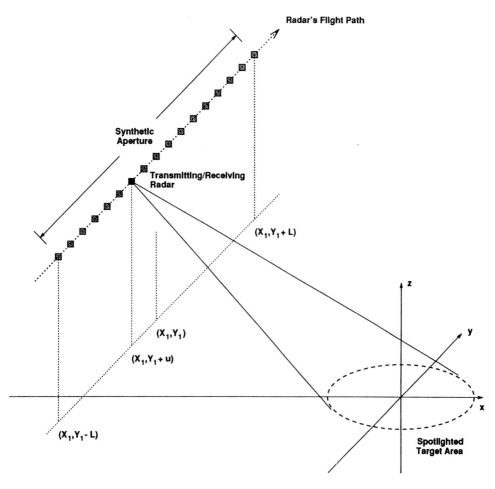

Figure 4.16 Imaging system geometry for slant-plane SAR imaging.

System Model and Inversion

Consider the (x, z) system geometry on the plane $y = u$ as shown in Figure 4.17. We define the *slant-range* domain by

$$x_s \equiv X_1 - \sqrt{(X_1 - x)^2 + z^2}. \tag{4.34}$$

Thus, the system model for the SAR's slant-plane geometry becomes

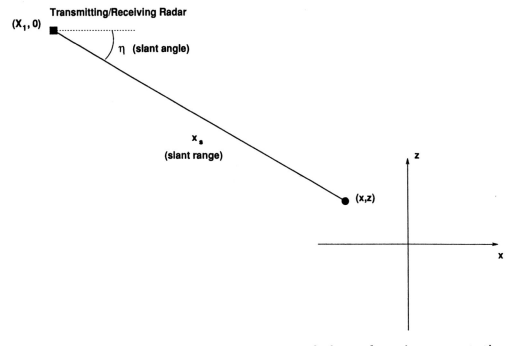

Figure 4.17 Geometrical representation of slant-plane in monostatic SAR imaging.

$$s(u, \omega) = \int \int \int dx \; dy \; dz \; f(x, y, z) \; \times$$

$$\exp[j2k\sqrt{(X_1 - x)^2 + (Y_1 + u - y)^2 + z^2}]$$

$$= \int \int f_s(x_s, y) \exp[j2k\sqrt{(X_1 - x_s)^2 + (Y_1 + u - y)^2}] \; dx_s dy,$$

$$(4.35)$$

where

$$f_s(x_s, y) \equiv \int_{-\pi}^{\pi} f(x, y, z) \; d\eta, \qquad (4.36)$$

with

$$\eta \equiv \arctan(\frac{z}{X_1 - x}). \qquad (4.37)$$

η is called the **slant angle**. $f_s(x_s, y)$ is called the slant-plane reflectivity function. [The Jacobian of the transformation from (x, z) to (x_s, η) is an amplitude function and is neglected on the second line of (4.35).]

The system model in (4.35) is the same as (4.3) with the range x replaced with the slant-range, that is, x_s, and the the two-dimensional reflectivity function $f(x, y)$ replaced with $f_s(x_s, y)$. Hence, we can use the same procedure that yielded the inversion (4.7) to derive the following inversion in slant-plane SAR imaging:

$$F_s(\sqrt{4k^2 - k_u^2}, k_u) = \exp(-j\sqrt{4k^2 - k_u^2}X_1 - jk_uY_1) \, S(k_u, \omega). \quad (4.38)$$

Note that this inversion provides a two-dimensional reconstruction of the slant-plane reflectivity function from the one-dimensional measurements in the synthetic aperture domain of y, that is, u. *The three-dimensional imaging capability may be obtained when additional measurements are made in a synthetic aperture domain for z*, or when $f(x, y, z)$ is nonzero only on a given plane, for example, the plane $z = z_0$. Next, we consider the latter case and obtain the resolution for its reconstructed image.

Planar Targets

Suppose the target function can be expressed in the following form:

$$f(x, y, z) = f(x, y) \, \delta(z - z_0),$$

that is, a delta sheet target on the plane $z = z_0$. Then, from (4.36), we obtain the following mapping of $f(x, y)$:

$$f_s(x_s, y) \equiv f(x, y),$$

where x_s is a nonlinear one-to-one transformation of x defined via [see (4.34)]

$$x_s \equiv X_1 - \sqrt{(X_1 - x)^2 + z_0^2}. \quad (4.39)$$

Using (4.38), one can reconstruct $f_s(x_s, y)$. The result can be utilized in an interpolation technique that maps the reconstructed $f_s(x_s, y)$ to $f(x, y)$ based on the transformation (4.39).

We denote the *effective range* by

$$X_e \equiv \sqrt{X_1^2 + z_0^2}. \quad (4.40)$$

From (4.39)-(4.40), we could write the following approximation:

$$x_s \approx X_1 - X_e + \frac{X_1}{X_e} x. \tag{4.41}$$

Using (4.15) and (4.41), the range resolution at broadside can be found to be the following:

$$\Delta_x = \frac{2\pi}{2(k_2 - k_1)} \frac{X_e}{X_1}. \tag{4.42}$$

Moreover, using (4.16), one can find the cross-range resolution via

$$\Delta_y = 2\pi \frac{X_e}{4k_c L}. \tag{4.43}$$

We observe from (4.42)-(4.43) that the resolutions in both the range and cross-range domains are deteriorated by the ratio of the effective range to the actual (x domain) range.

Three-Dimensional Imaging Using Interferometric (Stereo) SAR

An important application of SAR is in topographic terrain mapping of Earth and other planets [5]. In these imaging problems, the target is a nonplanar surface (delta sheet) in the three-dimensional spatial domain. This can be expressed as follows:

$$f(x, y, z) = f(x, y) \, \delta[z - z(x, y)],$$

where $z(x, y)$, which is unknown, represents the target's altitude as a function of its range. Then, the slant-range becomes

$$x_s \equiv X_1 - \sqrt{(X_1 - x)^2 + z^2(x, y)}.$$

In the following discussion, we consider the target function for a fixed cross-range y. Thus, for notational simplicity, we write the variable altitude as $z(x)$. Moreover, to simplify the analysis, we define the (x, y) domain (i.e., $z = 0$ plane) to be the plane that contains the radar's flight path and the center of the illuminated target area. This geometry implies that

$$|z(x)| \leq X_0 \ll X_1,$$

which simplifies the following discussion. (We mentioned earlier that the disk of radius X_0 centered at the origin is the physical radar's footprint.)

Provided that the mapping from $[x, z(x)]$ into x_s is one-to-one, we can write

$$f_s(x_s, y) \equiv f(x, y).$$

If the mapping of $[x, z(x)]$ into x_s is not one-to-one, the slant-plane reflectivity function, $f_s(x_s, y)$, could represent the superposition of the reflectivity values at two or more $[x, z(x)]$ points in the x_s domain.

For example, suppose two points, say $[x_1, z(x_1)]$ and $[x_2, z(x_2)]$, map into the same slant-range, that is,

$$
\begin{aligned}
x_s &= X_1 - \sqrt{(X_1 - x_1)^2 + z^2(x_1)} \\
&= X_1 - \sqrt{(X_1 - x_2)^2 + z^2(x_2)}.
\end{aligned}
$$

Then, from (4.36) we have

$$f_s(x_s, y) = f(x_1, y) + f(x_2, y).$$

Reference [5] provides an extensive discussion on this issue. We now examine three-dimensional SAR imaging based on the assumption that the mapping of $[x, z(x)]$ into x_s is one-to-one.

Suppose the radar carrying aircraft is equipped with another radar that makes another set of SAR measurements of the target scene along another trajectory, for example, the line $x = X_1$ on the plane $z = \Delta$. The resultant two sets of SAR measurements are called *stereo* SAR data. This stereo SAR measurement system is analogous to the stereo *monopulse* radar that is used for height finding (elevation angle measurements) [10]. Zebker and Goldstein [18] have developed a procedure for topographic terrain mapping from stereo SAR data that is described next.

We denote the slant-range for the second set of SAR measurements via

$$w_s \equiv X_1 - \sqrt{(X_1 - x)^2 + [\Delta - z(x)]^2}.$$

It is also assumed that the mapping from $[x, z(x)]$ into w_s is one-to-one. The resultant slant-plane reflectivity function is identified with $g_s(w_s, y)$. Thus, we have

$$g_s(w_s, y) = f(x, y).$$

Moreover, for a given x_s there exists a unique w_s such that

$$g_s(w_s, y) = f_s(x_s, y),$$

where (with $|z(x)| \ll X_1$)

$$w_s \approx x_s + \frac{\Delta^2 - 2\Delta z(x)}{2X_1}.$$

Thus, by identifying the common target points in the reconstructed images of $f_s(x_s, y)$ and $g_s(w_s, y)$, one can obtain an estimate of $z(x)$, call it $\hat{z}(x)$, from the following:

$$\hat{z}(x) \equiv \frac{X_1}{\Delta}(x_s - w_s) + .5\Delta.$$

The result can then be used to estimate range x from the knowledge of $[x_s, \hat{z}(x)]$ or $[w_s, \hat{z}(x)]$, for example,

$$\hat{x} \equiv X_1 - \sqrt{(X_1 - x_s)^2 - \hat{z}^2(x)}.$$

Zebker and Goldstein [18] performed the estimation of $z(x)$ via measuring the phase of the interference pattern generated from the complex reconstructions of $f_s(x_s, y)$ and $g_s(w_s, y)$ at a given target point.

4.7 STRIPMAP SAR: FRESNEL APPROXIMATION-BASED INVERSION

We develop the Fresnel approximation-based SAR inversion, also known as *stripmap SAR*, only for the broadside case, that is, $Y_1 = 0$. Consider the SAR system model developed in (4.3); that is,

$$s(u, \omega) = \int_x \int_y f(x, y) \, \exp[j2k\sqrt{(X_1 - x)^2 + (u - y)^2}] \, dx \, dy$$

Using the following (Fresnel) approximation:

$$2k\sqrt{(X_1 - x)^2 + (u - y)^2} \approx 2k(X_1 - x) + \frac{k(u - y)^2}{X_1},$$

in the system models, one obtains

$$s(u, \omega) \approx \int_x \int_y f(x, y) \ \exp[j2k(X_1 - x)] \ \exp[j\frac{k(u - y)^2}{X_1}] \ dx \, dy$$

$$= \exp(j2kX_1) \int_y \exp[j\frac{k(u - y)^2}{X_1}] [\underbrace{\int_x f(x, y) \ \exp(-j2kx) \ dx}_{Fourier\ integral}] \, dy$$

$$= \exp(j2kX_1) \int_y \exp[j\frac{k(u - y)^2}{X_1}] \ F_x(2k, y) \, dy$$

$$= \exp(j2kX_1) \ \exp(j\frac{ku^2}{X_1}) \ * \ F_x(2k, u)$$

$$= \exp(j2kX_1) \ c(u) \ * \ F_x(2k, u),$$

$$(4.44)$$

where $*$ denotes convolution in the u domain, and

$$c(u) \equiv \exp(j\frac{ku^2}{X_1}).$$

We also have

$$C(k_u) = \mathcal{F}_{(u)}[c(u)]$$

$$= \exp(-j\frac{k_u^2 X_1}{4k})$$

Taking the spatial Fourier transform of both sides of (4.44) with respect to u yields

$$S(k_u, \omega) \approx \exp(j2kX_1) \ F(2k, k_u) \ C(k_u), \qquad (4.45)$$

which results in the following inverse equation:

$$F(k_x, k_y) \approx \exp(-j2kX_1) \ \frac{S(k_u, \omega)}{C(k_u)}$$

$$= \exp(-j2kX_1) \ S(k_u, \omega) \ \exp(j\frac{k_u^2 X_1}{4k}),$$

$$(4.46)$$

where

$$k_x = 2k$$
$$k_y = k_u$$

(4.47)

Taking the inverse spatial Fourier transform of both sides of (4.46) with respect to k_u yields

$$F_x(2k, u) = \exp(-j2kX_1)\, s(u, \omega) \, * \, \exp[-jk\frac{u^2}{X_1}],$$

(4.48)

where $*$ denotes convolution in the u domain, and $F_x(k_x = 2k, u)$ is the one-dimensional Fourier transform of $f(x, u)$ with respect to x. Equation (4.48) is the Fresnel approximation-based inversion for what is known as strip map-mode SAR imaging.

Relation to the Spatial Doppler-Based Inversion

Using the following approximations:

$$k_x = \sqrt{4k^2 - k_u^2} \approx 2k,$$

and

$$\exp(-j\sqrt{4k^2 - k_u^2}\, X_1) = \exp[-j(2k - \frac{k_u^2}{4k} + ..)\, X_1]$$
$$\approx \exp(-j2kX_1)\, \exp(j\frac{k_u^2}{4k}X_1)$$

in the spatial Doppler-based inversion derived in (4.7)-(4.8) yields the Fresnel approximation-based inversion of (4.46)-(4.47).

Constraint for Validity

The Fresnel approximation-based inversion is a valid approach provided that the following constraint is satisfied [14]:

$$\frac{k(X_0 + L)^4}{4X_1^3} + \frac{kX_0(X_0 + L)^2}{X_1^2} \ll 1.$$

(4.49)

4.8 PLANE WAVE APPROXIMATION-BASED INVERSION

Consider the SAR imaging system geometry shown in Figure 4.18. We define the angle that the radar makes with respect to the broadside by the following:

$$\theta \equiv \arctan(\frac{Y_1 + u}{X_1}).$$

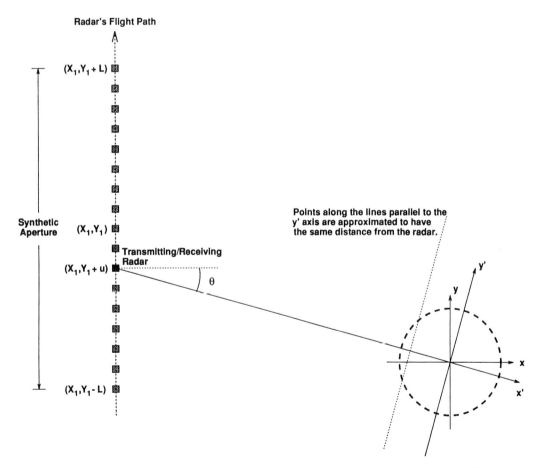

Figure 4.18 Imaging system geometry for SAR imaging: Plane wave approximation-based inversion.

Let

$$f'(x', y') = f(x, y),$$

where

$$\begin{bmatrix} x' \\ y' \end{bmatrix} = \begin{bmatrix} \cos\theta & \sin\theta \\ -\sin\theta & \cos\theta \end{bmatrix} \begin{bmatrix} x \\ y \end{bmatrix}$$

We showed in Section 2.4 that

$$F'(k_{x'}, k_{y'}) \equiv F(k_x, k_y)$$

where

$$\begin{bmatrix} k_{x'} \\ k_{y'} \end{bmatrix} = \begin{bmatrix} \cos\theta & \sin\theta \\ -\sin\theta & \cos\theta \end{bmatrix} \begin{bmatrix} k_x \\ k_y \end{bmatrix}$$

Making variable transformations from (x, y) to (x', y') in the SAR system model (4.3), one obtains

$$s(u, \omega) = \int_{x'} \int_{y'} dx' \, dy' \, f'(x', y') \times$$

$$\exp\left[j2k \sqrt{ \left(\sqrt{X_1^2 + (Y_1 + u)^2} - x' \right)^2 + y'^2 } \right] \tag{4.50}$$

Consider the following approximation

$$2k \sqrt{ \left(\sqrt{X_1^2 + (Y_1 + u)^2} - x' \right)^2 + y'^2 } \approx 2k \left(\sqrt{X_1^2 + (Y_1 + u)^2} - x' \right)$$

$$= 2k \left(\sqrt{X_1^2 + (Y_1 + u)^2} - x\cos\theta - y\sin\theta \right), \tag{4.51}$$

which approximates the spherical wave transmitted by the radar with a plane wave in the x' direction. Using (4.51) in the SAR system model in

(4.50) yields

$$s(u,\omega) \approx \int_{x'}\int_{y'} f'(x',y') \, \exp\left[\,j2k(\sqrt{X_1^2 + (Y_1 + u)^2} - x')\,\right] \, dx'dy'$$

$$= \exp(j2k\sqrt{X_1^2 + (Y_1 + u)^2}) \times$$

$$\underbrace{\int_{x'}\int_{y'} f'(x',y') \, \exp(-j2kx' - j0y')dx'dy'}_{Two \ dimensional \ Fourier \ integral}$$

$$= \exp(j2k\sqrt{X_1^2 + (Y_1 + u)^2}) \, F'(k_{x'}, k_{y'})$$

$$(4.52)$$

where

$$k_{x'} = 2k$$
$$k_{y'} = 0.$$

$$(4.53)$$

Making variable transformations from $(k_{x'}, k_{y'})$ to (k_x, k_y) in (4.52)-(4.53) yields

$$s(u,\omega) \approx \exp(j2k\sqrt{X_1^2 + (Y_1 + u)^2}) \, F(k_x, k_y),\qquad(4.54)$$

which yields the following inverse equation:

$$F'(k_x, k_y) \approx \exp(-j2k\sqrt{X_1^2 + (Y_1 + u)^2}) \, s(u,\omega),\qquad(4.55)$$

where

$$k_x = 2k\cos\theta = 2k \, \frac{X_1}{\sqrt{X_1^2 + (Y_1 + u)^2}}$$

$$k_y = 2k\sin\theta = 2k \, \frac{Y_1 + u}{\sqrt{X_1^2 + (Y_1 + u)^2}}$$

$$(4.56)$$

Equations (4.55)-(4.56) are known as the plane approximation-based inversion for spotlight-mode SAR imaging. *Note that the coverage dictated by (4.56) is polar.*

Constraints for Validity

We only consider the broadside case of $Y_1 = 0$. The phase error introduced due to the approximation in (4.51) can be shown to be (only significant terms are considered)

$$\frac{k(x^2 \sin^2 \theta + y^2 \cos^2 \theta + xy \sin 2\theta)}{X_1}. \tag{4.57}$$

With a target within a disk of radius X_0, the maximum phase error due to (4.57) can be found to be (with $2\theta \ll 1$)

$$\frac{kX_0^2(1 + \sin 2\theta)}{X_1} \approx \frac{kX_0^2}{X_1}, \tag{4.58}$$

which should be much smaller than one.

A milder restriction can be derived by rewriting (4.57) as follows:

$$\frac{k(x^2 \sin^2 \theta - y^2 \sin^2 \theta + xy \sin 2\theta)}{X_1} + \frac{ky^2}{X_1}. \tag{4.59}$$

The last term in (4.59), that is, $\frac{ky^2}{X_1}$, depends only on the point scatterer location and is invariant of the radar position, that is, u. Suppose we associate this term with the reflectivity function, that is, we define a new target function

$$f(x, y) \, \exp(j\frac{ky^2}{X_1}).$$

Provided that the radar bandwidth is much smaller than its center frequency, the new target function may be approximated as follows:

$$f(x, y) \, \exp(j\frac{ky^2}{X_1}) \approx f(x, y) \, \exp(j\frac{k_c y^2}{X_1}), \tag{4.60}$$

where k_c is the wavenumber of the center frequency. [We will examine the consequences of the approximation in (4.60).] Although the phase term $\frac{k_c y^2}{X_1}$ depends on the scatterer's cross range (y), it does not alter the magnitude of the reconstructed image using the plane wave approximation-based inversion. Hence, for the success of this inversion, we may only require that the first phase term in (4.59) be much less than one. This yields the following constraint (with $\sin^2 \theta \ll \sin 2\theta$):

$$\frac{k X_0^2 \sin 2\theta}{X_1} \ll 1. \tag{4.61}$$

We now consider the approximation in (4.60). We mentioned earlier that the range of the available wavenumbers in the radar signal is $[k_1, k_2]$; thus, $k_c = \frac{k_2 + k_1}{2}$. Hence, (4.60) is a good approximation if the following is satisfied (note that in (4.60) the maximum value that y can take is X_0):

$$\frac{(k_2 - k_1) X_0^2}{2 X_1} \ll 1. \tag{4.62}$$

Using the expression for the range resolution (4.15) in (4.62), one obtains

$$\frac{\pi X_0^2}{2 \Delta_x X_1} \ll 1,$$

which yields

$$\Delta_x \gg \frac{\pi X_0^2}{2 X_1}. \tag{4.63}$$

Thus, the approximation in (4.60) imposes the constraint (4.63) on the range resolution obtained via the plane wave approximation-based inversion.

Example: Figure 4.19 shows the reconstructions of a target scene that is composed of 17 reflectors in a broadside SAR problem. Figure 4.19a is obtained via the spatial Doppler-based inversion. Each target shows a different *point spread function* in the image that depends on the target's coordinates (see the discussion on resolution in Section 4.4 and Figure 4.9). The Fresnel approximation-based inversion in Figure 4.19b produces a highly out of focus and degraded image. It is difficult to analyze and/or predict image degradations for this approximation.

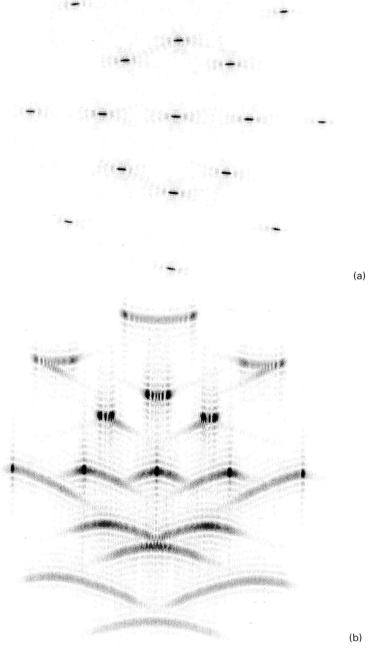

(a)

(b)

Figure 4.19 SAR reconstructions. (a) Spatial Doppler-based inversion. (b) Fresnel approximation-based inversion.

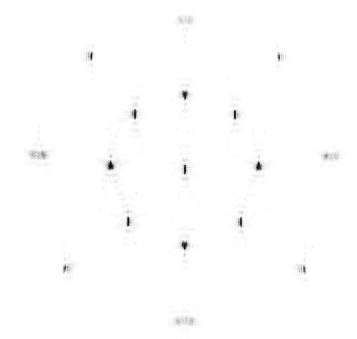

Figure 4.19 (*continued*) (c) Plane wave approximation-based inversion.

Figure 4.19c, the plane wave approximation-based inversion, shows loss of focus and degradations as a target is moved away from the origin. This can be attributed to the fact that the phase error in approximating a spherical wave by a plane wave increases with a target's radial distance from the origin.

4.9 DOPPLER BEAM SHARPENED CW SAR

The SAR inversions discussed in the previous sections are all based on the principle of *position-induced* synthetic aperture. One may also develop a SAR imaging method via utilizing the *fast-time* temporal Doppler shifts in the echoed signal caused by the difference between the radar and target velocities; this results in a *velocity-induced* synthetic aperture. (The fast-time temporal Doppler has a negligible effect in the pulsed SAR system models and inversions discussed earlier.) The temporal Doppler-based SAR is also known as *Doppler Beam Sharpened* (DBS) SAR.

System Model and Inversion

To make comparisons with the position-induced SAR imaging systems, we use the same notations for the DBS SAR imaging system variables. Suppose a transmitting/receiving radar positioned at $(X_1, Y_1 + u)$ illuminates a stationary target area as shown in Figure 4.20. (Note that u is not a variable in DBS SAR.) The transmitted radar signal is an FM-CW (see Chapter 1) for good resolution in both range and Doppler domains. The data acquisition system is similar to the one shown in Figure 4.5 expect for the transmitter/receiver that is now quasi-monostatic (see Figure 1.5) for the continuous wave transmission.

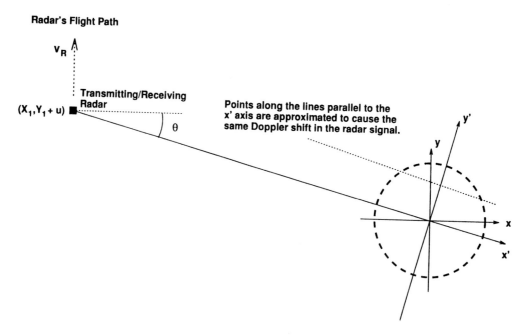

Figure 4.20 Imaging system geometry for Doppler beam sharpened CW SAR.

As in the previous section, we define the angle that the radar makes with respect to the broadside by the following:

$$\theta \equiv \arctan(\frac{Y_1 + u}{X_1}),$$

and let

$$f'(x', y') = f(x, y),$$

where

$$\begin{bmatrix} x' \\ y' \end{bmatrix} = \begin{bmatrix} \cos\theta & \sin\theta \\ -\sin\theta & \cos\theta \end{bmatrix} \begin{bmatrix} x \\ y \end{bmatrix}$$

Furthermore, from the results of Section 2.4 we have

$$F'(k_{x'}, k_{y'}) \equiv F(k_x, k_y)$$

where

$$\begin{bmatrix} k_{x'} \\ k_{y'} \end{bmatrix} = \begin{bmatrix} \cos\theta & \sin\theta \\ -\sin\theta & \cos\theta \end{bmatrix} \begin{bmatrix} k_x \\ k_y \end{bmatrix}.$$

The vehicle carrying radar has a known (cross-range) speed denoted by v_R. We assume that the radar's radiation pattern can be approximated by a plane wave. We consider one of the harmonics in the FM-CW radar signal, for example, $\omega_\ell \equiv \omega_c + \ell\omega_2$. At this harmonic, the echoed signal due to a reflector at (x', y') is temporally Doppler shifted by

$$\omega_D(x', y') \approx 2k_\ell v_R \sin\theta + \frac{2k_\ell v_R \cos\theta}{R_1} y', \tag{4.64}$$

where $k_\ell \equiv \frac{\omega_\ell}{c}$.

Using (4.64) and (4.51) for the plane wave approximation, we can write the following for the DBS SAR system model:

$$s_\ell(u, t) \approx \int_{x'} \int_{y'} f'(x', y') \, \exp[-j\omega_\ell t - j\omega_D(x', y')t]$$

$$\times \exp\left[j2k_\ell(\sqrt{X_1^2 + (Y_1 + u)^2} - x') \right] \, dx'dy'$$

which after some rearrangements yields

$$s_\ell(u,t) \approx \exp[j2k_\ell\sqrt{X_1^2 + (Y_1 + u)^2} - j(\omega_\ell + 2k_\ell v_R \sin\theta)t] \times$$

$$\underbrace{\int_{x'}\int_{y'} f'(x',y') \exp(-j2k_\ell x' - j\frac{2k_\ell v_R \cos\theta\ t}{R_1}y')dx'dy'}_{Two\ dimensional\ Fourier\ integral}$$

$$= \exp[j2k_\ell\sqrt{X_1^2 + (Y_1 + u)^2} - j(\omega_\ell + 2k_\ell v_R \sin\theta)t]\ F'(k_{x'}, k_{y'})$$
$$(4.65)$$

where

$$k_{x'} = 2k_\ell$$
$$k_{y'} = \frac{2k_\ell v_R \cos\theta\ t}{R_1}. \qquad (4.66)$$

Making variable transformations from $(k_{x'}, k_{y'})$ to (k_x, k_y) in (4.65) and after some rearrangements, one obtains the following inversion:

$$F(k_x, k_y) \approx \exp[-j2k_\ell\sqrt{X_1^2 + (Y_1 + u)^2} + j(\omega_\ell + 2k_\ell v_R \sin\theta)t]\ s_\ell(u,t),$$
$$(4.67)$$

with

$$k_x = 2k_\ell\cos\theta - \frac{2k_\ell v_R\cos\theta\ t}{R_1}\sin\theta$$
$$k_y = 2k_\ell\sin\theta + \frac{2k_\ell v_R\cos\theta\ t}{R_1}\cos\theta \qquad (4.68)$$

- *There is an amplitude and phase associated with the ℓ-th harmonic that is $A_1(\ell\omega_2)$ (see Chapter 1). Thus, the right side of (4.67) should be divided by $A_1(\ell\omega_2)$ (source deconvolution), or, in the matched filtered form, multiplied with the conjugate of $A_1(\ell\omega_2)$; that is,*

$$F(k_x, k_y) \approx A_1^*(\ell\omega_2)\ s_\ell(u,t)$$

$$\times\ \exp[-j2k_\ell\sqrt{X_1^2 + (Y_1 + u)^2} + j(\omega_\ell + 2k_\ell v_R \sin\theta)t].$$

By substituting the slow-time domain in terms of the fast-time domain, that is,

$$u = v_R t,$$

in (4.67), and

$$\theta = \arctan(\frac{Y_1 + v_R t}{X_1}),$$

in (4.68), and after certain approximations, one obtains an inverse equation that is identical to the SAR's plane wave approximation-based inversion used in conjunction with a pulsed radar.

The spatial frequency coverage (bandwidth) in the (k_x, k_y) domain is constructed via varying (ω_ℓ, t), that is, the harmonic of the FM-CW radar signal and its observation (processing) time. These dictate the imaging system's resolution as shown next.

Resolution

As we mentioned earlier, DBS SAR does not rely on varying u for image formation. We denote the time duration for illuminating the target with the radar's (continuous wave) signal and recording the resultant echoed signals by t_0 (also called the coherent processing time that is equal to t_3 defined earlier for an FM-CW radar signal). Based on (4.65), this time duration, which yields the observation time range $t \in [0, t_0]$, determines the bandwidth of the available data in the $k_{y'}$ domain. Thus, the cross-range resolution is found from (4.65) to be

$$\Delta_{y'} = \frac{\pi R_1}{k_\ell v_R \cos \theta_1 \, t_0}, \tag{4.69}$$

where $\theta_1 = \arctan(\frac{Y_1}{X_1})$. The range resolution is determined from the classical radar equations to be

$$\Delta_{x'} = \frac{\pi c}{\omega_1}, \tag{4.70}$$

where $2\omega_1$ is the baseband bandwidth of the transmitted FM-CW signal.

By examining (4.69), one can observe that the cross-range resolution can be improved by increasing the coherent processing time t_0. On the other hand, the Doppler shift equation (4.64) assumes that the target's cross-range y' (or the target's aspect angle with respect to the radar that varies with u) is approximately a constant during the coherent processing time $[0, t_0]$. However, since the radar (or the target in ISAR) is moving, this aspect angle might change significantly if t_0 (radar signal illumination and processing time) was chosen to be too long. This issue, which limits mainly the broadside cross-range resolution, is referred to as the problem of *motion through resolution cells* [1],[4].

4.10 FM-CW SAR/ISAR IMAGING

In this section, we reformulate FM-CW SAR/ISAR imaging in the framework of a spherical wave decomposition in terms of plane waves. This analysis is not based on the approximations used in DBS SAR and, thus, does not suffer from the problem of motion through resolution cells. This is true despite the fact that the system model and inversion do incorporate variations of a target's aspect angle with respect to the radar (corresponding to variations of u) during the coherent processing time. The approach is based on a temporal Doppler processing of FM-CW SAR data when the slow-time and fast-time domains are represented by the same variable.

System Model

As in the previous section, we assume FM-CW illumination and reception via a quasi-monostatic radar. We consider the SAR system model in (4.2) at one of the harmonics of the FM-CW radar signal, for example, $\omega_\ell \equiv \omega_c + \ell\omega_2$; that is, the transmitted signal is

$$p_\ell(t) = \exp(j\omega_\ell t),$$

and

$$P_\ell(\omega) = \delta(\omega - \omega_\ell).$$

- *We showed in Chapter 1 that the spectral distribution of the ℓ-th harmonic of an FM-CW signal is*

$$P_\ell(\omega) = A_1(\ell\omega_2)\, A_3(\omega - \omega_\ell).$$

$A_1(\ell\omega_2)$ *is a constant that can be dealt with later. At the present time, we assume measurements are made for* $t \in (-\infty, \infty)$, *i.e,* $t_3 = \infty$, *that implies*

$$A_3(\omega - \omega_\ell) = \delta(\omega - \omega_\ell).$$

We will examine finite aperture effects, that is, $t_3 < \infty$ *and* $A_3(\cdot)$ *is a sinc function, in our later discussions.*

In this case, the SAR system model in (4.2) becomes

$$s_\ell(u,t) \equiv \int\int f(x,y)\exp\left[j\omega_\ell[t - \frac{2\sqrt{(X_1 - x)^2 + (Y_1 + u - y)^2}}{c}]\right]dxdy$$

$$(4.71)$$

Suppose the aircraft's speed in the cross-range domain is v_R. The synthetic aperture variable u is equal to the slow-time, call it τ, multiplied by the aircraft's speed; that is,

$$u \equiv v_R\ \tau.$$

We rewrite the system model in (4.71) using the slow-time variable τ (instead of u) and the fast-time variable t, and, for notational simplicity, keep the functional $s_\ell(\cdot)$ to represent the resultant signal

$$s_\ell(\tau,t) \equiv \int\int dx\ dy\ f(x,y)\ \times$$

$$\exp\left[j\omega_\ell[t - \frac{2\sqrt{(X_1 - x)^2 + (Y_1 + v_R\tau - y)^2}}{c}]\right].$$

$$(4.72)$$

The Fourier transform of both sides of (4.72) with respect to t yields

$$s_\ell(\tau,\omega) = \int\int f(x,y)\ \exp[-j\frac{2\omega_\ell}{c}\sqrt{(X_1 - x)^2 + (Y_1 + v_R\tau - y)^2}]$$

$$\times\ \delta(\omega - \omega_\ell)\ dxdy.$$

$$(4.73)$$

With the help of the plane wave decomposition of a spherical wave, the Fourier transform of both sides of (4.73) with respect to τ can be found to be (Ω is the Fourier domain for τ)

$$S_\ell(\Omega,\omega) = \delta(\omega - \omega_\ell) \int\int f(x,y) \times$$

$$\exp[\ j\sqrt{\frac{4\omega_\ell^2}{c^2} - \frac{\Omega^2}{v_R^2}}(X_1 - x) + j\frac{\Omega}{v_R}(Y_1 - y)\ ]\ dxdy$$

$$=\delta(\omega - \omega_\ell)\ \exp(j\sqrt{\frac{4\omega_\ell^2}{c^2} - \frac{\Omega^2}{v_R^2}}\ X_1 + j\frac{\Omega}{v_R}Y_1) \times$$

$$\underbrace{\int\int f(x,y)\ \exp(-j\sqrt{\frac{4\omega_\ell^2}{c^2} - \frac{\Omega^2}{v_R^2}}\ x - j\frac{\Omega}{v_R}y)\ dxdy}_{Two\ dimensional\ Fourier\ integral}$$

$$=\delta(\omega - \omega_\ell)\exp(j\sqrt{\frac{4\omega_\ell^2}{c^2} - \frac{\Omega^2}{v_R^2}}X_1 + j\frac{\Omega}{v_R}Y_1)F(\sqrt{\frac{4\omega_\ell^2}{c^2} - \frac{\Omega^2}{v_R^2}},\frac{\Omega}{v_R})$$

$$(4.74)$$

Equation (4.74), which is obtained for CW illumination, is analogous to (4.6) that yielded the spatial Doppler-based inversion (4.7).

In reality, the slow-time and fast-time represent the same variable; that is,

$$\tau = t,$$

that we refer to as *real* time. Our objective is to solve the FM-CW SAR inverse problem based on the measurements of the real time signal

$$s(t,\omega_\ell) \equiv s_\ell(\tau,t)|_{\tau=t}$$
$$= s_\ell(t,t).$$
$$(4.75)$$

• *The harmonic of the FM-CW radar signal ω_ℓ is also a variable and, thus, the measured signal should be identified by $s(t,\omega_\ell)$.*

Inversion

To solve the inverse problem, we consider the following inverse two-dimensional Fourier transform:

$$s_\ell(\tau,t) = \int_\Omega \int_\omega S_\ell(\Omega,\omega)\ \exp[j(\Omega\tau + \omega t)]\ d\omega d\Omega. \qquad (4.76)$$

With $\tau = t$ and (4.75), (4.76) becomes

$$
s(t, \omega_\ell) = s_\ell(t, t)
$$
$$
= \int_\Omega \int_\omega S_\ell(\Omega, \omega) \, \exp[j(\Omega + \omega)t] \, d\omega d\Omega. \tag{4.77}
$$

We define the following two-dimensional transformation:

$$
\alpha \equiv \omega + \Omega
$$
$$
\beta \equiv \omega - \Omega \tag{4.78}
$$

Making variable transformations from (Ω, ω) to (α, β) in the integrals of (4.77), one obtains

$$
s(t, \omega_\ell) = \int_\alpha \int_\beta S_\ell(\frac{\alpha - \beta}{2}, \frac{\alpha + \beta}{2}) \, \exp(j\alpha t) \, d\alpha d\beta. \tag{4.79}
$$

Taking the Fourier transform of both sides of (4.79) with respect to the real time t yields

$$
S(\alpha, \omega_\ell) = \int_\beta S_\ell(\frac{\alpha - \beta}{2}, \frac{\alpha + \beta}{2}) \, d\beta, \tag{4.80}
$$

where α is the temporal frequency domain for the real time t.

Substituting (4.74) in (4.80), and carrying out the integral over the delta function, yields

$$
S(\alpha, \omega_\ell) = \exp\left[j\sqrt{\frac{4\omega_\ell^2}{c^2} - \frac{(\alpha - \omega_\ell)^2}{v_R^2}} \, X_1 + j\frac{(\alpha - \omega_\ell)}{v_R} Y_1 \right]
$$
$$
\times \, F\left[\sqrt{\frac{4\omega_\ell^2}{c^2} - \frac{(\alpha - \omega_\ell)^2}{v_R^2}}, \frac{(\alpha - \omega_\ell)}{v_R} \right]. \tag{4.81}
$$

Finally, from (4.81), we have the following inversion:

$$
F(k_x, k_y) = \exp(-jk_x \, X_1 - jk_y Y_1) \, S(\alpha, \omega_\ell), \tag{4.82}
$$

where

$$k_x \equiv \sqrt{\frac{4\omega_\ell^2}{c^2} - \frac{(\alpha - \omega_\ell)^2}{v_R^2}}$$

$$k_y \equiv \frac{(\alpha - \omega_\ell)}{v_R}$$

(4.83)

- *There is an amplitude and phase associated with the ℓ-th harmonic that is $A_1(\ell\omega_2)$ (see Chapter 1). Thus, the right side of (4.82) should be divided by $A_1(\ell\omega_2)$ (source deconvolution), or, in the matched-filtered form, multiplied with the conjugate of $A_1(\ell\omega_2)$; that is,*

$$F(k_x, k_y) = A_1^*(\ell\omega_2) \, \exp(-jk_x \, X_1 - jk_y Y_1) \, S(\alpha, \omega_\ell).$$

Relation to Pulsed SAR

For simplicity of notation as well as correspondence with pulsed SAR imaging, suppose the FM-CW SAR measurements are made for $t \in [\frac{-t_0}{2}, \frac{t_0}{2}]$ or $t \in [\frac{-t_3}{2}, \frac{t_3}{2}]$, where $t_3 = t_0$ is the parameter of the FM-CW radar signal. We define the following spatial frequency variable:

$$k_u \equiv \frac{\alpha - \omega_\ell}{v_R}.$$

(4.84)

Using (4.84) in the inverse equations (4.82)-(4.83) results in the following:

$$F(k_x, k_y) = \exp(-jk_x \, X_1 - jk_y Y_1) \, S(\alpha, \omega_\ell),$$

with

$$k_x \equiv \sqrt{4k_\ell^2 - k_u^2}$$

$$k_y \equiv k_u$$

which are identical to the inverse equations (4.7)-(4.8) that were derived for pulsed SAR imaging.

- *This result indicates that FM-CW SAR data around each harmonic of the radar signal (i.e., the baseband temporal Doppler data for each harmonic) is equivalent to pulsed SAR data.*

- *When $a_1(t)$ is a short-duration rectangular pulse, FM-CW SAR signaling corresponds to a pulsed radar signal if the echoed signal for the pulse $a_1(t - \ell t_2)$ arrives prior to the transmission of the next pulse, that is, $a_1[t - (\ell + 1)t_2]$. This is true when*

$$\frac{2(R_1 + X_0)}{c} < t_2 - t_1.$$

Thus, pulsed SAR imaging may be viewed as a special case of FM-CW SAR imaging (though the two SAR imaging methods use different principles for image formation).

- *The SAR inverse method presented in this section provides an accurate and unifying approach for SAR image formation that is applicable in both pulsed SAR and FM-CW SAR imaging systems. This is achieved via performing a long one-dimensional DFT on the real time SAR data for either of the two SAR systems. In pulsed SAR imaging, this long one-dimensional DFT can be converted into a smaller two-dimensional DFT. In FM-CW SAR imaging, the long one-dimensional DFT can be converted into a set of smaller one-dimensional DFTs via first passing the echoed signal through a set of digital (or analog) bandpass filters. FM-CW SAR has the advantage of a better signal-to-noise power ratio in its echoed signal due to its continuous wave transmission.*

Sampling Constraints and Resolution

The length of the coherent processing time for FM-CW is limited to t_3. Thus, using a finite aperture (coherent processing time) analysis similar to the one shown for pulse SAR equation (4.9a), the measured data in the α domain should be represented by the convolution of $S(\cdot)$ with the aperture transfer function, that is, the sinc function

$$A_3(\alpha) = t_3 \frac{\sin(.5t_3\alpha)}{.5t_3\alpha}.$$

Thus, the temporal Fourier transform of the measured data is

$$S(\alpha, \omega_\ell) \; * \; A_3(\alpha) = S(\alpha, \omega_\ell) \; * \; t_3\frac{\sin(.5t_3\alpha)}{.5t_3\alpha},$$

where $*$ denotes convolution in the α domain. Using (4.84) to transform α to k_u in the above convolution, we obtain an equation equivalent to (4.9a).

Thus, the sampling constraints and resolution for FM-CW SAR can be obtained via the spatial Doppler analysis performed for pulsed SAR. The resolution equations for FM-CW SAR are identical to the ones for pulsed SAR when the synthetic aperture in the u domain is within $[-L, L]$, where

$$L = \frac{v_R t_3}{2}.$$

The sampling rate in the fast-time domain of pulsed SAR imaging and the sampling rate in the real time domain of FM-CW SAR imaging are both dictated by the bandwidth of $a_1(t)$; that is,

$$\Delta_t \leq \frac{2\pi}{2\omega_1}.$$

The support band of the pulsed SAR signal in the k_u domain was shown to be [see (4.12)]

$$\Omega_s = [2k\sin\theta_1 - 2k\frac{L+X_0}{R_1}\cos^2\theta_1, 2k\sin\theta_1 + 2k\frac{L+X_0}{R_1}\cos^2\theta_1].$$

Thus, using the transformation in (4.84), the support band of the temporal Doppler data around the harmonic ω_ℓ is

$$\Omega_\ell \equiv [\omega_\ell + 2k_\ell v_R \sin\theta_1 - 2k_\ell v_R \frac{L+X_0}{R_1}\cos^2\theta_1, \omega_\ell + 2k_\ell v_R \sin\theta_1$$
$$+ 2k_\ell v_R \frac{L+X_0}{R_1}\cos^2\theta_1],$$

with $2L = v_R t_3$. The temporal Doppler shifted components for this harmonic would not overlap with the temporal Doppler shifted components of the other harmonics provided that (with $v_R \ll c$)

$$\omega_2 = \frac{2\pi}{t_2} > 4k_\ell v_R \frac{L+X_0}{R_1}\cos^2\theta_1.$$

This constraint is identical to

$$\Delta_u \leq 2\pi \frac{R_1}{4k(L + X_0)\cos^2 \theta_1},$$

that is, the sampling constraint in the aperture domain for the pulsed SAR signal [see (4.13)]. We will find milder constraints on t_2 based on compressing the FM-CW SAR signal in the next section.

We showed in (4.14) that pulsed SAR's spatial frequency coverage can be approximated via the following hexagonal transformation:

$$k_x \approx \tan\theta_1 \left(\frac{2k}{\sin\theta_1} - k_u\right)$$

$$k_y = k_u.$$

Using the sampling principles for hexagonal transformation, we obtained constraints for sample spacing in the measurement domain (k, k_u). With the equivalence of pulsed SAR and FM-CW SAR, we may use the above hexagonal transformation with

$$k_u \equiv \frac{\alpha - \omega_\ell}{v R},$$

as defined in (4.84), and k replaced with k_ℓ. Moreover, we have

$$\Delta_{k_\ell} \equiv \frac{\omega_2}{c},$$

and

$$\Delta_\alpha = \frac{2\pi}{t_3}.$$

The hexagonal sampling principles may also be used in this case to obtain constraints on Δ_{k_ℓ} (or t_2) and Δ_α. We do not develop the detailed forms of those constraints. An interesting result of those constraints is the following restriction on the pulse repetition interval:

$$t_2 > \frac{4X_0}{c}. \tag{4.85}$$

This constraint states that the pri should be greater than the arrival time difference between the echoes coming from the nearest point in the target region and the farthest point in the target region. A similar constraint was obtained in (1.48) for one-dimensional echo imaging via FM-CW signaling. We will obtain additional constraints on t_2 in the next section.

The hexagonal sampling constraints also yield the following restriction:

$$T_0 \equiv \frac{2\pi}{\Delta_\alpha} > \frac{2X_0}{v_R}.$$

If $T_0 > t_3$, this constraint can be met by zero-padding the measured FM-CW SAR signal in the time domain, that is, a process that we also used for pulsed SAR imaging.

FM-CW SAR Signal Compression

Consider the echoed signal for the ℓ-th harmonic of the FM-CW signal from a unit reflector located at (x, y), that is,

$$\exp\left[j\omega_\ell [t - \frac{2\sqrt{(X_1 - x)^2 + (Y_1 + v_R t - y)^2}}{c}] \right].$$

Suppose this signal is normalized (compressed) by multiplying it with

$$\exp\left[-j\omega_c [t - \frac{2\sqrt{X_1^2 + (Y_1 + v_R t)^2}}{c}] \right],$$

that is the complex conjugate of the echoed signal for the zero-th harmonic (i.e., the carrier) of the FM-CW signal from a unit reflector located at $(0, 0)$. The resultant phase function is

$$\phi(t) \equiv (\omega_\ell - \omega_c)\, t - 2k_\ell \sqrt{(X_1 - x)^2 + (Y_1 + v_R t - y)^2}$$
$$+ 2k_c \sqrt{X_1^2 + (Y_1 + v_R t)^2}.$$

The instantaneous frequency of this signal is approximately equal to (with $v_R \ll c$)

$$\frac{d\phi(t)}{dt} \approx (\omega_\ell - \omega_c)\left[1 - \frac{v_R(Y_1 + v_R t)}{cR_1}\right] + 2k_\ell v_R \frac{y}{R_1}$$
$$\approx (\omega_\ell - \omega_c) + 2k_\ell v_R \frac{y}{R_1}.$$

We also know that the target's cross-range falls within the radar's foot-print, that is, $y \in [-X_0, X_0]$. Thus, the support band of the normalized FM-CW SAR signal at the ℓ-th harmonic is

$$\Omega_{\ell_c} = \bigcup_{|y| \leq X_0} [(\omega_\ell - \omega_c) + 2k_\ell v_R \frac{y}{R_1}]$$

$$= [(\omega_\ell - \omega_c) - 2k_\ell v_R \frac{X_0}{R_1}, (\omega_\ell - \omega_c) + 2k_\ell v_R \frac{X_0}{R_1}],$$

that is a bandpass region centered at $\omega_\ell - \omega_c$ with a baseband bandwidth equal to $4k_\ell v_R \frac{X_0}{R_1}$. *Note that this result is identical to (4.21) with $u = v_R t$.*

Thus, the target's signatures at two adjacent harmonics of the FM-CW signal would not overlap with each other provided that

$$4k_\ell v_R \frac{X_0}{R_1} < \omega_2.$$

Thus, we have a milder constraint on the radar signal's pri (pulse repetition interval) that becomes

$$t_2 < \frac{2\pi R_1}{4k_\ell v_R X_0}.$$

Combining this result and (4.85), we obtain

$$\frac{4X_0}{c} < t_2 < \frac{2\pi R_1}{4k_\ell v_R X_0}. \tag{4.86}$$

(The largest available k_ℓ is used in (4.86) to determine t_2.)

- *The compression does not alter the sampling interval in the time domain that is still dictated by the bandwidth of $a_1(t)$. The compression provides a signal processing tool for alias-free handling of FM-CW SAR data while fully utilizing the power of the radar antenna.*

The compressed FM-CW SAR signal is in the form of a frequency division multiplexed (FDM) signal. Thus, one can pass this signal through a bank of bandpass filters followed by decompression, that is, multiplication with

$$\exp\left[j\omega_c[t - \frac{2\sqrt{X_1^2 + (Y_1 + v_R t)^2}}{c}]\right],$$

to recover the target's signature at each individual harmonic of the FM-CW signal.

- *The recovery of the target's signature at the ℓ-th harmonic may also be achieved via normalization with*

$$\exp\left[-j\omega_\ell[t - \frac{2\sqrt{X_1^2 + (Y_1 + v_R t)^2}}{c}]\right],$$

  followed by lowpass filtering and decompression with the conjugate of the above phase function. One should consider the cost effectiveness of the two procedures based on the available signal processing software and hardware.

Example: Consider an FM-CW SAR system with the following parameters: $(X_1, Y_1) = (10000, 3000)$ meters; $f_c = .3$ GHz; there are 4,096 time samples in the data acquisition time interval with $t_3 = 1.024$ seconds, that is, $\Delta_t = 250$ microseconds; $t_1 = t_2 = 16$ milliseconds; $a_1(t)$ is a baseband chirp signal; $v_R = 1,000$ meters/second, that is, $2L = 1,024$ meters. Four unit-reflectors are randomly positioned in the disk of radius 64 meters centered at the origin. For this measurement scenario, the FM-CW SAR signal suffers from overlapping of the target's signature (around the harmonics) in the frequency domain. The same is not true for the compressed FM-CW SAR signal.

Figure 4.21a shows the FM-CW SAR signal in the time domain; Figure 4.21b shows a portion of this signal over a smaller time interval. Figure 4.22a shows the compressed FM-CW SAR signal in the time domain; Figure 4.22b shows a portion of this signal over a smaller time interval. Figure 4.23a shows the FM-CW SAR signal in the frequency domain; Figure 4.23b shows a portion of this signal over a smaller frequency interval. Figure 4.24a shows the compressed FM-CW SAR signal in the frequency domain; Figure 4.24b shows a portion of this signal over a smaller frequency interval.

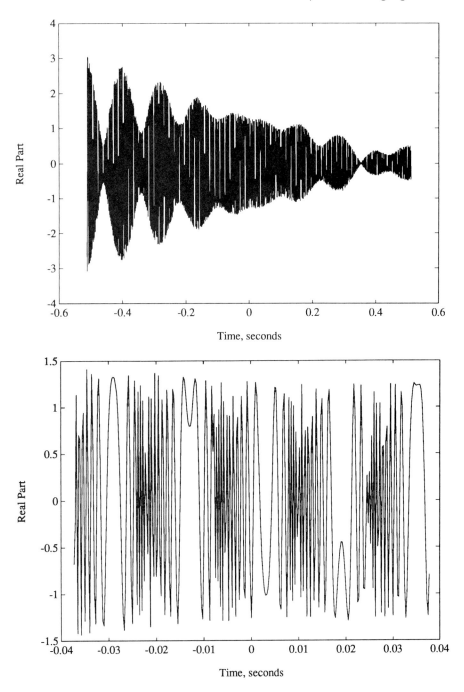

Figure 4.21 FM-CW SAR signal.

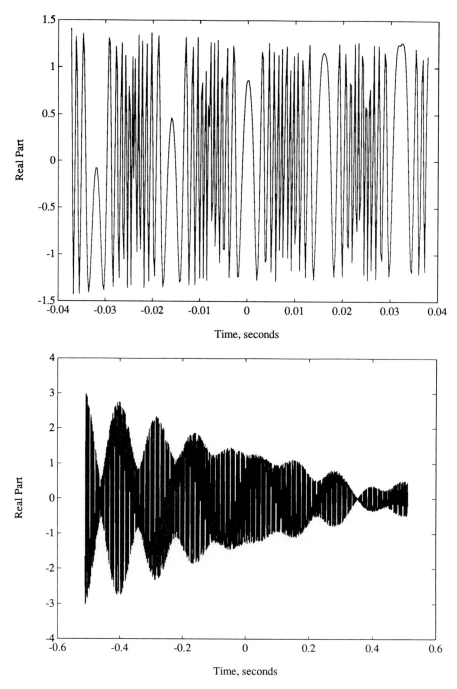

Figure 4.22 Compressed FM-CW SAR signal

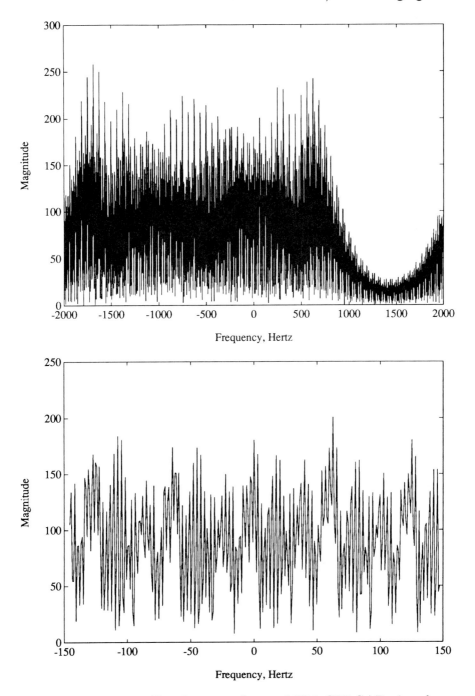

Figure 4.23 Fourier transform of FM-CW SAR signal.

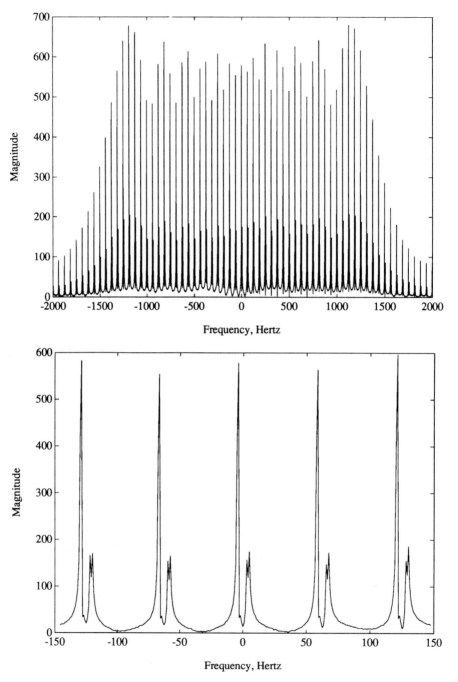

Figure 4.24 Fourier transform of compressed FM-CW SAR signal.

4.11 BISTATIC SAR/ISAR IMAGING

A bistatic synthetic aperture radar imaging problem arises in high-resolution terrain imaging using transmitting and receiving radars that are mounted on two different aircrafts. Such bistatic measurements are useful when the terrain's monostatic radar cross section is not strong [10]. Bistatic SAR measurements may involve several runs with varying bistatic angles by the radar-carrying aircrafts to obtain powerful echoed signals from the terrain that is to be imaged.

Bistatic SAR also has military reconnaissance applications. For these problems, a high-powered transmitter stationed at, for example, a ground station or a satellite illuminates the target scene from a distant and safe location. A receiver, mounted on a vehicle that flies much closer to the target scene (to improve resolution), makes bistatic measurements of the signals reflecting from the target area.

The bistatic SAR formulation also brings out certain functional properties of a physical array's data that is useful for developing inversion in multistatic echo imaging problems. An example of such an imaging scenario that illuminates a dynamic object with a single transmission and makes multiple (multistatic) measurements of the resultant echoed signal along a physical linear array is discussed in [13]. It is shown that such multistatic measurements can be translated into the data from a monostatic synthesized linear array.

System Model and Inversion

Figure 4.25 shows the imaging system geometry for bistatic SAR imaging. In the bistatic SAR or ISAR problem, a radar illuminates the object at the coordinates identified via $(X_1, Y_1 + u)$, $u \in [-L, +L]$ (synthesized aperture), on the (x, y) plane (x is the slant-range). For a given u, a receiving radar records the signal echoed from the object at $(X_2 + au, Y_2 + bu)$; (X_1, Y_1), (X_2, Y_2), and (a, b) are known or estimated constants. (In most applications (a, b), are estimated to maintain coherence between the transmitter and the receiver.) We denote the polar coordinates for (X_1, Y_1) and (X_2, Y_2) by (θ_1, R_1) and (θ_2, R_2), respectively.

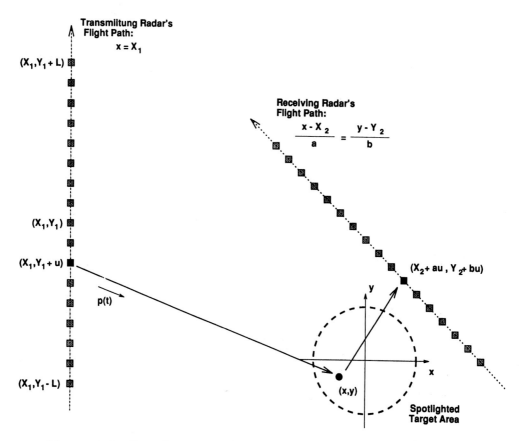

Figure 4.25 Imaging system geometry for bistatic SAR imaging.

The round-trip phase delay of the echoed signal by a point scatterer at (x, y) is

$$k\sqrt{(X_1 - x)^2 + (Y_1 + u - y)^2} + k\sqrt{(X_2 + au - x)^2 + (Y_2 + bu - y)^2}.$$

Thus, the total recorded echoed signal becomes

$$
\begin{aligned}
s(u, \omega) = \int\int \; dx\,dy \; f(x, y) \\
\times \exp[jk\sqrt{(X_1 - x)^2 + (Y_1 + u - y)^2}] \\
\times \exp[jk\sqrt{(X_2 + au - x)^2 + (Y_2 + bu - y)^2}].
\end{aligned}
\tag{4.87}
$$

The two spherical wave functions that appear on the right side of (4.87) have the following Fourier decompositions:

$$\exp[jk\sqrt{(X_1 - x)^2 + (Y_1 + u - y)^2}]$$
$$= \int d\alpha \exp[j\sqrt{k^2 - \alpha^2}(X_1 - x) + j\alpha(Y_1 + u - y)]$$
$$\exp[jk\sqrt{(X_2 + au - x)^2 + (Y_2 + bu - y)^2}]$$
$$= \int d\beta \exp[j\sqrt{k^2 - \beta^2}(X_2 + au - x) + j\beta(Y_2 + bu - y)].$$

$$(4.88)$$

α and β signify two distinct characteristics of the scattering phenomenon: (i) α represents the spatial frequency domain for the transmitted waves from the radar impinging on the object; (ii) β is the spatial frequency domain for the waves reflected from the object traveling back toward the radar.

Substituting (4.88) in the system model (4.87), one obtains a spatial Doppler decomposition for the SAR signal. Using a phase modulation analysis of the Doppler data via the method of stationary phase, one obtains a one-to-one mapping between $S(k_u, \omega)$ and $F(k_x, k_y)$, that is, the inverse equation [13]. The sampling constraints and processing issues for bistatic SAR could be obtained via the same procedures outlined in Section 4.4 (see [13]).

4.12 SPACEBORNE (CIRCULAR) SAR IMAGING

Spaceborne SAR imaging is a synthetic aperture radar modality that utilizes the motion of a satellite (transmitter/receiver) in an orbit. Such orbits can be accurately modeled as *circular* trajectories. Our discussion in this section is concerned with system modeling, inversion and certain processing issues associated with circular SAR/ISAR imaging. We first present a detailed analysis of system modeling, inversion and processing issues for circular SAR imaging with a pulsed radar. Then, the system model and inversion for circular SAR imaging with an FM-CW radar signal are outlined.

System Model

Consider an imaging system where a transmitting/receiving radar moves along a circle of radius R in the the spatial (x, y) domain (ground-plane geometry) as shown in Figure 4.26. This radar makes a transmission and its corresponding reception at the coordinates $(R\cos\theta, R\sin\theta)$ for $\theta \in [-\theta_0, \theta_0]$ (circular synthetic aperture). θ represents the slow-time domain; θ is equal to the constant angular speed of the satellite multiplied with the slow-time.

At a given temporal frequency of the pulsed radar signal, for example, ω, the round-trip delay for the signal echoed from a reflector at (x, y) is

$$2k \sqrt{(R\cos\theta - x)^2 + (R\sin\theta - y)^2}.$$

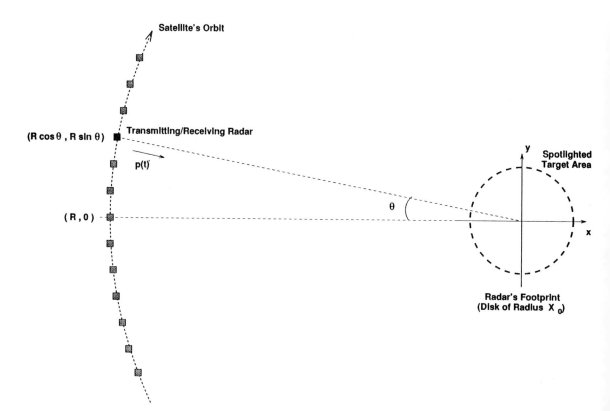

Figure 4.26 Imaging system geometry for spaceborne SAR imaging.

Thus, the total recorded echoed signal is

$$s(\theta, \omega) = \int_x \int_y f(x, y) \, \exp[j2k \, \sqrt{(R \cos \theta - x)^2 + (R \sin \theta - y)^2}] \, dx \, dy.$$

$$(4.89)$$

The system model in (4.89) is also applicable in the slant-plane geometry with the slant-range defined by the following:

$$x_s \equiv R \cos \theta - \sqrt{(R \cos \theta - x)^2 + z^2}.$$

We have the following plane wave decomposition for the spherical wave function on the right side of (4.89) [8, eq. 7.2.43]:

$$\exp[j2k \, \sqrt{(R \cos \theta - x)^2 + (R \sin \theta - y)^2}]$$

$$= \int_{-\pi/2}^{\pi/2} \exp[j2k \cos \phi \, (R \cos \theta - x) + j2k \sin \phi \, (R \sin \theta - y)] \, d\phi,$$

where ϕ's represent the angular directions of the plane waves. Using this decomposition in (4.89) yields

$$s(\theta, \omega) = \int_{-\pi/2}^{\pi/2} d\phi \, \exp[j2kR \cos(\theta - \phi)]$$

$$\times \left[\int_x \int_y f(x, y) \, \exp(-j2k \cos \phi x - j2k \sin \phi y) \, dx \, dy \right].$$

$$(4.90)$$

The two-dimensional integral over the target region (x, y) on the right side of (4.90) is a Fourier integral. Hence, we can write

$$s(\theta, \omega) = \int_{-\pi/2}^{\pi/2} \exp[j2kR \cos(\theta - \phi)] \, F(2k \cos \phi, 2k \sin \phi) \, d\phi. \quad (4.91)$$

We define the polar mapping of $F(2k \cos \phi, 2k \sin \phi)$ by $F_p(\phi, 2k)$; that is,

$$F(2k \cos \phi, 2k \sin \phi) = F_p(\phi, 2k).$$

We also define
$$g(\theta, \omega) \equiv \exp(j2kR\cos\theta).$$

Thus, we can rewrite the system model in (4.91) as follows:

$$
\begin{aligned}
s(\theta, \omega) &= \int_{-\pi/2}^{\pi/2} F_p(\phi, 2k)\ g(\theta - \phi, \omega)d\phi \\
&= F_p(\theta, 2k)\ *\ g(\theta, \omega),
\end{aligned}
\tag{4.92}
$$

where $*$ denotes convolution in the θ domain.

Inversion

We denote the Fourier transform domain for ϕ by ξ. Taking the Fourier transform of both sides of (4.92) with respect to θ yields

$$S(\xi, \omega) = \tilde{F}_p(\xi, 2k)\ G(\xi, \omega), \tag{4.93}$$

with

$$\tilde{F}_p(\xi, 2k) \equiv \mathcal{F}_{(\theta)}\big[\ F_p(\theta, 2k)\ \big],$$

and [see [8] for the following equation]

$$
\begin{aligned}
G(\xi, \omega) &\equiv \mathcal{F}_{(\theta)}\big[\ g(\theta, \omega)\ \big] \\
&= H_\xi(2kR)\ \exp(j\frac{\pi\xi}{2}),
\end{aligned}
$$

where $H_\xi(\cdot)$ is the Hankel function of the first kind, ξ order.

- *With $\theta_0 = \pi$, ξ takes on only integer values, and $\tilde{F}_p$ and G represent Fourier coefficients for the periodic signals F_p and g, respectively.*

From (4.93), we obtain the following inversion in the (ξ, ω) domain:

$$\tilde{F}_p(\xi, 2k) = \frac{S(\xi, \omega)}{H_\xi(2kR)\ \exp(j\frac{\pi\xi}{2})}, \tag{4.94}$$

or equivalently

$$F(2k\cos\theta, 2k\sin\theta) = \mathcal{F}_{(\xi)}^{-1}\left[\ \frac{S(\xi, \omega)}{H_\xi(2kR)\ \exp(j\frac{\pi\xi}{2})}\ \right]. \tag{4.95}$$

Note that the spatial frequency coverage as dictated by (4.95) is polar. The deconvolution kernel in (4.95) can be simplified without affecting the accuracy of the inversion. This will be shown in (4.105).

Sampling Constraint in the Aperture Domain

Consider the echoed signal in the (θ, ω) domain for a unit reflector at (x, y), that is,

$$\exp[j2k\sqrt{(R\cos\theta - x)^2 + (R\sin\theta - y)^2}].$$

Denote the polar coordinates for (x, y) by (r, α); thus, $r \leq X_0$ and $\alpha \in [0, 2\pi]$. The instantaneous frequency of this PM signal in the θ domain is (with $r \leq X_0 \ll R$)

$$\frac{\partial}{\partial\theta}[2k\sqrt{(R\cos\theta - x)^2 + (R\sin\theta - y)^2}]$$

$$= \frac{2kRr\sin(\theta - \alpha)}{\sqrt{(R\cos\theta - x)^2 + (R\sin\theta - y)^2}} \qquad (4.96)$$

$$\approx 2kr\sin(\theta - \alpha)$$

Thus, the instantaneous frequency in (4.96) falls in the interval $[-\xi_0, \xi_0]$ where

$$\xi_0 \equiv 2kX_0. \qquad (4.97)$$

Note that this band is invariant of the range of available θ values.

Using (4.97), we observe that the sample spacing in the θ domain should satisfy

$$\Delta_\theta \leq \frac{2\pi}{2\xi_0} = \frac{2\pi}{4kX_0} \qquad (4.98)$$

to avoid aliasing. Substituting for the radar's footprint from (4.1), i.e, $X_0 = \frac{R\lambda}{D}$, in (4.98), one obtains

$$\Delta_\theta = \frac{D}{4R}. \qquad (4.99)$$

Thus, the distance that the satellite travels between two successive measurements is

$$R\,\Delta_\theta = \frac{D}{4},\tag{4.100}$$

which is identical to the sample spacing obtained in (4.23) for the compressed SAR signal measured in translational SAR imaging.

The constraint in (4.98) is also identical to the constraint required on the sample spacing in the angular domain of polar data to avoid nonlinear aliasing in the reconstruction (interpolation) phase of the algorithm [11].

Plane Wave Approximation-Based Inversion

Using eq. (5.3.77) in [8] to approximate the Hankel function in (4.95), we obtain (with $\xi \leq 2kX_0 \ll 2kR$)

$$H_\xi(2kR)\ \exp(j\pi\xi/2) \approx \exp(j\sqrt{4k^2R^2 - \xi^2}).\tag{4.101}$$

Note that if the effect of ξ in the exponent on the right side of (4.101) could be neglected, that is,

$$\exp(j\sqrt{4k^2R^2 - \xi^2}) \approx \exp(j2kR),\tag{4.102}$$

then we have

$$H_\xi(2kR)\ \exp(j\pi\xi/2) \approx \exp(j2kR).\tag{4.103}$$

In this case, the denominator inside the inverse Fourier transform in (4.95), that is,

$$H_\xi(2kR)\ \exp(j\pi\xi/2),$$

is independent of ξ. Thus, the Fourier transform with respect to θ and the deconvolution on the right side of (4.95) is not essential. In this case, (4.95) becomes the same as circular SAR/ISAR inversion based on the plane wave approximation [1,16].

Clearly, the worst scenario encountered in (4.103) is when $\xi = \xi_0 = 2kX_0$. In this case, (4.103) becomes

$$\exp(j2k\sqrt{R^2 - X_0^2}) \approx \exp(j2kR).\tag{4.104}$$

Equation (4.104) is a valid approximation if

$$\frac{kX_0^2}{R} \ll 1.$$

This constraint, which is identical to the constraint (4.58) for airborne (translational) SAR, can be shown to be too restricted based on the arguments that were presented in Section 4.8. Using the steps that resulted in the constraints (4.61) and (4.63) for airborne SAR, one can show that the same constraints, that is,

$$\frac{kX_0^2 \sin 2\theta}{X_1} \ll 1,$$

and

$$\Delta_x \gg \frac{\pi X_0^2}{2X_1},$$

should be met in spaceborne SAR for the plane wave approximation-based inversion to be valid.

Deconvolution Implementation

We next consider the processing issues associated with the deconvolution in (4.95). With the help of (4.101), we can rewrite the deconvolution on the right side of (4.95) as follows: [constants and slowly-fluctuating amplitude functions are suppressed on the second line of (4.105)]

$$F(2k \cos \theta, 2k \sin \theta) = \mathcal{F}_{(\xi)}^{-1} \left[S(\xi, \omega) \, \exp(-j\sqrt{4k^2 R^2 - \xi^2}) \right] \tag{4.105}$$
$$\approx s(\theta, \omega) \, * \, g^*(\theta, \omega),$$

where g^* denotes the complex conjugate of g; $g^*(\theta, \omega)$ is called the deconvolution kernel. The instantaneous frequency of the phase modulated term on the right side of (4.105), that is, $\exp(-j\sqrt{4k^2 R^2 - \xi^2})$, is

$$\frac{d}{d\xi}(-\sqrt{4k^2 R^2 - \xi^2}) = \frac{\xi}{\sqrt{4k^2 R^2 - \xi^2}}.$$

This instantaneous frequency attains its maximum when $|\xi| = \xi_0 = 2kX_0$; that is,

$$\frac{\xi_0}{\sqrt{4k^2R^2 - \xi_0^2}} \approx \frac{2kX_0}{2kR} = \frac{X_0}{R}.$$

$\pm\frac{X_0}{R}$ represents the support of the deconvolution kernel, $g^*(\theta,\omega)$, in the θ domain. Thus, to avoid circular convolution aliasing in the discrete implementation of (4.105), the zero-padded processed aperture, call it $[-\psi_0, \psi_0]$, should satisfy

$$\theta_0 + 2\eta\frac{X_0}{R} \leq \psi_0, \tag{4.106}$$

where η, based on the Carson's rule, is a number between one and two.

After the deconvolution operation (4.95) with the zero-padded data, the resultant data in the region $|\theta| \leq \theta_0 + \eta\frac{X_0}{R}$ are preserved and used in the reconstruction phase of the inversion. However, the deconvolved data in the region $\theta_0 + \eta\frac{X_0}{R} < |\theta| \leq \psi_0$, that contain circular convolution aliasing, are discarded.

FM-CW Signaling

System Model: We next consider circular SAR/ISAR imaging using FM-CW signaling. The circular SAR system model at one of the harmonics of the FM-CW radar, for example, $\omega_\ell \equiv \omega_c + \ell\omega_2$, is

$$s_\ell(\theta,t) = \int_x \int_y dx\ dy\ f(x,y)\ \times$$
$$\exp\left[j\omega_\ell[t - \frac{2\sqrt{(R\cos\theta - x)^2 + (R\sin\theta - y)^2}}{c}] \right], \tag{4.107}$$

where θ is the circular synthetic aperture domain and t is the fast-time domain. We denote the satellite's angular speed by ω_R. Thus, the angular position of the satellite in the synthetic aperture domain in terms of the slow-time domain, call it τ, is

$$\theta = \omega_R\tau.$$

The system model in (4.107) in terms of τ can be expressed as follows (the functional $s_\ell(\cdot)$ is kept for notational simplicity):

$$s_\ell(\tau, t) = \int_x \int_y dx\ dy\ f(x, y) \times$$

$$\exp\left[j\omega_\ell[t - \frac{2\sqrt{[R\cos(\omega_R\tau) - x]^2 + [R\sin(\omega_R\tau) - y]^2}}{c}] \right],$$
$$(4.108)$$

The Fourier transform of both sides of (4.108) with respect to the fast-time domain t is

$$s_\ell(\tau, \omega) = \delta(\omega - \omega_\ell) \int_x \int_y f(x, y) \times$$

$$\exp[-j\frac{2\omega_\ell}{c} \frac{\sqrt{[R\cos(\omega_R\tau) - x]^2 + [R\sin(\omega_R\tau) - y]^2}}{c}]\ dx\ dy.$$
$$(4.109)$$

Using [8, eq. 7.2.43], the Fourier transform of both sides of (4.109) with respect to the slow-time domain τ can be found to be (Ω is the Fourier domain for τ)

$$S_\ell(\Omega, \omega) = \delta(\omega - \omega_\ell)\ \tilde{F}_p(\frac{\Omega}{\omega_R}, 2k)\ H_{\frac{\Omega}{\omega_R}}(2kR)\ \exp(j\frac{\pi\frac{\Omega}{\omega_R}}{2}), \qquad (4.110)$$

with

$$\tilde{F}_p(\frac{\Omega}{\omega_R}, 2k) \equiv \mathcal{F}_{(\tau)}\left[F_p(\omega_R\tau, 2k) \right],$$

where $H_{\frac{\Omega}{\omega_R}}(\cdot)$ is the Hankel function of the first kind, $\frac{\Omega}{\omega_R}$ order.

Our objective is to solve the FM-CW SAR inverse problem based on the measurements of the real time signal

$$s(t, \omega_\ell) \equiv s_\ell(\tau, t)|_{\tau=t}$$
$$= s_\ell(t, t). \qquad (4.111)$$

Inversion: The functional property shown in (4.80) for the linear array SAR signal is also applicable for the circular array SAR signal; that is, the temporal Fourier transform of $s(t, \omega_\ell)$ with respect to the real time t is

$$S(\alpha, \omega_\ell) = \int_\beta S_\ell(\frac{\alpha - \beta}{2}, \frac{\alpha + \beta}{2}) \, d\beta, \qquad (4.112)$$

where

$$\alpha \equiv \omega + \Omega$$
$$\beta \equiv \omega - \Omega.$$

Substituting (4.110) in (4.112), and carrying out the integral over the delta function, yields

$$S(\alpha, \omega_\ell) = \tilde{F}_p(\frac{\alpha - \omega_\ell}{\omega_R}, 2k_\ell) \, H_{\frac{\alpha - \omega_\ell}{\omega_R}}(2k_\ell R) \, \exp[j\frac{\pi(\alpha - \omega_\ell)}{2\omega_R}], \qquad (4.113)$$

which results in the following inversion:

$$\tilde{F}_p(\frac{\alpha - \omega_\ell}{\omega_R}, 2k_\ell) = \frac{S(\alpha, \omega_\ell)}{H_{\frac{\alpha - \omega_\ell}{\omega_R}}(2k_\ell R) \, \exp[j\frac{\pi(\alpha - \omega_\ell)}{2\omega_R}]}. \qquad (4.114)$$

- *There is an amplitude and phase associated with the ℓ-th harmonic that is $A_1(\ell\omega_2)$ (see Chapter 1). Thus, the right side of (4.114) should be divided by $A_1(\ell\omega_2)$ (source deconvolution), or, in the matched-filtered form, multiplied with the conjugate of $A_1(\ell\omega_2)$; that is,*

$$\tilde{F}_p(\frac{\alpha - \omega_\ell}{\omega_R}, 2k_\ell) = \frac{A_1^*(\ell\omega_2) \, S(\alpha, \omega_\ell)}{H_{\frac{\alpha - \omega_\ell}{\omega_R}}(2k_\ell R) \, \exp[j\frac{\pi(\alpha - \omega_\ell)}{2\omega_R}]}.$$

PROJECTS

1. Simulate a ground-plane airborne (linear synthetic aperture) SAR imaging system.

   a. Obtain the SAR signal in the (u, t), (u, ω), (k_u, t), and (k_u, ω) domains for a single target and multiple targets at broadside and squint modes.

b. Obtain the normalized SAR signal in the (u, ω) and (k_u, ω) domains. Interpolate the SAR signal from its normalized version and compare with the actual SAR signal.

c. Image the target scene using the three SAR inverse methods, that is, spatial Doppler-based, plane wave approximation-based, and Fresnel approximation-based. Observe the limitations of these methods as the parameters of the imaging system are varied.

d. Repeat Projects (1.a) and (1.c) using pulse and frequency diversity.

e. Repeat Project (1.a) with the data obtained by an aircraft with a flight path that deviates from a straight line. Use both a random number generator and an analytical nonlinear function of u to simulate these deviations. First examine the data when the deviations are much smaller than the wavelength. Then, gradually increase the deviations such that they become comparable to the wavelength. Finally, compensate for these deviations in the observed SAR data and repeat Project (1.c) on the compensated data.

2. Repeat Project 1 for a slant-plane linear array SAR imaging system with multiple targets possessing varying altitudes (z values).

3. Simulate a spaceborne (circular synthetic aperture) SAR imaging system.

a. Obtain the SAR signal in the (θ, t), (θ, ω), (ξ, t), and (ξ, ω) domains for a single target and multiple targets.

b. Image the target scene using the two circular SAR inverse methods, that is, spatial Doppler-based and plane wave approximation-based.

4. Simulate a temporal Doppler-based SAR imaging system. Examine the effect of varying the duration of the transmitted pulse on the range resolution and the cross-range resolution.

REFERENCES

1. D. Ausherman, A. Kozma, J. Walker, H. Jones, and E. Poggio, "Developments in radar imaging," *IEEE Trans. Aerospace and Electronic Systems,* 20:363, July 1984.

2. D. Blacknell, A. Freeman, R. White, and J. Wood, "The prediction of geometric distortions in airborne synthetic aperture radar imagery from autofocus measurements," *IEEE Trans. Geoscience and Remote Sensing,* 25, p. 775, November 1987.

3. N. Bojarski, "Three-dimensional electromagnetic short pulse inverse scattering," Syracuse University Res. Corp., February 1967.

4. W. Brown and R. Fredricks, "Range-Doppler imaging with motion through resolution cells," *IEEE Trans. Aerospace and Electronic Systems,* vol. 5, p. 98, January 1969.

5. J. C. Curlander and R. N. McDonough, *Synthetic Aperture Radar,* New York: Wiley, 1991.

6. L. Cutrona, E. Leith, L. Porcello, and W. Vivian, "On the application of coherent optical processing techniques to synthetic aperture radar," *Proc. IEEE,* vol. 54, p. 1026, 1966.

7. R. M. Lewis, "Physical optics inverse diffraction," *IEEE Transactions on Antennas and Propagation,"* vol. AP-17, no. 3, pp. 308-314, May 1969.

8. P. Morse and H. Feshbach, *Methods of Theoretical Physics,* New York: McGraw-Hill, 1968.

9. D. Munson, J. O'Brien, and W. Jenkins, "A tomographic formulation of spotlight-mode synthetic aperture radar," *Proc. IEEE,* vol. 71, p. 917, August 1983.

10. M. I. Skolnik, *Introduction to Radar Systems,* New York: McGraw-Hill, 1980.

11. M. Soumekh, "Band-limited interpolation from unevenly spaced sampled data," *IEEE Trans. on Acoustics, Speech and Signal Processing,* vol. 36, p. 110, January 1988.

12. M. Soumekh, "Echo imaging using physical and synthesized arrays," *Optical Engineering,* vol. 29, no. 5, pp. 545-554, May 1990.

13. M. Soumekh, "Bistatic synthetic aperture radar inversion with application in dynamic object imaging," *IEEE Trans. on Acoustics, Speech and Signal Processing,* September 1991.

14. M. Soumekh, "A system model and inversion for synthetic aperture radar imaging," *IEEE Transactions on Image Processing,* January 1992.

15. M. Soumekh and J. Choi, "Phase and amplitude-phase restoration in synthetic aperture radar imaging," *IEEE Transactions on Image Processing,* April 1992.

16. J. Walker, "Range - Doppler imaging of rotating objects," *IEEE Trans. Aerospace and Electronic Systems,* vol. 16, p. 23, January 1980.

17. D. R. Wehner, *High Resolution Radar,* Artech House, 1987.

18. H. A. Zebker and R. M. Goldstein, "Topographic mapping from interferometric synthetic aperture radar observations," *Journal of Geophysical Research,* vol. 91:B5, pp. 4993-4999, April 1986.

Chapter 5

BLIND-VELOCITY SAR/ISAR IMAGING

SAR and ISAR imaging are based on coherent signal processing methods that mold various radiation patterns of a synthesized array to extract cross-range (spatial Doppler) information. The success of such coherent processing algorithms depends greatly on correct phase synchronization of the collected data. Uncertainties in the relative position of the radar with respect to dynamic targets in SAR/ISAR result in erroneous Doppler information and, consequently, severe degradations in the reconstructed image.

Motion of a target in a stationary SAR background has been studied by Raney [1]. It is shown that for even relatively small values of the moving target's velocity, uncompensated motion results in both smearing and shifts in the reconstructed image (see also Appendix). A major difficulty associated with target motion compensation in SAR is to develop computationally invertible system models. This is a difficult task due to the presence of nonlinear phase functions of the moving target's velocity in the system model.

Incoherent methods for detecting a moving target in an image (obtained via SAR or other imaging modalities) are available (e.g., [4]) that do not exploit the phase information in the measured data. In this chapter, we show that the SAR signal's (coherent) spectral decomposition in the aperture domain also facilitates the analysis, estimation and compensation in the system model, and inversion for a moving target in SAR/ISAR imaging.

We first introduce the principle of *mean spatial Doppler shift* that is the basis of the blind-velocity synthetic aperture array imaging methods that are discussed in Chapters 5 and 6. We then discuss blind-velocity SAR imaging via a simplified model that assumes the target is at broadside, and the target's speed is much smaller than the speed of the aircraft that carries the radar. This scenario corresponds to SAR imaging of slowly moving ground targets. The resultant analysis, which is based on *short-time* Fourier analysis of SAR data, enables the reader to develop an intuition for the problem.

The generalized blind-velocity SAR problem, which involves squint targets with speeds comparable to the aircraft's speed (e.g., aerial combat), is examined in Section 5.3. Our approach in this section is based on the study of the *instantaneous frequency* of SAR signal. This method is a more mathematically direct approach than the short-time Fourier analysis of SAR data. However, both methods are derivatives of spatial Doppler principle. Other related SAR/ISAR imaging problems are also examined. The resultant algorithms are used to image an airborne DC-9 from its real ISAR data.

5.1 MEAN SPATIAL DOPPLER SHIFT

As mentioned in Section 4.4, the spectral support of the SAR signal in the spatial frequency domain of the aperture depends on the wavenumber of the radar signal, k, and the parameters of the imaging system, such as range, cross-range and synthetic aperture size. We now define a parameter called mean spatial Doppler shift that will be used in the latter sections for estimating a moving target's velocity. This spatial frequency information is analogous to the temporal Doppler shifts used in blind-speed MTI (moving target indication) or AMTI (airborne MTI) [2, Chapter 4].

Consider the general squint-mode SAR problem with the synthetic aperture identified by v and the center of the synthetic aperture at (X_s, Y_s), and

$$\theta \equiv \arctan \frac{Y_s}{X_s}.$$

(The new notation is used to accommodate our analysis in the next sections.)

From (4.12), one can observe that the spatial frequency (k_v) support for the echoed signal is centered around

$$K_v \equiv 2k \sin \theta.$$

K_v is referred to as the mean spatial frequency (Doppler) shift. K_v can be estimated from the energy distribution of the SAR data in the spatial Fourier domain via the following first moment formula:

$$K_v \approx \frac{\sum_j k_{v_j} |S(k_{v_j}, \omega)|^2}{\sum_j |S(k_{v_j}, \omega)|^2}.$$

A similar measure has been used to determine temporal Doppler shifts for MTI [3].

Clearly, for a broadside SAR problem the mean spatial frequency shift is approximately equal to zero in the spatial frequency domain for the synthetic aperture.

5.2 SAR IMAGING OF SLOWLY MOVING GROUND TARGETS

We now examine the problem of SAR imaging of a target scene composed of moving targets as well as a stationary background. An airborne radar illuminates a stationary background confined in the disk with radius X_{0f} centered at the origin in the spatial domain (the radar's footprint). A broadside SAR geometry is assumed for the stationary target area. During the data acquisition, a dynamic target with a constant velocity (vector) (A, B) is assumed to be moving within the stationary background. It is assumed that the echo from the moving target can be separated from the total return signal; this is true under certain constraints that are discussed later.

System Model and Inversion

Let $g(x, y)$ denote the reflectivity function of the moving target when the radar is at $(X_1, 0)$ on its flight path. We define the normalized velocity (a, b) as the ratio of the real velocity to the radar speed, that is,

$$(a, b) \equiv \left(\frac{A}{v_R}, \frac{B}{v_R} \right).$$

Thus, when the radar is at (X_1, u), the reflectivity function of the moving target becomes $g(x - au, y - bu)$ (see Figures 5.1a-b).

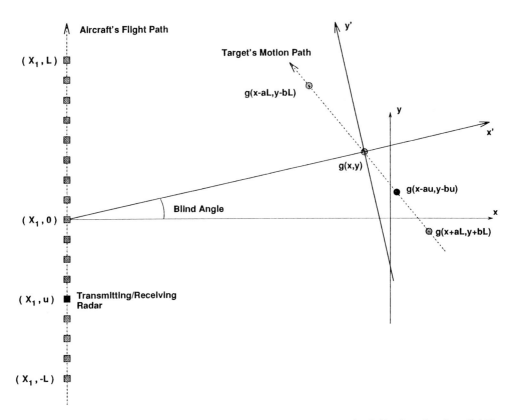

Figure 5.1a Imaging system geometry in blind-velocity SAR imaging (with a blind angle).

$g(x,y)$ generally corresponds to a target distribution that is *not* at broadside as shown in Figure 5.1a. The squint angle for $g(x,y)$ is identified as the *blind angle* in Figure 5.1a; the magnitude of the blind angle is less than the radar antenna's beamwidth. The blind angle is unknown and would not be recovered via the blind-velocity SAR/ISAR imaging algorithms described in this chapter. In fact, it turns out that these algorithms solve for the target's velocity in the (x',y') domain instead of the (x,y) domain; the (x',y') domain is the rotated version of the (x,y) domain by the blind angle.

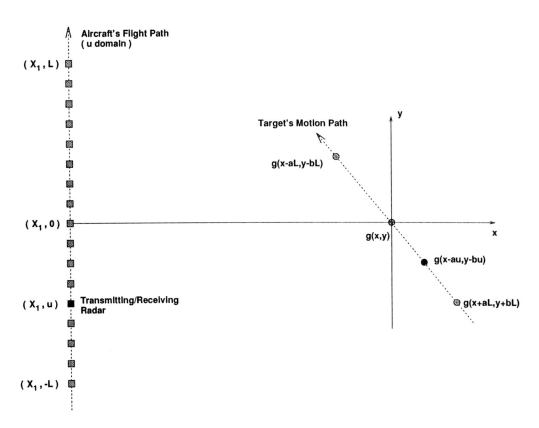

Figure 5.1b Imaging system geometry in blind-velocity SAR imaging

Moreover, these algorithms yield the moving target distribution in the (x', y') domain. These effects as well as the existence of the blind angle are transparent to these algorithms and what the user might deduce from them. One way to remove the blind angle ambiguity is to make simultaneous SAR measurements with two different aircrafts. We are not concerned with the blind angle effects and use the broadside model shown in Figure 5.1b in the following discussions.

- *There exists another source of ambiguity that is due to the lack of exact knowledge of the target range when $u = 0$. The blind range effects can be shown to be negligible in the blind-velocity SAR/ISAR imaging algorithms.*

We first develop the system model for the temporal Fourier transform of the moving target's echoed signal. In most practical circumstances, the temporal Doppler shift in the echoed signal due to the target and radar motions is very small; this is due to the fact that the radar and target's speeds are much smaller than the wave's speed of propagation. Thus, the effect of the temporal Doppler shift in the envelope of the radar signal is negligible [5, Chapter 13],[6]. In this case, one obtains the following system model for the echoed signal:

$$s(u,\omega) = \int\int dx\ dy\ g(x - au, y - bu)$$
$$\times\ \exp\left[j2k\ \sqrt{(x - X_1)^2 + (y - u)^2}\ \right]. \tag{5.1}$$

Making the following variable transformations:

$$\begin{aligned} x - au &= X \\ y - bu &= Y \end{aligned} \tag{5.2}$$

in the integrals of (5.1), one obtains

$$s(u,\omega) = \int\int dX\ dY\ g(X,Y)$$
$$\times\ \exp\left[j2k\ \sqrt{(X + au - X_1)^2 + (Y + bu - u)^2}\ \right]. \tag{5.3}$$

$s(u,\omega)$ in (5.3) can be interpreted as a signal echoed from a stationary target with reflectivity function $g(X,Y)$ when the measurements are made along the line $(X_1 - au, u - bu)$, $u \in [-L, L]$ (see Figure 5.2).

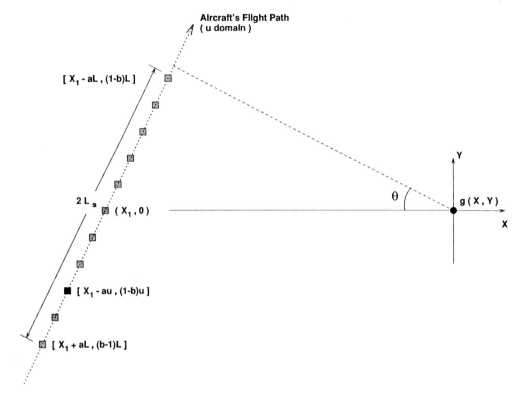

Figure 5.2 Blind-velocity SAR imaging: First transformation.

Next, we define the following mapping:

$$g_1(x_1, y_1) \equiv g(X, Y) \tag{5.4}$$

where

$$\begin{bmatrix} x_1 \\ y_1 \end{bmatrix} \equiv \begin{bmatrix} \cos\theta & \sin\theta \\ -\sin\theta & \cos\theta \end{bmatrix} \begin{bmatrix} X \\ Y \end{bmatrix} \tag{5.5}$$

and [*Note that θ depends on (a, b)*]

$$\theta \equiv \arctan\left(\frac{a}{1-b}\right). \tag{5.6}$$

We define the following variables to formulate the SAR system model in the (x_1, y_1) domain:

$$v \equiv u\sqrt{a^2 + (1-b)^2}$$

$$k_v \equiv \frac{k_u}{\sqrt{a^2 + (1-b)^2}} \tag{5.7}$$

Using (5.4)-(5.7), (5.3) can be rewritten as follows:

$$s_1(v, \omega) \equiv s(u, \omega)$$

$$= \int \int dx_1 \, dy_1 \, g_1(x_1, y_1) \tag{5.8}$$

$$\times \, \exp\left[\, j2k \, \sqrt{(x_1 - X_s)^2 + (y_1 - Y_s - v)^2} \, \right],$$

where

$$X_s = X_1 \cos\theta$$

$$Y_s = X_1 \sin\theta.$$

The signal $s_1(v, \omega)$ in (5.8) can be viewed as the SAR signal for squint-mode geometry [see (2.5)], with target spatial domain (x_1, y_1), squint range and cross-range coordinate (X_s, Y_s) and synthetic aperture domain $v \in [-L_s, L_s]$, where

$$L_s \equiv L\sqrt{a^2 + (1-b)^2}$$

(see Figure 5.3).

Based on the results of Chapter 4, the inversion formula and the spectral support of the radar echoes for this squint mode SAR system are

$$G_1(\sqrt{4k^2 - k_v^2}, k_v) = \exp\left[\, j(\sqrt{4k^2 - k_v^2} \, X_s + k_v \, Y_s) \, \right]$$

$$\times \, \sqrt{4k^2 - k_v^2} \, S_1(k_v, \omega), \tag{5.9}$$

for

$$2k\sin\theta - 2k\frac{X_{0g} + L_s}{X_1} \leq k_v \leq 2k\sin\theta + 2k\frac{X_{0g} + L_s}{X_1} \tag{5.10}$$

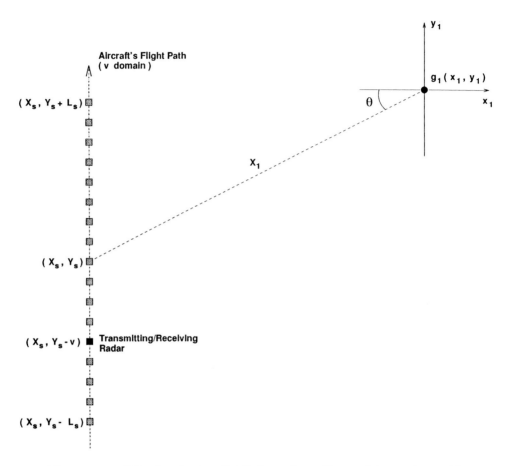

Figure 5.3 Blind-velocity SAR imaging: Second transformation.

where X_{0g} is the radius of the smallest disk that encloses the moving target. (The exact value of X_{0g}, that is less than the radar's footprint, is not essential for the algorithms that we will develop.) Clearly, to construct the inversion in (5.9) needed to reconstruct the moving target, we must know the target's velocity for the geometrical conversion into the squint-mode SAR imaging system shown in (5.8). In the next section, we present a method to estimate the target's velocity.

Velocity Estimation via Subaperture Processing

Equation (5.10) implies that the mean spatial Doppler shift for the echoed signals due to the moving target of interest is

$$K_v \simeq 2k \sin \theta \qquad (5.11)$$

It should be noted that the echoed signals are measured in the u domain. Thus, it is not K_v, but K_u that can be estimated. Hence, using (5.7) and (5.11), we can write the following:

$$K_u = K_v \sqrt{a^2 + (1 - b)^2} \simeq 2ka. \qquad (5.12)$$

Equation (5.12) states that a can be estimated from K_u. Clearly, we need other means/information to recover b. Next, we examine the spatial Doppler information in the **subapertures** of the synthetic aperture to obtain an estimate for b.

Let N denote the number of samples on the synthetic aperture. Then, for a given ω, we can have N recorded radar echoes. With the recorded data set of N elements, we generate a finite number of subsets with the same size M, what we call subapertures, by sequentially over-lapping one element for each subaperture. Based on the above-mentioned synthetic aperture and subaperture sizes, the following $N - M + 1$ subapertures can be constructed:

$$
\begin{aligned}
SA_1 &: \quad i = 1, 2, \quad \ldots \quad , M \\
SA_2 &: \quad i = 2, 3, \quad \ldots \quad , M + 1 \\
&\quad \vdots \qquad\qquad \vdots \\
SA_{N-M+1} &: \quad i = N - M + 1, \ldots, N
\end{aligned}
$$

SA_j denotes the j-th subaperture. Figures 5.4 and 5.5 illustrate that any subaperture in the (x, y) domain has a corresponding subaperture in the (x_1, y_1) domain.

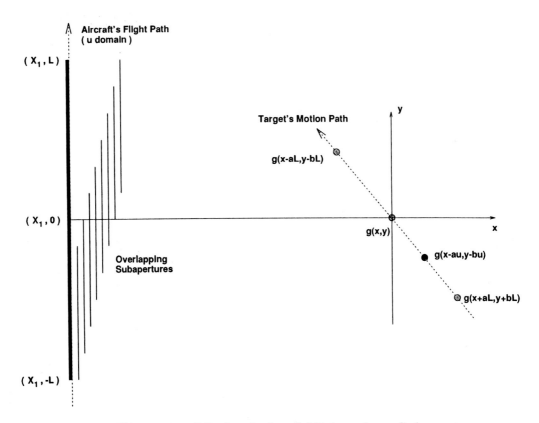

Figure 5.4 Blind-velocity SAR imaging: Subaperture processing in the u domain.

Consider the i-th subaperture in the (x_1, y_1) domain, as shown in Figure 5.6. Let $\theta + \Delta\theta_i$ denote the angle between the x_1-axis and the line joining the origin and the center of the i-th subaperture $(X_s, Y_s + v_i)$. Since $L_s \ll X_1$, then $\Delta\theta_i \ll 1$. Thus, we can write

$$\Delta\theta_i \simeq \frac{\delta_i}{X_1} \tag{5.13}$$

where

$$\delta_i \equiv v_i \cos\theta.$$

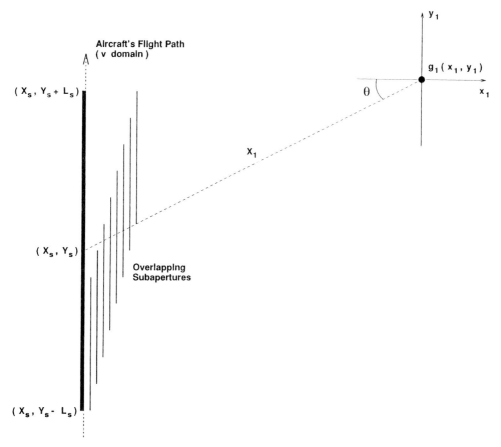

Figure 5.5 Blind-velocity SAR imaging: Subaperture processing in the v domain.

With the relation $v_i = u_i \sqrt{a^2 + (1-b)^2}$ and (5.6), $\Delta\theta_i$ can be approximated by the following:

$$\Delta\theta_i \simeq \frac{(1-b)u_i}{X_1} \tag{5.14}$$

Now consider the squint-mode SAR data within the i-th subaperture in the v domain. The mean spatial Doppler shift for this subset of the acquired SAR data can be found from

$$K_{v_i} \simeq 2k \sin(\theta + \Delta\theta_i) \quad \text{for} \quad i = 1, \ldots, N - M + 1. \tag{5.15}$$

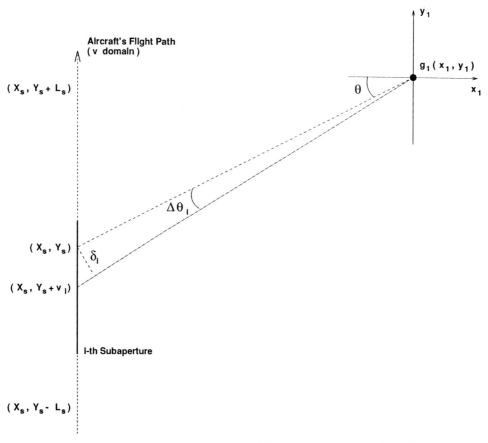

Figure 5.6 Blind-velocity SAR imaging: i-th subaperture in the v domain.

Let u_i be the mapping of v_i in the u domain; that is, u_i is the center of the i-th subaperture on the u-axis. Using (5.7), (5.14), and (5.15), we have

$$a + \frac{(1-b)^2}{X_1}u_i \simeq \frac{K_{u_i}}{2k} \qquad \text{for} \quad i = 1, \ldots, N - M + 1. \tag{5.16}$$

Again, it should be noted that since (a, b) is unknown, one can only determine K_{u_i} from the measured data.

The mean spatial frequency shift K_{u_i} is estimated by the following:

$$K_{u_i} = \frac{\sum_j k_{u_j} |S_i(k_{u_j}, \omega)|^2}{\sum_j |S_i(k_{u_j}, \omega)|^2} \tag{5.17}$$

where $S_i(k_{u_j}, \omega)$ is the spatial Fourier transform of the echoed signals pertaining to the i-th subaperture. *Note that (5.16) is a linear function of u_i,* and all u_i's are evenly spaced in the u domain. Hence, taking the zero-th and first moments on both sides of (5.16) with respect to u_i yields

$$\sum_i a \simeq \frac{1}{2k} \sum_i K_{u_i}$$

$$\sum_i \frac{(1-b)^2}{X_1} u_i^2 \simeq \frac{1}{2k} \sum_i K_{u_i} u_i \tag{5.18}$$

where $\sum_i$ is an abbreviation for $\sum_{i=1}^{N-M+1}$. Using (5.18) and after some manipulations, one can obtain the following estimate for (a, b):

$$\hat{a} = \frac{1}{N-M+1} \frac{\sum_i K_{u_i}}{2k} \tag{5.19}$$

$$\hat{b} = \begin{cases} 1 - \left(\frac{X_1}{2k \sum_i u_i^2} \left| \sum_i K_{u_i} u_i \right| \right)^{\frac{1}{2}} & \text{for } b \leq 1 \\ 1 + \left(\frac{X_1}{2k \sum_i u_i^2} \left| \sum_i K_{u_i} u_i \right| \right)^{\frac{1}{2}} & \text{for } b > 1 \end{cases} \tag{5.20}$$

The estimate $(\hat{a}, \hat{b})$ shown in (5.19) and (5.20) is obtained via processing the received signal at one temporal radian frequency, that is, ω. However, the transmitting radar signal is a wide-band signal (to achieve high resolution in the reconstructed image). Thus, one can obtain a number of estimates for (a, b) that correspond to the available temporal frequencies of the radar signal. Combining these estimates in a certain way, such as averaging them after rejecting the outliers, will improve the accuracy of the estimate for (a, b).

- *The performance of the subaperture processing method is invariant of the radar signal's temporal frequency bandwidth. The same is not true for the temporal Doppler processing method that is examined later in this chapter.*

Subaperture Size Selection

We next consider the problem of choosing the subaperture size. In the subaperture processing method, the accuracy of the velocity estimation mainly depends on the evaluation of the mean spatial Doppler shifts in the subapertures [see (5.17)]. Heuristically, the least ambiguity in evaluating the mean spatial Doppler shift for a subaperture will occur when the spatial frequency bandwidth for that subaperture is minimum. Consider the squint-mode geometry illustrated in Figure 5.6. For the i-th subaperture centered at $(X_s, Y_s + v_i)$, the actual spectral support of the moving target's echoes pertaining to the i-th subaperture is

$$2k\frac{(Y_s + v_i - X_{0g} - v_s)}{X_1} - \frac{\pi}{v_s}\eta \le k_v \le 2k\frac{(Y_s + v_i + X_{0g} + v_s)}{X_1} + \frac{\pi}{v_s}\eta \tag{5.21}$$

where $2v_s$ is the subaperture size and η is a chosen constant $(\eta \ge 1)$. Equation (5.21) is a more accurate version of (2.7) since it includes $\frac{\pi}{v_s}\eta$ which is the effective bandwidth for the aperture function, that is, the (approximate) support for $\text{sinc}(k_v \ v_s)$. (The aperture function's bandwidth is negligible in most SAR problems. However, this may not be true for the spatial Doppler data within a subaperture.) Thus, the spatial frequency bandwidth for the SAR data in the i-th subaperture can be expressed by the following:

$$BW = 2k\frac{X_{0g} + v_s}{X_1} + \frac{\pi}{v_s}\eta \tag{5.22}$$

BW is a function of the subaperture size v_s. The derivative of BW with respect to v_s provides the desired minimum bandwidth (spatial frequency dispersion) that corresponds to

$$v_s = \sqrt{\frac{\pi\eta X_1}{2k}}. \tag{5.23}$$

The actual subaperture size u_s in the (x, y) domain is related to v_s by the following:

$$u_s = v_s / \sqrt{a^2 + (1 - b)^2}. \tag{5.24}$$

Thus, u_s cannot be chosen unless (a, b) is known in advance. However, assuming $a, b \ll 1$, which is the case in practice, we may roughly choose the subaperture size as follows:

$$\tilde{u}_s = \sqrt{\frac{\pi \eta X_1}{2k}}. \tag{5.25}$$

To estimate a via (5.13) is clearly a special case of the subaperture processing with $M = N$. Once a and b are estimated, (5.9) is used for imaging the moving target.

Clutter Signature Filtering

The above-mentioned SAR velocity estimation and imaging of a moving target is applicable only when the moving target's echoes can be separated from the returns due to the stationary background and other moving targets residing in the stationary background. In this section, we develop constraints on (a, b) for the above-mentioned spectral separation. For convenience, we consider a stationary SAR background with a single moving target. The echoed signal at (X_1, u) can be expressed as follows:

$$s(u, \omega) = \int \int dx \, dy \, [f(x, y) + g(x - au, y - bu)] \\ \times \exp \left[j2k \sqrt{(x - X_1)^2 + (y - u)^2} \right], \tag{5.26}$$

where $f(x, y)$ and $g(x, y)$ are, respectively, the reflectivity functions of the stationary background and the moving target. Equation (5.26) can be rewritten as

$$s(u, \omega) = s_B(u, \omega) + s_M(u, \omega), \tag{5.27}$$

where

$$s_B(u, \omega) = \int \int f(x, y) \, \exp \left[j2k \sqrt{(x - X_1)^2 + (y - u)^2} \right] dx dy, \tag{5.28}$$

and

$$s_M(u,\omega) = \int\int g(x,y)\exp\left[j2k\sqrt{(x+au-X_1)^2+(y+bu-u)^2}\right]dxdy$$
$$(5.29)$$

The spatial frequency support of the stationary background is

$$-2k\frac{L+X_{0f}}{X_1} \leq k_u \leq 2k\frac{L+X_{0f}}{X_1}. \tag{5.30}$$

On the other hand, the spatial frequency support of the moving target is [see (5.10)]

$$2k\frac{(Y_s-L_s-X_{0g})}{X_1} \leq k_v \leq 2k\frac{(Y_s+L_s+X_{0g})}{X_1}. \tag{5.31}$$

By multiplying the upper and lower bounds in (5.31) with $\sqrt{a^2+(1-b)^2}$, the moving target's spatial frequency support in the k_u domain can be obtained.

Hence, the total echoed signal spectrum $S(k_u,\omega)$ consists of the background's spectrum, that is, $S_B(k_u,\omega)$, and the moving target's spectrum, that is, $S_M(k_u,\omega)$. The spatial frequency support for $S_B(k_u,\omega)$ is centered around the origin in the k_u domain, while the spatial frequency support for $S_M(k_u,\omega)$ is approximately off-centered by $2ka$. Thus, the two spectral supports are separable if they are disjoint in the k_u domain. Using (5.30) and (5.31), it can be shown that $s_M(u,\omega)$ (the echoes due to the moving target) can be separated from the total echoed signal provided that

$$\frac{X_{0f}+L}{X_1} < |a| - \frac{(X_{0g}+L_s)(1-b)^2}{X_1\sqrt{a^2+(1-b)^2}}. \tag{5.32}$$

The bandwidth of the aperture function can be incorporated in (5.30) and (5.31) to develop a more strict constraint than the one shown in (5.32). However, in most practical SAR problems, the spatial frequency bandwidth extensions due to the finite synthetic aperture size, that is, $\frac{\pi}{L}\eta$ [η is the same parameter defined in (5.22)], in the k_u domain for the echoes from the stationary background and moving target, are negligible compared with the bandwidths identified in (5.30) and (5.31).

The system block diagram shown in Figure 5.7 illustrates the scheme for imaging the stationary background and the moving target where the separation is attained via passing the echoed signals through a lowpass filter with cut-off spatial frequency $2k\frac{X_{0f}+L}{X_1}$.

- *Some of the spatial domain points in the stationary background are covered by the moving target for certain values of u and, thus, are* **invisible** *to the radar for these values of u. For each of those (x,y) points, the effective synthetic aperture is composed of two disjoint squint-mode subapertures. Thus, one should anticipate the resolution for these points to depend on the point spread function corresponding to the disjoint synthetic subapertures.*

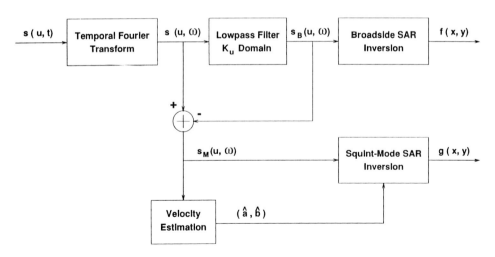

Figure 5.7 Reconstruction algorithm for blind-velocity SAR/ISAR imaging.

5.3 SAR IMAGING OF MOVING TARGETS IN AERIAL COMBAT

The principles developed in Section 5.2 are also applicable for a squint moving target where its speed, $\sqrt{A^2 + B^2}$, is comparable to v_R, that is, the speed of the aircraft that carries the radar. We formulate the generalized SAR imaging of a moving target via the analysis of the instantaneous frequency of SAR signal.

For our current analysis, it is more convenient to let u represent the slow-time domain instead of the synthetic aperture position. The coordinates of the radar as a function of the slow-time are $(X_1, Y_1 + v_R u)$; (X_1, Y_1) are known squint-mode parameters that are controlled by the manner in which the physical radar steers its beam (see Chapter 4). The target's reflectivity function at slow-time u is $g(x - Au, y - Bu)$. Thus, for a given fast-time temporal frequency ω and slow-time u, the SAR signal is

$$s(u, \omega) = \int_x \int_y dx \, dy \; g(x - Au, y - Bu)$$

$$\times \; \exp \left[j2k \; \sqrt{(X_1 + x)^2 + (Y_1 + v_R u + y)^2} \; \right].$$

(For notational simplicity in our future analysis, the signs of x and y are changed to positive in the above PM wave.) Making the following variable transformations:

$$x \; - \; Au \; = \; X$$
$$y \; - \; Bu \; = \; Y,$$

in the integrals of the above SAR system model, one obtains

$$s(u, \omega) = \int_X \int_Y dX \, dY \; g(X, Y)$$

$$\times \; \exp \left[j2k \; \sqrt{(X_1 + X + Au)^2 \; + \; (Y_1 + v_R u + Y + Bu)^2} \right].$$

Consider the PM wave (phase delay function) associated with the reflector at (X, Y) in the above SAR system model, that is,

$$\exp \left[j2k \; \sqrt{(X_1 + X + Au)^2 \; + \; (Y_1 + v_R u + Y + Bu)^2} \right].$$

The instantaneous frequency of this signal in the u domain is

$$
\begin{aligned}
K_u(X,Y) &\equiv \frac{\partial}{\partial u}\left[2k\sqrt{(X_1 + X + Au)^2 + (Y_1 + v_R u + Y + Bu)^2}\right] \\
&= 2k\frac{A\,(X_1 + X + Au) + (v_R + B)\,(Y_1 + v_R u + Y + Bu)}{\sqrt{(X_1 + X + Au)^2 + (Y_1 + v_R u + Y + Bu)^2}} \\
&\approx 2k\frac{A\,(X_1 + X + Au) + (v_R + B)\,(Y + v_R u + Y + Bu)}{R_1} \\
&= 2k\frac{A(X_1 + X) + (v_R + B)(Y_1 + Y)}{R_1} + 2k\frac{A^2 + (v_R + B)^2}{R_1}u.
\end{aligned}
$$

The SAR signal, that is, $s(u,\omega)$, is a linear combination of the above-mentioned PM waves, where $X \in [-X_{0g}, X_{0g}]$ and $Y \in [-X_{0g}, X_{0g}]$ with $X_{0g} \ll R_1$. Thus, the instantaneous frequency of the SAR signal can be approximated via the average value of $K_u(X,Y)$ in the (X,Y) domain; that is,

$$
K_u \approx 2k\frac{A\,X_1 + (v_R + B)\,Y_1}{R_1} + 2k\frac{A^2 + (v_R + B)^2}{R_1}\,u,
$$

which is a linear function of u. In this case, we can write

$$
K_u \approx K_{u0} + K_{u1}\,u,
$$

where

$$
K_{u0} \equiv 2k\frac{A\,X_1 + (v_R + B)\,Y_1}{R_1}
$$

$$
K_{u1} \equiv 2k\frac{A^2 + (v_R + B)^2}{R_1}.
$$

Thus, if K_u is known, then (K_{u0}, K_{u1}) and, consequently, (A,B) could be estimated from the zero-th and first moments of K_u with respect to the available discrete values of $u = u_i$.

- With $Y_1 = 0$ and $\sqrt{A^2 + B^2}$, the linear parameters of the instantaneous function become

$$
K_{u0} \equiv 2kA
$$

$$
K_{u1} \equiv 2k\frac{(v_R + B)^2}{X_1}.
$$

This model is identical to the one described in (5.16) that was developed in Section 5.2 for a slowly moving broadside target.

The subaperture processing for velocity estimation discussed in Section 5.2 is in fact the *short-time Fourier transform* method to estimate the instantaneous frequency K_u from the measurements. To reduce the ambiguity in performing this estimation, Section 5.2 provided a procedure to select a subaperture around a given u_i based on the following two constraints:

i. The subaperture length is large enough such that the ambiguity due to the aperture (sinc) function is negligible in the k_u domain; and

ii. The subaperture length is small enough such that the variations of K_u from K_{u_i} is small in the subaperture centered around $u = u_i$.

For the generalized blind-velocity SAR imaging, one can also determine the subaperture length based on a priori knowledge of (X_1, Y_1, v_R) and an estimate of (A, B). Clearly, one can utilize other methods, for example, a noncausal discrete-time Phase-Lock Loop (PLL), to estimate the instantaneous frequency function. Similar to the selection of subaperture length for short-time Fourier analysis, the parameters of the PLL, for example, the bandwidth of its filters, should be selected based on a priori knowledge of the SAR system parameters.

5.4 ISAR IMAGING OF MOVING TARGETS

In this section, we address the problem of ISAR imaging of a moving target with an unknown constant velocity. Consider a two-dimensional ISAR imaging system geometry on the (x, y) plane. A radar is fixed at $(X_1, 0)$, making transmissions and corresponding receptions at discrete times $u \in (-u_0, u_0)$ while a target is moving within the radar footprint (see Figure 5.8a-b). The moving target is assumed to have a constant velocity (A, B) during the radar's data acquisition. u is now a time variable but different from time variable t that is the Fourier counterpart for the temporal radian frequency ω. In this case, the received signal $s(u, \omega)$ is the sum of two radar returns

$$s(u, \omega) = s_F(u, \omega) + s_G(u, \omega) \tag{5.33}$$

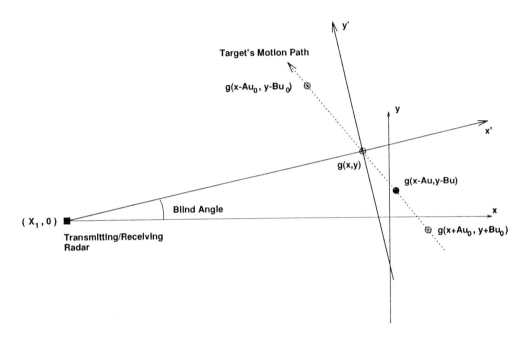

Figure 5.8a Imaging system geometry in blind-velocity ISAR imaging (with a blind angle).

where

$$s_F(u,\omega) = \int \int f(x,y) \exp \left[j2k \sqrt{(x - X_1)^2 + y^2} \right] dx dy$$

$$s_G(u,\omega) = \int \int g(x - Au, y - Bu) \exp \left[j2k \sqrt{(x - X_1)^2 + y^2} \right] dx dy$$

where $f(x,y)$ and $g(x,y)$ are the reflectivity functions of the stationary background and the moving target, respectively.

- *Note that the echoed signal due to the stationary background, that is, $s_F(u,\omega)$, is constant with respect to u.*

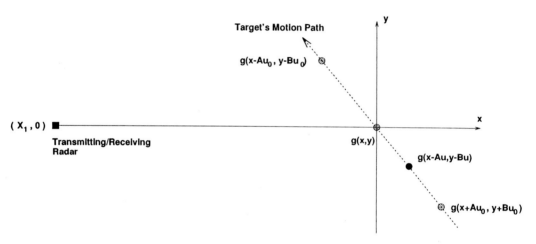

Figure 5.8b Imaging system geometry in blind-velocity ISAR imaging.

Let the spatial domain (x_1, y_1), $g_1(x_1, y_1)$, and (X_s, Y_s) be defined in the same way as in (5.4)-(5.8) except for the rotation angle θ that is now equal to

$$\theta = \arctan\left(-\frac{A}{B}\right).$$

Then, following the procedures analogous to (5.1)-(5.10), the moving target's echo $s_G(u, \omega)$ is alternatively represented in the (x_1, y_1) domain as follows (see Figure 5.3):

$$\tilde{s}_G(v,\omega) \equiv s_G(u,\omega)$$

$$= \int\int g_1(x_1, y_1) \exp\left[j2k\sqrt{(x_1 - X_s)^2 + (y_1 - Y_s - v)^2} \right] dx_1 dy_1$$
(5.34)

where $v \equiv u\sqrt{A^2 + B^2}$. It should be noted that the time variable (u) function $s_G(u,\omega)$ is converted into the spatial variable (v) function $\tilde{s}_G(v,\omega)$. Taking the Fourier transform of (5.33) with respect to u (or v), we obtain

$$S(k_u, \omega) = S_F(k_u, \omega) + \tilde{S}_G(k_v, \omega)$$
(5.35)

$$S_F(k_u, \omega) \propto \text{sinc}(k_u \, u_0)$$
(5.36)

and

$$\tilde{S}_G(k_v, \omega) = G_1(\sqrt{4k^2 - k_v^2}, k_v) \frac{\exp\left[j\left(\sqrt{4k^2 - k_v^2}X_s + k_v Y_s \right) \right]}{\sqrt{4k^2 - k_v^2}}$$
(5.37)

where

$$k_v = \frac{k_u}{\sqrt{A^2 + B^2}}.$$

Equation (5.37) implies that if we know the moving target's velocity, then this ISAR imaging problem is, by a rotational transformation, reduced to the problem of imaging a stationary target in a squint-mode SAR geometry.

The results of Section 5.2 can also be used here to separate the moving target's signature from the stationary background echoes. For this purpose, the spatial frequency bandwidth for the background's echoes can be chosen to be approximately equal to $\frac{\pi\eta}{u_0}$ [see (5.36)]. After extracting the moving target's echo via filtering in the k_u domain, the next step is to estimate the velocity of the moving target. For this, we use the subaperture processing method introduced earlier. The estimates for (A, B) are determined by the following:

$$\hat{A} = \frac{1}{N - M + 1} \frac{\sum_i K_{u_i}}{2k}$$

$$\hat{B} = \sqrt{\frac{X_1}{2k} \frac{\sum |K_{u_i} u_i|}{\sum u_i^2}}$$
(5.38)

where N denotes the number of ISAR measurement in $[-u_0, u_0]$, M is the number of measurement per subaperture, and K_{u_i} is the mean Doppler shift of the i-th subaperture estimated from the echoed signals [see (5.17)].

5.5 TEMPORAL DOPPLER PROCESSING

Thus far, the spatial Doppler information has been used for motion estimation and spectral separation. We now address this problem via processing the temporal Doppler information in SAR data. Later, we will point out the limitation encountered in this method and accentuate the advantage of the use of the spatial Doppler information.

Temporal Doppler Shift for Velocity Estimation

Due to the relative motion between the radar and the moving target, the echoed signal experiences a temporal Doppler shift. In practice, the size of the moving target is much smaller than the extent of the stationary background. Hence, in the following analysis, the moving target is modeled by a point scatterer. Let N represent the number of samples on the synthetic aperture and (x_0, y_0) be the coordinate of the moving target when a radar is at $(X_1, 0)$ on its flight path.

The relative target/radar temporal Doppler speed is found by adding the projections of the moving target's velocity and the radar's velocity onto the line that joins the moving target and the radar as shown in Figure 5.9. Then, the relative Doppler speed at the radar location (X_1, u_i) can be written as

$$v_d(u_i) \equiv v_R \cos\left(\frac{\pi}{2} - \theta_i\right) + v_R \sqrt{a^2 + b^2} \cos(\theta_0 + \theta_i) \qquad (5.39)$$

where θ_i denotes the angle between a line parallel to the x-axis and the line connecting the radar with the moving target.

Since X_1 is significantly greater than L, we may use the following approximation:

$$\cos\theta_i \simeq 1$$

$$\sin\theta_i \simeq \theta_i \simeq \tan\theta_i \simeq \frac{(y_0 + bu_i - u_i)}{X_1}. \qquad (5.40)$$

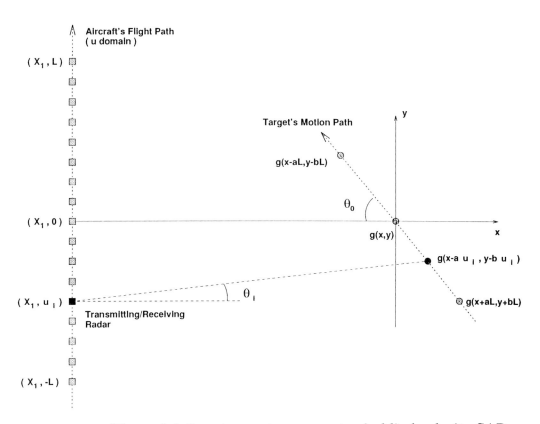

Figure 5.9 Imaging system geometry in blind-velocity SAR Imaging: Temporal Doppler processing.

With the help of these approximations, (5.39) becomes

$$v_d(u_i) = v_R \left(a + \frac{y_0}{X_1}(1-b) \right) - u_i \frac{(1-b)^2}{X_1} v_R. \tag{5.41}$$

Note that the relative Doppler speed is a linear function of u_i, and measurements are made at equally spaced positions within $[-L, L]$. Taking the zero-th and first moments of $v_d(u_i)$ with respect to u_i, we obtain

$$\sum_{i=1}^{N} v_d(u_i) = v_R \left(a + \frac{y_0}{X_1}(1-b) \right) N$$

$$\sum_{i=1}^{N} v_d(u_i)u_i = -\frac{(1-b)^2}{X_1} v_R \sum_{i=1}^{N} u_i^2$$

(5.42)

From the two equations in (5.42), the estimate for (a, b) can be determined as follows:

$$\hat{a} = -\frac{(1-b)}{X_1} y_0 + \frac{\sum_i v_d(u_i)}{v_R N} \tag{5.43}$$

$$\hat{b} = \begin{cases} 1 - \left[-\dfrac{\sum_i v_d(u_i)u_i}{v_R \sum_i u_i^2} \right]^{\frac{1}{2}}, & \text{for } b \leq 1; \\ 1 + \left[-\dfrac{\sum_i v_d(u_i)u_i}{v_R \sum_i u_i^2} \right]^{\frac{1}{2}}, & \text{for } b > 1 \end{cases} \tag{5.44}$$

Since $X_1 \gg y_0$, the term $-\frac{(1-b)}{X_1}y_0$ in (5.44) is unknown but can be assumed to be negligible.

The success of this method depends on the measurement accuracy of the temporal Doppler shift in echoed signals across the synthetic aperture. However, due to the fact that the transmitting pulse duration should be much less than half of the pulse repetition period, the echoed signal in general has a large temporal frequency bandwidth, which makes it difficult to estimate Doppler speed v_d accurately [1],[7]. Even if the radar transmits a long duration pulse (maintaining the pulse duration less than half of the pulse repetition period), that is, a narrow temporal frequency bandwidth for the velocity estimation, the long pulse return is not appropriate for imaging the moving target, in that the narrow bandwidth of the radar signal will degrade the range resolution of the moving target's image. Thus, in addition to using a short pulse for the imaging purpose, it requires another transmitting pulse exclusively used for estimating the velocity.

This can be achieved via utilizing a pilot tone. In this case, the temporal frequency band of the pilot tone should not overlap with that of the short transmitting pulse used for imaging the moving target such that they can be separable through filtering in the temporal frequency domain. However, the use of an extra pulse will degrade range resolution due to the loss of a portion of the temporal band for the pilot tone and a guard band. Furthermore, this will add to the complexity of the overall hardware structure.

Another advantage in using the spatial Doppler information becomes clear in the clutter rejection problem. In the next section, we point out the difficulty of the spectral separation when the temporal Doppler information is utilized.

Clutter Signature Filtering

Earlier we discussed the problem of separating two spectral supports due to stationary background and a moving target. In this section, we examine the spectral separability via temporal frequency domain processing. Consider the SAR imaging system geometry. The moving target is, again, assumed to be a point scatterer. A temporal Doppler velocity resulting from the radar motion and the moving scatterer with the velocity (A, B) is expressed as

$$v_d(u_i) = v_R \cos\left(\frac{\pi}{2} - \theta_i\right) + v_R \sqrt{a^2 + b^2} \cos(\theta_0 + \theta_i) \qquad (5.45)$$

where $(a, b) \equiv (A/v_R, B/v_R)$ and $\theta_0 = \arctan(b/a)$. Following the procedure used to derive (5.41), we have the following equation:

$$v_d(u_i) \simeq v_R\left(a + \frac{y_0}{X_1}(1 - b)\right) - u_i \frac{(1 - b)^2}{X_1} v_R. \qquad (5.46)$$

The temporal Doppler velocity due to the relative motion between the radar and the stationary background falls in the following interval:

$$\left[-v_R \frac{X_{0f} + u_i}{X_1}, v_R \frac{X_{0f} + u_i}{X_1}\right],$$

that depends on $u_i \in [-L, L]$. Thus, the two radar returns are separable if the target's velocity (a, b) satisfies the following condition:

$$
\begin{aligned}
v_R \frac{X_{0f} + L}{X_1} &< \min\left[v_d(u_i)\right] \quad for \quad a > 0 \\
-v_R \frac{X_{0f} + L}{X_1} &> \max\left[v_d(u_i)\right] \quad for \quad a < 0
\end{aligned}
\tag{5.47}
$$

After some manipulations, (5.47) becomes

$$
\frac{X_{0f} + L}{X_1} < |a| - \frac{X_{0g}|1 - b| + L(1 - b)^2}{X_1}.
\tag{5.48}
$$

The condition in (5.48) is approximately the same as the condition (5.32) for separating the two radar returns in the spatial frequency domain. Thus, theoretically, the separability condition is nearly the same for the two Doppler processing methods. However, (5.48) is true only when the radar signal is a narrow-band function. This, as mentioned earlier, results in a poor range resolution in the reconstructed image.

5.6 ISAR IMAGING OF MANEUVERING TARGETS

The velocity of a maneuvering target is a nonlinear function of u (see Figure 5.10). In this section, we present a general solution for estimating the velocity of a maneuvering target based on ISAR measurements.

We begin with a target whose motion is modeled via velocity and acceleration vectors (A, B) and (C, D) in the spatial domain. We denote the synthetic aperture (slow-time) domain with u. For a given fast-temporal frequency of the illuminated radar signal ω, the measured ISAR signal at the slow-time u is

$$
s(u, \omega) = \int_x \int_y dx \, dy \, g(x, y)
$$

$$
\times \, \exp\left[j2k\sqrt{(X_1 + x + Au + .5Cu^2)^2 + (y + Bu + .5Du^2)^2}\right],
$$

where $g(x, y)$ is the target's reflectivity function, $k \equiv \omega/c$ is the wavenumber.

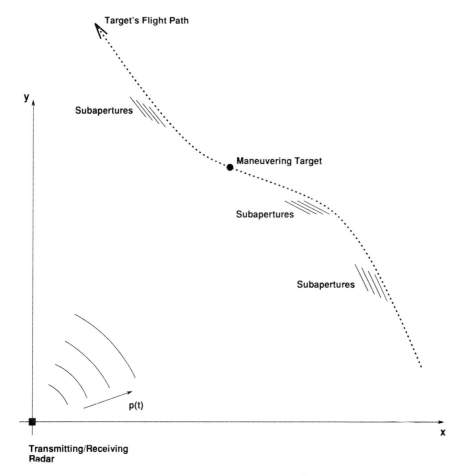

Figure 5.10 Blind-velocity ISAR imaging of a maneuvering target

We assume that at time $u = 0$ the center-of-mass of the target is at $(X_1, 0)$; X_1 is estimated from the time of arrival of the echoed signal; the actual off-broadside angle of the target, though it cannot be retrieved from ISAR measurements, does not play any role in the estimation problem. Thus, the phase delay signal (PM wave) associated with the echoed signal from the center-of-mass of this target is

$$\exp[j2k\sqrt{(X_1 + Au + .5Cu^2)^2 + (Bu + .5Du^2)^2}].$$

The instantaneous frequency of this signal in the u domain is

$$
\begin{aligned}
K_u &\equiv \frac{\partial}{\partial u}[2k\sqrt{(X_1 + Au + .5Cu^2)^2 + (Bu + .5Du^2)^2}] \\
&= 2k\frac{(A + Cu)(X_1 + Au + .5Cu^2) + (B + Du)(Bu + .5Du^2)}{\sqrt{(X_1 + Au + .5Cu^2)^2 + (Bu + .5Du^2)^2}} \\
&\approx 2k\frac{(A + Cu)(X_1 + Au + .5Cu^2) + (B + Du)(Bu + .5Du^2)}{X_1 + Au + .5Cu^2} \\
&\approx 2k(A + Cu) + 2k\frac{(B + Du)(Bu + .5Du^2)}{X_1} \\
&= 2kA + 2k(C + \frac{B^2}{X_1})u + 3k\frac{BD}{X_1}u^2 + k\frac{D^2}{X_1}u^3,
\end{aligned}
$$

$$(5.49)$$

which is a third order polynomial of u. Thus, if K_u is known at discrete values of $u = u_i$, then (A, B, C, D) could be obtained via a least-squares algorithm, for example, the zero-th, first, second, and third moments of K_u with respect to the available discrete values of $u = u_i$.

One can use the subaperture processing described earlier or any other method for retrieving the instantaneous frequency function, for example, a discrete-time PLL, to estimate K_{u_i}'s. As we mentioned earlier, the subaperture processing discussed in Section 5.2 is the short-time Fourier transform method to estimate K_{u_i}'s from the measurements.

Figure 5.10 shows a maneuvering target and the subapertures taken over its path to estimate K_{u_i}'s. One can develop a procedure similar to the one shown in Section 5.2 to determine the optimal subaperture size that reduces ambiguity in estimating K_{u_i}'s [based on some a priori knowledge or constraints on (A, B, C, D)].

Once the target trajectory is determined, one can convert this data to the ISAR data for a straight line target trajectory using the algorithm to compensate for deviations from flight path (see Chapter 4). The resultant data can then be used to image the target.

This principle can be extended to the case when the target's motion can be modeled as, for example, an N-th order polynomial of u in both

x and y domains. In this case, K_u can be expressed as a $2N - 1$ order polynomial of u that can be used to determine the target trajectory.

These algorithms that utilize higher order polynomials of u can fail rapidly when some of the coefficients of the polynomial model are small relative to the others. It might be more practical for the user to use lower polynomials to get an estimate of the target trajectory. Then, an algorithm that compensates for phase degradations in SAR data, for example, [10] can be used to refine the estimator.

Flight Path Projection onto a Line

After estimating the maneuvering target's trajectory, one can use the procedure described in Section 4.5 (compensation for deviations from the flight path) to project the maneuvering target's ISAR data to the target's ISAR data on a straight line. Once this is achieved, one can utilize the ISAR inversion for a target moving on a straight line to image the maneuvering target.

We develop this procedure for a target with velocity and acceleration vectors (A, B) and (C, D). The compensated phase for the flight path projection onto a line can be obtained by considering the following approximation:

$$\sqrt{(X_1 + Au + .5Cu^2)^2 + (Bu + .5Du^2)^2} \approx \sqrt{(X_1 + Au)^2 + (Bu)^2}$$
$$+ .5Cu^2 + \frac{BDu^3}{2(X_1 + Au)}$$

Thus, the phase correction function for this purpose is

$$\exp\left[j2k[.5Cu^2 + \frac{BDu^3}{2(X_1 + Au)}]\right]. \tag{5.50}$$

A Target Moving on a Straight Line

Consider a target moving on a straight line that makes an angle, for example, θ_0 with respect to the x-axis. We denote the speed and acceleration of this target on the *line* by v_0 and a_0, respectively. Thus, we can write the following for the speed and acceleration of the target along the x and y axes:

$$A = v_0 \cos \theta_0$$

$$B = v_0 \sin \theta_0$$

$$C = a_0 \cos \theta_0$$

$$D = a_0 \cos \theta_0.$$

In this case, the instantaneous frequency function defined in (5.49) can be used to solve for *three* unknown parameters (θ_0, v_0, a_0).

5.7 ISAR DETECTION AND IMAGING IN HEAVY CLUTTER

The subaperture processing discussed in the previous sections relies on determining spectral shifts in the target's ISAR signature in the slow-time domain. The success of this approach hinges on the dominance of the target's ISAR signature over noise and clutter in the slow-time spectral (Fourier) domain. In presence of heavy dynamic clutter, the desired target's spectral shifts may not be clearly recognizable in the measured ISAR data and, thus, yield an inaccurate velocity estimator.

In this section, we address blind-velocity ISAR imaging when the target's signature is not identifiable due to heavy noise and clutter. We first develop an ISAR coherent system model for multiple moving targets. Then, we present a *blind-velocity* multiple target detection method via a coherent transformation of ISAR data. This procedure enables us to *localize* a moving target's signature and reject (filter out) most of the clutter and noise signatures. The resultant database, which possesses a much higher signal-to-noise and clutter power ratio, is passed through the subaperture processing algorithm for target velocity estimation and imaging.

ISAR System Model for Multiple Moving Targets

Consider a two-dimensional ISAR imaging system geometry on the (x, y) plane as shown in Figures 5.11a-b. A radar that is located at $(0, 0)$ in the spatial domain illuminates the target area with a time dependent pulsed signal $p(t)$ and records the resultant echoed signals.

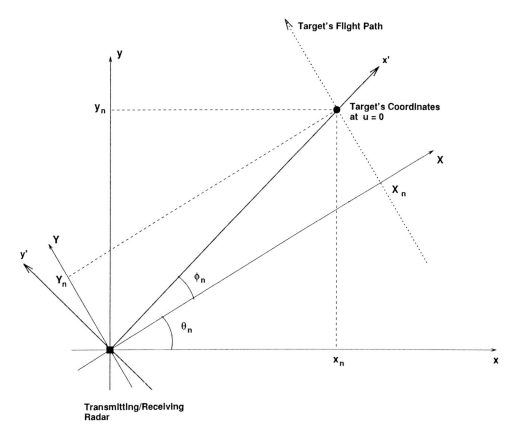

Figure 5.11a System geometry for ISAR detection of moving targets: $u = 0$.

The radar makes such transmissions and corresponding receptions at discrete times of $u \in [-u_0, u_0]$ while an unknown number of targets are moving within the radar's footprint. The moving targets are assumed to have constant velocities identified by (A_n, B_n), $n = 1, 2, 3, ...$, during the radar's data acquisition. u is called the *slow-time* domain; t is referred to as the *fast-time* domain.

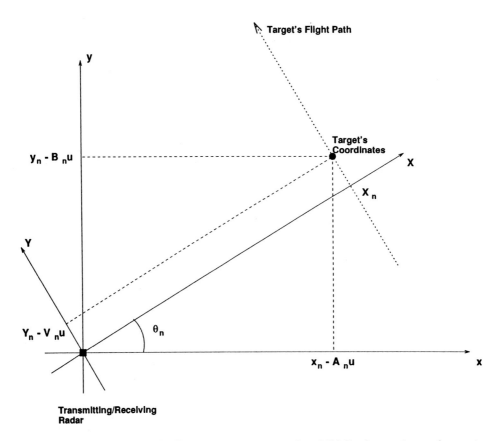

Figure 5.11b System geometry for ISAR detection of moving targets: arbitrary u.

For the detection problem, we assume that each target is a point scatterer located at its center-of-mass; this condition will be removed for the imaging problem. The targets' coordinates at $u = 0$ are denoted by (x_n, y_n), $n = 1, 2, 3, \ldots$. Thus, the n-th target at time u is located at the following spatial coordinates (see Figure 5.11b):

$$(x, y) \; = \; (x_n - A_n u \; , \; y_n - B_n u).$$

For a fixed u, the round-trip time delay in the echoed signal due to the n-th target is

$$\frac{2\sqrt{(x_n - A_n u)^2 + (y_n - B_n u)^2}}{c},$$

where c is the propagation speed. Thus, the two-dimensional recorded signal is

$$s(u,t) \equiv \sum_n \frac{g_n}{R_n^2(u)} p\left[t - \frac{2\,R_n(u)}{c} \right] + s_c(t) + s_N(u,t), \quad (5.51)$$

where $s_c(t)$ is the **static** clutter signature that can be assumed to be invariant of u, $s_N(u,t)$ is the sum of the measurement noise and the **dynamic** clutter that is assumed to be a white process with variance σ^2, g_n is the n-th target's reflectance (this parameter also contains the square root of the radar antenna's transmitting/receiving power and propagation path loss), and

$$R_n(u) \equiv \sqrt{(x_n - A_n u)^2 + (y_n - B_n u)^2}.$$

We will show that the contribution of the static clutter, $s_c(t)$, can be removed from the measurements via a filtering process. In our analysis, we are concerned with the corrupting effects of $s_N(u,t)$. For a given u, the ratio of the power received from the n-th target to the power of $s_N(u,t)$ is (input SNR; the power of $p(t)$ is assumed to be one or absorbed in g_n^2)

$$\begin{aligned}
\left(\frac{S_n}{N}\right)_i &= \frac{g_n^2}{R_n^4(u)\sigma^2} \\
&\approx \frac{g_n^2}{R_n^4 \sigma^2},
\end{aligned} \quad (5.52)$$

where

$$R_n \equiv \sqrt{x_n^2 + y_n^2} = R_n(0). \quad (5.53)$$

The term $\frac{1}{R_n^4}$ on the right side of (5.52) is one of the factors that results in a low input SNR for the ISAR detection/imaging problem.

Temporal (Fast-Time) Fourier Processing

Taking the one-dimensional Fourier transform of both sides of (5.51) with respect to t yields

$$s(u,\omega) \equiv P(\omega) \sum_n g_n \frac{\exp[j2k\sqrt{(x_n - A_n u)^2 + (y_n - B_n u)^2}]}{(x_n - A_n u)^2 + (y_n - B_n u)^2} \qquad (5.54)$$
$$+ S_c(\omega) + s_N(u,\omega),$$

where ω is the temporal frequency domain for t. (For notational simplicity, the Fourier transforms of $s(u,t)$ and $s_N(u,t)$ with respect to t are identified by $s(u,\omega)$ and $s_N(u,\omega)$, respectively.)

We define the following (squint) angle and speed values for the n-th target

$$\theta_n \equiv \arctan(\frac{A_n}{B_n})$$
$$V_n \equiv \sqrt{A_n^2 + B_n^2} \qquad (5.55)$$

We also define the following rotational transformation of the n-th target's coordinates (see Figure 5.11):

$$\begin{bmatrix} X_n \\ Y_n \end{bmatrix} \equiv \begin{bmatrix} \cos\theta_n & -\sin\theta_n \\ \sin\theta_n & \cos\theta_n \end{bmatrix} \begin{bmatrix} x_n \\ y_n \end{bmatrix} \qquad (5.56)$$

- *θ_n is referred to as the **blind angle** for the n-th target. The blind angle represents an ambiguity that cannot be resolved via ISAR data. The magnitude of the blind angle is less than or equal to half of the physical radar antenna's beamwidth. The blind-velocity ISAR imaging described earlier solves for the n-th target's parameters (velocity and coordinates) in the (X,Y) domain (not the (x,y) domain) shown in Figure 5.11. (The (X,Y) domain is constructed by rotating the (x,y) domain by θ_n.) The blind angle does not have any effect in the algorithm and is unknown to the user. (The blind angle may be recovered via, for example, combining the outputs of **two** ISAR systems that are used to image the target simultaneously.)*

Using (5.55)-(5.56) in the system model of (5.54) yields

$$s(u,\omega) \equiv P(\omega) \sum_n g_n \frac{\exp[j2k\sqrt{X_n^2 + (Y_n - V_n u)^2}]}{X_n^2 + (Y_n - V_n u)^2} + S_c(\omega) + s_N(u,\omega).$$

$$(5.57)$$

The system model in (5.57) shows that the n-th target is located at (X_n, Y_n) when $u = 0$ and moves with speed V_n parallel to the Y-axis.

- *The **relative** (X, Y) domain is different for each target since the blind angle θ_n varies with n. θ_n is transparent in the processing that is shown in the following sections.*

Spatial (Slow-Time) Fourier Processing

We denote the pulse repetition frequency (the number of transmitted pulses per unit time in the u domain) by f_0. Taking the Fourier transform of both sides of (5.57) with respect to $u \in [-u_0, u_0]$ yields [11, eq. 5.3.89]

$$
\begin{aligned}
S(k_u, \omega) =& P(\omega) \sum_n \frac{\exp(-j\frac{\pi}{4})g_n}{V_n \cos\phi_n} \left(\frac{\pi f_0}{2u_0 k R_n^3}\right)^{\frac{1}{2}} \\
& \times \exp[j\sqrt{4k^2 - (\frac{k_u}{V_n})^2}X_n + j\frac{k_u}{V_n}Y_n]I_n(\frac{k_u}{k}) \\
& + S_c(\omega)\,\mathrm{sinc}(k_u u_0) + S_N(k_u, \omega),
\end{aligned}
$$

$$(5.58)$$

where $I_n(\cdot)$ is an indicator (band) function defined by (see the discussion on finite aperture effects in [9])

$$I_n(\frac{k_u}{k}) = \begin{cases} 1 & \frac{k_u}{k} \in [2V_n \sin\phi_n - \frac{2u_0 V_n^2 \cos^2 \phi_n}{R_n}, 2V_n \sin\phi_n + \frac{2u_0 V_n^2 \cos^2 \phi_n}{R_n}] \\ 0 & \text{otherwise} \end{cases}$$

$$(5.59)$$

with

$$R_n \equiv \sqrt{X_n^2 + Y_n^2} = \sqrt{x_n^2 + y_n^2},$$

and

$$\phi_n \equiv \arctan(\frac{Y_n}{X_n}). \qquad (5.60)$$

- *Equation (5.58) is obtained via the following approximations for slowly fluctuating amplitude functions (for the n-th target with $V_n \ll c$):*

$$\frac{1}{[\sqrt{X_n^2 + (Y_n - V_n u)^2}]^3} \approx \frac{1}{\sqrt{R_n^3}},$$

and

$$\frac{1}{\sqrt{4k^2 - (\frac{k_u}{V_n})^2}} \approx \frac{1}{2k \cos \phi_n}.$$

- *The signature of the n-th target is centered around*

$$H_n \equiv 2V_n \sin \phi_n, \tag{5.61}$$

in the $\frac{k_u}{k}$ domain. The length of this support band is

$$2W_n \equiv \frac{4u_0 V_n^2 \cos^2 \phi_n}{R_n}, \tag{5.62}$$

*in the $\frac{k_u}{k}$ domain. Both H_n and W_n are **invariant** of k (or ω). Furthermore, the range-dependent amplitude function $\frac{1}{R_n^2}$ on the right side of (5.51) or (5.57) is converted to $\frac{1}{\sqrt{R_n^3}}$ on the right side of (5.58) via the spatial Doppler processing.*

It is assumed that the signature of each target does not overlap with the static clutter signature; that is,

$$I_n(\alpha) \, I_c(\alpha) = 0 \quad \text{for all } n \text{ and } \alpha$$

where $I_c(\cdot)$ is the support band for the static clutter signature $\text{sinc}(k_u u_0)$. Thus, we may use a highpass filter with a rejection band identified by

$$[-\frac{\pi}{u_0}, \frac{\pi}{u_0}],$$

to filter the static clutter signature in the k_u domain. In the discussion that follows, we assume that this filtering operation is performed and, thus, we do not carry the static clutter signature in the equations.

We also require spectral separability among the targets' signatures, that is,

$$I_n(\alpha)\ I_m(\alpha) = 0 \quad \text{for all } m \neq n \text{ and } \alpha,$$

for a given range cell (t cell) that is equal to the time duration of the transmitted pulsed signal $p(t)$. (This should be true in the domain of the signal $Q(h_u, t)$ that is defined in the next section.)

Next, we develop methods for detecting the targets from their signatures in the presence of heavy measurement noise and dynamic clutter.

Target Detection and Signature Extraction

In the above formulation, we presented the ISAR signal information content via $s(u, t)$ in (5.51), $s(u, \omega)$ in (5.54), and $S(k_u, \omega)$ in (5.58). The detection problem can be viewed as the most reliable way to process the ISAR signal for identifying the moving targets.

Maximum Likelihood-Based Method: Using the white Gaussian model for the dynamic clutter, the sufficient statistic (likelihood function) for the detection problem is achieved via the following coherent processing:

$$\ell(X_0, Y_0, V_0, \phi_0) \equiv \left| \sum_{k_u} \sum_{\omega} S(k_u, \omega) \right.$$

$$\left. \times \ \exp[-j\sqrt{4k^2 - (\frac{k_u}{V_0})^2}\ X_0 - j\frac{k_u}{V_0}Y_0]\ I_0(\frac{k_u}{k}) \right|,$$
$$(5.63)$$

where (X_0, Y_0, V_0, ϕ_0) identify the target parameter space over which the statistic ℓ should be maximized. (The magnitude of the sum is used in (5.63) since a target's radar cross section is generally a complex number and affects both the in-phase and quadrature channels.) This procedure is computationally intensive.

The other alternative is, for a given (V_0, ϕ_0), using the ISAR *imaging* algorithm to reconstruct the target region. If there existed a target with parameters (V_0, ϕ_0), then this target would appear in the reconstructed image. The reconstructed image around the target location should show significantly higher target-to-clutter ratio [the same as the target-to-clutter ratio for the statistic in (5.63)] than the target-to-clutter ratio in the measurement (u, t) domain. This is due to the fact that the reconstruction algorithm coherently combines and localizes the target signature for image formation. This process should be repeated for all values of (V_0, ϕ_0) in its prescribed parameter space. This approach also requires a significant computation time.

Transformation Method: The ISAR imaging basically achieves higher target-to-clutter ratio by localizing the target contribution in the received signal around a single point in the image domain. We now examine the detection problem through a transformed version of the ISAR signal that also localizes the target contribution in its domain.

We define the following linear mapping:

$$h_u \equiv \frac{k_u}{k}. \tag{5.64}$$

From (5.64), we denote the following functional mapping of the ISAR signal (the static clutter signature is filtered; $S_N(k_u, \omega)$ is suppressed for notational simplicity):

$$
\begin{aligned}
Q(h_u, \omega) &\equiv \frac{\sqrt{2u_0 k}}{\exp(-j\frac{\pi}{4})\sqrt{\pi f_0}}\, S(k_u, \omega) \\
&= P(\omega) \sum_n \frac{g_n}{\sqrt{R_n^3}\, V_n\, \cos\phi_n} \\
&\quad \times \exp\!\left[\, j\frac{\omega}{c}[\sqrt{4 - (\frac{h_u}{V_n})^2}\, X_n + \frac{h_u}{V_n} Y_n]\,\right] I_n(h_u),
\end{aligned}
\tag{5.65}
$$

with

$$I_n(h_u) = \begin{cases} 1 & h_u \in [H_n - W_n, H_n + W_n]; \\ 0 & \text{otherwise} \end{cases}$$

Taking the inverse Fourier transform of both sides of (5.65) with respect to ω yields

$$
Q(h_u, t) = \sum_n \frac{g_n}{\sqrt{R_n^3}\, V_n\, \cos\phi_n}\, p\!\left[\, t - \sqrt{4 - (\frac{h_u}{V_n})^2}\, \frac{X_n}{c} - \frac{h_u}{V_n}\frac{Y_n}{c}\right] I_n(h_u).
\tag{5.66}
$$

[For notational simplicity, the inverse Fourier transform of Q is also called Q in (5.66).]

The transformed signal $Q(h_u, t)$ localizes the n-th target's signature, that is,

$$p\left[t - \sqrt{4 - (\frac{h_u}{V_n})^2} \; \frac{X_n}{c} - \frac{h_u}{V_n} \frac{Y_n}{c} \right] I_n(h_u),$$

in an interval equal to the duration of $p(t)$ in the time domain and an interval equal to $2W_n$ in the h_u domain. The locus of this signature resembles a portion of a parabola.

For a given $h_u \in [H_n - W_n, H_n + W_n]$, the power of the n-th target to the power of measurement noise/dynamic clutter power in $Q(h_u, t)$ can be found from (5.58) to be (output SNR)

$$(\frac{S_n}{N})_o \approx \frac{\pi}{2} \; \frac{f_0 \; g_n^2}{u_0 \; R_n^3 \; k V_n^2 \; \cos^2 \phi_n \; \sigma^2}, \tag{5.67}$$

where k_c is the wavenumber of the radar signal's center (carrier) temporal frequency. Using (5.52) in (5.67) yields

$$\frac{(\frac{S_n}{N})_o}{(\frac{S_n}{N})_i} = \frac{\pi}{2} \; \frac{R_n \; f_0}{u_0 \; k \; V_n^2 \; \cos^2 \phi_n}. \tag{5.68}$$

For most practical values of (R_n, f_0, u_0, k, V_n) (e.g., detecting long-range missiles using high-powered HF radars), (5.68) shows an improvement for the target-to-clutter ratio in the (h_u, t) domain as compared to the (u, t) domain. In this case, one anticipates the target's parabolic locus in the (h_u, t) domain to be more prominent in presence of clutter than the noisy target signature in the (u, t) domain. If the noise level is too high for this locus to be visible, image processing techniques for shape/contour detection may be used to identify parabolic contours in $|Q(h_u, t)|$.

Target's Velocity Estimation and Imaging

In this section, we present a method for ISAR imaging of moving targets based on the transformation method described in the previous section. It is assumed that each moving target's signature is localized visually and filtered by the user in the (h_u, t) domain. (Image processing methods may be used to localize the targets' signatures without manual supervision.) We showed earlier in this chapter that that SAR/ISAR imaging of a moving target can be converted into imaging the target in a stationary squint-mode SAR problem where the parameters of the squint-mode geometry depend on the target's velocity. Thus, the target's velocity should be estimated in advance. The blind-velocity ISAR imaging method is as follows:

Step 1: Obtain the signature of the moving target via bandpass filtering in the (h_u, t) domain. Thus, this operation rejects added noise and other moving targets' signatures.

Step 2: Take the Fourier transform of the target's signature with respect to t. Now the signal is represented in the (h_u, ω) domain.

Step 3: Perform the linear mapping of the signal in the (h_u, ω) domain into the (k_u, ω) domain, in accordance with the relation $k_u = h_u k$. The resultant (k_u, ω) domain data should be stored to image the moving target after Step 5.

Step 4: Take the inverse Fourier transform of the (k_u, ω) domain data with respect to k_u, which leads to the data in the (u, ω) domain.

Step 5: Use the subaperture processing method to estimate the target's velocity $(\hat{A}_n, \hat{B}_n)$.

Step 6: Use ISAR imaging algorithm with the data from Step 3 and the estimated velocity from Step 5 to reconstruct the target.

Example: Next, we examine the merits of the above-mentioned detection and reconstruction algorithm via computer simulations. The parameters of the ISAR system geometry used in the simulation are as follow: For 1024 discrete slow-time points in the time interval $u \in [0.213, -0.213]$ (sec), the radar, which is located at $(0., 0.)$, transmits a rectangular pulse that is amplitude modulating a $f_c = 90$ MHz carrier and receives corresponding echoed signals. There exist two moving targets within the radar footprint that is a disk with radius 1,024 m, centered at (10000.,0.)(m). Each target is simulated as an object with four point reflectors.

Target 1 has a velocity vector $(-900.,-1500.)$ (m/sec) and is located at $(9970.,10.)$ (m) when $u = 0$. This target's velocity in the coordinate system where the target's cross-range is zero for $u = 0$ is $(-901.504,-1499.096)$. Target 2 has the velocity vector $(450.,1800.)$ (m/sec) and its coordinates at $u = 0$ are $(10200.,400.)$ (m). Using (5.68), the theoretical improvement in SNR can be found to be 16.2 dB.

Gaussian noise is added to the echoed signal such that the signal-to-noise ratio (input SNR) for a single scatterer is -3.03 dB. Thus, one anticipates the output SNR to be $16.2 - 3.03 = 13.17$ dB. Figures 5.12 and 5.13 show the distribution of the (u,t) domain data for the noise-free and noisy cases, respectively.

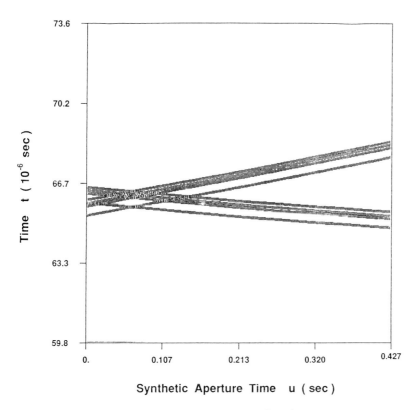

Figure 5.12 ISAR signature $s(u,t)$.

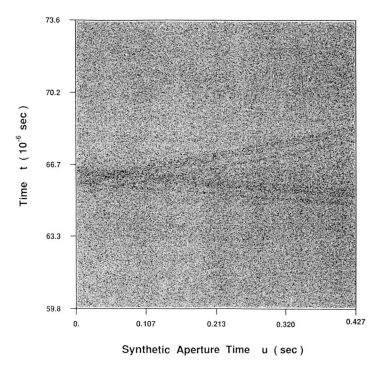

Figure 5.13 ISAR signature $s(u,t)$ with additive noise (SNR = -3.03 dB).

Figures 5.14 and 5.15 are the (k_u, ω) and (h_u, ω) domains data for the noise-free case. Figures 5.16 and 5.17 show the distribution of the (h_u, t) domain data for the noise-free and noisy cases, respectively.

The following figures illustrate the reconstruction procedure and output images of a moving target. Suppose we are interested in reconstructing target 1. Figure 5.18 depicts the filtering performed in the (h_u, t) domain to extract target 1's signature when SNR = -3.03 dB. The filtered data is first inverse Fourier transformed and then interpolated into the (k_u, ω) domain (see Figure 5.19). After taking inverse Fourier transform of the data with respect to u, the resultant data which is in the (u, ω) domain, is processed in the subaperture processing algorithm. The estimated velocity is $(-900.68, -1424.80)$ (m/sec).

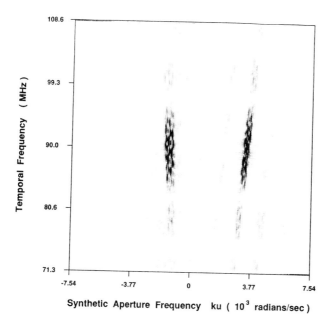

Figure 5.14 ISAR signature $S(k_u, \omega)$.

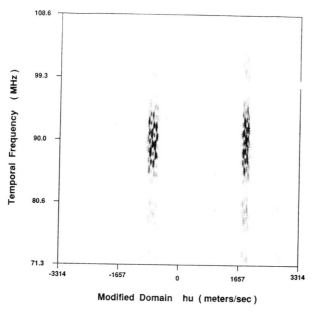

Figure 5.15 ISAR signature $Q(h_u, \omega)$.

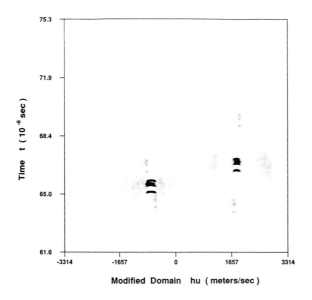

Figure 5.16 ISAR signature $Q(h_u, t)$.

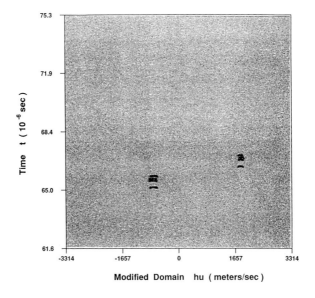

Figure 5.17 ISAR signature $Q(h_u, t)$ with additive noise (SNR = -3.03 dB).

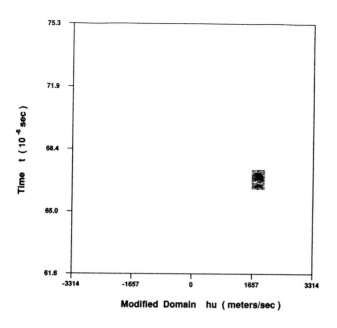

Figure 5.18 Filtered ISAR signature $Q(h_u, t)$.

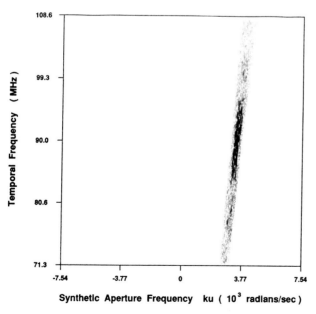

Figure 5.19 Filtered ISAR signature $S(k_u, \omega)$.

Figure 5.20 is the image of target 1 reconstructed with an actual velocity and uncorrupted echoed signal. The image in Figure 5.21 is the reconstructed target with the estimated velocity, using original noisy ISAR data, which means the filtering in the (h_u, t) domain is not performed (target 2 is removed for this experiment). Figure 5.22 is the reconstructed image with the estimated velocity using the filtered data in the (h_u, t) domain.

Note that the noise level in Figure 5.22 is reduced significantly as compared with the noise level in Figure 5.21.

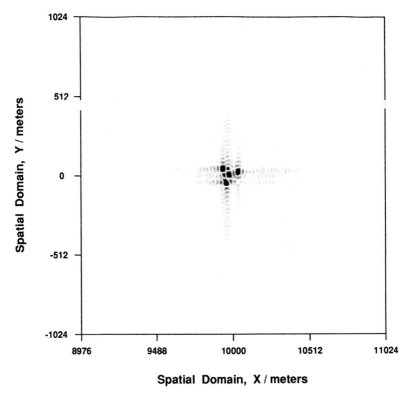

Figure 5.20 ISAR reconstruction with actual velocity and no additive noise.

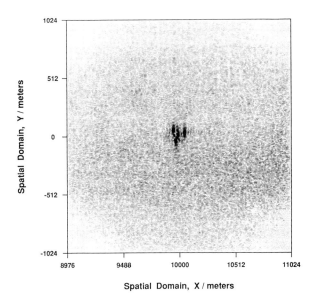

Figure 5.21 ISAR reconstruction with estimated velocity and additive noise; target signature is not filtered in (h_u, t) domain.

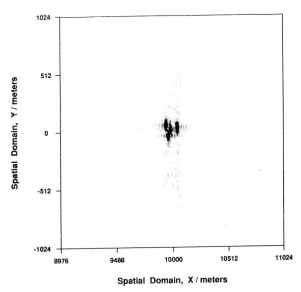

Figure 5.22 ISAR reconstruction with estimated velocity and additive noise; target signature is filtered in (h_u, t) domain.

Figures 5.23 and 5.24 illustrate the returned signal in the (u, t) and (h_u, t) domains, respectively, for SNR $= -12.5$ dB. Moreover, the target's signature is invisible in the (u, t) domain while it is still distinguishable in the (h_u, t) domain (i.e., the detection can be performed; the output SNR is $16.2 - 12.5 = 3.7$ dB). In this case, the results for velocity estimation and reconstruction were not good. We were able to obtain fair results (velocity estimator and reconstruction) when the SNR was lowered to about -9.1 dB level. At lower SNR's, the velocity estimator algorithm was not successful.

- *These results indicate that at lower SNR levels, the subaperture processing for the target's velocity estimation may fail though the target may still be detectable in the transformed domain* (h_u, t).

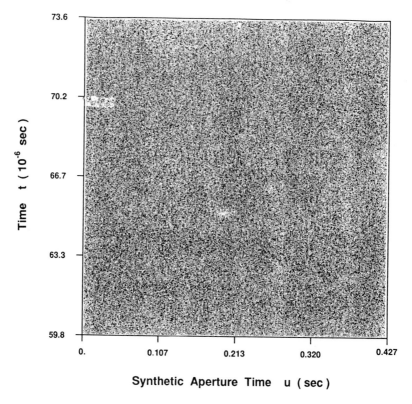

Figure 5.23 ISAR signature $s(u, t)$ with additive noise (SNR = -12.5 dB).

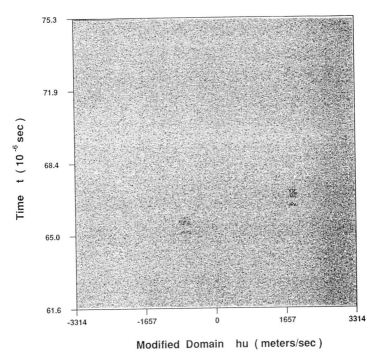

Figure 5.24 ISAR signature $Q(h_u, t)$ with additive noise (SNR = -12.5 dB).

5.8 ISAR IMAGING OF AN AIRBORNE DC-9

In this section, we present results on blind-velocity ISAR imaging of a DC-9 aircraft over Lindbergh Field at San Diego. The data were provided by the radar group at the Naval Command, Control and Ocean Surveillance Center (NCCOSC), San Diego.

Blind-Velocity ISAR Imaging

The DC-9's stepped-frequency ISAR database used in this analysis, and similar SAR/ISAR databases obtained over the past decade, are insufficient (aliased) in the slow-time domain when viewed in the framework of the recently developed high-resolution (relatively large synthetic aperture) SAR/ISAR imaging methods.

We utilize SAR/ISAR signal compression in the synthetic aperture domain to retrieve the target's unaliased ISAR signature. *This in turn allows us to incorporate ISAR data taken over large synthetic aperture intervals in the inversion algorithm that results in better cross-range resolution.* ISAR images obtained via these coherent techniques show clear and focused *dominant* reflectors, such as the aircraft's engines and tail (the corner of horizontal-vertical stabilizers), which possess the resolution anticipated by the ISAR theory. However, the side lobes (point spread function) associated with these dominant reflectors deteriorate other parts of the target structure in the reconstructed image; this is known as the *coherent speckle* effect. We present a method for reducing coherent speckle via separating the dominant reflector signature in the compressed ISAR signal. As a result, more details about the aircraft can be extracted from the ISAR data. The radar parameters used in collecting the ISAR data are as follows. The moving aircraft is located at $(4952., 0.)$ at $u = 0$. The radar transmits a stepped-frequency modulated signal and receives corresponding echoed signal. Sixty-four temporal step frequencies, with frequency spacing 4 MHz in a bandpass region identified via $f \in [9.01, 9.266]$ (GHz), are used. The radar's pulse repetition frequency (prf) is 6859.

ISAR Signal Interpolation: The radar makes 256 slow-time measurements in the time interval $u \in [-1.194, 1.194]$ (sec). The length of a DC-9 aircraft is more than 40 meters. In this case, the u (slow-time) domain ISAR data for the DC-9 can be shown to be undersampled and, thus, aliased. Figure 5.25a is the real part of aliased $s(u, \omega)$ for a fixed value of ω (the center frequency of the radar signal). Figure 5.25b shows the distribution of aliased $|S(k_u, \omega)|$. To overcome the aliasing problem, we use a rough estimate of (A, B) (obtained from a tracking instrument) to compress the ISAR data in the slow-time domain. The magnitude distribution of the compressed data in the (k_u, ω) domain is given in Figure 5.26. We then zero-pad the compressed data in the k_u domain such that the sampling rate in the u domain is increased by eight times; that is, the number of samples for $u \in [-1.194, 1.194]$ (sec) becomes 2048. The resultant data is then decompressed to retrieve the DC-9's unaliased ISAR data. Figure 5.27a is the real part of $s(u, \omega)$ at the center frequency of the radar signal. Figure 5.27b shows the distribution of $|S(k_u, \omega)|$.

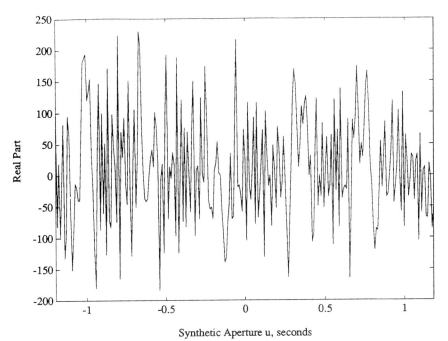

Figure 5.25a Aliased ISAR signal $s(u, \omega_c)$.

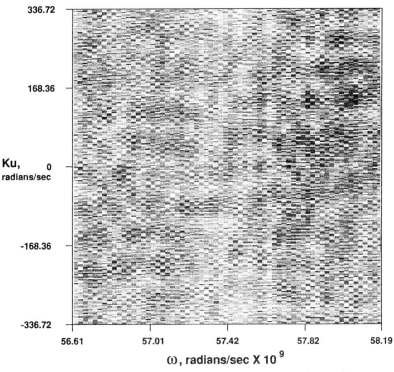

Figure 5.25b Aliased ISAR signal $S(k_u, \omega)$.

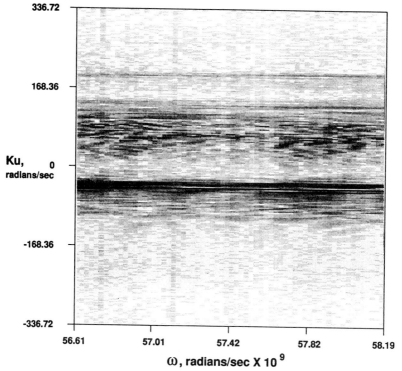

Figure 5.26 Compressed ISAR signal $S_c(k_u, \omega)$.

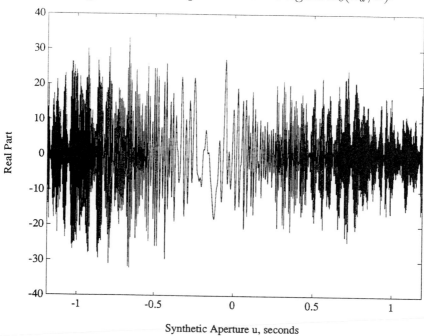

Figure 5.27a Interpolated ISAR signal $s(u, \omega_c)$.

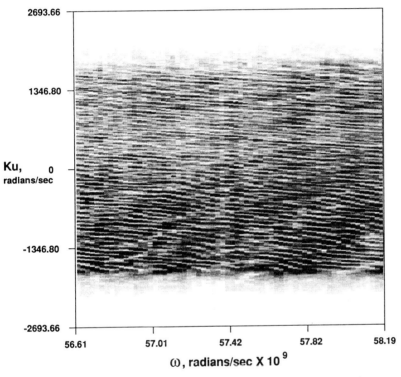

Figure 5.27b Interpolated ISAR signal $S(k_u, \omega)$.

Constant Velocity Target Model: After recovering the unaliased ISAR data, we apply the subaperture processing to estimate the DC-9's motion parameters. First, we assume the target possesses no acceleration, that is, $C = D = 0$. The estimate for the velocity is found to be

$$(A, B) = (-42.7774, 137.1446) \text{ m/sec.}$$

The resultant reconstructed image is shown in Figure 5.28.

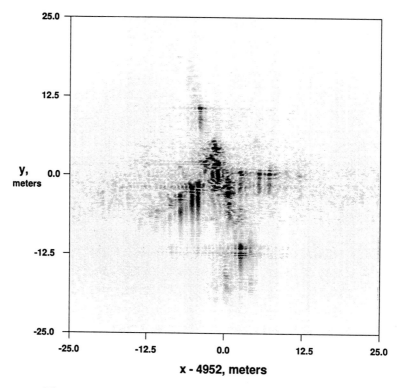

Figure 5.28 Reconstructed ISAR image with (A, B).

The dominant reflector on the DC-9 is around its tail section. The dominant reflector's signature is visible at $k_u \approx -40.$ radians/sec in Figure 5.26. To reduce its effect, the signature of the tail in the compressed ISAR signal is filtered and processed separately in the inversion algorithm. For this purpose, we divide the compressed ISAR data into two regions: $k_u < 0$ and $k_u \geq 0$. We then process each of the two signatures separately in the zero-padding, decompression, and reconstruction algorithms. The magnitudes of the resultant two reconstructed images are quantized (256 gray levels). The two gray scale images are added to each other to yield the final image.

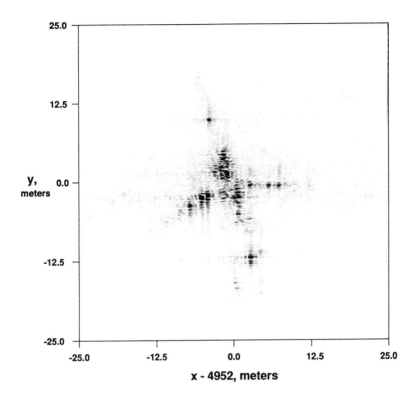

Figure 5.29 Reconstructed ISAR image with $(A, B, C, D) \equiv (v_0, a_0, \theta_0)$.

Velocity and Acceleration Target Model on a Straight Line: Next, we assume the target is moving on a straight line and possesses nonzero acceleration. In this case, we obtain the following estimates:

$$(A, B) = (-42.8034, 143.591) \text{ m/sec},$$

$$(C, D) = (.3664538, -1.229329) \text{ m/sec}^2.$$

Figure 5.29 shows the reconstructed image based on the above estimates.

Velocity and Acceleration Maneuvering Target Model: Next, we model the target as an accelerating one that is not moving on a straight line. Based on this general model, the estimates become

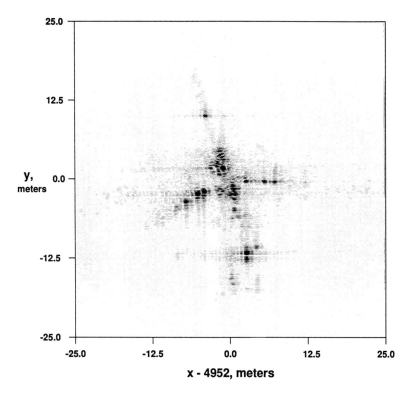

Figure 5.30 Reconstructed ISAR image with (A, B, C, D).

$$(A, B) = (-42.7995, 302.797) \text{ m/sec},$$

$$(C, D) = (14.736524, 1.487397) \text{ m/sec}^2.$$

Note that the estimate $B = 302.8$ m/sec and $C = 14.74$ m/sec^2 are quite different from the other two estimates and are unrealistic. However, these numbers provide the best fit for the instantaneous frequency function based on our presumed model. In this case, to map the target's ISAR data into a straight line based on the above estimates, we choose the straight line to be defined via the (A, B) estimates that are obtained from the model that assumes the target has no acceleration. The result is shown in Figure 5.30, which is similar to the reconstruction shown in Figure 5.29.

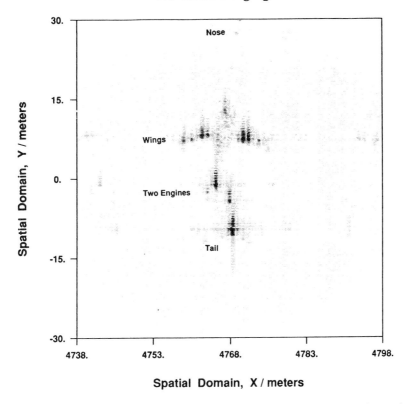

Figure 5.31 Reconstructed ISAR image with (A, B) (no acceleration in the target motion).

Constant Velocity Target Model: The airborne aircraft does not possess acceleration at all phases of its flight path. Figure 5.31 shows the DC-9 reconstruction for such a case with

$$(A, B) = (-16.4105, 148.991) \text{ m/sec.}$$

For this case, 1024 slow-time samples are available for $u \in [0., 1.194]$ (sec). (This phase of the DC-9's flight path has a different reference time point and does not overlap with the longer flight path phase that was discussed earlier.) To exhibit the dominant reflector effect, we present this image without processing the dominant reflector signature separately. Note that in this orientation of the aircraft, its two side engines (the corner reflectors generated by the fuselage and the engines) are clearly visible.

ISAR Detection and Imaging in Heavy Clutter

Next, we examine the merits of the algorithms for ISAR detection and imaging, which were discussed in Section 5.7, using the DC-9 data of Figure 5.31. Based on (5.68), the theoretical improvement in SNR for the DC-9 data is 4.1 dB.

- *The SNR improvement for this case is relatively small. This is due to the fact that the target is at close range (about 5 kilometers) and the radar frequency (9 GHz) is well above the HF frequency range.*

Figures 5.32a and 5.32b show the DC-9's signature in the (u, t) and (h_u, t) domains, respectively. The (u, t) domain data are generated via the inverse Fourier transform of the ISAR data with respect to the step frequency (i.e., the fast-time temporal frequency domain).

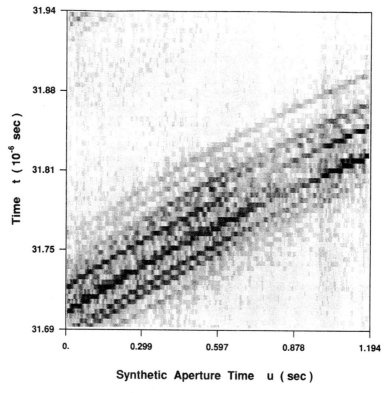

Figure 5.32a DC-9's ISAR signature $s(u, t)$.

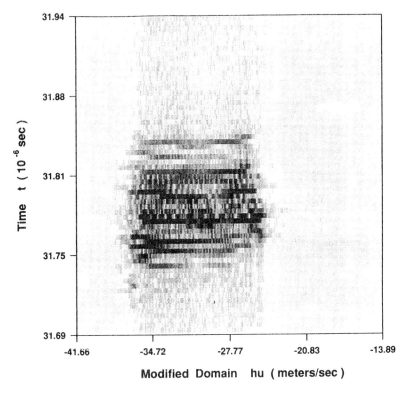

Figure 5.32b DC-9's ISAR signature $Q(h_u, t)$.

White Gaussian noise is added to the DC-9 data such that the input SNR becomes -11.82 dB. Figures 5.33a and 5.33b show the corrupted ISAR signal in the (u, t) and (h_u, t) domains. With the filtered data, aircraft's velocity is estimated to be $(-16.30227, 146.4909)$ (m/sec). The aircraft's reconstructions using the noisy data and the noisy data that are filtered are shown in Figures 5.34 and 5.35, respectively. Due to the estimator error, the output images appear shifted (see Appendix).

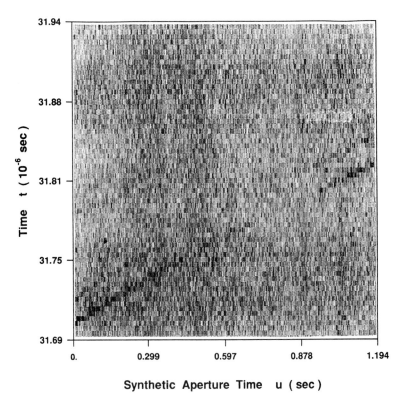

Figure 5.33a DC-9's ISAR signature $s(u,t)$ with additive noise.

- *While the filtered data yields a good velocity estimator, the image reconstructed by this database shows fading in certain parts of the target structure. This is due to the fact that the entire target's signature is not visible in the noisy (h_u, t) domain data. The filter used for this experiment only picked the dominant component that appears above the noise level in Figure 5.33b. As a result, a portion of the target's signature corresponding to the low energy reflectors on the aircraft is lost in the filtering process.*

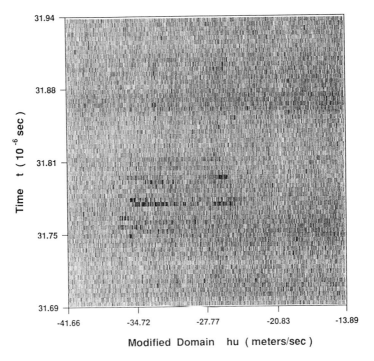

Figure 5.33b DC-9's ISAR signature $Q(h_u, t)$ with additive
noise.

- *The results with the DC-9 data show that while the data filtered in the*
  (h_u, t) are suitable for velocity estimation, it caused fading degrada-
  tions in the reconstructed image. Thus, the user may decide to utilize
  reconstructed images from both filtered and noisy data for, for example,
  target identification.

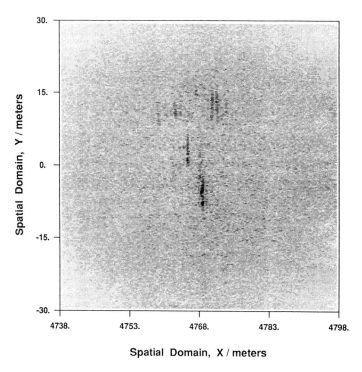

Figure 5.34 DC-9's ISAR reconstruction without filtering.

Representation via FM-CW Signaling

In Chapter 4, we showed that pulsed stepped-frequency SAR signaling is a special case of FM-CW SAR signaling; that is,

$$a(t) = a_3(t) \sum_{\ell} a_1(t - \ell t_2),$$

where $a_1(t)$ is composed of a finite number of evenly spaced rectangular pulses that are amplitude-modulating sinusoids with frequencies that are being increased (stepped) linearly:

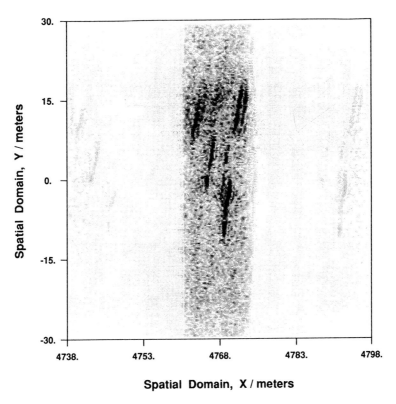

Figure 5.35 DC-9's ISAR reconstruction with filtering.

$$a_1(t) \equiv \sum_{m=1}^{M} a_0(t - m\Delta_t) \, \exp\big[jm\Delta_\omega(t - m\Delta_t)\big],$$

and $a_0(t)$ is a rectangular pulse.

We now exhibit this fact using the DC-9's stepped-frequency ISAR data. As we mentioned earlier, there are 64 stepped-frequencies with frequency spacing 4 MHz. Thus, the bandwidth of the FM-CW signal is 256 MHz, which should also be the sampling rate for the resultant FM-CW ISAR signal. However, this constraint is severely violated by the radar's prf, which is 6,859 Hz.

The coherent integration time for the A/D converter does apply an *analog* filter (the integrator in the electronic circuitry of the A/D converter) on the FM-CW ISAR signal and reduces its bandwidth. However, the data is still severely aliased. This small FM-CW ISAR bandwidth also results in a poor range resolution. Clearly, the same is not true if the measurements are treated and processed as pulsed stepped-frequency ISAR data.

In spite of severe aliasing and poor range resolution for the DC-9's FM-CW ISAR database, we can still observe the compression property of FM-CW ISAR signals in the available data. This is due to the fact that t_2 is an integer multiple of Δ_t; thus, an aliased harmonic, which is an integer multiple of ω_2, falls exactly on another harmonic.

We consider 4096 real-time stepped-frequency samples taken over $t \in [0, .597]$ second. In this data set, there are 64 periods each containing 64 step frequencies. We mentioned earlier that the radar's prf is 6859 Hertz. Thus, the repetition rate of the FM-CW signal is

$$f_2 \equiv \frac{1}{t_2} = \frac{6859}{64} = 107 \text{ Hertz.}$$

The DC-9's velocity was estimated to be $(a_0, b_0) = (-15.1, 147.1)$ meters/second for the segment of the target's flight path studied here. The compression function for the ISAR scenario is

$$\exp\left[-j\omega_c[t - \frac{2\sqrt{(X_1 + a_0 \ t)^2 + (b_0 \ t)^2}}{c}]\right].$$

Figure 5.36a is the DC-9's FM-CW baseband ISAR signature in the frequency domain. Figure 5.36b shows a portion of this signal over a smaller frequency interval. Based on the sampling constraints for an FM-CW ISAR signal that were developed earlier, the DC-9's signatures at the harmonics of the FM-CW signal overlap with each other.

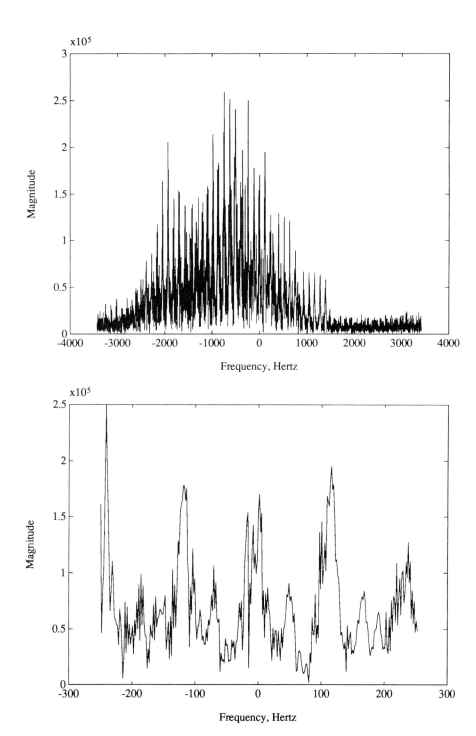

Figure 5.36 DC-9's FM-CW ISAR signature in the frequency domain.

Figure 5.37a is the DC-9's Compressed FM-CW ISAR signature in the frequency domain. Figure 5.37b shows a portion of this signal over a smaller frequency interval. Note that the target's compressed signature shows distinct energy concentrations around the harmonics of $f_2 = 107$ Hertz. However, unlike the compressed signal for the DC-9's pulsed ISAR data, the DC-9's aliased FM-CW compressed distribution does not show the signatures of the aircraft's tail, engines, wings and noise.

5.9 AUTOMATIC TARGET DETECTION FROM INCOHERENT ISAR DATA

The coherent ISAR detection and imaging described in Section 5.7 assumes an additive clutter-noise model that varies with both slow-time and fast-time. We mentioned earlier that in the presence of multiplicative noise, which is due to the target's nonlinear motion and random turbulence, the coherent information in SAR/ISAR data could be totally lost. The coherent ISAR detection algorithm is also highly vulnerable to phase errors, and fails when the deviations of the target from its presumed straight line path is on the order of $\frac{\lambda}{4}$, where λ is the smallest wavelength in the pulsed signal.

We now examine this issue and discuss a method that utilizes the *magnitude* of ISAR data for detecting a moving target that possesses random motion. The basis of our formulation for incoherent ISAR detection is that the *signal-to-clutter power ratio in the ISAR signature is greater than 0 dB*. This simply translates into the condition that the target signature is in fact *visible* in the incoherent ISAR signature. Such an assumption is the basis of all automatic (machine-based) moving target detection methods that utilize incoherent data, for example, [4], and many image processing algorithms for detecting *lines* in an image. The main message of this section is that incoherent ISAR data may also be interpreted as being a *baseband* ISAR database and, thus, possesses the functional properties of ISAR signals. The (h_u, t) transformation on incoherent ISAR data, which yields localized information for a target, is based on those ISAR signal properties.

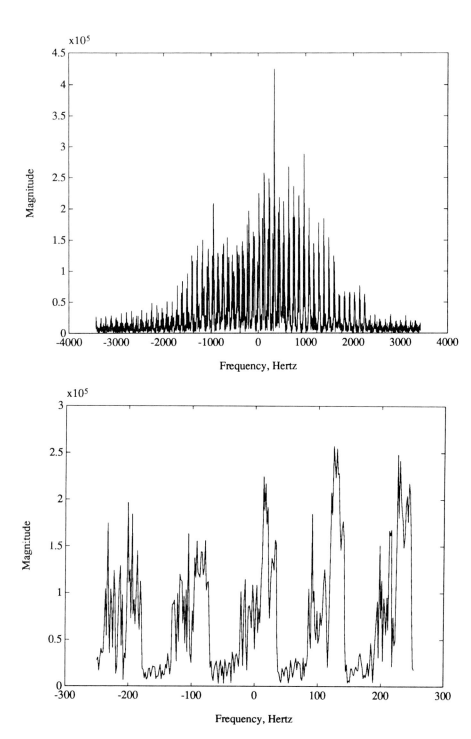

Figure 5.37 DC-9's compressed FM-CW ISAR signature in the frequency domain.

We begin with the two-dimensional ISAR imaging system geometry on the (x, y) plane shown in Figures 5.11a-b. A radar that is located at $(0, 0)$ in the spatial domain illuminates the target area with a time-dependent pulsed signal $p(t)$ and records the resultant echoed signals. The radar makes such transmissions and corresponding receptions at discrete times of $u \in [-u_0, u_0]$ while an unknown number of targets are moving within the radar's footprint.

In Section 5.7, we assumed that the moving targets have constant velocities identified by (A_n, B_n), $n = 1, 2, 3, ...,$ during the radar's data acquisition. Thus, if the targets' coordinates at the slow-time $u = 0$ are denoted by (x_n, y_n), $n = 1, 2, 3, ...,$ then the n-th target at slow-time u is located at the following spatial coordinates:

$$(x, y) = (x_n - A_n u , \; y_n - B_n u).$$

In our present formulation, we associate a nonlinear component of the slow-time, call it $[\alpha_n(u), \beta_n(u)]$, to the n-th target's linear motion model; that is,

$$(x, y) = [x_n - A_n u - \alpha_n(u) , \; y_n - B_n u - \beta_n(u)].$$

Thus, the two-dimensional recorded signal in the slow-time fast-time domain becomes

$$s(u, t) \equiv \sum_n \frac{g_n}{R_n^2(u)} \, p\left[t - \frac{2 \, R_n(u)}{c} \right] + s_N(u, t),$$

where $s_N(u, t)$ is the sum of the measurement noise and the dynamic clutter, and

$$R_n(u) \equiv \sqrt{[x_n - A_n u - \alpha_n(u)]^2 + [y_n - B_n u - \beta_n(u)]^2}.$$

Consider the analytical representation of the pulsed signal, that is,

$$p(t) = a(t) \; \exp(j\omega_c t),$$

where $a(t)$ is a lowpass signal in $[-\omega_0, \omega_0]$. Thus, we have the following for the echoed signal from the n-th target:

$$p\Big[\, t - \frac{2\, R_n(u)}{c}\,\Big] = a\Big[\, t - \frac{2\, R_n(u)}{c}\,\Big]\; \exp\Big[\, j\omega_c[t - \frac{2\, R_n(u)}{c}]\,\Big]$$

$$= \int_{-\omega_0}^{\omega_0} A(\omega)\; \exp\Big[-j(\omega + \omega_c)\frac{2\, R_n(u)}{c}\Big]\; \exp[j(\omega + \omega_c)t]\; d\omega.$$

The support band of $p(t)$ in the fast-time frequency domain is $[\omega_c - \omega_0, \omega_c + \omega_0]$. In practical **high-resolution** SAR/ISAR imaging problems, the wavelengths in this band could be on the order of one millimeter to one centimeter. Thus, even small values of the nonlinear target motion, that is, (α_n, β_n), could have catastrophic effects. With $\omega_c \gg \omega_0$, these errors could be traced to large phase error functions that are due to the contribution of the nonlinear motion in the phase function

$$\exp\Big[-j\omega_c\frac{2\, R_n(u)}{c}\Big].$$

Figure 5.38 shows the magnitude of ISAR data (incoherent ISAR signature) for a target scene off the coast of San Diego. In this scene, one target is a free-floating structure that has no forced motion other than the motion caused by the ocean waves; the signature of this target appears around the fast-time $t \approx 1$ microsecond. The other target is a small moving boat; its signature appears as a straight line extending approximately within the fast-time interval $t \in [1, 2]$ (microseconds). The other lines seen in the ISAR signature are due to the ocean waves. Figure 5.39 is the magnitude of the two-dimensional Fourier transform of coherent ISAR signature, that is, $|S(k_u, \omega)|$. Due to the random motion of the boat and floating target that is caused by the ocean waves, one anticipates the coherent ISAR data to contain large phase errors. The spectrum shown in Figure 5.39 is severely degraded and does not show the signatures of the two targets.

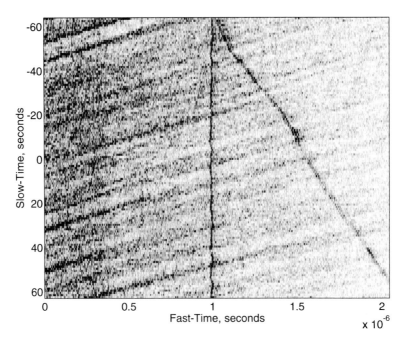

Figure 5.38 Incoherent ISAR signature $|s(u,t)|$.

Suppose the signal-to-clutter power ratio is **greater** than 0 dB in the measured ISAR signal. In this case, we can make the following approximation for the magnitude of the ISAR signal:

$$b(u,t) \equiv |s(u,t)|$$

$$\approx \sum_n \frac{g_n}{R_n^2(u)} \; a_0 \Big[\, t \; - \; \frac{2 \, R_n(u)}{c} \, \Big] \; + \; |s_N(u,t)|, \qquad (5.69)$$

where $a_0(t) \equiv |a(t)|$ is a lowpass signal in $[-\omega_{00}, \omega_{00}]$, with $\omega_{00} \leq \omega_0$.

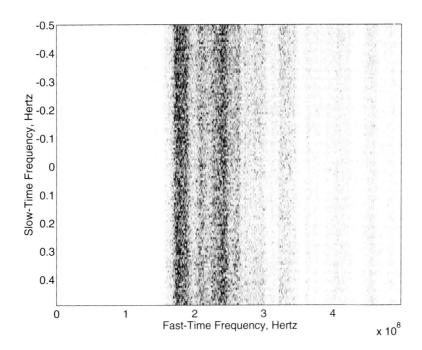

Figure 5.39 Coherent ISAR signature $S(k_u, \omega)$.

(In the following discussion, $|s_N(u,t)|$ is suppressed for notational simplicity.) Equation (5.69) corresponds to an ISAR system model where the illuminated signal is $a_0(t)$, that is, a lowpass signal, and the received ISAR signal is $b(u,t)$.

The main difference between the original coherent ISAR system model and the ISAR magnitude-transformed system model in (5.69) is the disappearance of the phase function

$$\exp[-j\omega_c \frac{2\,R_n(u)}{c}],$$

which contains the major portion of the phase error that is due to the nonlinear motion. The Fourier transform of both sides of (5.69) with respect to the fast-time is

$$b(u, \omega) \equiv A_0(\omega) \sum_n g_n \frac{\exp[j2kR_n(u)]}{R_n^2(u)},$$

for $\omega \in [-\omega_{00}, \omega_{00}]$. The wavelengths in this lowpass support band are significantly larger than the fast-time frequency support band for the coherent ISAR signal.

Thus, in the signature of the n-th target, the phase error term due to the nonlinear motion is negligible, that is,

$$\exp[-j\omega \frac{2\,R_n(u)}{c}] \approx \exp[-j\frac{2\sqrt{(x_n - A_n u)^2 + (y_n - B_n u)^2}}{c}],$$

for a *portion* of the lowpass band that we denote via $[-\omega_{0n}, \omega_{0n}]$, $\omega_{0n} \leq \omega_{00}$; the extent of this portion depends on the magnitude of the n-th target's nonlinear motion. Using this approximation, the system model in (5.69) becomes

$$b(u, \omega) \equiv A_0(\omega) \sum_n \frac{g_n}{R_n^2} \exp[-j2k\sqrt{(x_n - A_n u)^2 + (y_n - B_n u)^2},$$

which is an ISAR system model involving targets that possess linear motion. Thus, we may use $b(u, \omega)$, for $\omega \in [-\omega_{0n}, \omega_{0n}]$ where the nonlinear motion of the n-th target causes negligible phase errors in its incoherent ISAR signature, to detect this target.

The above system model for the n-th target is true only for $\omega \in [-\omega_{0n}, \omega_{0n}]$. The exact knowledge of the band $[-\omega_{0n}, \omega_{0n}]$ is not required for the processing shown in the following discussion. In fact, the contaminated incoherent ISAR signature of the n-th target for $|\omega| > \omega_{0n}$ is smeared (convolved withe Fourier transform of the multiplicative noise) and possesses much lower energy than the its incoherent ISAR signature in the lowpass band $[-\omega_{0n}, \omega_{0n}]$.

The formulation of ISAR detection from $b(u, \omega)$ involves its Fourier transformation with respect to the slow-time; that is,

$$B(k_u, \omega) = A_0(\omega) \sum_n \frac{\exp(-j\frac{\pi}{4})g_n}{V_n \cos \phi_n} \left(\frac{\pi f_0}{2u_0 k R_n^3} \right)^{\frac{1}{2}}$$

$$\times \exp[j\sqrt{4k^2 - (\frac{k_u}{V_n})^2}X_n + j\frac{k_u}{V_n}Y_n]I_n(\frac{k_u}{k}),$$

(5.70)

for $\omega \in [-\omega_0, \omega_0]$, where $I_n(\cdot)$ is the indicator (band) function defined in (5.59). (The spherical wave decomposition is not valid for $\omega = 0$. In practice, we discard the fast-time d.c. component of the database in (5.70); that is, we set $B(k_u, 0) = 0$.)

Figure 5.40 shows $|B(k_u, \omega)|$ for the incoherent ISAR data of Figure 5.38. The maximum value of this image is more than six times the maximum value of the image in Figure 5.39 for the coherent ISAR signature in the (k_u, ω) domain; this, as we mentioned earlier, is due to the fact that the incoherent data are less sensitive to the smearing caused by the motion phase errors than the coherent data. In Figure 5.40, one can distinguish three distinct signatures: one along the line $k_u = 0$ is due to the free-floating target; the *thick* line on the second and fourth quadrants, which represents a variety of Doppler spreads, is the ocean clutter (waves) signature; the thin and slanted line in the first and third quadrants is the moving boat's signature.

Note that each target possesses a different support band region, that is, $[-\omega_{0n}, \omega_{0n}]$. For the boat and ocean waves that contain more random movements than the free-floating target, that is, larger $[\alpha(u), \beta(u)]$ values, $\omega_{0n} \approx 15$ MHz. However, the free-floating target, which is more stable than the boat, has a passband value of $\omega_{0n} > 30$ MHz.

The transformation of $B(k_u, \omega)$ domain data into the $h_u, \omega)$ domain is

$$D(h_u, \omega) \equiv \frac{\sqrt{2u_0 k}}{\exp(-j\frac{\pi}{4})\sqrt{\pi f_0}} B(k_u, \omega),$$

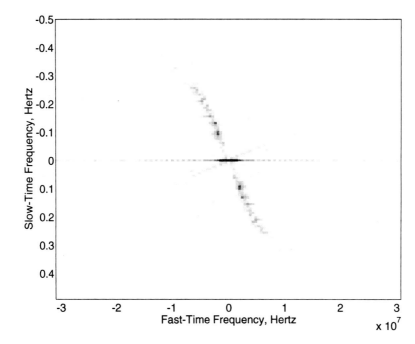

Figure 5.40 Incoherent ISAR signature $B(k_u, \omega)$.

that after substitution for $B(k_u, \omega)$ from (5.70) yields

$$
\begin{aligned}
D(h_u, \omega) = A_0(\omega) \sum_n \frac{g_n}{\sqrt{R_n^3 \, V_n \, \cos\phi_n}} \\
\times \, \exp\Big[\, j\frac{\omega}{c}\Big[\sqrt{4 - (\frac{h_u}{V_n})^2} \, X_n \, + \, \frac{h_u}{V_n}Y_n\Big] \, \Big] \, I_n(h_u).
\end{aligned}
\tag{5.71}
$$

[For the lowpass incoherent ISAR data, it is critical to include the multiplicative term $\sqrt{k}$ on the right side of (5.71).]

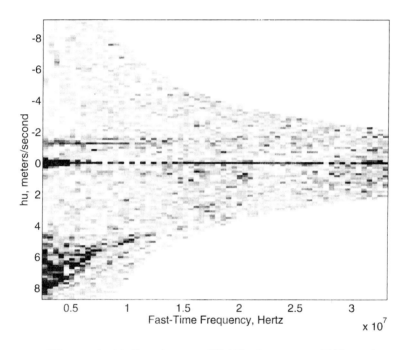

Figure 5.41 Incoherent ISAR signature $D(h_u, \omega)$.

Figure 5.41 depicts the magnitude of $D(h_u, \omega)$ that is the transformed version of the ISAR signature in Figure 5.40. This image, and other two-dimensional signals that depend on h_u and will be shown later, is labeled according to $h_u \equiv \frac{k_u}{2k}$ since $H_n = V_n \sin \phi_n$ represents the n-th target's speed in the broadside. In this image, the free-floating target appears at $h_u = 0$, that is, a motionless structure. The moving boat's signature is at $h_u \approx -1.5$ meters/second. The ocean clutter has its signature approximately within the interval $h_u \in [5, 8]$ (meters/second).

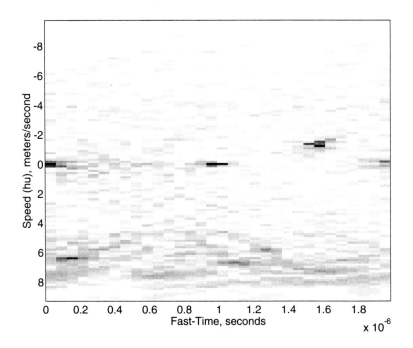

Figure 5.42 Incoherent ISAR signature $D(h_u, t)$ (bandwidth= [2,17] MHz).

The inverse Fourier transform of this signal yields the database for the ISAR detection problem:

$$D(h_u, t) = \sum_n \frac{g_n}{\sqrt{R_n^3} V_n \cos \phi_n} a_0 \left[t - \sqrt{4 - (\frac{h_u}{V_n})^2} \, \frac{X_n}{c} - \frac{h_u}{V_n} \frac{Y_n}{c} \right] I_n(h_u).$$

The signature of a target in the transformed (h_u, t) domain is now localized based on its mid-range and broadside speed; that is, at $t = \frac{2R_n}{c}$ and $h_u = 2V_n \sin \phi_n$. This localized statistic is suitable for automatic, that is, machine-based, detection of stationary as well as moving targets in the scene. Example are shown in Figures 5.42 and 5.43.

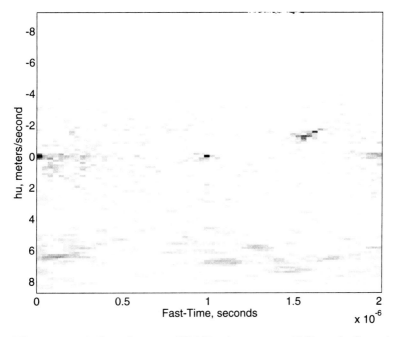

Figure 5.43 Incoherent ISAR signature $D(h_u, t)$ (bandwidth=
[2,32] MHz).

Figure 5.42 is the magnitude of $D(h_u, t)$ for the moving boat and free-
floating target in the ocean that was explained earlier. This is obtained
by the inverse Fourier transform of $D(h_u, \omega)$, for $\omega \in [2, 17]$ MHz, with
respect to ω. The free-floating target's signature appears at the fast-time
$t \approx 1$ microsecond. The moving boat shows a more *faded* and *smeared*
signature (due to its longer range and more random movements) at the
fast-time $t \approx 1.5$ microseconds; this fast-time point represents the boat's
range at the slow-time $u = 0$. The ocean clutter signature appears at all
fast-time (range) values as anticipated.

Another target appears at $(h_u, t) \approx (0, 0)$. This signature is likely to be due to the transient signals in the radar antenna circuitry when the receiver is turned on. Another likely scenario is that this target is the signature of a motionless structure (e.g., a building) near the beach. The faded signature at $(h_u, t) \approx (0, 2 \text{ microsecond})$ is a circular aliasing artifact caused by the smearing of the target signature at $(h_u, t) = (0, 0)$.

Figure 5.43 shows $|D(h_u, t)|$ when the support band of the data processed is chosen to be [2,32] Mhz. With the doubling of the fast-time frequency band, the free-floating target exhibits a distinct and focused signature at the fast-time $t \approx 1$ microsecond. However, there is no significant change in the signatures of the boat and ocean waves. (These two signatures appear less intense than their corresponding signatures in Figure 5.42 since the image in Figure 5.43 is quantized with respect to a much stronger peak value for the free-floating target's signature.)

5.10 ISAR IMAGING OF A ROTATING TARGET

We consider an ISAR system involving a target rotating with angular speed ω_R about the origin in the spatial domain. The transmitting/receiver radar is located at $(R, 0)$. The center-of-mass for the target is at the polar coordinates (θ_0, r_0). Thus, for a given slow-time τ, the coordinates of the target's center-of-mass is

$$[\, r_0 \cos(\omega_R \tau + \theta_0) \,, \; r_0 \sin(\omega_R \tau + \theta_0) \,].$$

Thus, for a given fast-time temporal frequency ω, the phase delay associated with the echoed signal coming from the target's center-of-mass is

$$\exp\left[j2k\sqrt{[R - r_0 \cos(\omega_R \tau + \theta_0)]^2 + [r_0 \sin(\omega_R \tau + \theta_0)]^2} \right].$$

The instantaneous frequency of this signal in the τ domain is

$$\Omega_\tau \equiv \frac{\partial}{\partial \tau} \left[2k\sqrt{[R - r_0 \cos(\omega_R \tau + \theta_0)]^2 + [r_0 \sin(\omega_R \tau + \theta_0)]^2} \right] \tag{5.72}$$
$$\approx 2k\omega_R r_0 \sin(\omega_R \tau + \theta_0),$$

which is a sinusoidal function of τ.

One can estimate Ω_τ via measuring the instantaneous frequency of the echoed signal in the slow-time domain (e.g., use the subaperture processing). Then, one should fit a *sinusoid* to this estimate. By measuring the period, the phase at $\tau = 0$, and the amplitude of this sinusoid, the three parameters $(\omega_r, r_0, \theta_0)$ could be estimated. The estimate of ω_r can then be used to reconstruct the target.

For the case of spaceborne SAR imaging where the satellite's angular speed is not known exactly, the phase delay function due to the target's center-of-mass is

$$\exp\left[j2k\sqrt{[R\cos(\omega_R\tau) - r_0\cos\theta_0]^2 + [R\sin(\omega_R\tau) - r_0\sin\theta_0]^2}\right].$$

The instantaneous frequency of this PM wave is equal to the right side of (5.72). Thus, the subaperture processing used in ISAR imaging of a rotating target can be used for blind-velocity spaceborne SAR imaging.

APPENDIX

Effect of the Estimation Error

We showed that the moving target can be imaged if its velocity is known. In this section, we examine the effect of the velocity estimation error on the reconstructed image with the estimated velocity $(\hat{a}, \hat{b})$. Our analysis is carried out in the (x_1, y_1) domain. This can then be carried over to the (x, y) domain via the coordinate transformation shown in (5.5). For our discussion, we use the following variables:

$$\hat{\theta} \equiv \arctan\left(\frac{\hat{a}}{1 - \hat{b}}\right)$$

$$(k_{x_1}, k_{y_1}) \equiv (\sqrt{4k^2 - k_v^2}, k_v) \tag{A1}$$

$$(\hat{k}_{x_1}, \hat{k}_{y_1}) \equiv (\sqrt{4k^2 - \hat{k}_v^2}, \hat{k}_v)$$

where

$$\hat{k}_v = \frac{k_u}{\sqrt{\hat{a}^2 + (1 - \hat{b})^2}}.$$

Using the Taylor series expansion, (k_{x_1}, k_{y_1}) is related to $(\hat{k}_{x_1}, \hat{k}_{y_1})$ by the following:

$$k_{x_1} \simeq \hat{k}_{x_1} + \frac{\hat{k}_{y_1}^2 (1 - \Pi^2)}{2\hat{k}_{x_1}} \qquad (A2)$$

$$k_{y_1} = \Pi \hat{k}_{y_1}$$

where

$$\Pi \equiv \frac{k_v}{\hat{k}_v} = \frac{k_{y_1}}{\hat{k}_{y_1}} = \sqrt{\frac{\hat{a}^2 + (1 - \hat{b})^2}{a^2 + (1 - b)^2}}.$$

Let $\hat{g}_1(x_1, y_1)$ represent the moving target image reconstructed with the estimated velocity $(\hat{a}, \hat{b})$. Then, $\hat{g}_1(x_1, y_1)$ is obtained by taking the two dimensional inverse Fourier transform of $S(k_u, \omega) \exp[-j\hat{\Omega}]$, that is,

$$\hat{g}_1(x_1, y_1) = \int\int S(k_u, \omega) \exp[-j(\hat{\Omega})] \exp\left[j(\hat{k}_{x_1} x_1 + \hat{k}_{y_1} y_1)\right] d\hat{k}_{x_1}\, d\hat{k}_{y_1} \tag{A3}$$

where $S(k_u, \omega)$ is the spatial Fourier transform of the echoed signals from the moving target and

$$\hat{\Omega} \equiv \sqrt{4k^2 - \hat{k}_v^2}\, X_1 \cos\hat{\theta} + \hat{k}_v X_1 \sin\hat{\theta}. \tag{A4}$$

Noting that

$$S(k_u, \omega) \equiv S_1(k_v, \omega) = G_1\left(\sqrt{4k^2 - k_v^2}, k_v\right) \exp[j\Omega] \tag{A5}$$

where

$$\Omega = \sqrt{4k^2 - k_v^2}\, X_1 \cos\theta + k_v X_1 \sin\theta$$

(A3) becomes

$$\hat{g}_1(x_1, y_1) = \int\int G_1\left(\sqrt{4k^2 - k_v^2}, k_v\right) \exp\left[j(\Omega - \hat{\Omega})\right]$$

$$\times \exp\left[j(\hat{k}_{x_1} x_1 + \hat{k}_{y_1} y_1)\right] d\hat{k}_{x_1}\, d\hat{k}_{y_1} \tag{A6}$$

$$= \tilde{g}_1(x_1, y_1) * *h(x_1, y_1)$$

where

$$\tilde{g}_1(x_1, y_1) \equiv \int \int G_1(k_{x_1}, k_{y_1}) \exp\left[j(\hat{k}_{x_1}x + \hat{k}_{y_1}y)\right] d\hat{k}_{x_1} d\hat{k}_{y_1}$$

$$h(x_1, y_1) \equiv \int \int \exp\left[j(\Omega - \hat{\Omega})\right] \exp\left[j(\hat{k}_{x_1}x + \hat{k}_{y_1}y)\right] d\hat{k}_{x_1} d\hat{k}_{y_1}$$

$$(A7)$$

$\tilde{g}_1(x_1, y_1)$ can be shown to be approximately equal to $g_1(x_1, y_1)$.

- *One function is a jittered version of the other function in the spatial frequency domain. This jitter error corresponds to a phase error that is significantly smaller than the phase error in (A8) when $X_{0g} \ll X_1$ and, thus, is negligible.*

Thus, the output image, that is, $\hat{g}_1(x_1, y_1)$, can be approximated by the actual image $g_1(x_1, y_1)$ convolved with a point spread function $h(x_1, y_1)$.

We now examine the behavior of $h(x_1, y_1)$ that determines the extent of smearing and shifting in the reconstructed image. Using the Taylor series expansion, the phase term $\Omega - \hat{\Omega}$ in (A7) is approximated as follows:

$$\Omega - \hat{\Omega} \simeq \sqrt{4k^2 - \hat{k}_v^2}\, X_1(\cos\theta - \cos\hat{\theta})$$

$$+ \frac{\hat{k}_v^2(1 - \Pi^2)}{2\sqrt{4k^2 - \hat{k}_v^2}} X_1 \cos\theta \qquad (A8)$$

$$+ \hat{k}_v X_1(\Pi\sin\theta - \sin\hat{\theta})$$

Using (A8), $h(x_1, y_1)$ can be rewritten as follows:

$$h(x_1, y_1) = \int \int \exp\left[j\left(\Delta_r \hat{k}_{x_1} + \Delta_{cr}\hat{k}_{y_1} + \frac{\hat{k}_{y_1}^2}{2\hat{k}_{x_1}}(1 - \Pi^2)X_1\cos\theta\right)\right]$$

$$\exp\left[j(\hat{k}_{x_1}x + \hat{k}_{y_1}y)\right] d\hat{k}_{x_1} d\hat{k}_{y_1}$$

$$(A9)$$

where

$$\Delta_r = X_1(\cos\theta - \cos\hat{\theta}) \qquad (A10)$$

$$\Delta_{cr} = X_1(\Pi\sin\theta - \sin\hat{\theta}). \qquad (A11)$$

With the aid of convolution theorem, (A9) becomes

$$h(x_1, y_1) = \delta(x_1 - \Delta_r, y_1 - \Delta_{cr}) * *h_1(x_1, y_1) \qquad (A12)$$

where

$$h_1(x_1, y_1) = \int \int \exp\left[j \frac{\hat{k}_{y_1}^2}{2\hat{k}_{x_1}} (1 - \Pi^2) X_1 \cos\theta \right]$$
$$\times \exp\left[j \left(\hat{k}_{x_1} x_1 + \hat{k}_{y_1} y_1 \right) \right] d\hat{k}_{x_1} d\hat{k}_{y_1}. \qquad (A13)$$

Consequently, due to the velocity estimation error, the point spread function $h(x_1, y_1)$ is not only shifted by Δ_r in range and Δ_{cr} in cross-range, but also smeared depending on the behavior of $h_1(x_1, y_1)$. $h_1(x_1, y_1)$ is the inverse Fourier transform of

$$\exp\left[j \frac{\hat{k}_{y_1}^2}{2\hat{k}_{x_1}} (1 - \Pi^2) X_1 \cos\theta \right] \qquad (A14)$$

which is a phase modulated signal with respect to $\hat{k}_{x_1}$ ($\hat{k}_{y_1}$). Thus, the spatial dispersion of $h_1(x_1, y_1)$ in range (cross-range) can be found by taking the derivative of (A14) with respect to $\hat{k}_{x_1}$ ($\hat{k}_{y_1}$). Let x_{sm} and y_{sm} denote the maximum spatial dispersion in range and cross-range, respectively. Then

$$x_{sm} = max \left(\frac{\partial}{\partial \hat{k}_{x_1}} \left[\frac{\hat{k}_{y_1}^2}{2\hat{k}_{x_1}} (1 - \Pi^2) X_1 \cos\theta \right] \right)$$
$$= max \left(\frac{\hat{k}_{y_1}^2}{2\hat{k}_{x_1}^2} (1 - \Pi^2) X_1 \cos\theta \right)$$
$$y_{sm} = max \left(\frac{\partial}{\partial \hat{k}_{y_1}} \left[\frac{\hat{k}_{y_1}^2}{2\hat{k}_{x_1}} (1 - \Pi^2) X_1 \cos\theta \right] \right)$$
$$= max \left(\frac{\hat{k}_{y_1}}{\hat{k}_{x_1}} (1 - \Pi^2) X_1 \cos\theta \right). \qquad (A15)$$

Since most of the radar signal energy reflected from the moving target is contained within the region

$$2k \left(\sin\theta - \frac{X_{0g} + L_s}{X_1} \right) \leq k_v \ (\text{ or } k_{y_1}) \ \leq 2k \left(\sin\theta + \frac{X_{0g} + L_s}{X_1} \right)$$

the maximum spatial frequency support of the echoed signal in the k_{y_1} domain is

$$max \ (\hat{k}_{y_1}) = \frac{2k}{\Pi} \left(\sin\theta + \frac{X_{0g} + L_s}{X_1} \right) \qquad (A16)$$

Since $\hat{k}_{x_1} \simeq 2k \cos\theta$, x_{sm} and y_{sm}, respectively, become

$$x_{sm} = \left| \frac{(1 - \Pi^2)X_1}{2\Pi^2 \cos\theta} \left(\sin\theta + \frac{X_{0g} + L_s}{X_1} \right)^2 \right|$$
$$y_{sm} = \left| \frac{1 - \Pi^2}{\Pi} X_1 \left(\sin\theta + \frac{X_{0g} + L_s}{X_1} \right) \right| \qquad (A17)$$

Note that for small θ, x_{sm} is significantly less than y_{sm}. If the reconstructed image is not to be smeared, x_{sm} and y_{sm} should be less than resolution in x_1 and resolution in y_1, respectively.

The above analysis provides the extent of shifts and smearing [see (A10), (A11), and (A17)] in the (x_1, y_1) domain. Corresponding shifts and smearing in the (x, y) domain can be evaluated with the help of (5.5).

PROJECTS

1. Simulate a SAR imaging system involving a stationary background and a moving target.

   a. Obtain the SAR data in the (u, t), (u, ω), (k_u, t), and (k_u, ω) domains.

   b. Perform clutter signature filtering on the data and estimate the moving target's velocity via subaperture processing.

   c. Reconstruct the moving target using its estimated velocity. Observe the effect of the estimator error in the reconstructed image by varying the velocity estimator.

2. Repeat Project 1 via the temporal Doppler processing method. Examine the sensitivity of the velocity estimator to the duration of the transmitted pulse.

3. Repeat Project 1 for a maneuvering target.

4. Simulate an ISAR imaging system involving multiple moving targets.
    a. Obtain the ISAR data in the (u, t), (u, ω), (k_u, t), (k_u, ω), (h_u, ω), and (h_u, t) in a clutter/noise-free and a heavy clutter/noise environments. Use a random number generator (e.g., Gaussian) to simulate a white clutter/noise signature.
    b. Identify the target's signature in the (h_u, t) domain via hypothesis testing (select an appropriate threshold for your decision device), and extract each target's signature.
    c. Repeat Project 1 on the extracted targets' signatures.

REFERENCES

1. R. K. Raney, "Synthetic aperture imaging radar and moving targets," *IEEE Trans. Aerospace and Electronic Systems,* p. 499, May 1971.

2. M. I. Skolnik, *Introduction to Radar Systems,* New York: McGraw-Hill, 1980.

3. W. M. Brown and C. J. Palermo, *Random Processes, Communications and Radar,* New York: McGraw-Hill, 1969.

4. S. D. Blostein and T.S. Huang, "Detecting small moving object in image sequence using sequential hypothesis testing," *IEEE Trans. on Signal Processing,* vol. 39, p. 1611, July 1991.

5. H. L. Van Trees, *Detection, Estimation, and Modulation Theory,* Part III, Wiley, pp. 238-243, 1971.

6. A. W. Rihaczek, "Radar resolution of moving targets," *IEEE Trans. on Information Theory,* vol. IT-13, pp. 51-56, January 1967.

7. A. Oppenheim, *Applications of Digital Signal Processing,* Englewood Cliffs, NJ: Prentice Hall, pp.239-327, 1978.

8. D. Blacknell, A. Freeman, R. White, and J. Wood, "The Prediction of Geometric Distortions in Airborne Synthetic Aperture Radar Imagery from Autofocus Measurements," *IEEE Trans. Geoscience and Remote Sensing*, 25, p.775, November 1987.

9. M. Soumekh, "A system model and inversion for synthetic aperture radar imaging," *IEEE Trans. on Image Processing*, January 1992.

10. M. Soumekh and J. Choi, "Phase and amplitude-phase restoration in synthetic aperture radar imaging," *IEEE Trans. on Image Processing*, July 1992.

11. P. Morse and H. Feshbach, *Methods of Theoretical Physics*, New York: McGraw-Hill, 1968.

Chapter 6

PASSIVE ARRAY IMAGING AND DETECTION

A passive array records radiated signals from the targets in its environment due to a source that is commonly *unknown* to the passive array's receiver structure. (The source and the receiver's local oscillator are not synchronized.) The radiation could be due to an internal or external source. The common types of target radiation recorded in passive array imaging/detection are acoustic, infrared, and visible (red to blue) light. A classic (continuous) passive aperture is the human eye. In this case, the sun or a light source is the radiation field. This radiation results in partial absorption and reflection from the targets in the environment. The portion of the light spectrum that is reflected is processed by the human eye via a lens for image formation on the retina. In Section 6.2 we will examine incoherent narrow-band passive array imaging that has similarities to the processing used by the human eye for image formation.

Passive array imaging has applications in artificial vision for vision-impaired individuals and robots. Passive array imaging and detection is also a valuable tool in covert reconnaissance of targets in air (infrared radiation) and water (acoustic radiation) as well as celestial exploration. There are also passive array detection scenarios involving on-line non-destructive testing of industrial equipments that produce acoustic waves during their operation. In diagnostic medicine, passive heat (infrared) sensors have been used to detect inflammation and irregularities inside the human body.

The main obstacle in passive array imaging is the lack of coherence in the incoming *time* signals impinging on a passive array. The same is not true for the signals that appear in the aperture domain. In this chapter, we show that the coherent spatial Doppler principle, which was introduced in Chapter 4 for synthetic aperture radar imaging, is also applicable for developing methods for passive array imaging and detection. We first introduce spatial Doppler phenomenon for passive arrays via a temporally coherent system. We then examine incoherent passive array imaging and bistatic detection of multiple targets. Motion-induced and position-induced passive synthetic aperture imaging via interferometric processing are also discussed. Our study is based on analysis of two-dimensional imaging geometries using linear passive arrays. The same principles are also applicable in three-dimensional imaging problems with planar passive arrays.

6.1 COHERENT WIDE-BAND IMAGING

We examine imaging a target that radiates a known temporal signal, call it $p(t)$ [$p(t)$ is not a pulsed signal], from all points within its body; that is, the signals emitted by the target points are *coherent* with respect to each other *and* the receiver structure for the passive array. This passive array imaging may not be encountered in practice. However, it is the simplest passive array imaging problem for demonstrating the spatial Doppler principle that is the basis of the work presented in Sections 6.2-6.5.

System Model

We begin by considering a two-dimensional imaging system shown in Figure 6.1. The x-coordinate is used to identify range, and y specifies the cross-range domain.

The elements of a passive array are positioned on the line $x = X_1$ in the (x, y) domain and are identified by the coordinates (X_1, u) for $u \in [-L, +L]$ (aperture) on the (x, y) plane; X_1 (target's range) is a known constant. The target area is within the disk of radius X_0 centered at the origin in the spatial domain.

The target emits a time-dependent signal $p(t)$. The time delay associated with the signal propagation from (x, y) in the target region to an array element is

$$\frac{\sqrt{(X_1 - x)^2 + (u - y)^2}}{c}.$$

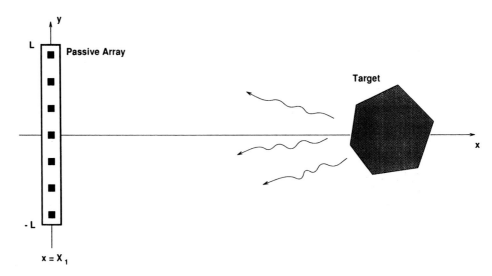

Figure 6.1 Coherent wide-band passive array imaging.

Thus, the total recorded echoed signal becomes (amplitude functions are suppressed)

$$s(u,t) \equiv \int \int f(x,y) \ p[t - \frac{\sqrt{(X_1 - x)^2 + (u - y)^2}}{c}] \ dxdy, \qquad (6.1)$$

where $f(x,y)$ is the target area's radiance function and c is the wave propagation speed; the integral in the (x,y) domain is over the target region, that is, the disk of radius X_0 centered at the origin.

Taking the temporal Fourier transform of both sides of (6.1) yields [for notational simplicity, we use $s(u,\omega)$ to represent the temporal Fourier transform of $s(u,t)$]

$$s(u,\omega) = P(\omega) \int \int f(x,y) \ \exp[-jk\sqrt{(X_1 - x)^2 + (u - y)^2}] \ dxdy.$$
$$(6.2)$$

Spatial Doppler-Based Inversion

The spherical wave with wavenumber k on the right side of (6.2), that is,

$$\exp[-jk\sqrt{(X_1 - x)^2 + (u - y)^2}],$$

has the following spatial Fourier (Doppler) decomposition in terms of plane waves [9],[10]:

$$\int_{-k}^{k} \frac{1}{\sqrt{k^2 - k_u^2}} \exp[j\sqrt{k^2 - k_u^2}\,(X_1 - x) + jk_u(u - y)]\,dk_u. \qquad (6.3)$$

The significance of this decomposition (spatial Doppler) is in the fact that it transforms nonlinear phase functions of (x, y, u) into linear phase functions of (x, y, u).

Substituting (6.3) for the spherical wave function in the system model (6.2) yields

$$
\begin{aligned}
s(u, \omega) = &P(\omega) \int_{-k}^{k} \frac{\exp(j\sqrt{k^2 - k_u^2}\,X_1)}{\sqrt{k^2 - k_u^2}} \\
&\times \underbrace{\left[\int\int f(x, y)\exp[-j(\sqrt{k^2 - k_u^2}\,x + k_u y)]dxdy\right]}_{Two\ dimensional\ Fourier\ integral}\,\exp(jk_u u)dk_u \\
= &P(\omega) \int_{-k}^{k} \frac{\exp(j\sqrt{k^2 - k_u^2}\,X_1)}{\sqrt{k^2 - k_u^2}} F(\sqrt{k^2 - k_u^2}, k_u)\exp(jk_u u)dk_u
\end{aligned}
$$

$$(6.4)$$

At the present time, we assume that the measurements are made for $u \in (-\infty, \infty)$; we will examine finite aperture effects in the later sections. Taking the spatial Fourier transform of both sides of (6.4) with respect to u (Doppler processing) yields the following:

$$S(k_u, \omega) = \frac{\exp(j\sqrt{k^2 - k_u^2}\,X_1)}{\sqrt{k^2 - k_u^2}} P(\omega)\,F(\sqrt{k^2 - k_u^2}, k_u). \qquad (6.5)$$

Finally, from (6.5), we can write the following inversion:

$$F(k_x, k_y) = \frac{\sqrt{k^2 - k_u^2}\,\exp(-j\sqrt{k^2 - k_u^2}\,X_1)}{P(\omega)}S(k_u, \omega), \qquad (6.6)$$

where

$$k_x \equiv \sqrt{k^2 - k_u^2}$$
$$k_y \equiv k_u$$

(6.7)

represent the contours of the available data to reconstruct $F(\cdot,\cdot)$ from the spatial Doppler data. An example of the spatial frequency coverage dictated by (6.7) is depicted in Figure 6.2. This spatial frequency coverage is similar to the one shown in Chapter 4 for monostatic SAR imaging.

The discussions that follow are invariant of $P(\omega)$. For notational simplicity, we do not carry $P(\omega)$.

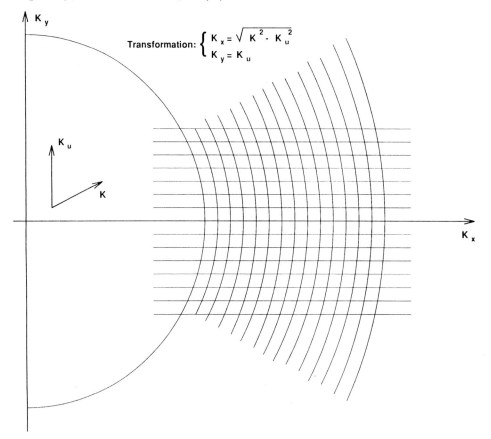

Figure 6.2 Mapping of the measurement domain (k_u, k) into the target's spatial frequency domain (k_x, k_y) in coherent wide-band passive array imaging.

Spatial Doppler Phenomenon

There are various processing issues associated with the inversion in (6.6) that are not examined in this section. These principles are similar to the processing issues associated with active synthetic array imaging systems that are discussed in [10]. We now only present the principle of spatial Doppler that is the main essence of the topics we will cover in the next two sections.

The starting point for our analysis is to consider finite aperture effects in the spatial Fourier transform of the measured data. We rewrite the system model (6.2) using the spatial Fourier decomposition of the spherical wave (the amplitude function $\frac{1}{\sqrt{k^2 - k_u^2}}$ is suppressed):

$$
\begin{aligned}
s(u, \omega) &= \int \int dx\; dy\; f(x, y) \\
&\quad \times \left[\int_{-k}^{k} \exp[j\sqrt{k^2 - k_u^2}\,(X_1 - x) + j k_u(u - y)]\; dk_u \right] \\
&= \int \int f(x, y)\; \mathcal{F}_{(k_u)}^{-1}\left[\exp[j\sqrt{k^2 - k_u^2}\,(X_1 - x) - j k_u y] \right]\; dx dy
\end{aligned}
$$
(6.8)

for $u \in [-L, L]$, and zero otherwise. We next perform the Doppler analysis (Fourier transform with respect to u) on $s(u, \omega)$ and take into account finite aperture effects (i.e., $L < \infty$).

By incorporating the fact that we have access only to the values of $u \in [-L, L]$, the Fourier transform with respect to u of both sides of (6.8) yields

$$
\begin{aligned}
S(k_u, \omega) &= \int \int dx\; dy\; f(x, y) \\
&\quad \times \left[\exp[j\sqrt{k^2 - k_u^2}\,(X_1 - x) - j k_u y] \;*\; 2L\frac{\sin(L k_u)}{L k_u} \right],
\end{aligned}
$$
(6.9)

where $*$ denotes convolution in the k_u domain.

The aperture transfer function, that is, $2L\frac{\sin(L k_u)}{L k_u}$ (sinc function), is a lowpass filter. Hence, the convolution of this filter with the phase modulated function $\exp[j\sqrt{k^2-k_u^2}\,(X_1-x)-jk_uy]$ approximately results in the suppression (filtering) of the components of the PM wave at the values of k_u where the instantaneous frequency of the PM wave falls outside the interval $[-L, L]$.

For a point scatterer at (x, y), the instantaneous frequency of the phase modulated function in the k_u domain is found via

$$\frac{\partial}{\partial k_u}\left[\sqrt{k^2-k_u^2}\,(X_1-x)-k_uy\right] = \frac{-k_u}{\sqrt{k^2-k_u^2}}(X_1-x)-y.$$

Hence, the range of k_u values where the PM wave is not suppressed is found from the following inequalities:

$$-L \;\leq\; \frac{-k_u}{\sqrt{k^2-k_u^2}}(X_1-x)-y \;\leq\; L. \tag{6.10}$$

Solving for this interval from (6.10), one obtains the following band in the k_u domain (with $x, y, L << X_1$):

$$\Omega(y) \equiv \left[\; k\sin[\arctan(\frac{y-L}{X_1-x})]\;,\; k\sin[\arctan(\frac{y+L}{X_1-x})]\;\right]$$

$$\approx [\; k\frac{y-L}{X_1}\;,\; k\frac{y+L}{X_1}\;]. \tag{6.11}$$

Note that this band is centered around $k\sin\theta(x,y)$ where

$$\theta(x, y) \equiv \arctan(\frac{y}{X_1-x}) \approx \frac{y}{X_1},$$

is the point scatterer's angle with respect to the broadside. We refer to this as the spatial Doppler phenomenon in passive array imaging. This is depicted in Figure 6.3 for a broadside and an off-broadside targets.

Chapter 4 shows that for a broadside target the cross-range (y) resolution is proportional to the length of the band $\Omega(y)$. The range (x) resolution is primary dictated by the bandwidth of $p(t)$ and is invariant of the array's aperture length.

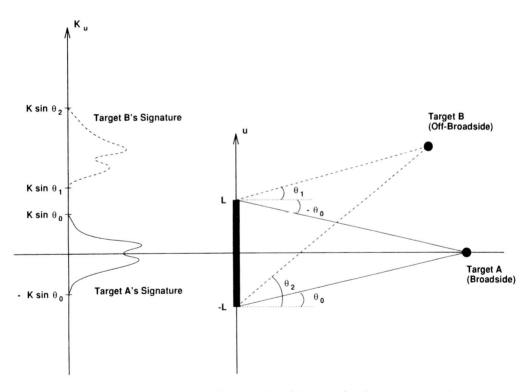

Figure 6.3 Spatial Doppler (Fourier) phenomenon in passive array imaging.

Fresnel Approximation-Based Inversion

Consider the system model developed in (6.2); that is,

$$s(u, \omega) = \int_x \int_y f(x, y) \ \exp[jk\sqrt{(X_1 - x)^2 + (u - y)^2}] \ dx dy.$$

Using the following (Fresnel) approximation:

$$k\sqrt{(X_1 - x)^2 + (u - y)^2} \approx k(X_1 - x) + \frac{k(u - y)^2}{2X_1},$$

in the system model (6.2), one obtains

$$
\begin{aligned}
s(u, \omega) &\approx \int_x \int_y f(x, y) \ \exp[jk(X_1 - x)] \ \exp[j\frac{k(u - y)^2}{2X_1}] \ dx dy \\
&= \exp(jkX_1) \int_y \exp[j\frac{k(u - y)^2}{2X_1}] \ [\underbrace{\int_x f(x, y) \ \exp(-jkx) \ dx}_{Fourier\ integral}] \ dy \\
&= \exp(jkX_1) \int_y \exp[j\frac{k(u - y)^2}{2X_1}] \ F_x(k, y) \ dy \\
&= \exp(jkX_1) \ \exp(j\frac{ku^2}{2X_1}) \ * \ F_x(k, u),
\end{aligned}
$$

$$(6.12)$$

where $*$ denotes convolution in the u domain.

Taking the spatial Fourier transform of both sides of (6.12) with respect to u and using the following Fourier pair relationship:

$$\mathcal{F}_{(u)}[\exp(j\frac{ku^2}{2X_1})] = \exp(-j\frac{k_u^2 X_1}{2k}),$$

one obtains

$$S(k_u, \omega) \approx \exp(jkX_1) \ F(k, k_u) \ \exp(-j\frac{k_u^2 X_1}{2k}),$$

which results in the following inverse equation:

$$F(k_x, k_y) \approx \exp(-jkX_1) \; S(k_u, \omega) \; \exp(j\frac{k_u^2 X_1}{2k}), \qquad (6.13)$$

where

$$\begin{aligned} k_x &= k \\ k_y &= k_u \end{aligned} \qquad (6.14)$$

Taking the inverse spatial Fourier transform of both sides of (6.13) with respect to $k_y = k_u$ yields

$$F_x(k, y) \approx \exp(-jkX_1) \; s(y, \omega) \; * \; \exp(-jk\frac{y^2}{2X_1}), \qquad (6.15)$$

where $*$ denotes convolution in the u domain, and $F_x(k_x = k, u)$ is the one-dimensional Fourier transform of $f(x, u)$ with respect to x. Equation (6.15) is the Fresnel approximation-based inversion for coherent wide-band passive array imaging.

6.2 INCOHERENT NARROW-BAND IMAGING

We next examine a passive array imaging problem where the condition of coherent radiation is relaxed. With this, we are forced to lower our expectations in retrieving useful imaging information from the measurements. More specifically, the range information (resolution) is lost due to incoherence of the target radiation. However, we show that the cross-range information is still recoverable from the aperture measurements based on a user-controllable parameter (X_1, the focal line; the focal plane in three-dimensional imaging problems).

Planar Targets

It is assumed that the target is a surface located at a distance X_1 from the array in the range domain (see Figure 6.4). (The line $x = X_1$ is analogous to the focal plane/line for a camera.) The target radiates a single-frequency (narrow-band) temporal signal with a wavenumber k.

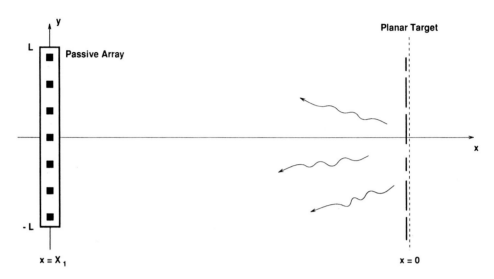

Figure 6.4 Incoherent narrow-band passive array imaging
of planar targets.

The time-dependent signal recorded across the passive array's aperture (u domain; $u \in [-L, L]$) is

$$s(u,t) = \int_y f(y,t) \, \exp[j\omega t + j\phi(y,t)] \, \exp[jk\sqrt{X_1^2 + (u-y)^2}] \, dy; \quad (6.16)$$

$f(y,t) > 0$ is the reflectance map function (related to the desired image) that contains both the target's physical properties and fluctuations of the amplitude of the radiating source (e.g., a light bulb energized by a 60 Hz electronic source); and $\phi(y,t)$ is an unknown phase function that represents the relative phase delay of the impinging wave on a target point (related to the distance between the source and the point target and the unknown phase fluctuations of the source), and the lack of coherence among the target's radiating points and the receiver structure for the passive array.

For notational simplicity, we define

$$g(y,t) \equiv f(y,t) \ \exp[j\phi(y,t)],$$

and rewrite (6.16) as follows:

$$s(u,t) = \int_y g(y,t) \ \exp(j\omega t)\exp[jk\sqrt{X_1^2 + (u-y)^2}] \, dy. \qquad (6.17)$$

Taking the spatial Fourier transform of both sides of (6.17) with respect to u yields (for notational simplicity, the amplitude function $\frac{1}{\sqrt{k^2-k_u^2}}$ is suppressed):

$$S(k_u,t) = \int_y g(y,t) \ \exp(j\omega t) \ \exp(j\sqrt{k^2 - k_u^2}X_1 - jk_u y) \, dy$$

$$= \exp(j\omega t + j\sqrt{k^2 - k_u^2} \ X_1) \underbrace{\int_y g(y,t) \ \exp(-jk_u y) \, dy}_{Fourier \ integral} \qquad (6.18)$$

$$= \exp(j\omega t + j\sqrt{k^2 - k_u^2} \ X_1) \ G_y(k_u,t)$$

where

$$G_y(k_y,t) \equiv \mathcal{F}_{(y)}\Big[g(y,t)\Big].$$

Equation (6.18) yields the following inversion:

$$G_y(k_u,t) = \exp(-j\omega t) \ \exp(-j\sqrt{k^2 - k_u^2}X_1) \ S(k_u,t). \qquad (6.19)$$

The inverse spatial Fourier transform of both sides of (6.19) with respect to $k_y = k_u$ yields

$$g(y,t) = \exp(-j\omega t) \ \mathcal{F}_{(k_y)}^{-1}\Big[\exp(-j\sqrt{k^2 - k_y^2} \ X_1) \ S(k_y,t)\Big]. \qquad (6.20)$$

Suppose the measurements are made for $t \in [0, T_0]$. We define the average reflectance map function by

$$\begin{aligned}
\bar{f}(y) &\equiv \int_0^{T_0} f(y,t) \, dt \\
&= \int_0^{T_0} |g(y,t)| \, dt
\end{aligned} \qquad (6.21)$$

Using (6.20) in (6.21), one obtains

$$\bar{f}(y) = \int_0^{T_0} \left| \exp(-j\omega t) \, \mathcal{F}_{(k_y)}^{-1} \left[\exp(-j\sqrt{k^2 - k_y^2} \, X_1) \, S(k_y, t) \right] \right| \, dt.$$
(6.22)

Equation (6.22) represents the spatial Doppler inversion of the average reflectance function from the passive array measurements at temporal frequency ω. We have left the phase function $\exp(-j\omega t)$ inside the magnitude operation on the right side of (6.22) to represent the fact that one may image targets radiating at various temporal frequencies (e.g., targets with different *colors*) via passing the passive array data through a bank of narrow-band bandpass filters in the temporal frequency domain prior to constructing the inversion shown in (6.22).

We consider three targets located at the range $X_1 = 1000$ meters with cross-range values $y_1 = 200$ meters, $y_2 = 0$ meters and $y_3 = -100$ meters, with relative amplitudes of 1.5, 2 and 1, respectively. These three targets emit a monochromatic signal with wavenumber $k = \pi$ radians/meter. Figure 6.5 shows $\bar{f}(y)$ (magnitude) for $L = 100$ meters (resolution = 10.5 meters approximately for all targets), and $L = 50$ meters (resolution = 21 meters). (The fluctuating signal is the real part of the reconstruction prior to the magnitude operation.) *Note from (6.11) that the signature of each target in the k_u domain is observable only in the band*

$$k_u \in [k \frac{y_n - L}{X_1}, k \frac{y_n + L}{X_1}],$$

$n = 1, 2, 3$, *due to the finite aperture of the passive array.* Thus, the reconstructed signal (prior to the magnitude operation) for the n-th target in the y domain is a sinc pattern modulating a sinusoidal carrier with frequency $k_u = k \frac{y_n}{X_1}$. The magnitude of this signal, that is, $\bar{f}(y)$, is used to identify targets in the cross-range domain.

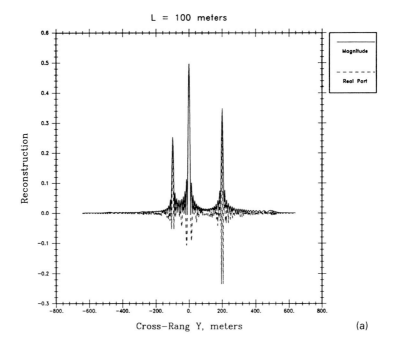

(a)

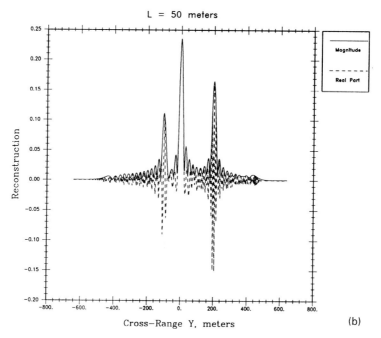

(b)

Figure 6.5 Cross-range reconstruction of a planar target.
(a) $L = 100$ meters. (b) $L = 50$ meters.

Using a procedure similar to the one shown in Section 6.1, the Fresnel approximation-based inversion for the system model (6.16) can be found to be

$$\bar{f}(y) \approx \int_0^{T_0} \left| \exp(-j\omega t) \, \mathcal{F}_{(k_y)}^{-1} \left[\exp[-j(k - \frac{k_y^2}{2k}) \, X_1] \, S(k_y, t) \right] \right| \, dt$$

$$= \int_0^{T_0} \left| \exp(-j\omega t) \, \mathcal{F}_{(k_y)}^{-1} \left[\exp(j\frac{k_y^2}{2k} \, X_1) \, S(k_y, t) \right] \right| \, dt$$

$$= \int_0^{T_0} \left| \exp(-j\omega t) \left[s(y, \omega) \, * \, \exp(-jk\frac{y^2}{2X_1}) \right] \right| \, dt,$$

$$(6.23)$$

where $*$ denotes convolution in the y domain. Equation (6.23) is the governing equation for analog image formation with lenses. Human vision is also based on this principle.

Nonplanar Targets

We next examine imaging a nonplanar surface in the (x, y) domain that radiates an incoherent narrow-band signal (see Figure 6.6). The system model in (6.16) should be modified as follows:

$$s(u, t) = \int_y f(y, t) \exp[j\omega t + j\phi(y, t)] \exp[jk\sqrt{[X_1 + x(y)]^2 + (u - y)^2}] dy$$

$$(6.24)$$

where $x(y)$ represents the deviations of the surface from the focused plane (line $x = 0$). Using the procedure that led to (6.18) from (6.16), we can obtain the following from (6.24):

$$S(k_u, t) = \exp(j\omega t + j\sqrt{k^2 - k_u^2} \, X_1)$$
$$\times \int_y g(y, t) \, \exp[j\sqrt{k^2 - k_u^2} \, x(y)] \, \exp(-jk_u y) \, dy.$$

$$(6.25)$$

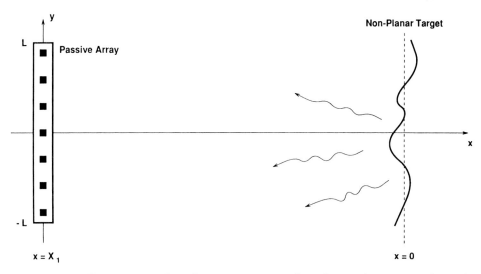

Figure 6.6 Incoherent narrow-band passive array imaging of nonplanar targets.

The phase function $\exp[j\sqrt{k^2 - k_u^2}\, x(y)]$ is the factor that separates (6.25) from (6.18). This term is unknown and cannot be compensated for in the inversion. If one attempts inversion (6.22) for nonplanar targets, the phase function $\exp[j\sqrt{k^2 - k_u^2}\, x(y)]$ would result in a shift-varying (y-dependent) *shift and smearing* of the points that are not located on the focusing plane, that is, the line $x = 0$.

The instantaneous frequency of the phase error function is

$$\frac{\partial}{\partial k_u}\left[\sqrt{k^2 - k_u^2}\, x(y)\right] = \frac{k_u}{\sqrt{k^2 - k_u^2}} x(y).$$

The amount of the undesired shift (error in the cross-range domain, y_e) for a target off the focal plane is approximately equal to this instantaneous frequency evaluated at the k_u value at the center of the target's signature in the k_u domain; that is,

$$y_e(y) \approx \frac{y}{X_1 + x(y)} x(y).$$

This effect is more severe for off-broadside points (i.e., as y moves away from the origin) on the target's surface.

The amount of the undesired smearing (Δ_e) for a target off the focal plane is determined from the difference of the above instantaneous frequency at the lower and upper k_u values of the target's signature in the k_u domain:

$$\Delta_e \approx \frac{2L\,|x(y)|}{X_1 + x(y)}.$$

This smearing effect is invariant of y [though a function of $x(y)$].

Consider the target scene examined for Figure 6.5a ($L = 100$ meters). Suppose the targets at $y_1 = 200$ and $y_2 = 0$ meters are moved to the range 800 meters (i.e., $x(y_1) = x(y_2) = -200$ meters). Figure 6.7 shows the reconstructed target region for this scenario. Note that both off focused plane targets exhibit the same smearing. The off-broadside target at $y_1 = 200$ meters also shows a shift of approximately $y_e(y_1) = -50$ meters.

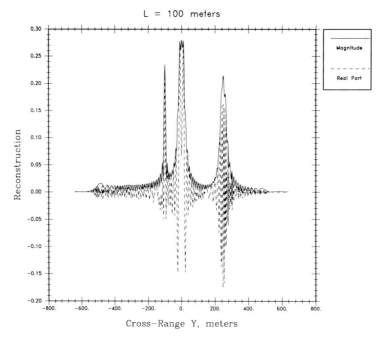

Figure 6.7 Cross-range reconstruction of a nonplanar target.

As we mentioned earlier, X_1, that is, the focal line, is a parameter that is controlled by the user. The measurements made in the (u,t) domain may be processed with different X_1 values by the user to obtain the sharpest possible image and/or imaging at different range values. This procedure is similar to the range focusing performed with cameras.

6.3 BISTATIC (STEREO) DETECTION OF MULTIPLE TARGETS

In the previous section, we showed that coherent spatial Doppler processing may be used to resolve targets in the cross-range domain. However, due to the incoherence of the incoming time signals, targets are not resolvable in the range domain. We now examine a passive array problem where a bistatic combination of passive arrays is used to detect and locate multiple targets in an imaging scene.

System Model

Consider a two-dimensional passive array imaging system geometry on the (x, y) plane as shown in Figure 6.8. The target scene is composed of a finite/infinite number of targets at the unknown coordinates (x_n, y_n), $n = 1, 2, 3, \ldots$ in the spatial domain. (Unlike the imaging problems that we discussed in the previous sections, we now assume that the target scene is not centered at the origin in the spatial domain.) The n-th target transmits an unknown signal, call it $p_n(t)$ ($p_n(t)$ is not a pulsed signal), during the data acquisition period. A passive linear array located at $x = 0$ with sensors at $u \in [-L, L]$ records the signals transmitted by the targets. (Note that the passive array located on the line $x = 0$ is not in the middle of the target region; it is assumed that $\sqrt{x_n^2 + y_n^2} \gg L$.) The signal recorded at the sensor located at $(0, u)$ is

$$s(u,t) \equiv \sum_n p_n \Big[t - \frac{\sqrt{x_n^2 + (y_n - u)^2}}{c} \Big]. \qquad (6.26)$$

Taking the one-dimensional Fourier transform of both sides of (6.26) with respect to t yields

$$s(u,\omega) = \sum_n P_n(\omega) \, \exp[j2k\sqrt{x_n^2 + (y_n - u)^2}], \qquad (6.27)$$

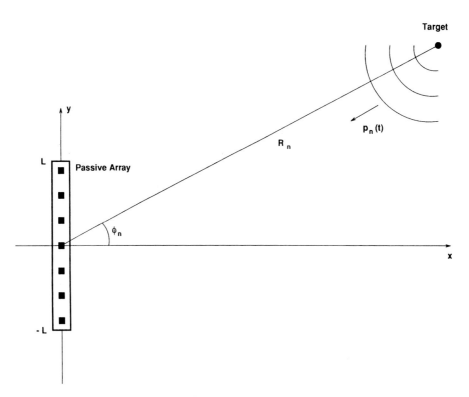

Figure 6.8 A radiating target illuminating a passive array.

where ω is the temporal frequency domain for t. [For notational simplicity, the Fourier transform of $s(u,t)$ with respect to t is identified by $s(u,\omega)$.]

Spatial Doppler Processing

Taking the Fourier transform of both sides of (6.27) with respect to $u \in [-L, L]$ yields

$$S(k_u, \omega) = \sum_n \frac{P_n(\omega)}{\sqrt{k^2 - k_u^2}} \; \exp(j\sqrt{k^2 - k_u^2}\; x_n + j k_u y_n)\; I_n(\frac{k_u}{k}), \quad (6.28)$$

where $I_n(\cdot)$ is an indicator (spatial Doppler band) function defined by

$$I_n(\frac{k_u}{k}) = \begin{cases} 1 & \frac{k_u}{k} \in [\sin\phi_n - \frac{L}{R_n}\cos^2\phi_n, \sin\phi_n + \frac{L}{R_n}\cos^2\phi_n]; \\ 0 & \text{otherwise} \end{cases} \quad (6.29)$$

with

$$R_n \equiv \sqrt{x_n^2 + y_n^2},$$

and

$$\phi_n \equiv \arctan(\frac{y_n}{x_n}). \quad (6.30)$$

- *The signature of the n-th target is centered around*

$$H_n \equiv \sin\phi_n = \frac{y_n}{R_n}, \quad (6.31)$$

in the $\frac{k_u}{k}$ domain. The length of this support band is

$$2W_n \equiv \frac{2L}{R_n}\cos^2\phi_n, \quad (6.32)$$

*in the $\frac{k_u}{k}$ domain. Both H_n and W_n are **invariant** of k (or ω).*

Next, we develop a method for detecting the targets from their signatures.

Target Detection

We define the following linear mapping:

$$h_u \equiv \frac{k_u}{k}. \quad (6.33)$$

From (6.33), we denote the following functional mapping of the spatial Doppler signal:

$$\begin{aligned} Q(h_u, \omega) &\equiv \sqrt{k^2 - k_u^2} \; S(k_u, \omega) \\ &= \sum_n P_n(\omega) \; \exp\left[j\frac{\omega}{c}(\sqrt{1 - h_u^2} \; x_n + h_u y_n) \right] I_n(h_u), \end{aligned}$$

$$(6.34)$$

with

$$I_n(h_u) = \begin{cases} 1 & h_u \in [H_n - W_n, H_n + W_n]; \\ 0 & \text{otherwise} \end{cases}$$

Taking the inverse Fourier transform of both sides of (6.34) with respect to ω yields

$$Q(h_u, t) = \sum_n p_n\left[t - \sqrt{1 - h_u^2}\, \frac{x_n}{c} - h_u \frac{y_n}{c} \right] I_n(h_u). \qquad (6.35)$$

(For notational simplicity, the inverse Fourier transform of Q is also called Q in (6.35).)

The transformed signal $Q(h_u, t)$ localizes the n-th target's signature, that is,

$$p_n\left[t - \sqrt{1 - h_u^2}\, \frac{x_n}{c} - h_u \frac{y_n}{c} \right] I_n(h_u),$$

in an interval equal to $2W_n$ in the h_u domain.

Suppose two passive arrays with sensors at, for example, $(0, u - \Delta)$ and $(0, u + \Delta)$ with $u \in [-L, L]$, are used to record the signals emitted by the targets in the scene (see Figure 6.9). (The two passive arrays could be overlapping or nonoverlapping subapertures of a larger passive array.) Δ is a known constant that is much smaller than R_n's. The signals recorded by the two passive arrays are

$$s_1(u, t) \equiv \sum_n p_n\left[t - \frac{\sqrt{x_n^2 + (y_n + \Delta - u)^2}}{c} \right]$$

$$s_2(u, t) \equiv \sum_n p_n\left[t - \frac{\sqrt{x_n^2 + (y_n - \Delta - u)^2}}{c} \right]. \qquad (6.36)$$

Using the procedure that resulted in (6.35) from (6.26), we can obtain the following from (6.36) (with Δ and L both much smaller than R_n's):

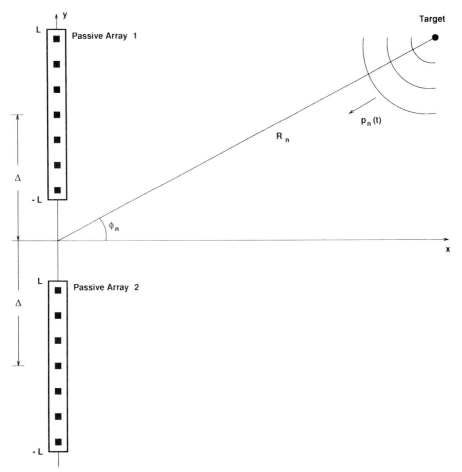

Figure 6.9 Bistatic detection of multiple targets with passive arrays.

$$Q_1(h_u, t) = \sum_n p_n \Big[t - \sqrt{1 - h_u^2} \, \frac{x_n}{c} - h_u \frac{y_n + \Delta}{c} \Big] I_{n1}(h_u)$$

$$Q_2(h_u, t) = \sum_n p_n \Big[t - \sqrt{1 - h_u^2} \, \frac{x_n}{c} - h_u \frac{y_n - \Delta}{c} \Big] I_{n2}(h_u), \qquad (6.37)$$

where

$$I_{ni}(h_u) = \begin{cases} 1 & h_u \in [H_{ni} - W_n, H_{ni} + W_n]; \\ 0 & \text{otherwise} \end{cases} \qquad (6.38)$$

for $i = 1, 2$, with

$$H_{n1} \equiv \frac{y_n + \Delta \cos^2 \phi_n}{R_n}$$

$$H_{n2} \equiv \frac{y_n - \Delta \cos^2 \phi_n}{R_n},$$

(6.39)

and

$$2W_n \equiv \frac{2L}{R_n} \cos^2 \phi_n.$$

(6.40)

By examining (6.37)-(6.40), one can observe that the signature of the n-th target in $Q_2(h_u, t)$ is a shifted version of its signature in $Q_1(h_u, t)$; the value of the shift is

$$
\begin{aligned}
(h_n, t_n) &\equiv \left(H_{n1} - H_{n2} , \sqrt{1 - H_{n1}^2}\, \frac{x_n}{c} + H_{n1} \frac{y_n + \Delta}{c} \right. \\
&\quad \left. - \sqrt{1 - H_{n2}^2}\, \frac{x_n}{c} - H_{n2} \frac{y_n - \Delta}{c} \right) \\
&= \left(\frac{2\Delta \cos^2 \phi_n}{R_n} , \frac{2\Delta \sin \phi_n}{c} \right).
\end{aligned}
$$

(6.41)

Thus, the two-dimensional correlation function

$$\rho_{12}(h_u, t) = Q_1(h_u, t) \; * * \; Q_2^*(h_u, t)$$

(6.42)

should exhibit peaks at $(h_u, t) = (h_n, t_n)$, $n = 1, 2, 3, ...$ (Q_2^* is the conjugate of Q_2). (It is clear from (6.41) that $h_n \geq 0$.) These peaks not only identify/detect the targets but also may be used to estimate the targets' coordinates, that is, (R_n, ϕ_n)'s. *Note that the matching performed via (6.42) is achieved without the knowledge of $p_n(t)$'s.*

Suppose the signals emitted by two targets in the scene are correlated, for example, one is the delay version of the other (multipath effect). In this case, the two show correlation in (6.42) only if the signatures of the two targets in the (h_u, t) domain have the same shape. This may or may not occur depending on the two targets' coordinates and the passive arrays' parameters.

From (6.39), one can show that the undesirable cross terms for two correlated targets appear at the following two h_u values:

$$h_{12} \equiv \Delta \left(\frac{\cos^2 \phi_1}{R_1} + \frac{\cos^2 \phi_2}{R_2} \right) + \left(\frac{y_1}{R_1} - \frac{y_2}{R_2} \right)$$

$$h_{21} \equiv \Delta \left(\frac{\cos^2 \phi_1}{R_1} + \frac{\cos^2 \phi_2}{R_2} \right) - \left(\frac{y_1}{R_1} - \frac{y_2}{R_2} \right)$$

One may also envision a set of multistatic passive arrays, for example, subapertures within a passive array, that are used for target detection and parameter estimation via the above-mentioned two-dimensional correlation. In the case of partitioning an array into subapertures, we are interested in finding the optimal (in some sense) size for the subaperture sizes. Suppose the optimal subaperture size is the one that yields the most compact support for a target signature in the k_u (or h_u) domain.

The spatial Doppler dispersion of a target signature in the k_u domain with the inclusion of the effective bandwidth for the aperture function [i.e., $\mathrm{sinc}(k_u L)$] is

$$BW \equiv k \frac{L}{R_n} + \frac{\pi}{L} \eta, \tag{6.43}$$

where $\eta \geq 1$ is a chosen constant. The derivative of (6.43) with respect to L provides the desired minimum spatial Doppler dispersion that corresponds to

$$L = \sqrt{\frac{\pi \eta R_n}{k}}. \tag{6.44}$$

Since R_n is unknown and varying from one target to another, one may use an estimate of the range of the targets in (6.44).

Example: Consider a system geometry for bistatic detection based on the following parameters: There are 128 sensor elements on each of the two passive arrays with $L = 100$ meters and $\Delta = 4500$ meters; there are 128 time samples in a 100 microsecond observation interval; there are two targets in the scene positioned at $(x_1, y_1) = (14000, 5500)$ meters and $(x_2, y_2) = (30000, -19500)$ meters.

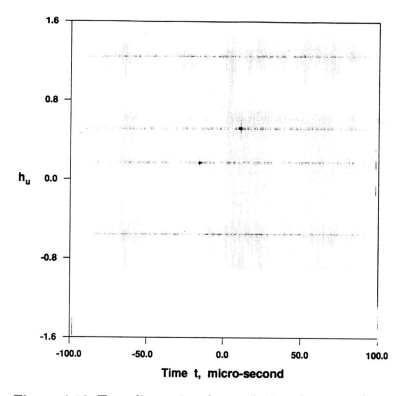

Figure 6.10 Two-dimensional correlation function for two un-correlated targets.

These two targets emit a time-dependent signal composed of 121 sinusoidal harmonics at frequencies separated by 10 KHz in the band 125 MHz ±600 KHz; the (Fourier) coefficients of these sinusoids were created via a complex normal random generator with mean zero and standard deviation one for both the real and imaginary parts; the speed of propagation in the medium is 3×10^8 meters/second.

Substituting the above specifications in (6.41), one obtains

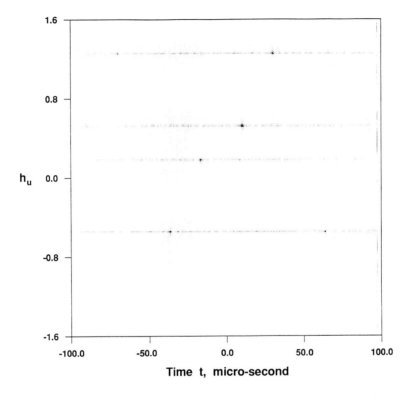

Figure 6.11 Two-dimensional correlation function for two correlated targets.

$$(h_1, t_1) = (.52, 11. \text{ microseconds})$$
$$(h_2, t_2) = (.18, -16.4 \text{ microseconds})$$

Using the specifications for the cited example, we have

$$h_{12} = 1.26 \quad \text{and} \quad h_{21} = -.56.$$

It should be noted that the two cross terms' h_u values do not always have opposite polarities that could have been exploited to identify and remove the cross terms. The corresponding time points for the cross terms are $t_{12} = -70.8$ microseconds and $t_{21} = 65.$ microseconds.

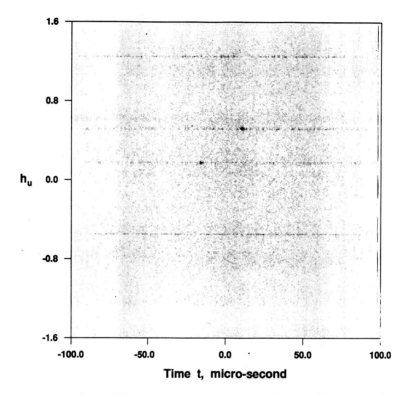

Figure 6.12 Two-dimensional correlation function for two uncorrelated targets with additive noise (SNR= -5.2
dB).

Figure 6.10 shows the two-dimensional correlation function ρ_{12} when
the temporal Fourier coefficients for the signals radiating from the two
targets were generated using two separate calls of the random number
generator. The correlation function shows two weak cross terms, one of
which appears at a negative h_n value. Figure 6.11 shows ρ_{12} when the
signal transmitted from the second target is a delayed version (by 98.94
microseconds) of the signal transmitted by the first target. In this case,
the cross-correlation of the two targets shows a stronger signature that
is comparable to the targets' signatures.

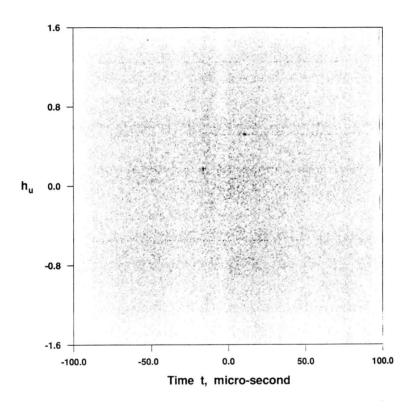

Figure 6.13 Two-dimensional correlation function for two uncorrelated targets with additive noise (SNR= -11.2
dB).

Figures 6.12 and 6.13 show ρ_{12} when the received signal is corrupted by a zero-mean additive complex noise with standard deviations (for both the real and imaginary parts) of 20 (SNR = -5.2 dB) and 40 (SNR = -11.2 dB), respectively. Figure 6.14 is the two-dimensional correlation function ρ_{12} for the geometry described above with $\Delta = 100$ meters. For this scenario, the signatures of the two targets are not separable.

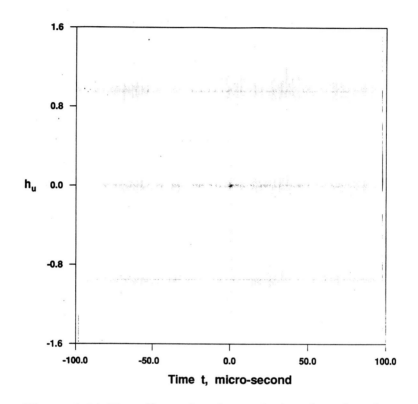

Figure 6.14 Two-dimensional correlation function for two uncorrelated targets ($\Delta = 100$ meters).

One might argue that the targets could be identifiable in the two-dimensional correlation function of the original measurements, that is,

$$s_1(u,t) \,**\, s_2^*(u,t).$$

Figure 6.15 shows this correlation function for the case of uncorrelated targets and noise-free measurements.

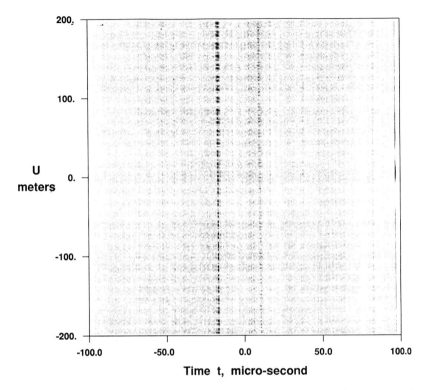

Figure 6.15 Two-dimensional correlation function of original measurements.

6.4 PASSIVE SYNTHETIC APERTURE ARRAY IMAGING

In the next two sections, we examine passive array imaging systems involving a receiver and a radiating target, one of which moves relative to the other during the data acquisition period. The receiver could be an array or a single antenna. The physical aperture of the receiver is too small for high-resolution imaging. Due to this fact, we are interested in exploiting the motion of the receiver or the target to synthesize the effect of a large aperture antenna, that is, a process similar to the *motion-induced* active synthetic aperture array imaging that was discussed in Chapters 4 and 5.

Passive synthetic aperture and passive inverse synthetic aperture array imaging are relatively new concepts. Groutage [12],[13] has suggested using two antennas mounted on a moving vehicle (e.g., an aircraft or a satellite) to collect electromagnetic waves being radiated from a target scene. The target scene is imaged via an interferometric processing of passive synthetic aperture array data acquired by the two antennas. Reference [14] is a special issue on acoustic synthetic aperture array imaging that contains several papers on passive synthetic aperture systems. These systems utilize arrays that are towed by moving ships or submarines for synthetic aperture formation. Another potential application of passive synthetic aperture array imaging is in assessing damage in a battlefield using satellites that can record infrared radiation, that is, emission from targets that are on fire.

Our discussion on passive synthetic aperture array imaging is based on a system model that is similar to the system model for active FM-CW SAR imaging. However, to develop a computationally manageable inversion for *passive* sources, we are forced to assume simpler models for the target scene and signals being emitted from it. These limitations will prevent us from obtaining *imaging* algorithms for the inverse problem. The inversion of the simplified system models for passive synthetic aperture arrays results in *parameter estimation* methods to locate the radiating targets.

Wide-Band System Model

We consider the two-dimensional imaging geometry that is shown in Figure 6.16. This two-dimensional domain is the transformation of the three-dimensional range, cross-range and altitude domain into the two-dimensional slant-range and cross-range domain; the slant-range is the square root of the sum of the squares of the range and altitude. x is used to denote the slant-range domain, and y is the cross-range (along the track) domain.

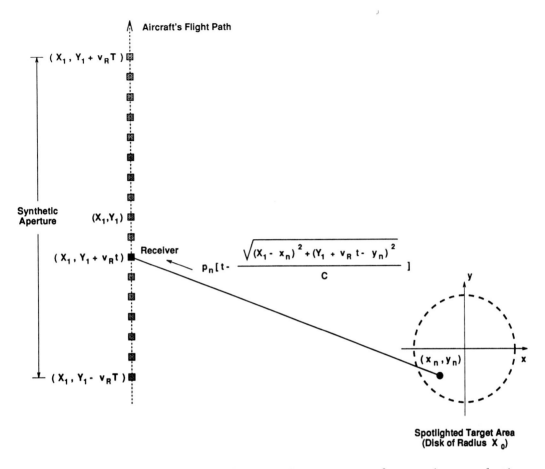

Figure 6.16 Imaging system geometry for passive synthetic aperture array imaging.

The passive physical array moves along the line $x = X_1$ with speed v_R in the (x, y) domain. Along this path, the physical array records a time-dependent signal (from the sources in the target scene) at the coordinates $(X_1, Y_1 + v_R t)$ for $t \in [-T, T]$ (synthesized aperture) on the (x, y) plane; X_1 and Y_1 (squint-mode parameters) are known constants; $Y_1 = 0$ corresponds to the broadside case. We denote the polar coordinates for (X_1, Y_1) by (R_1, θ_1). By properly phasing and adding the signals recorded by the physical array's elements, the physical array's beam is electronically focused on the desired target area (spotlighting).

Suppose we are interested in the target scene centered around the origin in the spatial (x, y) domain. In this case, when the vehicle is at the coordinates $(X_1, Y_1 + v_R t)$, the steer angle for spotlighting is

$$\arctan(\frac{Y_1 + v_R t}{X_1}).$$

Thus, the target area illuminated (spotlighted) by the physical array is the disk of radius X_0 centered at the origin in the spatial domain. X_0, which is defined by

$$X_0 = \frac{R_1 \lambda}{D},$$

is a known constant; λ is the wavelength, and D is the physical array's diameter. X_0 represents the resolution of the physical array without being moved to synthesize the effects of a larger aperture.

The recorded signal from the spotlighted target scene is

$$s(t) \equiv \sum_n s_n(t),$$

where $s_n(t)$ is the incoming signal from the n-th radiating target. This signal can be represented as follows:

$$s_n(t) \equiv p_n \left[t - \frac{\sqrt{(X_1 - x_n)^2 + (Y_1 + v_R t - y_n)^2}}{c} \right], \qquad (6.45)$$

where c is the wave propagation speed, and $p_n(t)$ is the signal transmitted by the n-th target that is located at (x_n, y_n) in the spatial domain. [The loss associated with the propagation path and the array's gain are absorbed in $p_n(t)$.] We assume that the radiating sources in the target scene are uncorrelated. Thus, we can analyze $s_n(t)$ separately for retrieving information on the n-th target.

Based on the decomposition of a spherical wave in terms of plane waves [9] and the principles we developed earlier for FM-CW SAR imaging, we can find the temporal Fourier transform of $s_n(t)$ to be the following:

$$S_n(\omega) = \int_{\alpha} d\alpha \ P_n(\alpha)$$

$$\times \exp\left[-j\sqrt{\frac{\alpha^2}{c^2} - (\frac{\omega - \alpha}{v_R})^2} \ (X_1 - x_n) - j(\frac{\omega - \alpha}{v_R}) \ (Y_1 - y_n)\right].$$

$$(6.46)$$

A practical inversion for the above system model, which assumes the target source is a wide-band signal, is not available.

Wide-Band Inversion via Stereo Measurements

Let us consider the stereo passive synthetic aperture array data for the above-mentioned wide-band model. Suppose two passive antennas are mounted on the aircraft with time-varying coordinates $(X_1, Y_1 + \Delta + v_R t)$ and $(X_1, Y_1 - \Delta + v_R t)$, where Δ is a known constant; 2Δ is the distance between the two antennas. Thus, the two passive measurements made by these two antennas are

$$s_{n1}(t) \equiv p_n\left[t - \frac{\sqrt{(X_1 - x_n)^2 + (Y_1 + \Delta + v_R t - y_n)^2}}{c}\right],$$

and

$$s_{n2}(t) \equiv p_n\left[t - \frac{\sqrt{(X_1 - x_n)^2 + (Y_1 - \Delta + v_R t - y_n)^2}}{c}\right].$$

We have the following approximation:

$$\sqrt{(X_1 - x_n)^2 + (Y_1 \pm \Delta + v_R t - y_n)^2}$$

$$\approx \sqrt{(X_1 - x_n)^2 + (Y_1 + v_R t - y_n)^2} + \frac{\pm \Delta(Y_1 - y_n) \pm \Delta v_R t + .5\Delta^2}{R_1}.$$

Suppose the target's signature in the temporal frequency domain is approximately centered at $\omega = \omega_n$. Moreover, it is assumed that ω_n is much larger than the bandwidth of the measured signals, that is, $s_{n1}(t)$ and $s_{n2}(t)$. In this case, the signal

$$q_{n1}(t) \equiv s_{n1}(t) \ \exp(j\frac{\Delta v_R \omega_n t}{R_1 c})$$

is a delayed version of the signal

$$q_{n2}(t) \equiv s_{n2}(t) \ \exp(-j\frac{\Delta v_R \omega_n t}{R_1 c}).$$

The amount of the delay is

$$\tau_n \equiv \frac{2\Delta(Y_1 - y_n)}{R_1 c},$$

which carries information on the target's cross-range, that is, y_n.

To estimate τ_n, one can construct the following cross-correlation function:

$$\Gamma_n(\tau) \equiv \int_{-T}^{T} q_{n1}(t) \ q_{n2}^*(t+\tau) \ dt.$$

This cross-correlation function should exhibit a peak (or its center-of-mass is located) at $\tau = \tau_n$. After estimating τ_n from the location of this peak, call it $\hat{\tau}_n$, the result can be used to estimate y_n via

$$\hat{y}_n \equiv Y_1 - \frac{R_1 c}{2\Delta}\hat{\tau}_n.$$

The accuracy of this method depends on the extent of the side lobes of $\Gamma_n(\tau)$ around $\tau = \tau_n$ as well as the distance between the two antennas 2Δ and $R_1 c$. (Note that τ_n is proportional to $\frac{2\Delta}{R_1 c}$.) The side lobes of $\Gamma_n(\tau)$ are related to the integration time $2T$ and the spectral properties (baseband bandwidth) of

$$p_n\left[t - \frac{\sqrt{X_1^2 + (Y_1 + v_R t)^2}}{c}\right].$$

The baseband bandwidth of the above signal is approximately equal to

$$\Omega_n \equiv 2\omega_{0n} + \frac{2v_R^2\omega_n T}{R_1 c},$$

where $2\omega_{0n}$ is the baseband bandwidth of $p_n(t)$. Thus, the cross-range resolution is found via

$$\Delta_y \equiv \frac{R_1 c}{2\Delta} \frac{2\pi}{\Omega_n}.$$

- *The baseband bandwidth Ω_n increases as $v_R T$ or, equivalently, the size of the synthetic aperture increases.*

- *The above correlation method is applicable even when the target emits a narrow-band signal, that is, $\omega_{0n} \approx 0$. In this case, the temporal frequency bandwidth generated via the aircraft motion (temporal Doppler phenomenon), that is, $\frac{2v_R^2\omega_n T}{R_1 c}$, determines Ω_n and, thus, the accuracy of the method. For this scenario, one has to have a priori knowledge of ω_n.*

The above stereo measurements in the **cross-range** domain do not provide additional information to estimate the target's range, that is, x_n. However, stereo measurements in the **range** domain may be used to estimate the target's range. For this, suppose two passive antennas are mounted on the aircraft with time-varying coordinates $(X_1 + \Delta, Y_1 + v_R t)$ and $(X_1 - \Delta, Y_1 + v_R t)$, where Δ is a known constant; 2Δ is the distance between the two antennas. Thus, the two passive measurements made by these two antennas are

$$s_{n1}(t) \equiv p_n\left[t - \frac{\sqrt{(X_1 + \Delta - x_n)^2 + (Y_1 + v_R t - y_n)^2}}{c}\right],$$

and

$$s_{n2}(t) \equiv p_n\left[t - \frac{\sqrt{(X_1 - \Delta - x_n)^2 + (Y_1 + v_R t - y_n)^2}}{c}\right].$$

We have the following approximation:

$$\sqrt{(X_1 \pm \Delta - x_n)^2 + (Y_1 + v_R t - y_n)^2}$$
$$\approx \sqrt{(X_1 - x_n)^2 + (Y_1 + v_R t - y_n)^2} + \frac{\pm\Delta(X_1 - x_n) + .5\Delta^2}{R_1}.$$

In this case, $s_{n1}(t)$ is a delayed version of $s_{n2}(t)$. The amount of the delay is

$$\tau_n \equiv \frac{2\Delta(X_1 - x_n)}{R_1 c},$$

which carries information on the target's range, that is, x_n.

The following cross-correlation function

$$\Gamma_n(\tau) \equiv \int_{-T}^{T} s_{n1}(t) \; s_{n2}^*(t + \tau) \, dt$$

possesses a peak at $\tau = \tau_n$. After estimating τ_n from the location of this peak, call it $\hat{\tau}_n$, the result can be used to estimate x_n via

$$\hat{x}_n \equiv X_1 - \frac{R_1 c}{2\Delta}\hat{\tau}_n.$$

The accuracy of this method also depends on the extent of the sidelobes of $\Gamma_n(\tau)$ around $\tau = \tau_n$ as well as the distance between the two antennas 2Δ and $R_1 c$. Thus, the range resolution is

$$\Delta_x \equiv \frac{R_1 c}{2\Delta} \frac{2\pi}{\Omega_n},$$

where

$$\Omega_n \equiv 2\omega_{0n} + \frac{2v_R^2 \omega_n T}{R_1 c},$$

and $2\omega_{0n}$ is the baseband bandwidth of $p_n(t)$.

Finally, one may use *three* receiving antennas with time-varying coordinates $(X_1, Y_1 + v_R t)$, $(X_1 + \Delta, Y_1 + v_R t)$, and $(X_1, Y_1 + \Delta + v_R t)$ (an L-shaped configuration) to record the necessary data to obtain both range and cross-range information via the above-mentioned correlation methods.

Narrow-Band System Model

We next examine information contents of a single passive receiver under the assumption that the target emits a narrow-band signal. Suppose the n-th target transmits a tone of the form

$$p_n(t) \equiv g_n \ \exp(j\omega_n t),$$

where g_n is a complex constant that represents the relative power and phase of the source, and ω_n is its unknown frequency. Thus, we have

$$P_n(\omega) = g_n \ \delta(\omega - \omega_n).$$

The recorded signal due to the n-th target becomes

$$s_n(t) = g_n \ \exp\left[j\omega_n t - jk_n\sqrt{(X_1 - x_n)^2 + (Y_1 + v_R t - y_n)^2}\right], \quad (6.47)$$

where $k_n \equiv \frac{\omega_n}{c}$ is the wavenumber. The temporal Fourier transform of the measured signal is

$$S_n(\omega) = g_n \ \exp\left[-j\sqrt{k_n^2 - (\frac{\omega - \omega_n}{v_R})^2} \ (X_1 - x_n) - j(\frac{\omega - \omega_n}{v_R})(Y_1 - y_n)\right].$$
$$(6.48)$$

One can develop practical methods for retrieving target data based on the above narrow-band system model. This is described next.

Narrow-Band Inversion

Consider the time domain data after baseband conversion of $s_n(t)$ based on a known estimate of ω_n, call it $\hat{\omega}_n$, as shown in the following:

$$s_n(t) \ \exp(-j\hat{\omega}_n t) = g_n \ \exp\left[j\gamma(t)\right], \quad (6.49)$$

where

$$\gamma(t) \equiv (\omega_n - \hat{\omega}_n)t - k_n\sqrt{(X_1 - x_n)^2 + (Y_1 + v_R t - y_n)^2}. \quad (6.50)$$

The instantaneous frequency of $s_n(t)$ is

$$\frac{d\gamma(t)}{dt} \approx (\omega_n - \hat{\omega}_n) - k_n \frac{v_R(Y_1 + v_R t - y_n)}{R_1} \qquad (6.51)$$

$$\equiv \gamma_0 + \gamma_1\, t,$$

where

$$\gamma_0 \equiv \omega_n - \hat{\omega}_n - \frac{k_n v_R(Y_1 - y_n)}{R_1}$$

$$\gamma_1 \equiv \frac{-k_n v_R^2}{R_1}. \qquad (6.52)$$

Note that the instantaneous frequency signal is a linear function of time. Thus, one can estimate (γ_0, γ_1) from the zero-th and first moments of the instantaneous frequency signal. The result can then be used to estimate (k_n, y_n) or, equivalently, (ω_n, y_n). To retrieve the instantaneous frequency function from the discrete measurements of $s_n(t)$, one may use, for example, the subaperture processing used in blind-velocity active SAR/ISAR imaging.

- *If the left side of (6.49) contains a compression function, that is,*

$$s_n(t)\ \exp\left[-j\hat{\omega}_n t + j\hat{k}_n \sqrt{(X_1 - x_n)^2 + (Y_1 + v_R t - y_n)^2}\right] = g_n\ \exp\left[j\gamma(t)\right],$$

where $\hat{k}_n \equiv \frac{\hat{\omega}_n}{c}$, then (6.52) becomes

$$\gamma_0 \equiv (\omega_n - \hat{\omega}_n)\left[1 - \frac{v_R Y_1}{c\ R_1}\right] + \frac{k_n v_R y_n}{R_1}$$

$$\gamma_1 \equiv \frac{-(k_n - \hat{k}_n)v_R^2}{R_1}.$$

From (6.48), we have the following that can be viewed as a form of baseband conversion on the ω domain data:

$$S_n(\omega)\ \exp\left[j\sqrt{k_n^2 - (\frac{\omega - \omega_n}{v_R})^2}\ X_1 + j(\frac{\omega - \omega_n}{v_R})\ Y_1\right] = g_n\ \exp\left[j\eta(\omega)\right], \qquad (6.53)$$

where

$$\eta(\omega) \equiv \sqrt{k_n^2 - (\frac{\omega - \omega_n}{v_R})^2} \; x_n + j(\frac{\omega - \omega_n}{v_R}) \; y_n. \qquad (6.54)$$

The instantaneous frequency of $S_n(\omega)$ is

$$\frac{d\eta(\omega)}{d\omega} \approx \frac{\frac{\omega_n - \omega}{v_R^2}}{k_n \cos \theta_1} x_n + \frac{1}{v_R} y_n \qquad (6.55)$$

$$\equiv \eta_0 + \eta_1 \; \omega,$$

where

$$\eta_0 \equiv \frac{c x_n}{v_R^2 \cos \theta_1} + \frac{y_n}{v_R}$$

$$\eta_1 \equiv \frac{-x_n}{k_n v_R^2 \cos \theta_1}. \qquad (6.56)$$

The above instantaneous frequency signal is a *linear* function of ω. Thus, we can estimate (η_0, η_1) from the zero-th and first moments of the instantaneous frequency signal. The result and the estimates of (k_n, y_n) from (6.52) can be used in (6.56) to estimate x_n. To retrieve the instantaneous frequency function from the discrete measurements of $S_n(\omega)$, we may also use the subaperture processing on the frequency domain data.

6.5 PASSIVE INVERSE SYNTHETIC APERTURE ARRAY IMAGING

Consider a two-dimensional imaging system geometry on the (x, y) plane as shown in Figures 6.17a-6.17b. In this discussion, it is more convenient to assume that a passive physical array is located at $(0, 0)$ in the spatial domain. The physical array records the incoming signals from a spotlighted target scene while a number of targets are moving within that spotlighted area. The moving targets are assumed to have constant velocities identified by (A_n, B_n), $n = 1, 2, 3, \dots$. The targets' coordinates at $t = 0$ are denoted by (x_n, y_n), $n = 1, 2, 3, \dots$. Thus, the n-th target at time t is located at the following spatial coordinates (see Figure 6.17b)

$$(x, y) \; = \; (x_n - A_n t \;, \; y_n - B_n t).$$

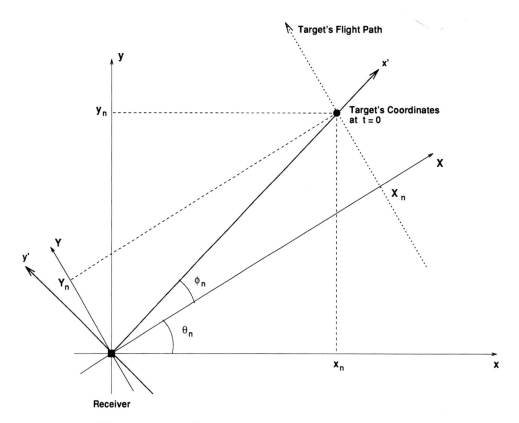

Figure 6.17a System geometry for passive inverse synthetic aperture array imaging: $t = 0$.

The n-th target transmits a tone with unknown frequency ω_n. Thus, the n-th target's signature in the recorded signal is

$$s_n(t) \equiv g_n \, \exp\left[j\omega_n t - k_n \sqrt{(x_n - A_n t)^2 + (y_n - B_n t)^2}\right]. \qquad (6.57)$$

We define the *squint* angle and speed values for the n-th target via

$$\theta_n \equiv \arctan\left(\frac{A_n}{B_n}\right)$$
$$V_n \equiv \sqrt{A_n^2 + B_n^2}. \qquad (6.58)$$

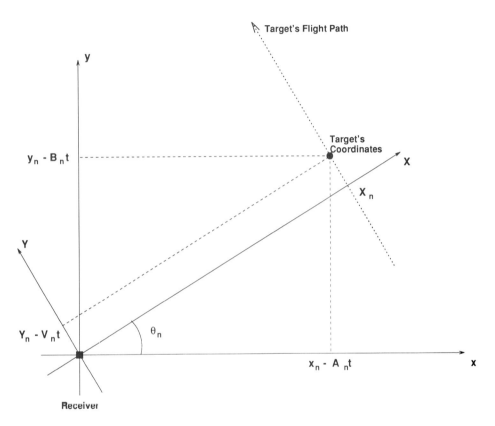

Figure 6.17b System geometry for passive inverse synthetic aperture array imaging: arbitrary t.

We also define the following rotational transformation of the n-th target's coordinates (see Figure 6.17a):

$$\begin{bmatrix} X_n \\ Y_n \end{bmatrix} \equiv \begin{bmatrix} \cos\theta_n & -\sin\theta_n \\ \sin\theta_n & \cos\theta_n \end{bmatrix} \begin{bmatrix} x_n \\ y_n \end{bmatrix}. \qquad (6.59)$$

θ_n is referred to as the *blind angle* for the n-th target.

The blind angle represents an ambiguity that cannot be resolved via passive array data. The magnitude of the blind angle is less than or equal to half of the physical array's beamwidth. The inverse passive synthetic aperture array that is described here solves for the n-th target's parameters (velocity and coordinates) in the (X, Y) domain (not the (x, y) domain) shown in Figure 6.17a. (The (X, Y) domain is constructed by rotating the (x, y) domain by θ_n.) Although the blind angle is unknown to the user, it does not have any effect in the imaging algorithm.

Using (6.58)-(6.59) in the system model of (6.57) yields

$$s_n(t) = g_n \, \exp\!\left[j\omega_n t - k_n \sqrt{X_n^2 + (Y_n - V_n t)^2}\right]. \qquad (6.60)$$

The system model in (6.60) shows that the n-th target is located at (X_n, Y_n) when $t = 0$ and moves with speed V_n parallel to the Y-axis.

- *The relative (X, Y) domain is different for each target since the blind angle θ_n varies with n. θ_n is transparent in the processing of $s_n(t)$.*

Define the target's range at $t = 0$ to be

$$R_n \equiv \sqrt{x_n^2 + y_n^2}$$
$$= \sqrt{X_n^2 + Y_n^2}.$$

Suppose the passive array's beam, a disk of radius of X_0, is focused around (X_1, Y_1) in the spatial domain. In most practical applications, we have

$$X_0 \ll R_1 = \sqrt{X_1^2 + Y_1^2}.$$

Thus, for the n-th target that falls in that beam, we have

$$\frac{1}{R_n} \approx \frac{1}{R_1}.$$

This is used in the following discussion.

Using the results of the previous section on passive synthetic aperture array imaging, that is, (6.49)-(6.56), we can write the following based on the system model in (6.60):

$$s_n(t) \, \exp(-j\hat{\omega}_n t) = g_n \, \exp\!\left[j\gamma(t)\right],$$

where

$$\gamma(t) \equiv (\omega_n - \hat{\omega}_n)t - k_n\sqrt{X_n^2 + (Y_n - V_n t)^2}.$$

The instantaneous frequency of $s_n(t)$ is

$$\frac{d\gamma(t)}{dt} \approx (\omega_n - \hat{\omega}_n) - k_n \frac{V_n(Y_n - V_n t)}{R_1}$$

$$\equiv \gamma_0 + \gamma_1\, t,$$

where

$$\gamma_0 \equiv \omega_n - \hat{\omega}_n - \frac{k_n V_n Y_n}{R_1}$$

$$\gamma_1 \equiv \frac{-k_n V_n^2}{R_1}. \tag{6.61}$$

For the temporal Fourier transform of the measured signal, we have

$$S_n(\omega)\, \exp\left[j\sqrt{k_n^2 - (\frac{\omega - \omega_n}{V_n})^2}\, X_1 + j(\frac{\omega - \omega_n}{V_n})\, Y_1\right] = g_n\, \exp\left[j\eta(\omega)\right],$$

where

$$\eta(\omega) \equiv \sqrt{k_n^2 - (\frac{\omega - \omega_n}{V_n})^2}\, (X_n - X_1) + j(\frac{\omega - \omega_n}{V_n})\, (Y_n - Y_1).$$

The instantaneous frequency of $S_n(\omega)$ is

$$\frac{d\eta(\omega)}{d\omega} \approx \frac{\frac{\omega_n - \omega}{V_n^2}}{k_n \cos\theta_1}(X_n - X_1) + \frac{1}{V_n}(Y_n - Y_1)$$

$$\equiv \eta_0 + \eta_1\, \omega,$$

where

$$\eta_0 \equiv \frac{c(X_n - X_1)}{V_n^2 \cos\theta_1} + \frac{(Y_n - Y_1)}{V_n}$$

$$\eta_1 \equiv \frac{(X_1 - X_n)}{k_n V_n^2 \cos\theta_1}. \tag{6.62}$$

One can estimate (γ_0, γ_1) and (η_0, η_1) from the zero-th and first moments of the instantaneous frequency functions of $s_n(t)$ and $S_n(\omega)$, respectively. The resultant estimates and the four equations in (6.61) and (6.62) are used to solve for the four unknown targets' parameters, that is, $(X_n, Y_n, V_n, \omega_n)$.

6.6 INTERFEROMETRIC APERTURE SYNTHESIS FOR CELESTIAL IMAGING

Observing celestial targets using waves being emitted from them has been an active area of research since the invention of the telescope. In the 1920s, Michelson introduced a procedure for imaging celestial targets via an interferometric processing of the waves being radiated from them [8]. In this section, we present the basic principles for a synthetic aperture-based celestial imaging system that utilizes Michelson interferometry [15],[16].

System Model and Inversion

We formulate the problem in the two-dimensional spatial domain with aperture synthesis in a one-dimensional linear array; generalization of this concept to the three-dimensional spatial domain using a synthesized planar array is trivial. We assume the target region is a planar structure on the line $x = X_1$ in the (x, y) domain. The receivers are located at $(0, u_i)$, $i = 1, \ldots, N$. The analog circuitry of th receivers is tuned such that they are capable of measuring a bandpass portion in the electromagnetic spectrum that is commonly in the visible band. For simplicity, we assume that the radiation pattern of each receiver is *omnidirectional*. A general receiver radiation pattern can be incorporated in the following analysis; this will be shown later.

The i-th receiver records the following time-dependent signal from the radiating target:

$$s(u_i, t) \equiv \int_y p_y\left[t - \frac{\sqrt{X_1^2 + (y - u_i)^2}}{c} \right] dy, \qquad (6.63)$$

where $p_y(t)$ is the bandpass portion of the wave that is transmitted by the target located at (X_1, y). This signal can be expressed in the following analytical form:

$$p_y(t) \equiv a_y(t) \ \exp(j\omega t),$$

where ω is the center frequency of the receiver's band.

Provided that $X_1 \gg y, u_i$ and $a_y(t)$ is a slowly fluctuating signal, we have the following Fresnel approximation for the spherical wave on the right side of (6.63):

$$p_y\left[t - \frac{\sqrt{X_1^2 + (y - u_i)^2}}{c} \right] = a_y\left[t - \frac{\sqrt{X_1^2 + (y - u_i)^2}}{c} \right]$$

$$\times \exp\left[j\omega[t - \frac{\sqrt{X_1^2 + (y - u_i)^2}}{c}] \right]$$

$$\approx a_y(t - \frac{X_1}{c})$$

$$\times \exp(j\omega t - jkX_1) \ \exp\left[-j\frac{k(y - u_i)^2}{2X_1}\right].$$

$$(6.64)$$

The signal that is recorded by the imaging system is the magnitude of the optical correlation of the signals measured by the two receivers over an integration time $t \in [0, T_0]$ that is chosen by the user; that is,

$$\Gamma_{ij} \equiv \left| \int_0^{T_0} s(u_i, t) \ s^*(u_j, t) \ dt \right|,$$

$$(6.65)$$

where the coherent processing time, over which the receivers and the target are assumed to be motionless, is a parameter chosen by the user. This is referred to as *interferometric* processing of the aperture data.

Suppose the signals being emitted from the various points in the target region are uncorrelated over the time interval of observations; that is,

$$\int_0^{T_0} a_{y_1}(t) \ a_{y_2}^*(t) \ dt = \begin{cases} f(y_1) & \text{for } y_1 = y_2; \\ 0 & \text{otherwise.} \end{cases}$$

Using this assumption and the approximation in (6.64) in the expression for the interferogram of (6.65), one obtains

$$\Gamma_{ij} \approx \left| \int_y f(y) \, \exp\left[-j\frac{k}{2X_1}[(y-u_i)^2 - (y-u_j)^2]\right] \, dy \right|$$

$$= \left| \underbrace{\int_y f(y) \, \exp\left[-j\frac{k(u_i-u_j)}{X_1}y\right] \, dy}_{Fourier\ integral} \right| \qquad (6.66)$$

$$= \left| F\left[\frac{k(u_i-u_j)}{X_1}\right] \right|.$$

Based on (6.66), the interferometric data provide the samples of $|F(k_y)|$ at

$$k_{yij} \equiv \frac{k(u_i-u_j)}{X_1}.$$

Nonideal Receivers: We showed in Chapter 3 that the radiation pattern of a nonideal receiver located at the origin, that is, (0,0), at frequency ω possesses an amplitude function in the spatial domain that we denoted via $a(x,y,\omega)$. For instance, for a flat receiver with an aperture of $2L_e$, $a(x = X_1, y, \omega)$ is a sinc function with its main-lobe at

$$y \equiv \pm X_0 = \pm\frac{X_1\lambda}{2L_e};$$

that is, the extent of the main-lobe in the y domain is $2X_0 = \frac{X_1\lambda}{L_e}$ that is the Rayleigh resolution for a single receiving element. Earlier, we refer to $2X_0$ as the *effective* target area that is being imaged.

By incorporating the amplitude pattern in (6.63), the resultant incoming signal becomes

$$s(u_i,t) \equiv \int_y a(X_1, y-u_i,\omega) \, p_y\left[t - \frac{\sqrt{X_1^2 + (y-u_i)^2}}{c}\right] \, dy.$$

In practical celestial imaging problems, u_i's are much smaller than X_1, the target's range, and $2X_0$, the effective target area. Also, $a(X_1, y, \omega)$ is a slowly-fluctuating amplitude signal. In this case, we have the following approximation:

$$a(X_1, y - u_i, \omega) \approx a(X_1, y, \omega).$$

Using this approximation and the steps that led to (6.66), we obtain the following for the interferometer data:

$$\Gamma_{ij} \approx |\int_y |a(X_1, y, \omega)|^2 \ f(y) \ \exp[-j\frac{k(u_i - u_j)}{X_1}y] \ dy|$$

$$\equiv |\int_y f_w(y) \ \exp[-j\frac{k(u_i - u_j)}{X_1}y] \ dy|$$

$$= |F_w[\frac{k(u_i - u_j)}{X_1}]|,$$

where we define the *windowed* target function via

$$f_w(y) \equiv w(y) \ f(y),$$

and the window function to be

$$w(y) \equiv |a(X_1, y, \omega)|^2.$$

Thus, the interferometric data provide the samples of the windowed target function $|F_w(k_y)|$. Clearly, we have

$$F_w(k_y) = F(k_y) \ * \ W(k_y),$$

where $*$ denotes convolution in the k_y domain. For a flat receiver, that is, when $a(x, y, \omega)$ is a sinc function, $w(y)$ is a sinc-squared signal. Thus, $W(k_y)$ is a triangular pulse.

Three-Dimensional Geometries: In three-dimensional imaging problems, the objective is to image a planar radiating target $f(y, z)$ that is located at range $x = X_1$. The receivers are positioned on the plane $x = 0$ and their coordinates are identified via $\mathbf{u}_i = (u_i, v_i)$, $i = 1, 2, 3, 4, \ldots$, in the $\mathbf{u} = (u, v)$ domain, that is, a planar array. (For the Earth-based sensor systems, a better model for the receiver array is a portion of a sphere, representing the Earth's surface, that moves with the Earth's rotation; this will be discussed.)

The distance of a radiating source at (X_1, y, z) from the receiver at $(0, u_i, v_i)$ is

$$\sqrt{X_1^2 + (y - u_i)^2 + (z - v_i)^2}.$$

The total signal that reaches the i-th receiver from the radiating target scene is

$$s(u_i, v_i, t) \equiv \int_y \int_z p_{yz} \left[t - \frac{\sqrt{X_1^2 + (y - u_i)^2 + (z - v_i)^2}}{c} \right] dy\ dz.$$

Using the steps similar to the ones that led to (6.66) for the two-dimensional systems, one can obtain the following for the interferometric processing of the signals of the i-th and j-th receivers in three-dimensional systems:

$$\Gamma_{ij} \approx |F(k_{yij}, k_{zij})|,$$

where

$$k_{yij} \equiv \frac{k(u_i - u_j)}{X_1}$$

$$k_{zij} \equiv \frac{k(v_i - v_j)}{X_1}.$$

If we connect the i-th receiver's coordinates to the j-th receiver's coordinates in the spatial domain of $\mathbf{u} = (u, v)$, the resultant vector in the $\mathbf{u}$ domain is

$$\mathbf{u}_i - \mathbf{u}_j = (u_i - u_j, v_i - v_j).$$

The direction (angle) of this vector is the angle of the interferometer datum sample vector (k_{yij}, k_{zij}) in the (k_y, k_z) domain. Moreover, the length of the vector (k_{yij}, k_{zij}) is equal to the length of the vector $\mathbf{u}_i - \mathbf{u}_j$ multiplied with $\frac{k}{X_1}$.

Due to cost constraints, only a few receivers are used in practice. By varying the locations of the receivers relative to the target position (e.g., the Earth's rotation in three-dimensional problems that involves reconstruction in the (k_y, k_z) domain) or relative to each other (e.g., using *mobile* receivers), one can recover different samples of $|F(k_y)|$ or $|F(k_y, k_z)|$. This process is a *position-induced* synthetic aperture array imaging. In some systems, the use of target emission at various frequency bands (e.g., infrared, red, blue and ultraviolet in the optical systems) has been suggested to obtain better coverages in the spatial frequency domain.

The resultant sampled data coverage in the spatial frequency domain, that is, k_y in two-dimensional problems or (k_y, k_z) in three-dimensional problems, frequently contains large gaps where the sampling rate violates the Nyquist rate. In this case, it is difficult to extrapolate the desired target function in those gaps from the available measurements. Later in this section, we will discuss synthesis of nonredundant arrays that reduce the extent of these gaps.

The other impasse for generating the spatial image, that is, $f(y)$ (or $f(y, z)$), is the lack of knowledge of the phase of $F(k_y)$ (or $F(k_y, k_z)$) in this imaging scheme. Recovery of phase of a signal from its magnitude has been an active area of research in celestial imaging. In addition to the classical energy reduction algorithms suggested by Gerchberg and Saxton that are based on a priori information on the properties of the target function (e.g., it is *positive* and *space-limited* in the spatial domain), the use of triple correlation or bispectrum [15] was recently suggested to solve the phase ambiguity problem. We will examine the phase retrieval problem later in this section.

Sampling Constraints and Resolution

We consider the linear array problem. The largest distance between the two receivers, that is, $u_i - u_j$ determines the extent of the band of the available interferometric data in the spatial frequency domain. Moreover, we have $-2L \leq u_i i - u_j \leq 2L$. Thus, the resolution band, the Rayleigh resolution band, for a linear aperture with $u_i \in [-L, L]$ is

$$k_y \in \left[\frac{-2kL}{X_1}, \frac{2kL}{X_1} \right].$$

Thus, the resolution in the y domain is

$$\Delta_y = \frac{X_1 \lambda}{4L}.$$

The Rayleigh band for a passive interferometric synthetic aperture imaging system is twice the size of the Rayleigh band for the other passive imaging systems that we examined earlier in this chapter; see Sections 6.1 and 6.2, and equation (6.11). Moreover, this Rayleigh band is equal to the Rayleigh band for the *active* imaging systems that we discussed in Chapters 3-5.

- **Interferometric** *aperture synthesis generates a coherent processing environment similar to active imaging systems via mixing the output of one receiver with the output of another receiver that serves as a* **reference** *signal.*

- *The classical lens processing principles (Fresnel approximation-based) for imaging the average reflectance map function $\bar{f}(y)$ with a noninterferometric aperture (see (6.22)) utilize a photographic film to record the desired image [1],[2]. As we showed in (6.11), the Rayleigh band of $\bar{f}(y)$, that also dictates its resolution, is*

$$\left[\frac{-kL}{X_1}, \frac{kL}{X_1}\right].$$

However, the film produces a magnitude-squared of the reflectance map function. Thus, the bandwidth of the recorded image is twice the reflectance map function, that is,

$$\left[\frac{-2kL}{X_1}, \frac{2kL}{X_1}\right].$$

This bandwidth expansion is an artifact of the recording mechanism and should not be mistaken with the actual Rayleigh band of the passive imaging system.

If the number of the receiver elements is N, then there are N^2 interferometric pairings of these receivers. Suppose these yield M *distinct* interferometric sample points in the spatial frequency of k_y domain, where $M \leq N^2$. Clearly, $k_{yij} = 0$ when $i = j$, $i = 1, \ldots, N$. Thus, the maximum value that M can take is

$$M_{max} \equiv N^2 - N + 1.$$

If the target resides within the interval $[-X_0, X_0]$ in the spatial y domain, then the average Nyquist sampling rate for the k_{yij}'s (whether they are evenly-spaced or not) should satisfy the following:

$$\Delta_{k_y} \equiv \frac{\frac{4kL}{X_1}}{M} \leq \frac{2\pi}{4X_0}.$$

This yields the following constraint for the number of distinct interferometric data points:

$$\frac{4LX_0}{\lambda X_1} \leq M.$$

Next, we examine a method for maximizing M, that is, synthesis of nonredundant arrays.

Nonredundant Array Synthesis

Next, we consider the design of nonredundant synthetic arrays. To formulate this problem for two dimensional as well as one-dimensional synthetic arrays, we define $\mathbf{u}$ to be the continuous aperture domain and $\mathbf{u}_i$, $i = 1, \ldots, N$, to be the location of the array elements; $\mathbf{u} \equiv u$ for the one-dimensional arrays, and $\mathbf{u} \equiv (u, v)$ for the two-dimensional arrays.

We define the discrete array configuration function via the following:

$$\mathbf{a}(\mathbf{u}) \equiv \sum_{i=1}^{N} \delta(\mathbf{u} - \mathbf{u}_i),$$

where

$$\delta(\mathbf{u} - \mathbf{u}_i) \equiv \begin{cases} 1 & \text{for } \mathbf{u} = \mathbf{u}_i \\ 0 & \text{otherwise}, \end{cases}$$

is a discrete delta function. The discrete autocorrelation of the array configuration function is

$$r_{\mathbf{a}}(\mathbf{u}) \equiv \mathbf{a}(\mathbf{u}) \; * \; \mathbf{a}(-\mathbf{u})$$

$$= \sum_{i=1}^{N} \sum_{j=1}^{N} \delta(\mathbf{u} - \mathbf{u}_i + \mathbf{u}_j),$$

where $*$ denotes discrete convolution in the $\mathbf{u}$ domain.

The number of interferometric data points at a given spatial frequency $k_{\mathbf{y}} \equiv k_y$ or $k_{\mathbf{y}} \equiv (k_y, k_z)$ is

$$\mathbf{N}(k_{\mathbf{y}}) \equiv r_{\mathbf{a}}(\mathbf{u}),$$

where

$$k_{\mathbf{y}}(k, \mathbf{u}) \equiv \frac{k \; \mathbf{u}}{X_1}.$$

Note that this coverage depends on k or the wavelength of the target emission. Clearly, the spatial frequency coverage from one wavelength, for example, λ_1, to another wavelength, say λ_2, is simply the magnification or contraction of the coverage for λ_1 by $\frac{\lambda_1}{\lambda_2}$.

The ideal array configuration yields an $\mathbf{N}(k_{\mathbf{y}})$ function that is equal to one (i.e., *flat*) in the $k_{\mathbf{y}}$ domain except at $k_{\mathbf{y}} = 0$ or $(0,0)$ where $\mathbf{N}(0)$ or $\mathbf{N}(0,0) = N$. This implies that the interferometric data are likely to be distributed uniformly and without redundancy in the spatial frequency $k_{\mathbf{y}}$ domain.

For instance, for the one-dimensional arrays with evenly-spaced elements, that is, $u_i = i\Delta_u$, then $\mathbf{a}(u)$ is a discrete rectangular pulse and its autocorrelation, $r_{\mathbf{a}}(u)$, is a discrete triangular pulse. For this scenario, $M = N$ and the spatial frequency coverage of the interferometer contains too many redundancy.

Similar principles can be developed for three-dimensional geometries with Earth rotation. For this, suppose the array is centered around the polar coordinates $(r_0, 0, \phi_0)$ and is composed of N sensors that are located on the Earth's surface at the following time-varying coordinates:

$$u_i(\tau) \equiv r_0 \ \cos(\omega_0 \tau + \theta_i) \ \cos \phi_i$$
$$v_i(\tau) \equiv r_0 \ \sin(\omega_0 \tau + \theta_i) \ \cos \phi_i$$
$$w_i \equiv r_0 \sin \phi_i,$$

$i = 1, \ldots, N$, where r_0 is the Earth's radius, ω_0 is the Earth's rotational speed around its axis, and (r_0, θ_i, ϕ_i) are the polar coordinates of the i-th sensor. τ is the *slow-time* domain. Earlier, we denoted the fast-time domain for interferometric processing by t.

Moreover, suppose the target is a stationary plane, call it (y, z) plane, that is centered around the polar coordinates $(X_1, 0, \Phi_0)$ and is tangential to the sphere of radius X_1; the range axis, x, is the line joining the origin to the center of the (y, z) plane. Then, at a fixed slow-time τ, the mixing (interferometric processing) of the i-th and j-th sensors results in the following spatial frequency sample point:

$$k_{yij}(\tau) \equiv \frac{k \ \cos \Phi_0}{X_1} \ [v_i(\tau) - v_j(\tau)]$$
$$k_{zij}(\tau) \equiv \frac{k \ \cos \Phi_0}{X_1} \ (w_i - w_j) - \frac{k \ \sin \Phi_0}{X_1} \ [u_i(\tau) - u_j(\tau)].$$

During the fast-time coherent processing of $[0, T_0]$ for this mixing, the slow-time τ can be assumed to be fixed, that is, the Earth is motionless.

- *It is not necessary to mix all sensors simultaneously. If a sequential mixing of the sensors is utilized, then the user can appropriate a larger fast-time coherent processing period, that is, T_0, for each pairing of the sensors. This improves the signal-to-noise power ratio of the measurements.*

In practice, the extent of the array much smaller than the Earth's radius. In this case, we have $|\theta_i| \ll 1$ and $|\phi_i - \phi_0| \ll 1$, where $(r_0, 0, \phi_0)$ are the polar coordinates of the center of the synthetic aperture. Then, we have the following approximation for the spatial frequency sample locations:

$$k_{yij}(\tau) \approx \frac{k \, r_0 \cos \Phi_0}{X_1} \left[\cos \phi_0 \cos(\omega_0 \tau) \, (\theta_i - \theta_j) \right.$$

$$\left. - \sin \phi_0 \sin(\omega_0 \tau) \, (\phi_i - \phi_j) \right]$$

$$k_{zij}(\tau) \approx \frac{k \, r_0 \sin \Phi_0}{X_1} \left[\cos \phi_0 \sin(\omega_0 \tau) \, (\theta_i - \theta_j) \right.$$

$$\left. + \sin \phi_0 \cos(\omega_0 \tau) \, (\phi_i - \phi_j) \right]$$

$$+ \underbrace{\frac{k \, r_0 \cos \Phi_0}{X_1} \, \cos \phi_0 \, (\phi_i - \phi_j)}_{Slow-time \; invariant}.$$

For a fixed sensor pair (i, j) and varying slow-time τ, the locus of the spatial frequency contour $[k_{yij}(\tau), k_{zij}(\tau)]$ approximates a shifted elliptical contour. The amount of shift is equal to the *slow-time-invariant* component in the expression for $k_{zij}(\tau)$.

For the above-mentioned three-dimensional imaging geometries that involve data collection in the slow-time of the Earth's rotation that yields shifted elliptical contours of data in the spatial frequency domain, Y-shaped arrays are believed to contain less redundancy. These arrays are currently being used for interferometric celestial imaging of targets from their microwave (radio) emission. The Y-shaped arrays are also being considered for interferometric synthetic aperture imaging from the optical radiation of targets.

Figure 6.18 shows a Y-shaped synthetic aperture array and spatial frequency coverages that can be obtained with this array. The star-shaped coverage is for a single wavelength with no Earth rotation; this coverage contains large gaps in it. The coverage with a single wavelength and Earth rotation shows a more uniform density for the available samples though it also contains gaps. Finally, the use of three wavelengths with Earth rotation results in a coverage that is almost complete within the Rayleigh band.

Figure 6.19 shows target reconstructions with the Y-shaped array. The original target is a simulated spiral galaxy. The filled aperture reconstruction is for an interferometric disk array within the extent of the

Spatial Frequency Coverages for Y-Shaped Array

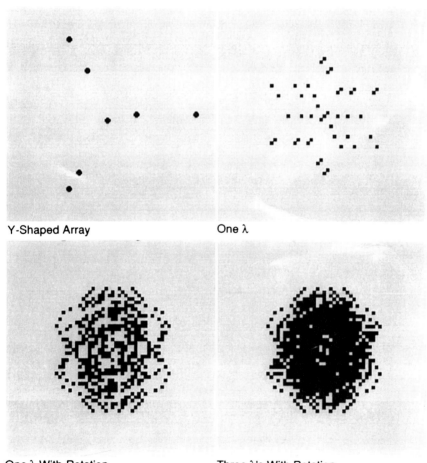

Y-Shaped Array   One λ

One λ With Rotation   Three λ's With Rotation

Figure 6.18 Y-shaped array and its spatial frequency coverages.

Reconstructions With Y-Shaped Array

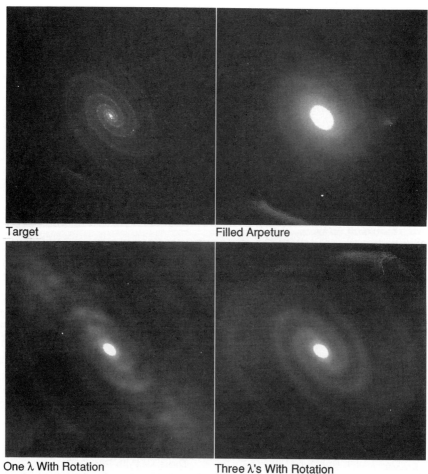

Target

Filled Arpeture

One λ With Rotation

Three λ's With Rotation

Figure 6.19 Target reconstructions with Y-shaped array.

Y-shaped array that is composed of regularly spaced elements. Its resulting coverage yields evenly spaced samples of the desired signal in the spatial frequency domain within the Rayleigh band. The reconstruction with a single wavelength and Earth rotation exhibits *streaks* or what is known as *ghosts* due to the gaps in its spatial frequency coverage. The same is not true for the image reconstructed with three wavelengths and Earth rotation.

This image shows more prominent high frequency features than the filled aperture reconstruction. This is due to the fact that the filled aperture image contains a cone window (Chinese hat function) in the spatial frequency domain that suppresses the high spatial frequency contents of the image. The cone window is the autocorrelation of the disk array that is composed of regularly spaced elements. Similar to the autocorrelation of the rectangular aperture for the one-dimensional measurements, that is, the triangular function, the cone window is a measure of the distribution of the number of available interferometric data samples in the spatial frequency domain and, thus, it represents the redundancy of the available samples in the frequency domain.

The effect of the cone window can be removed. However, this window is a Weiner type window that has the effect of suppressing additive noise where the signal is relatively weak. The same is not true for the autocorrelation of the Y-shaped array or other forms of sparse synthetic arrays. For those arrays, the user should first compensate for variations of the autocorrelation function via, for example, averaging the samples that fall within a spatial frequency pixel or interpolation, and then apply a Weiner type filter, for example, a cone window or a two-dimensional Hamming window, to reduce the noise effects.

There are methods to design arrays that do not contain redundancy [17]. A simple computer-based approach is to select $\mathbf{u}_i$'s via a random number generator in the aperture domain $[-L, L]$. Suppose the discrete probability density function that is used to generate these numbers is $g(\mathbf{u})$. Then, the discrete Fourier transform, DFT, of the array configuration function, that is, $\mathbf{a}(\mathbf{u})$, is

$$\mathbf{A}(k_{\mathbf{u}}) \equiv \sum_{i=1}^{N} \exp(j k_{\mathbf{u}} \mathbf{u}_i).$$

The spectrum of $\mathbf{u}(u)$ is found via the following:

$$S_{\mathbf{a}}(k_{\mathbf{u}}) \equiv E\big[|\mathbf{A}(k_{\mathbf{u}})|^2\big]$$
$$= (N^2 - N)\,|G(k_{\mathbf{u}})|^2 + N.$$

where $E[\cdot]$ is the expectation operator in the probability space of $\mathbf{u}_i$'s, and $G(k_{\mathbf{u}})$ is the DFT of $g(\mathbf{u})$ (i.e., the characteristic function).

The best design in this problem should yield a large d.c. value for the spectrum and negligible sidelobes. The uniform distribution provides such a distribution for the spectrum. Similar to the synthesis of aperiodic FM-CW signals that was discussed in Chapter 1, one may generate many of these array distributions using a computer and select the one that has the desired properties.

Another approach for this synthesis problem can be based on selecting a single-wavelength autocorrelation function, that is, $r_{\mathbf{a}}(\mathbf{u})$, or, equivalently, spectrum, $S_{\mathbf{a}}(k_{\mathbf{u}})$, for the discrete array configuration function and then working backwards to find the array pattern that best approximates that autocorrelation function. This solution is suited for scenarios where the user knows a priori the bias of the density of the available spatial frequency samples when the Earth's rotation or several wavelengths of the incoming signal are used.

This may be achieved via the following iterative method:

Step 1. Set the iteration step to zero: $\ell = 0$. Synthesize the zero-th solution of the iteration in the frequency domain via the following:

$$\mathbf{A}_0(k_{\mathbf{u}}) \equiv \sqrt{S_{\mathbf{a}}(k_{\mathbf{u}})}\ \exp[\phi_0(k_{\mathbf{u}})],$$

where $\phi_0(k_{\mathbf{u}})$ is a random phase function with odd symmetry, that is

$$\phi_0(k_{\mathbf{u}}) = -\phi_0(-k_{\mathbf{u}}),$$

to make $\mathbf{a}_0(\mathbf{u})$ a real function.

Step 2. Increment the iteration step: $\ell = \ell + 1$. Choose $\mathbf{u}_{i\ell}$, $i = 1, \ldots, N$, to be the location of the highest N values of $\mathbf{a}_{\ell-1}(\mathbf{u})$ within the extent of the aperture. Define the array configuration function to be the following:

$$\mathbf{a}_\ell(u) \equiv \sum_{i=1}^{N} \delta(\mathbf{u} - \mathbf{u}_{i\ell}).$$

The algorithm can be terminated here and the resultant solution is the synthesized array.

Step 3. Increment the iteration step: $\ell = \ell + 1$. The frequency domain solution at this iteration is defined to be

$$\mathbf{A}_\ell(k_{\mathbf{u}}) \equiv \sqrt{S_{\mathbf{a}}(k_{\mathbf{u}})} \, \exp[\phi_{\ell-1}(k_{\mathbf{u}})],$$

where $\phi_{\ell-1}(k_{\mathbf{u}})$ is the phase function of $\mathbf{A}_{\ell-1}(k_{\mathbf{u}})$.

Step 4. Go to Step 2.

After a few iterations, the algorithm converges to a unique solution. In this case, the iteration may be terminated at the end of Step 2 by the user. The resultant solution may still contain some redundancy. To obtain a *uniform* coverage or *density* in the spatial frequency domain, it is better to choose an autocorrelation function that is generated via slightly jittering the evenly-spaced samples of a uniform grid. *Note that $r_{\mathbf{a}}(0)$ or $r_{\mathbf{a}}(0,0)$ is always equal to N and its redundancy cannot be circumvented.*

Phase Retrieval via Sensor Fusion

Next, we examine an iterative method to address the problem of phase ambiguity in interferometric aperture synthesis celestial imaging. This is achieved by fusing the image data from the physical aperture of a telescope with the interferometric synthetic aperture data. As we will show, this procedure is based on iterative corrections in the spatial and spatial frequency domain that is also the basis of the Gerchberg-Saxton algorithm. The additional data provided by the physical aperture of a telescope helps the convergence of the algorithm to the actual image function.

Suppose we are capable of obtaining a low resolution image of the target region via a single telescope with diameter $2L_r$, where L_r is by an order of magnitude smaller than L. We call this image the reference target image and denote it with $f_r(y)$.

- *The reference image is a real signal that is obtained by associating alternative positive and negative signs to the fringe patterns of the telescope's intensity image. For the processing that follows, the important information in the reference image is its phase function in the spatial frequency domain, that is, the phase of $F_r(k_y)$. It turns out that this phase function is approximately equal to the phase function of the spatial Fourier transform of the recorded amplitude function $|f_r(y)|$. Thus, the recovery of $f_r(y)$ from the fringe patterns of $|f_r(y)|$ is not essential.*

Based on the Rayleigh resolution limit of the telescope, we have the following for the Fourier transform of the reference target function:

$$F_r(k_y) = \begin{cases} F(k_y) & \text{for } |k_y| \leq \frac{kL_r}{X_1}; \\ 0 & \text{otherwise.} \end{cases}$$

The phase of the above function in the Rayleigh band of the telescope is the critical information that is used in the following procedure.

We combine the magnitude data from the larger interferometer with the phase data from the telescope to generate the following signal:

$$F_0(k_y) \equiv \begin{cases} F_r(k_y) = F(k_y) & \text{for } |k_y| \leq \frac{kL_r}{X_1}; \\ |F(k_y)| & \text{for } \frac{kL_r}{X_1} < |k_y| \leq \frac{2kL}{X_1}; \\ 0 & \text{otherwise.} \end{cases}$$

We call $F_0(k_y)$ or its inverse Fourier transform $f_0(y)$ the zero-th solution of the iteration.

The next step of the iterative solution is to mask $f_0(y)$ with the telescope's intensity image; that is,

$$f_1(y) \equiv f_0(y)\,|f_r(y)|.$$

This operation is similar to the imposition of the space-limited constraint on the target's extent that is used in the Gerchberg-Saxton iterative solution. Other constraints on $f(y)$, for example, its dynamic range, may be imposed in this step.

Next, we take this solution in the spatial frequency domain. Suppose we have

$$F_1(k_y) \equiv |F_1(k_y)| \, \exp[j\phi_1(k_y)],$$

where $\phi_1(k_y)$ is the phase of $F_1(k_y)$. The solution at the next step of the iteration is

$$F_2(k_y) \equiv \begin{cases} F_r(k_y) = F(k_y) & \text{for } |k_y| \leq \frac{kL_r}{X_1}; \\ |F(k_y)| \, \exp[j\phi_1(k_y)] & \text{for } \frac{kL_r}{X_1} < |k_y| \leq \frac{2kL}{X_1}; \\ 0 & \text{otherwise.} \end{cases}$$

In general, we have the following operation at the odd steps of the algorithm:

$$f_{2n+1}(y) \equiv f_{2n}(y) \, |f_r(y)|.$$

The solution at the even steps of the iteration has the following form:

$$F_{2n}(k_y) \equiv \begin{cases} F_r(k_y) = F(k_y) & \text{for } |k_y| \leq \frac{kL_r}{X_1}; \\ |F(k_y)| \, \exp[j\phi_{2n-1}(k_y)] & \text{for } \frac{kL_r}{X_1} < |k_y| \leq \frac{2kL}{X_1}; \\ 0 & \text{otherwise,} \end{cases}$$

where $\phi_{2n-1}(k_y)$ is the phase of $F_{2n-1}(k_y)$.

Similar to the Gerchberg-Saxton method, the convergence of this algorithm cannot be shown. The main difference between this method and the Gerchberg-Saxton algorithm is the use of the phase of the reference signal in the spatial frequency domain to provide a *fair* initial guess for the algorithm. The use of an appropriate zero-th solution, that is, the initial guess, is a critical issue for the convergence of iterative reconstruction methods.

Figure 6.20 shows a target reconstructed with both phase and amplitude from the noisy interferometric data of a synthetic aperture (solid line). The reconstruction from the amplitude data is also shown in this figure (dashed line). The intensity image (reference image) of the same target with an aperture that is one-fifth of the synthetic aperture is presented via the dotted curve. Figure 6.21 is the reconstructed image from the synthetic aperture amplitude data and the reference image using the above-mentioned iterative algorithm.

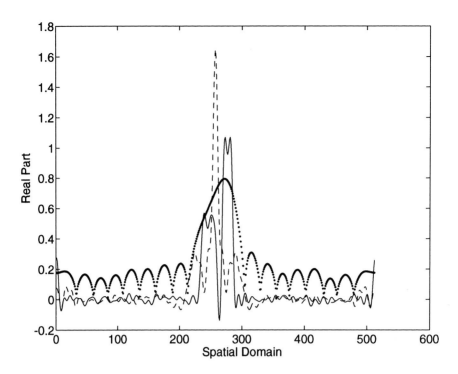

Figure 6.20 Target reconstructions without sensor fusion.

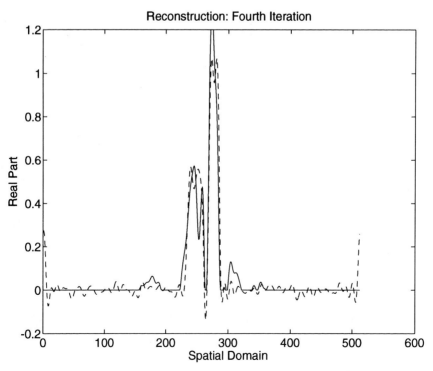

Figure 6.21 Target reconstruction with sensor fusion.

PROJECTS

1. Simulate an incoherent narrow-band passive array imaging system with a planar target region. Reconstruct the target region.

2. Simulate an incoherent narrow-band passive array imaging system with a nonplanar target region. Reconstruct the target region with various values for the focal plane X_1.

3. Simulate multiple targets radiating correlated/uncorrelated wideband signals that are recorded by two passive arrays. (Use a random number generator to simulate a set of Fourier series for each radiating target signal.) Obtain the passive array data for both arrays in the (u,t), (u,ω), (k_u,t), (k_u,ω), (h_u,ω), and (h_u,t) domains. Correlate the two (h_u,t) domain results. Observe the effect of varying Δ and the temporal bandwidth of the radiating signals.

REFERENCES

1. M. Born and E. Wolf, *Principles of Optics*, 6th edition, New York: Pergamon Press, 1983.

2. J. Goodman, *Introduction to Fourier Optics*, New York: McGraw-Hill, 1968.

3. H. P. Bucker, "Cross-sensor beam forming with a sparse line array," *J. Acoust. Soc. Am.*, vol. 26, no. 2, pp. 494-498, February 1977.

4. A. Papoulis, *Systems and Transforms with Applications in Optics*, New York: McGraw-Hill, 1968.

5. M. I. Skolnik, *Introduction to Radar Systems*, New York: McGraw-Hill, 1980.

6. B.D. Steinberg, *Principles of Aperture and Array System Design*, New York: Wiley, 1976.

7. D. E. Dudgeon and R. M. Mersereau, *Multidimensional Digital Signal Processing*, Englewood Cliffs, NJ: Prentice Hall, 1984.

8. A. Michelson and F. Pease, "Measurement of the diameter of Alpha Orionis with the interferometer," *Astrophysics Journal*, vol. 53, pp. 249-259, 1921.

9. P. M. Morse and H. Feshbach, *Methods of Theoretical Physics*, New York: McGraw-Hill, Parts 1 and 2, 1953.

10. M. Soumekh, "A system model and inversion for synthetic aperture radar imaging," *IEEE Transactions on Image Processing*, pp. 64-76, January 1992.

11. M. Soumekh, "Echo imaging using physical and synthesized arrays," *Optical Eng.*, pp. 545-554, May 1990.

12. D. Groutage and D. Gary, "The application of synthetic aperture techniques to radio location and passive imaging," *Proceedings of 21st Asilomar Conference on Signals, Systems and Computers*, pp. 634-640, November 1987.

13. D. Groutage, D. Gary, and R. Kollars, "The application of passive synthetic aperture techniques to the problem of geolocating electromagnetic emitters from spaceborne platforms," David Taylor Research Center, SADP-U89/32-1910, March 1989.

14. *IEEE Journal of Ocean Engineering*, special issue on acoustic synthetic aperture processing, vol. 17, no. 1, January 1992.

15. A. Lohmann, G. Weigelt, and B. Wirnitzer, "Speckle masking in astronomy: triple correlation and applications," *Applied Optics*, vol. 22, pp. 4028-4037, 1983.

16. P. Cruzalebes, G. Schumacher, and J. Starck, "Model-independent mapping by optical aperture synthesis: basic principles and computer simulation," *Journal of Optical Society of America*, vol. 9, pp. 708-724, May 1992.

17. F. Russell and J. Goodman, "Nonredundant arrays and postdetection processing for aberration compensation in incoherent imaging," *Journal of Optical Society of America*, vol. 61, no. 2, pp. 182-191, February 1971.

Chapter 7

BISTATIC ARRAY IMAGING

A *bistatic* measurement refers to a scenario where the transmitter and receiver do not possess identical coordinates in the spatial domain. We examined a bistatic imaging problem in Chapter 4, that is, bistatic SAR/ISAR imaging. This chapters outlines bistatic imaging problems that are encountered in diagnostic imaging, nondestructive testing, and geophysical exploration.

Three bistatic imaging systems are examined via the spatial Doppler (Fourier) decomposition principle. The formulation of the three imaging systems, as shown in (7.1)-(7.4), (7.5)-(7.8) and (7.9)-(7.12), are very similar to each other. More generalized bistatic imaging systems may be studied using similar mathematical methods [26].

The chapter closes with the application of *geometrical optics* approximation in formulating transmission-mode bistatic imaging. We will examine some of the imaging methods that have been extensively utilized in diagnostic medicine (also known as Computer Assisted Tomography, CAT or CT) and geophysical exploration in the past 20 years [1],[2],[10],[19].

To establish sampling constraints for bistatic array imaging systems, we use the assumption that the target area is confined within a disk of radius X_0. This area could be the actual target's support in the spatial domain (as is the case in diagnostic medicine), or a portion of an infinitely extended target that is illuminated by the radiation source (e.g., geophysical exploration).

7.1 ECHO IMAGING

Echo-mode bistatic imaging is not an imaging modality that is used in practice. In fact, the three-dimensional database for this system is difficult and cumbersome to acquire and process. The main message of our discussion in this section is on the equivalence of information in databases obtained in various echo-mode imaging systems. These include phased arrays (two-dimensional database; Chapter 3), synthetic aperture arrays (two-dimensional database; Chapter 4), and physical bistatic arrays (three-dimensional database).

System Model and Inversion

Consider a linear array located on the line $x = X_1$ in the spatial domain. The array's length is $2L$; the array is centered at $y = 0$. We now examine the measurement database when only one of the element's of the array located at, for example, (X_1, u), $u \in [-L, L]$, is used to illuminate the target region in the array's transmit mode, and the echoed signals are measured at (X_1, v), $v \in [-L, L]$, in the array's receive mode (see Figure 7.1). *Note that the same database may be acquired via a single mobile transmitter and a single mobile receiver.*

Suppose the transmitted pulsed signal is $p(t)$. The time delay associated with propagation from (X_1, u) to (x, y) is $\frac{\sqrt{(X_1-x)^2+(u-y)^2}}{c}$; and the time delay associated with propagation from (x, y) to (X_1, v) is $\frac{\sqrt{(X_1-x)^2+(v-y)^2}}{c}$. Thus, the measured signal due to a unit reflector at (x, y) is (amplitude functions are suppressed for notational simplicity)

$$s_{xy}(u, v, t) \equiv p\left[t - \frac{\sqrt{(X_1 - x)^2 + (u - y)^2}}{c} - \frac{\sqrt{(X_1 - x)^2 + (v - y)^2}}{c}\right].$$

The temporal Fourier transform of this signal is

$$s_{xy}(u, v, \omega) \equiv P(\omega) \ \exp[jk\sqrt{(X_1 - x)^2 + (u - y)^2}]$$
$$\times \ \exp[jk\sqrt{(X_1 - x)^2 + (v - y)^2}].$$

The total received signal from a target scene with reflectivity function $f(x, y)$ can be found from

$$s(u, v, \omega) \equiv \int_x \int_y f(x, y) \ s_{xy}(u, v, \omega) \ dxdy$$

$$= P(\omega) \int_x \int_y f(x, y) \ \exp[jk\sqrt{(X_1 - x)^2 + (u - y)^2}] \quad (7.1)$$

$$\times \ \exp[jk\sqrt{(X_1 - x)^2 + (v - y)^2}] \ dxdy.$$

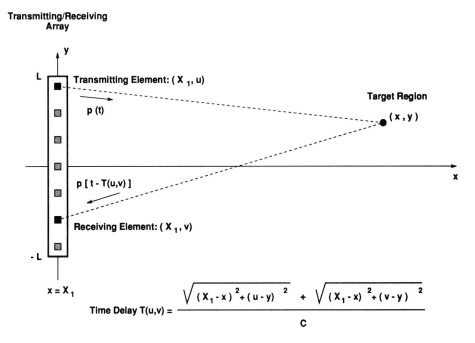

Figure 7.1 Imaging system geometry for echo-mode bistatic imaging.

We have the following for the Fourier transforms of the spherical wave functions on the right side of (7.1):

$$\mathcal{F}_{(u)}\left[\exp[jk\sqrt{(X_1 - x)^2 + (u - y)^2}]\right] = \exp[j\sqrt{k^2 - k_u^2}\,(X_1 - x) - jk_u y],$$

and

$$\mathcal{F}_{(v)}\left[\exp[jk\sqrt{(X_1 - x)^2 + (v - y)^2}]\right] = \exp[j\sqrt{k^2 - k_v^2}\,(X_1 - x) - jk_v y].$$

(Amplitude functions $1/\sqrt{k^2 - k_u^2}$ and $1/\sqrt{k^2 - k_v^2}$ are suppressed on the right side of the above.) Thus, the two-dimensional spatial Fourier transform of both sides of (7.1) with respect to (u, v) yields

$$S(k_u, k_v, \omega) = P(\omega) \int_x \int_y f(x, y) \exp[j\sqrt{k^2 - k_u^2}\,(X_1 - x) - jk_u y]$$

$$\times \ \exp[j\sqrt{k^2 - k_v^2}\,(X_1 - x) - jk_v y]\, dx dy$$

$$= P(\omega)\ \exp[j(\sqrt{k^2 - k_u^2} + \sqrt{k^2 - k_v^2})X_1]$$

$$\times \underbrace{\int_x \int_y f(x, y)\ \exp[-j(\sqrt{k^2 - k_u^2} + \sqrt{k^2 - k_v^2})x - j(k_u + k_v)y]\, dx dy}_{Two\ dimensional\ Fourier\ integral}$$

$$= P(\omega)\ \exp[j(\sqrt{k^2 - k_u^2} + \sqrt{k^2 - k_v^2})X_1]$$

$$\times \ F(\sqrt{k^2 - k_u^2} + \sqrt{k^2 - k_v^2}, k_u + k_v).$$

$$(7.2)$$

The inversion of the system model in (7.2) yields the following for the reflectivity function:

$$F(k_x, k_y) = \exp[-j(\sqrt{k^2 - k_u^2} + \sqrt{k^2 - k_v^2})X_1]\, \frac{S(k_u, k_v, \omega)}{P(\omega)}, \qquad (7.3)$$

[within the band that $P(\omega) \neq 0$], where

$$k_x \equiv \sqrt{k^2 - k_u^2} + \sqrt{k^2 - k_v^2}$$
$$k_y \equiv k_u + k_v. \qquad (7.4)$$

Figures 7.2a and 7.2b show the locus of available data in the (k_x, k_y) domain as dictated by (7.4) for a fixed ω.

In Figure 7.2a, the thick dashed line identifies the finite range (due to finite aperture effects) of available k_u (transmitting aperture's spatial frequency domain) values. For three values of k_u in that finite range, the finite range of available k_v (receiving aperture's spatial frequency domain) values are identified via thick solid lines in Figure 7.2a. These solid lines are the locus of the inverted data, that is, (7.4).

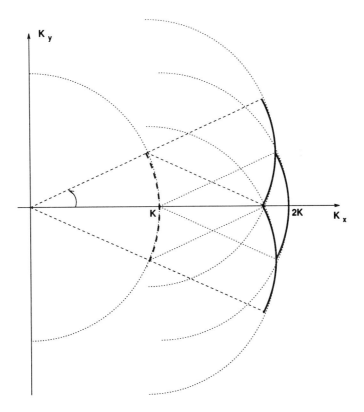

Figure 7.2a Spatial frequency coverage in echo-mode bistatic imaging for three values of k_u.

Figure 7.2b shows the locus of the available data for a set of values of k_u within its finite range. In most practical echo imaging systems where k is much larger than the finite range of k_u and k_v, this coverage does not provide more extensive information than the phased array data or synthetic aperture array data that lie on the circle of radius $2k$ for a fixed ω. When variations of ω [i.e., the transmitted signal, $p(t)$, is a wide-band signal] is incorporated in the spatial frequency coverage, then all three echo-mode databases become identical and convey the same imaging information. This is discussed next.

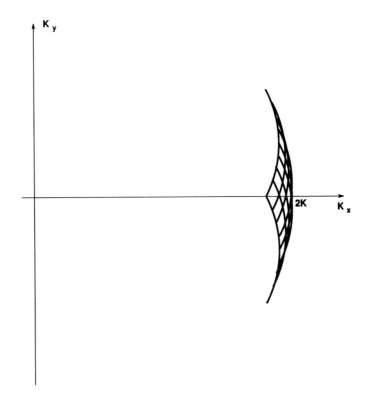

Figure 7.2b Spatial frequency coverage in echo-mode bistatic imaging for a range of values of k_u.

Generalized Array Synthesis

Three array imaging systems that we have examined, phased physical array, synthetic aperture array, and bistatic physical array, involve transmitting and receiving elements that reside within a single aperture. We have also demonstrated that all three array imaging systems provide information in a baseband region in the spatial frequency domain of the desired image that translates into what we referred to as the Rayleigh band/resolution.

The topic that we are now going to investigate is the *equivalence* of these three imaging systems. We begin our analysis by observing that the inversion methods for the three imaging systems recover the samples of $F(k_x, k_y)$ via an invertible *linear* processing (e.g., Fourier transform) of the measured data. Moreover, the bandpass region of the available $F(k_x, k_y)$ is the same for all three imaging systems. Thus, we can conclude that the measurements obtained by these three array imaging systems belong to the same linear signal subspace. This fact can also be established numerically via the Gram-Schmidt procedure.

This implies that the *three-dimensional* database obtained by the bistatic physical array, that is, $s(u, v, \omega)$, carries the same information (in its linear signal subspace) as the *two-dimensional* databases for the phased physical array, $s(\theta, \omega)$, and the synthetic aperture array, $s(u, \omega)$. The equivalence of the linear signal subspaces defined by these three databases also implies that one of these databases can be recovered from a linear processing of another one of the databases.

For instance, the bistatic physical array data can be converted to phased physical array data via the following linear operation:

$$s(\theta, \omega) = \int_u \int_v s(u, v, \omega) \ \exp[jk \ \sin\theta \ (u + v)] \ du \ dv.$$

The synthetic aperture data is obtained from the bistatic physical array data via

$$s(u, \omega) = s(u, v, \omega)|_{v=u}$$
$$= s(u, u, \omega).$$

The inverse of the above linear operations, that is, recovering $s(u, v, \omega)$ from one of the other two databases, is not as straightforward and compact; the procedure involves relating the databases to $F(k_x, k_y)$, that is, the inversion algorithms.

In general, any transmit-receive radiation pattern of the array may be synthesized via simple analytical equations (a linear model) from the bistatic physical array data, that is, $s(u, v, \omega)$.

Sampling Constraints and Resolution

Based on the spatial Doppler phenomenon (finite aperture effects) described in Chapter 1, the support band of the echo-mode bistatic array data in, respectively, transmit mode and receive mode are (with $X_0 + L \ll X_1$)

$$k_u \in \left[-k\frac{X_0 + L}{X_1}, k\frac{X_0 + L}{X_1} \right]$$

$$k_v \in \left[-k\frac{X_0 + L}{X_1}, k\frac{X_0 + L}{X_1} \right]$$

Thus, the Nyquist sampling constraints in the (u, v) domains are

$$\Delta_u \leq 2\pi \frac{X_1}{2k(X_0 + L)}$$

$$\Delta_v \leq 2\pi \frac{X_1}{2k(X_0 + L)}$$

In Chapter 4, we showed that the sampling rate for synthetic array data was twice the sampling rate obtained in the above.

The resolution for the echo-mode bistatic case is found from the following:

$$\Delta_y = 2\pi \frac{X_1}{4kL}$$

$$\Delta_x = \frac{\pi c}{2\omega_0}$$

that is identical to the results for synthetic aperture and phased array imaging ($[-\omega_0, \omega_0]$ is the baseband bandwidth of the transmitted pulsed signal). One should anticipate this result due to the equivalence of information in the databases for the three echo imaging systems.

7.2 TRANSMISSION IMAGING

Our discussion in this section brings out a major deviation from the echo-mode imaging systems that were examined in the previous chapters. Due to the bandpass nature of the transmitted signal in most echo-mode imaging systems, the inverted data yield the distribution of the target's *reflectivity* function in a bandpass region in the (k_x, k_y) domain. This limited the echo-mode imaging capability to formation of the target's boundaries.

As we will see in this section, the inverted data in transmit mode imaging problems provide a coverage at low spatial frequencies. Thus, the user may deduce quantitative as well as qualitative information from a transmit mode reconstructed image. Moreover, similar to the one-dimensional transmission imaging examined in Chapter 1, a wide-band illumination does not provide sufficient coverage in the spatial frequency domain of the range domain. To circumvent this problem, the transmitter/receiver aspect angle is varied with respect to the target. This data collection strategy is referred to as a *rotating* transmitter/receiver.

We present the analysis of transmit mode imaging systems via a method developed by Wolf [35] and is referred to as the *Born* or *single scattering* approximation or the method of *small perturbations*. This approximation was used throughout the echo-mode imaging systems that we discussed previously. There are two other approximations available to formulate the imaging problems that are examined in this book. One is called the *Rytov* approximation [24] or the method of *smooth perturbations* that was developed by Iwata and Nagata [13]. The third approximation is an approximation to the Rytov method and is referred to as the *geometrical optics* approximation. There exists an extensive analysis of these three methods for forward problems [7],[8],[12],[17],[18],[24],[32],[33] and inverse problems [1]-[3],[9],[13] [16],[20] [22],[25], [34],[35] in the literature.

The single scattering approximation (Born method) can be shown to fail under most practical imaging conditions/constraints, for example, when the target size becomes larger than the wavelength of the impinging field [8],[12],[16],[17],[25],[32]. In most radar inverse problems involving imaging a hard-scattering target (i.e., the transmitted signal cannot *penetrate* the target) from *high* spatial frequency echo-mode data, the single scattering approximation does not pose a major issue. The same is not true if one is interested in echo-mode or transmit mode imaging of penetrable targets in diagnostic medicine and geophysical exploration.

The problem becomes more severe in the transmit mode imaging problems involving a rotating transmitter/receiver [17],[25]. In these problems, the Rytov method has shown better performance. An important signal processing issue associated with the Rytov method is to determine the *unwrapped* phase of the measured signal [16]. In fact, many experimental researchers who unknowingly processed the wrapped phase (i.e., the phase's principal value) for the inverse or forward problem, were led to believe that the Rytov method failed more rapidly than the Born method.

The study of the relative merits of the three inverse methods is not the topic of this book, and the above explanation does not do justice in serving that purpose. We will formulate the inverse problem in transmit mode bistatic imaging via the Born method. The solution of this inverse problem via the Rytov method involves the same operations performed for the Born method except for replacing the measured scattered wave with the complex phase of the measured signal [20].

In Section 7.3, we will momentarily deviate from our analysis of transmit mode bistatic imaging systems and formulate the inverse problem for a geophysical bistatic imaging modality with the help of the Born method. The geometrical optics approximation-based inversion for transmit mode bistatic imaging systems will be discussed in Section 7.4.

We now proceed with linear array transmit mode bistatic imaging formulated in the framework of the Born method as presented by Nahamoo and Kak [22]. Witten, Tuggle, and Waag [34] have developed the inversion for circular array transmit mode bistatic imaging.

System Model and Inversion

Consider a target region centered around the origin in the spatial domain as shown in Figure 7.3. A linear array of transmitting elements are located on the line $x = X_1$ in the spatial domain. The array's length is $2L_1$; the array is centered at $y = 0$. A linear array of receiving elements is positioned on the line $x = X_2$ in the spatial domain. The receiving array's length is $2L_2$; the array is centered at $y = 0$. The target region is between the two arrays, that is, $X_1 X_2 < 0$.

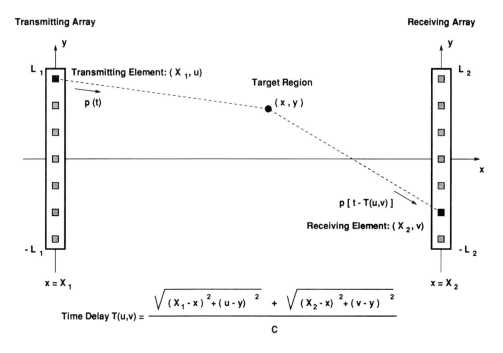

Transmitting Array

Receiving Array

L₁

Transmitting Element: (X ₁, u)

Target Region

p (t)

(x , y)

p [t - T(u,v)]

Receiving Element: (X ₂, v)

- L₁

- L₂

x = X₁

x = X₂

$$\text{Time Delay } T(u,v) = \frac{\sqrt{(X_1 - x)^2 + (u - y)^2} + \sqrt{(X_2 - x)^2 + (v - y)^2}}{c}$$

Figure 7.3 Imaging system geometry for transmission-mode bistatic imaging.

We consider the case when one of the elements of the transmitting array located at, for example, (X_1, u), $u \in [-L_1, L_1]$, is used to illuminate the target region, and the resultant waves *coming out* of the target are measured by the receiver at (X_2, v), $v \in [-L_2, L_2]$. Similar to the echo-mode bistatic system discussed in Section 7.1, the transmit mode bistatic database may be acquired via a single mobile transmitter and a single mobile receiver.

Suppose the transmitted pulsed signal is $p(t)$. The time delay associated with propagation from (X_1, u) to (x, y) is $\frac{\sqrt{(X_1-x)^2+(u-y)^2}}{c}$; and the time delay associated with propagation from (x, y) to (X_2, v) is $\frac{\sqrt{(X_2-x)^2+(v-y)^2}}{c}$. Thus, the measured signal due to a unit scatterer at (x, y) is

$$s_{xy}(u, v, t) \equiv p\left[t - \frac{\sqrt{(X_1 - x)^2 + (u - y)^2}}{c} - \frac{\sqrt{(X_2 - x)^2 + (v - y)^2}}{c}\right].$$

The temporal Fourier transform of this signal is

$$s_{xy}(u, v, \omega) \equiv P(\omega) \, \exp[jk\sqrt{(X_1 - x)^2 + (u - y)^2}]$$
$$\times \, \exp[jk\sqrt{(X_2 - x)^2 + (v - y)^2}].$$

The total received signal from a target scene with scattering function $f(x, y)$ can be found from

$$s(u, v, \omega) \equiv \int_x \int_y f(x, y) \, s_{xy}(u, v, \omega) \, dxdy$$

$$= P(\omega) \int_x \int_y f(x, y) \, \exp[jk\sqrt{(X_1 - x)^2 + (u - y)^2}] \quad (7.5)$$

$$\times \, \exp[jk\sqrt{(X_2 - x)^2 + (v - y)^2}] \, dxdy.$$

The scattering function $f(x, y)$ represents certain properties of the target under study that depends on the type of source used (e.g., optical or ultrasonic) [20],[21],[35].

We have the following for the Fourier transforms of the spherical wave functions on the right side of (7.5):

$$\mathcal{F}_{(u)}\left[\exp[jk\sqrt{(X_1 - x)^2 + (u - y)^2}]\right] = \exp[j\sqrt{k^2 - k_u^2} \, (X_1 - x) - jk_u y],$$

and

$$\mathcal{F}_{(v)}\left[\exp[jk\sqrt{(X_2 - x)^2 + (v - y)^2}]\right] = \exp[-j\sqrt{k^2 - k_v^2} \, (X_1 - x) - jk_v y].$$

(Amplitude functions $\dfrac{1}{\sqrt{k^2-k_u^2}}$ and $\dfrac{1}{\sqrt{k^2-k_v^2}}$ are suppressed on the right side of the above.) Thus, the two-dimensional spatial Fourier transform of both sides of (7.5) with respect to (u,v) yields

$$
\begin{aligned}
S(k_u, k_v, \omega) &= P(\omega) \int_x \int_y f(x,y) \, \exp[j\sqrt{k^2-k_u^2}\,(X_1 - x) - jk_u y] \\
&\quad \times \exp[-j\sqrt{k^2-k_v^2}\,(X_2 - x) - jk_v y] \, dx\,dy \\
&= P(\omega) \, \exp[j(\sqrt{k^2-k_u^2}X_1 - \sqrt{k^2-k_v^2}X_2)] \\
&\quad \times \underbrace{\int_x \int_y f(x,y) \, \exp[-j(\sqrt{k^2-k_u^2} - \sqrt{k^2-k_v^2})x - j(k_u + k_v)y] \, dx\,dy}_{Two\ dimensional\ Fourier\ integral} \\
&= P(\omega) \, \exp[j(\sqrt{k^2-k_u^2}X_1 - \sqrt{k^2-k_v^2}X_2)] \\
&\quad \times F(\sqrt{k^2-k_u^2} - \sqrt{k^2-k_v^2}, k_u + k_v).
\end{aligned}
$$
$$(7.6)$$

The inversion of the system model in (7.6) yields the following for the target function:

$$
F(k_x, k_y) = \exp[-j(\sqrt{k^2-k_u^2}X_1 - \sqrt{k^2-k_v^2}X_2)] \, \frac{S(k_u, k_v, \omega)}{P(\omega)}, \quad (7.7)
$$

(within the band that $P(\omega) \neq 0$), where

$$
\begin{aligned}
k_x &\equiv \sqrt{k^2-k_u^2} - \sqrt{k^2-k_v^2} \\
k_y &\equiv k_u + k_v.
\end{aligned}
$$
$$(7.8)$$

Figures 7.4a and 7.4b show the locus of available data in the (k_x, k_y) domain as dictated by (7.8) for a fixed ω.

In Figure 7.4a, the thick dashed line identifies the finite range (due to finite aperture effects) of available k_u (transmitting aperture's spatial frequency domain) values. For three values of k_u in that finite range, the finite range of available k_v (receiving aperture's spatial frequency domain) values are identified via thick solid lines in Figure 7.4a. These solid lines are the locus of the inverted data, that is, (7.8).

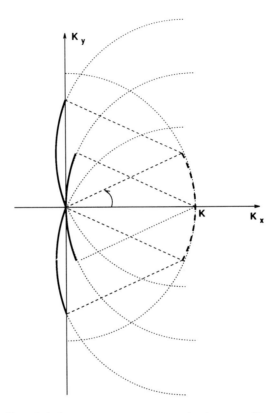

Figure 7.4a Spatial frequency coverage in transmit mode bistatic imaging for three values of k_u.

Figure 7.4b shows the locus of the available data for a set of values of k_u within its finite range. When variations of ω (i.e., the transmitted signal, $p(t)$, is a wide-band signal) is incorporated in the spatial frequency coverage, the available database suffers from irregular gaps in the coverage. Thus, the user is forced to use another data collection strategy to circumvent this problem. A rotating transmitter/receiver is a possible solution to this problem that is discussed next.

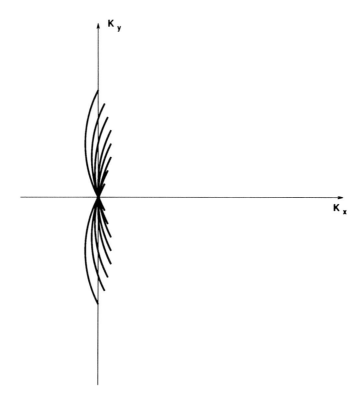

Figure 7.4b Spatial frequency coverage in transmit mode bistatic imaging for a range of values of k_u.

Rotating Narrow-Band Transmitter/Receiver

Figure 7.5 depicts a scenario where the transmitter and receiver in the imaging system shown in Figure 7.3 are rotated by an angle θ. For this system, we consider a mobile transmitter/receiver, though physical arrays, similar to the ones shown in Figure 7.3, may also be used. The target function in the rotated geometry is

$$f'(x',y') = f(x,y),$$

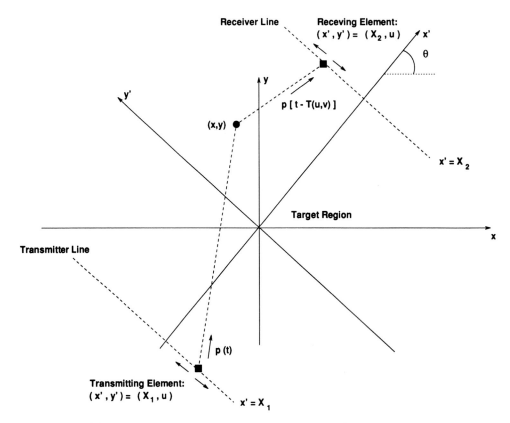

Figure 7.5 Imaging system geometry for transmission-mode
bistatic imaging: Rotating transmitter/receiver.

where

$$\begin{bmatrix} x' \\ y' \end{bmatrix} = \begin{bmatrix} \cos\theta & \sin\theta \\ -\sin\theta & \cos\theta \end{bmatrix} \begin{bmatrix} x \\ y \end{bmatrix}$$

which, based on the results of Chapter 2, has the following Fourier transform:

$$F'(k_{x'}, k_{y'}) \equiv F(k_x, k_y)$$

where

$$\begin{bmatrix} k_{x'} \\ k_{y'} \end{bmatrix} = \begin{bmatrix} \cos\theta & \sin\theta \\ -\sin\theta & \cos\theta \end{bmatrix} \begin{bmatrix} k_x \\ k_y \end{bmatrix}.$$

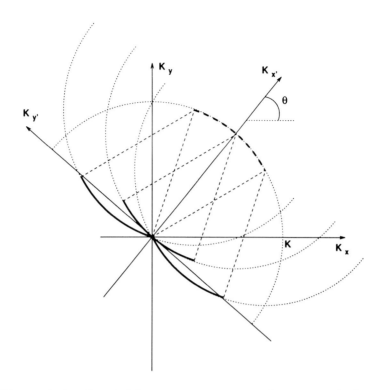

Figure 7.6a Spatial frequency coverage for transmission-mode
bistatic imaging: Rotating transmitter/receiver.

Using steps similar to (7.5)-(7.8) for the rotated geometry, we obtain
the following inversion:

$$F'(k_{x'}, k_{y'}) = \exp[-j(\sqrt{k^2 - k_u^2}X_1 - \sqrt{k^2 - k_v^2}X_2)] \frac{S(k_u, k_v, \omega)}{P(\omega)},$$

(within the band that $P(\omega) \neq 0$), where (see Figures 7.6a-c)

$$k_{x'} \equiv \sqrt{k^2 - k_u^2} - \sqrt{k^2 - k_v^2}$$
$$k_{y'} \equiv k_u + k_v.$$

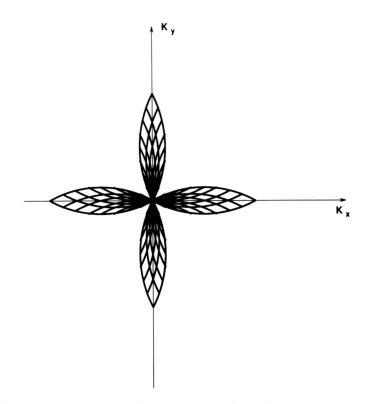

Figure 7.6b Spatial frequency coverage for transmission-mode bistatic imaging with rotation.

Using the inverse of the rotational transformation, the inverse equations can be rewritten as follows in the (k_x, k_y) domain:

$$F(k_x, k_y) = \exp[-j(\sqrt{k^2 - k_u^2}X_1 - \sqrt{k^2 - k_v^2}X_2)] \frac{S(k_u, k_v, \omega)}{P(\omega)},$$

where

$$k_x \equiv \left[\sqrt{k^2 - k_u^2} - \sqrt{k^2 - k_v^2}\right]\cos\theta - (k_u + k_v)\sin\theta$$

$$k_y \equiv (k_u + k_v)\cos\theta + \left[\sqrt{k^2 - k_u^2} - \sqrt{k^2 - k_v^2}\right]\sin\theta.$$

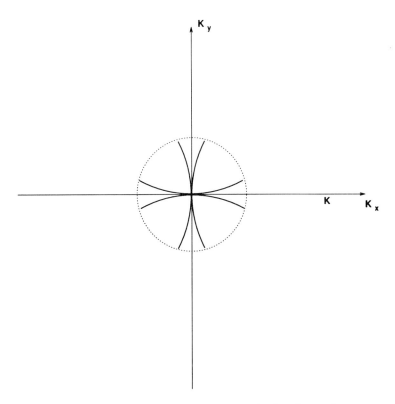

Figure 7.6c Same as Figure 7.6b for $k_u = 0$.

Figure 7.6a shows the locus of available data in the (k_x, k_y) domain for the rotated geometry and fixed values of ω and θ. By varying θ and under certain sampling constraints, one can reconstruct $F(k_x, k_y)$ in this rotating narrow-band transmitter/receiver system [29]. Figure 7.6b shows the resultant coverage for $\theta = 0, \frac{\pi}{2}, \pi, \frac{3\pi}{2}$. In practice, double or triple digit number of rotation angles are needed for alias-free reconstruction of $F(k_x, k_y)$ [14]-[16].

Plane Wave Radiation Source

Figure 7.6c shows a subset of the coverage shown in Figure 7.6b that corresponds to the fixed value of $k_u = 0$; that is,

$$k_x \equiv (k - \sqrt{k^2 - k_v^2}) \cos \theta - k_v \sin \theta$$
$$k_y \equiv k_v \cos \theta + (k - \sqrt{k^2 - k_v^2}) \sin \theta.$$

For a fixed θ (i.e., transmitter/receiver geometry), the case of $k_u = 0$ (the dc value) is equivalent to simultaneously turning on all the transmitting elements on the line $x' = X_1$ since

$$\int_u \exp[jk\sqrt{(X_1 - x')^2 + (u - y')^2}] \, du$$
$$= \exp[j\sqrt{k^2 - k_u^2} \, (X_1 - x') - jk_u y'] \, |_{k_u=0}$$
$$= \exp[jk \, (X_1 - x')].$$

This signal represents a *plane* wave propagating parallel to the x'-axis.

- *Generating a plane wave source is feasible with a physical transmitting array. A single mobile transmitter cannot be used for this purpose.*

The imaging system geometry considered by Wolf for his analysis did use a plane wave radiation source [35]. Kaveh and Mueller, who proposed the first practical imaging system with a rotating narrow-band transmitter/receiver [14],[20], also utilized plane wave radiation. The driving force behind their pioneering work may be traced back to the Fourier slice theorem and reconstruction from straight path projections (Radon transform), that is, the basis of the geometrical optics approximation-based inversion that will be discussed in Section 7.4.

In fact, the inversion described in this section for transmit mode bistatic imaging becomes equivalent to the geometrical optics-based inversion [that will be derived in (7.21)-(7.22)] when $|k_v| \ll k$ such that

$$\sqrt{k^2 - k_v^2} \approx k,$$

can be used in the expressions for (k_x, k_y). In this case, the curved loci of the available data shown in Figure 7.6c can be approximated by straight lines; that is,

$$k_x \approx -k_v \sin\theta$$
$$k_y \approx k_v \cos\theta.$$

This coverage is identical to the one that will be shown in (7.22) for the geometrical optics approximation.

The above approximations are valid under any of the following two circumstances:

i. *The wavenumber, k, becomes very large (or, equivalently, the wavelength becomes very small) as compared with the length of the loci shown. This is true, for example, for the case of X-ray radiation.*

ii. *The receiving aperture becomes too small compared to $|X_2|$. In this case, the ability of the receiver to record the components corresponding to larger values of k_v (also called **diffracted waves**) diminishes.*

Figure 7.6d shows the spatial frequency coverage for the case of $k_u = 0$, $k_v \in [-1, 1]$, $k = 1.1$, and $\theta \in [0, \pi)$. In this case the assumption

$$|k_v| \ll k$$

does not hold. This coverage shows a gap in the spatial frequency domain (the area between the third and fourth quadrants for negative values of k_y). This gap can be prevented by making measurements for $\theta \in [0, 2\pi)$ [20],[29].

Figure 7.6e shows the spatial frequency coverage for the case of $k_u = 0$, $k_v \in [-1, 1]$, $k = 10^6$, and $\theta \in [0, \pi)$. For this case, the assumption

$$|k_v| \ll k$$

does hold and, thus, the curved loci are transformed into straight lines of the Fourier slice theorem, that is, Radon transform. Note that this coverage does not suffer from a gap in the spatial frequency domain when $\theta \in [0, \pi)$.

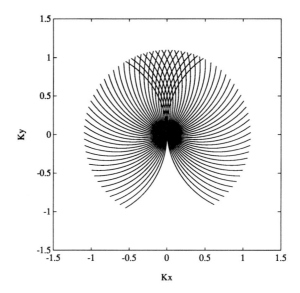

Figure 7.6d Spatial Frequency coverage when $|k_v| \ll k$ is not a valid assumption (diffraction imaging).

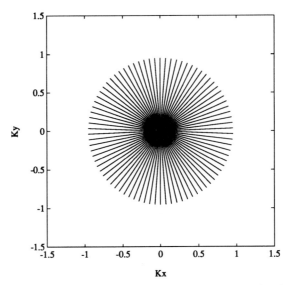

Figure 7.6e Spatial Frequency coverage when $|k_v| \ll k$ is a valid assumption (straight-path imaging; Radon transform).

Sampling Constraints and Resolution

Based on the spatial Doppler phenomenon that was described in Chapter 1, the support band of the transmission-mode bistatic array data in, respectively, transmit mode and receive mode are (with $X_0 + L_1 \ll X_1$ and $X_0 + L_2 \ll X_2$; the general case, which results in lengthy equations, may be formulated in a similar fashion)

$$k_u \in \left[-k\frac{X_0 + L_1}{X_1}, k\frac{X_0 + L_1}{X_1} \right]$$
$$k_v \in \left[-k\frac{X_0 + L_2}{X_2}, k\frac{X_0 + L_2}{X_2} \right].$$

Thus, the Nyquist sampling constraints in the (u, v) domains are

$$\Delta_u \leq 2\pi \frac{X_1}{2k(X_0 + L_1)}$$
$$\Delta_v \leq 2\pi \frac{X_2}{2k(X_0 + L_2)}.$$

For the plane wave radiation source (i.e., $k_u = 0$), the sampling constraint in the angular domain is discussed in [29].

For the rotating narrow-band transmitter/receiver, the resolution at the origin in the spatial domain can be found from the following:

$$\Delta_x = \Delta_y = 2\pi \frac{1}{2k(\frac{L_1}{X_1} + \frac{L_2}{X_2})}.$$

The resolution and the corresponding point spread function are slightly different at the other points in the target region.

7.3 A GEOPHYSICAL IMAGING MODALITY

One can envision various bistatic imaging geometries by varying the relative coordinates of the transmitter and receiver lines. The two systems that were examined in the previous sections represent only two of those imaging scenarios. We now consider another bistatic imaging problem that has been utilized in geophysical exploration. For this imaging system, a mobile transmitter is used at the ground level while a receiver line is positioned in a borehole as shown in Figure 7.7. The transmitter in these applications is an explosion set by the user to generate a powerful acoustic source (for deep penetration inside the ground). Due to this fact, the transmitter is not located in a borehole that might be damaged by the explosion.

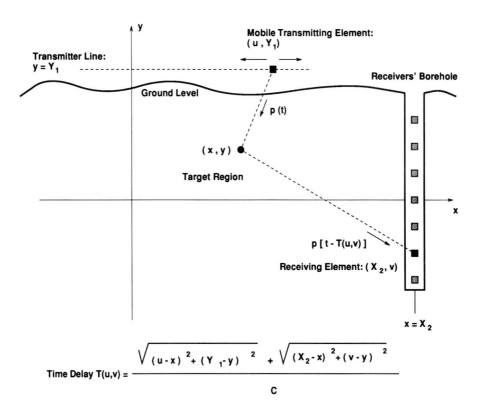

Figure 7.7 Imaging system geometry for geophysical bistatic imaging with a ground level transmitter.

System Model and Inversion

Consider a target region centered around the origin in the spatial domain as shown in Figure 7.7. A linear array of transmitting elements are located on the line $y = Y_1$ in the spatial domain. Equivalently, we may assume that a mobile transmitter with coordinates (u, Y_1), where u is a variable, is used to illuminate the target region (see Figure 7.7). A linear array of receiving elements is positioned on the line $x = X_2$ in the spatial domain. The receiving array's length is $2L_2$; the array is centered at $y = 0$.

We consider one of the fixed coordinates of the transmitter, (u, Y_1), and the resultant measurements made at (X_2, v), $v \in [-L_2, L_2]$. Suppose the transmitted pulsed signal is $p(t)$. The time delay associated with propagation from (u, Y_1) to (x, y) is $\frac{\sqrt{(u-x)^2+(Y_1-y)^2}}{c}$; and the time delay associated with propagation from (x, y) to (X_2, v) is $\frac{\sqrt{(X_2-x)^2+(v-y)^2}}{c}$. Thus, the measured signal due to a unit scatterer at (x, y) is

$$s_{xy}(u, v, t) \equiv p\left[t - \frac{\sqrt{(u-x)^2+(Y_1-y)^2}}{c} - \frac{\sqrt{(X_2-x)^2+(v-y)^2}}{c}\right].$$

The temporal Fourier transform of this signal is

$$s_{xy}(u, v, \omega) \equiv P(\omega) \ \exp[jk\sqrt{(u-x)^2+(Y_1-y)^2}]$$
$$\times \ \exp[jk\sqrt{(X_2-x)^2+(v-y)^2}].$$

The total received signal from a target scene with scattering function $f(x, y)$ can be found from

$$s(u, v, \omega) \equiv \int_x \int_y f(x, y) \ s_{xy}(u, v, \omega) \ dxdy$$
$$= P(\omega) \int_x \int_y f(x, y) \ \exp[jk\sqrt{(u-x)^2+(Y_1-y)^2}] \quad (7.9)$$
$$\times \ \exp[jk\sqrt{(X_2-x)^2+(v-y)^2}] \ dxdy.$$

We have the following for the Fourier transforms of the spherical wave functions on the right side of (7.9):

$$\mathcal{F}_{(u)}\left[\exp[jk\sqrt{(u-x)^2+(Y_1-y)^2}]\right]$$
$$= \exp[jk_u\,(u-x)+j\sqrt{k^2-k_u^2}\,(Y_1-y)],$$

and

$$\mathcal{F}_{(v)}\left[\exp[jk\sqrt{(X_2-x)^2+(v-y)^2}]\right]$$
$$= \exp[-j\sqrt{k^2-k_v^2}\,(u-x)-jk_v\,y].$$

(Amplitude functions $\frac{1}{\sqrt{k^2-k_u^2}}$ and $\frac{1}{\sqrt{k^2-k_v^2}}$ are suppressed on the right side of the above.) Thus, the two-dimensional spatial Fourier transform of both sides of (7.9) with respect to (u,v) yields

$$S(k_u,k_v,\omega)=P(\omega)\int_x\int_y f(x,y)\exp[jk_u(u-x)+\sqrt{k^2-k_u^2}(Y_1-y)]$$
$$\times\ \exp[-j\sqrt{k^2-k_v^2}\,(X_2-x)-jk_vy]\,dxdy$$
$$= P(\omega)\ \exp[j(\sqrt{k^2-k_u^2}Y_1-\sqrt{k^2-k_v^2}X_2)]$$
$$\times\underbrace{\int_x\int_y f(x,y)\ \exp[-j(k_u-\sqrt{k^2-k_v^2})x-j(\sqrt{k^2-k_u^2}+k_v)y]\,dxdy}_{Two-dimensional\ Fourier\ integral}$$
$$= P(\omega)\ \exp[j(\sqrt{k^2-k_u^2}Y_1-\sqrt{k^2-k_v^2}X_2)]$$
$$\times\ F(k_u-\sqrt{k^2-k_v^2},\sqrt{k^2-k_u^2}+k_v).$$

$$(7.10)$$

The inversion of the system model in (7.10) yields the following for the reflectivity function:

$$F(k_x,k_y)=\exp[-j(\sqrt{k^2-k_u^2}Y_1-\sqrt{k^2-k_v^2}X_2)]\ \frac{S(k_u,k_v,\omega)}{P(\omega)},\quad(7.11)$$

(within the band that $P(\omega)\neq0$), where

$$k_x\equiv k_u-\sqrt{k^2-k_v^2}$$
$$k_y\equiv\sqrt{k^2-k_u^2}+k_v.$$
$$(7.12)$$

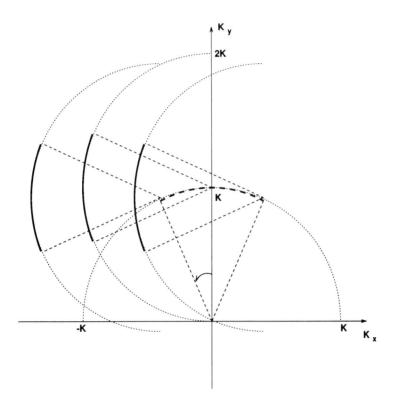

Figure 7.8a Spatial frequency coverage in geophysical bistatic imaging with a ground level transmitter for three values of k_u.

Figures 7.8a and 7.8b show the locus of available data in the (k_x, k_y) domain as dictated by (7.12) for a fixed ω. In Figure 7.8a, the thick dashed line identifies the finite range (due to finite aperture effects) of available k_u (transmitting aperture's spatial frequency domain) values. For three values of k_u in that finite range, the finite range of available k_v (receiving aperture's spatial frequency domain) values are identified via thick solid lines in Figure 7.8a. These solid lines are the locus of the inverted data, that is, (7.12).

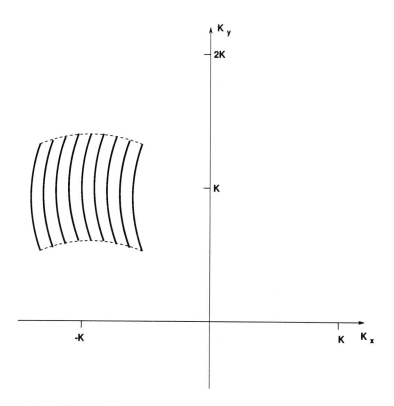

Figure 7.8b Spatial frequency coverage in geophysical bistatic imaging
with a ground level transmitter for a range of values of k_u.

Figure 7.8b shows the locus of the available data for a set of values of k_u within its finite range and a fixed value of ω. Unlike echo-mode bistatic systems, the spatial frequency coverage obtained via a narrow-band source is sufficient for reconstruction of a bandpass version of $F(k_x, k_y)$ in this geophysical bistatic imaging problem. Moreover, this imaging modality does not require a rotating transmitter/receiver that is used in transmission-mode bistatic systems.

Sampling Constraints and Resolution

Based on the spatial Doppler phenomenon (finite aperture effects) described in Chapter 1, the support band of the bistatic array data for the above-mentioned geophysical imaging problem in, respectively, transmit mode and receive mode are (with $X_0 + L_1 \ll Y_1$ and $X_0 + L_2 \ll X_2$)

$$k_u \in \left[-k\frac{X_0 + L_1}{Y_1}, k\frac{X_0 + L_1}{Y_1} \right]$$

$$k_v \in \left[-k\frac{X_0 + L_2}{X_2}, k\frac{X_0 + L_2}{X_2} \right].$$

Thus, the Nyquist sampling constraints in the (u, v) domains are

$$\Delta_u \leq 2\pi \frac{Y_1}{2k(X_0 + L_1)}$$

$$\Delta_v \leq 2\pi \frac{X_2}{2k(X_0 + L_2)}.$$

For a narrow-band source, the resolution at the origin in the spatial domain can be found from the following:

$$\Delta_x = 2\pi \frac{Y_1}{2kL_1}$$

$$\Delta_y = 2\pi \frac{X_2}{2kL_2}.$$

The resolution and the corresponding point spread function are slightly different at the other points in the target region.

7.4 GEOMETRICAL OPTICS APPROXIMATION-BASED IMAGING

In the past century, X-ray sources have been used to produce *shadows* of a bone for diagnostic purposes. A similar procedure has also been utilized for nondestructive testing in industrial inspection. Such shadows are practically the image of a midplane of the target under study in sharp focus with all other planes overlaid with various amounts of blurring [20].

One of the drawbacks of the shadow imaging technique is the lack of depth information about the target under study in the resultant X-ray pictures.

In the 1950s, the mathematical concept of using a set of $(N - M)$-dimensional information $(N > M > 0)$ to reconstruct an N-dimensional function became the basis for many coherent and incoherent imaging systems. This mathematical concept is due to the work of Radon at the beginning of the twentieth century. The pioneering work for imaging systems was performed by Bracewell in radio astronomy imaging [5],[6].

The inversion in these imaging problems is based on the Radon's theory that a three-dimensional functions can be determined from their two-dimensional *projections*. Projections are defined to be the line integrals along straight paths through the three-dimensional function. These projections are also referred to as the three-dimensional functions's *Radon transform*.

This concept proved to be an important tool to reconstruct the three-dimensional distribution of the attenuation coefficient within a target with the help of X-ray sources (incoherent narrow-band imaging) [2],[10]. By assuming that X-ray beams pass through the target in straight paths, the X-ray shadows of the target provide the desired two-dimensional projections of the attenuation coefficient function.

The straight-path assumption to model wave propagation through an inhomogeneous medium (target) is called the *geometrical optics* approximation. Coherent and incoherent ultrasonic/acoustic imaging systems have also been analyzed in the framework of the geometrical optics approximation. The images that are produced via these systems provide information about the distribution of the sound speed (also called *time-of-flight* reconstruction that is available only in the coherent imaging systems), and absorption coefficient (attenuation reconstruction) in the target under study. A survey of the imaging systems that utilize the Radon transform theory can be found in [20].

Our discussion in this section involves the study of some of the transmit mode bistatic imaging modalities that are based on the geometrical optics approximation. Our formulation is based on the reconstruction of two-dimensional functions from their one-dimensional projections. We examined the mathematical basis for reconstruction from this form of Radon transform data in Chapter 2 (Fourier slice theorem).

Rotating Linear Array with a Focused (Parallel) Beam

We begin with the system geometry that was envisioned by Bracewell to formulate radio astronomy imaging (see Figures 7.9a-b). This system became the basis for the first operational computerized tomography system developed by Houndsfield for diagnostic medicine in 1972 [20].

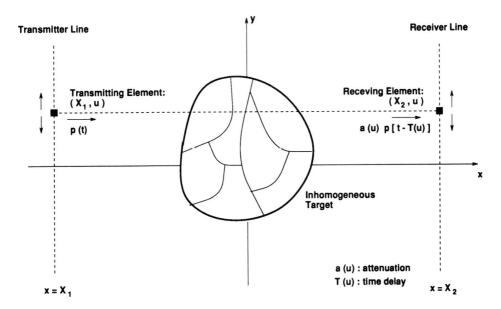

Figure 7.9a Transmission-mode coherent/incoherent bistatic imaging: Geometrical optics-based approximation with a focused beam ($\theta = 0$).

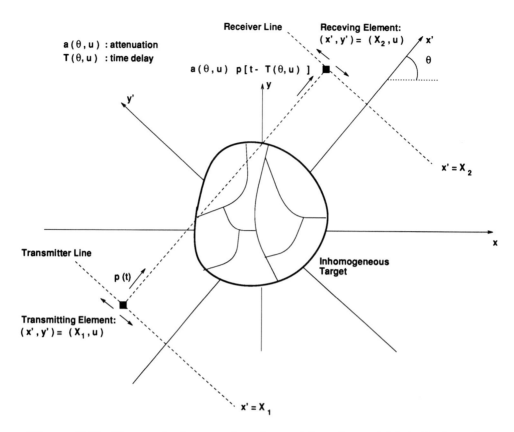

Figure 7.9b Transmission-mode coherent/incoherent bistatic imaging:
Geometrical optics-based approximation with a focused
beam (arbitrary θ).

Consider the imaging system shown in Figure 7.9a. (Notice the similarities between this system and the transmission-mode system shown in
Figure 7.3.) The target under study is composed of various inhomogeneous media (e.g., bone, tissue, fat, and blood in medical imaging, and
salt water, sand, gravel, gas, and oil in geophysical imaging), and resides
within the disk of radius X_0 at the origin in the spatial domain. The
transmitter is moved along the line $x = X_1$ and emits a *focused* beam
parallel to the x-axis. The receiver is moved along the line $x = X_2$ (on
the other side of the target region).

When the transmitter is at (X_1, u), $u \in [X_0, X_0]$, the receiver is positioned at (X_2, u) to record the focused beam that has gone through the target along the line $y = u$. The beam that has gone through the target along this line experiences attenuation and time delay. (This phenomenon is identical to the one-dimensional transmission imaging described in Chapter 1.) Let $p(t)$ be the signal transmitted by the transmitter. Then, for a given u, the signal that reaches the receiver is

$$e^{\gamma(u)} \, p[t - \tau(u)];$$

$\gamma(u)$ is the attenuation in the received signal; and $\tau(u)$ is the time delay associated with the signal propagation from the transmitter to the receiver, that is, $\tau(u)$ (time-of-flight). For a given u, the receiver's energy detector records the attenuation in the received signal, that is, $\gamma(u)$. In the case of a coherent system, the receiver's matched filter-peak detector also records the time-of-flight, that is, $\tau(u)$. Thus, we can identify the measured data in this experiment via the following:

$$s(u) \equiv \gamma(u) + j\tau(u). \tag{7.13}$$

In incoherent imaging systems, the imaginary part of $s(u)$, that is, the time-of-flight $\tau(u)$, is not available and is assumed to be zero in the processing that is done on $s(u)$ for image formation.

We denote the attenuation function and speed distribution within the target region by $\epsilon(x, y)$ and $c(x, y)$, respectively. We define the complex target function via its real and imaginary parts as follows:

$$f(x, y) \equiv f_r(x, y) + j f_i(x, y), \tag{7.14}$$

where

$$f_r(x, y) \equiv \begin{cases} \epsilon(x, y), & \text{if } \sqrt{x^2 + y^2} \le X_0; \\ 0, & \text{otherwise} \end{cases}$$

and

$$f_i(x, y) \equiv \begin{cases} \frac{1}{c(x,y)}, & \text{if } \sqrt{x^2 + y^2} \le X_0; \\ 0, & \text{otherwise} \end{cases}$$

Clearly, one can retrieve $\epsilon(x, y)$ by reconstructing $f_r(x, y)$. Moreover, information on $f_i(x, y)$ can be used to obtain $c(x, y)$. The inversion that will be shown is based on reconstructing $f(x, y)$ for coherent systems or $f_r(x, y)$ for incoherent systems.

Based on the principles presented in Section 1.9, we can write

$$\gamma(u) = \int_{-\infty}^{\infty} f_r(x, u) \, dx, \tag{7.15}$$

and

$$\tau(u) = \int_{-\infty}^{\infty} f_i(x, u) \, dx. \tag{7.16}$$

Using (7.14)-(7.16) in (7.13), we can write

$$s(u) = \int_{-\infty}^{\infty} f(x, u) \, dx. \tag{7.17}$$

(Note that $s(u) = 0$ for $|u| > X_0$ since the target support is the disk of radius X_0.) Taking the spatial Fourier transform of both sides of (7.17) yields

$$\begin{aligned} S(k_u) &= F(k_x, k_y)|_{(k_x=0, k_y=k_u)} \\ &= F(0, k_u) \end{aligned} \tag{7.18}$$

Consider the scenario in Figure 7.9b where the transmitter and receiver in the imaging system shown in Figure 7.9a are rotated by an angle θ. The target function in the rotated geometry is

$$f'(x', y') = f(x, y),$$

where

$$\begin{bmatrix} x' \\ y' \end{bmatrix} = \begin{bmatrix} \cos\theta & \sin\theta \\ -\sin\theta & \cos\theta \end{bmatrix} \begin{bmatrix} x \\ y \end{bmatrix}$$

which, based on the results of Chapter 2, has the following Fourier transform:

$$F'(k_{x'}, k_{y'}) \equiv F(k_x, k_y)$$

where

$$\begin{bmatrix} k_{x'} \\ k_{y'} \end{bmatrix} = \begin{bmatrix} \cos\theta & \sin\theta \\ -\sin\theta & \cos\theta \end{bmatrix} \begin{bmatrix} k_x \\ k_y \end{bmatrix}.$$

We denote the attenuation and time-of-flight in this rotated measurement by $s(\theta, u)$. Using steps similar to the ones that led to (7.17) for the rotated geometry, we obtain the following system model:

$$s(\theta, u) = \int_{-\infty}^{\infty} f'(x', u) \, dx'. \tag{7.19}$$

Taking the spatial Fourier transform of both sides of (7.19) with respect to u yields

$$S(\theta, k_u) = F'(k_{x'}, k_{y'})|_{(k_{x'}=0, k_{y'}=k_u)}$$
$$= F'(0, k_u) \tag{7.20}$$

Using the inverse of the rotational transformation from the $(k_{x'}, k_{y'})$ domain to the (k_x, k_y) domain, we obtain the following inverse equation from (7.20):

$$F(k_x, k_y) = S(\theta, k_u), \tag{7.21}$$

where

$$k_x = -k_u \sin\theta$$
$$k_y = k_u \cos\theta \tag{7.22}$$

- *The coverage in (7.22) is identical to the limiting case of the coverage for transmission-mode imaging based on the Born and Rytov methods that was shown in Figure 7.6c.*

The coverage dictated by (7.22) is polar. The inverse equations in (7.21)-(7.22) was referred to as the Fourier slice theorem in Chapter 2. We discussed methods for reconstructing from polar data in Chapter 2. For incoherent imaging systems, the reconstruction from $s(\theta, u) = \gamma(u)$ (i.e., $\tau(\theta, u) = 0$) only provides the distribution of $f_r(x, y)$ or the attenuation function $\epsilon(x, y)$.

Finally, (7.19) represents *line integrals* through the target function $f(x, y)$, also called the target function's Radon transform. Radon transform function, that is, $s(\theta, u)$, is the line integral of the target function along a line in the spatial domain that is identified via the following:

$$y = \tan \theta \; x \; + \; \frac{u}{\cos \theta}. \tag{7.23}$$

The nonzero values of the Radon transform are uniquely determined via measurements made for $\theta \in [0, \pi)$ or $\theta \in [-\frac{\pi}{2}, \frac{\pi}{2})$ and $u \in [-X_0, X_0]$. The (θ, u) domain data is called *parallel beam* projections data.

The imaging systems described in the next sections deal with scenarios where the measurement domain is a transformation of the (θ, u) domain. In this case, one may use an interpolation method, for example, the one outlined in Chapter 2 or [28], to recover $s(\theta, u)$ from the given measured data. Then, one can use the Fourier slice theorem on the interpolated data to reconstruct $f(x, y)$. [11] provides a formal proof of this concept.

Sampling Constraints and Resolution

The parameters for the rotating parallel beam imaging system are dictated by the size of the target under study and the resolution desired by the user. Suppose one requires the resolution to be Δ_0, that is,

$$\Delta_x = \Delta_y = \Delta_0.$$

(Note that due to the rotational symmetry of the polar data in the (k_x, k_y) domain, the resolution in the x and y domains are the same.) Thus, the coverage of the polar data in the spatial frequency domain should be within a disk of radius ρ_0, where

$$\rho_0 \equiv \frac{1}{2\Delta_0}.$$

In this case, the sampling constraints in the measurement domain become (see Chapter 2 or [28])

$$\Delta_\theta \leq \frac{\Delta_0}{X_0}$$

$$\Delta_u \leq \Delta_0.$$

Linear Array with a Diverging (Fan) Beam

Figure 7.10 depicts an imaging scenario used in geophysical exploration. A transmitting and receiving linear arrays are positioned in two boreholes. (One may use a mobile transmitter instead of a physical transmitter array as shown in Figure 7.10.) The target region to be imaged resides between the two boreholes. The transmitter located at (X_1, u) illuminates the target with a *diverging* beam, also called a *fan beam* source. The receivers at (X_2, v) (v is a variable) record the resultant waves.

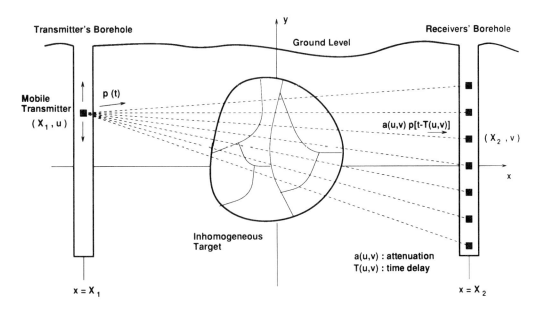

Figure 7.10 Imaging system geometry for geophysical transmission-mode coherent/incoherent bistatic imaging: Geometrical optics-based approximation with a diverging beam.

Geometrical optics approximation is used to model the wave propagation through the target. In this case, the attenuation and time-of-flight information recorded represent the line integrals through the target identified via the following:

$$y = \frac{v - u}{X_2 - X_1} \, x \; + \; \frac{u X_2 - v X_1}{X_2 - X_1}. \tag{7.24}$$

The measurement domain for this experiment is constructed via the variations of (u, v); that is, there are no rotations.

We denote the parallel beam measurement domain described in the previous section by (Θ, U). (These two variables are different from the ones used in the previous section to avoid confusion with the fan beam measurement domain (u, v) of this section.) Comparing (7.23) and (7.24), we can observe that the (Θ, U) and (u, v) domains are related via the following two-dimensional mapping:

$$\tan \Theta = \frac{v - u}{X_2 - X_1}$$
$$\frac{U}{\cos \Theta} = \frac{u X_2 - v X_1}{X_2 - X_1}$$

or

$$\Theta = \arctan\left(\frac{v - u}{X_2 - X_1}\right)$$
$$U = \frac{u X_2 - v X_1}{X_2 - X_1} \, \cos\left[\arctan\left(\frac{v - u}{X_2 - X_1}\right)\right]. \tag{7.25}$$

Thus, one can translate the fan beam data in the (u, v) domain data into the parallel beam projections data in the (Θ, U) domain data via an interpolation method.

However, for the (u, v) domain data to be mapped completely into the (Θ, U) domain data, it is required to make the fan beam measurements for $u \in (-\infty, \infty)$ and $v \in (-\infty, \infty)$ (even when the target is space-limited within the disk of radius X_0). This is clearly not feasible. This issue is known as the *incomplete* projection data problem (e.g., see [27]; [27] also provides a set references that examine this issue).

Figure 7.11 shows a coverage in the (Θ, U) domain obtained from mapping the (u, v) domain data (samples). The values shown for the U axis are normalized with X_0. The *complete* data in the (Θ, U) domain corresponds to a coverage that contains the rectangular region $U \in [-1, 1]$ and $\Theta \in [-\frac{\pi}{2}, \frac{\pi}{2})$. Clearly, the parallelogram coverage shown in Figure 7.11 cannot be considered as complete. The problem gets worse as X_1 and X_2 become larger as compared with the size of the transmitting and receiving apertures.

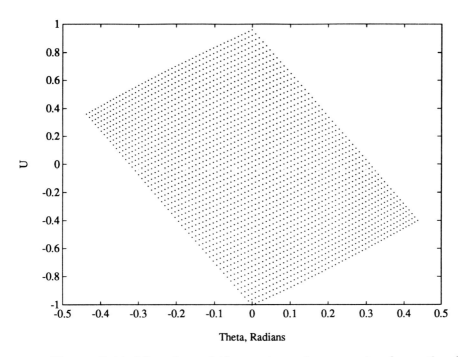

Figure 7.11 Mapping of the rectangular samples from the (u, v) domain to the (Θ, U) domain.

Rotating Circular Array with a Diverging (Fan) Beam

We next examine a fan beam data collection strategy that utilizes a rotating transmitter and a circular receiver aperture. This imaging geometry is currently used for X-ray computerized tomography problems of diagnostic medicine and industrial inspection [10],[19]. Figure 7.12a shows the imaging geometry involving a diverging (fan) beam and a set of receivers to make measurements (i.e., attenuation and, for coherent systems, time-of-flight).

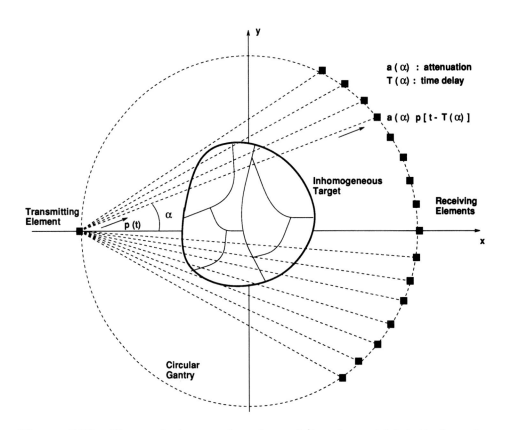

Figure 7.12a Transmission-mode coherent/incoherent bistatic imaging: Geometrical optics-based approximation with a diverging beam on a circular aperture ($\theta = 0$).

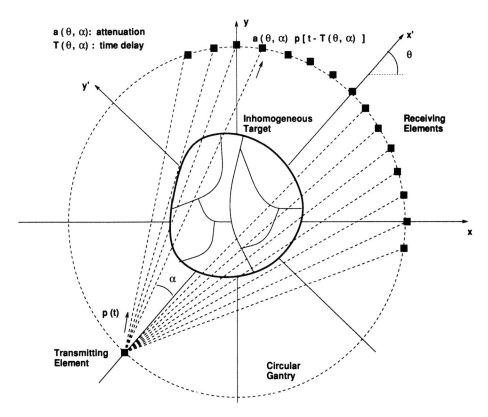

Figure 7.12b Transmission-mode coherent/incoherent bistatic imaging:
Geometrical optics-based approximation with a diverging
beam on a circular aperture (arbitrary θ).

Figure 7.12b depicts the imaging system when the transmitter is
rotated by an angle θ. The measurement domain for this system is identified via (θ, α); θ represents the rotation angle of the transmitter; and
α is the receiver angle with respect to the broadside of the transmitter.
For a given (θ, α), the equation of the line integral through the target is

$$y = \tan(\theta + \alpha)\, x \; + \; \frac{R \sin \alpha}{\cos(\theta + \alpha)}. \qquad (7.26)$$

Comparing the line integral equation for parallel beam data, that is, (7.23) and (7.26), we have the following mapping between the rotating parallel beam domain, (Θ, U), and the rotating fan beam domain, (θ, α):

$$\tan \Theta = \tan(\theta + \alpha)$$

$$\frac{U}{\cos \Theta} = \frac{R \sin \alpha}{\cos(\theta + \alpha)}$$

or

$$\begin{aligned} \Theta &= \theta + \alpha \\ U &= 2R \sin \alpha \end{aligned} \qquad (7.27)$$

This mapping is complete provided that the rotating fan beam data are measured for $\theta \in [0, \pi + 2\alpha_0]$ or $\theta \in [-\frac{\pi}{2} - \alpha_0, \frac{\pi}{2} + \alpha_0]$ and $\alpha \in [-\alpha_0, \alpha_0]$, where

$$\alpha_0 \equiv \arcsin(\frac{X_0}{R}).$$

Figure 7.13 shows a coverage in the (Θ, U) domain obtained from mapping the (θ, α) domain data (samples). The values shown for the U axis are normalized with X_0.

- *The samples mapped into the (Θ, U) domain do exhibit a complete coverage; that is, the coverage contains the rectangular region $U \in [-1, 1]$ and $\Theta \in [-\frac{\pi}{2}, \frac{\pi}{2})$. The coverage also contains some redundancy that cannot be prevented.*

Reference [27] presents a method for translating rotating fan beam data into rotating parallel beam data. The resultant, as we mentioned earlier, can be used to reconstruct the target function via the Fourier slice theorem.

Using (7.27) and sampling constraints resulting from a nonlinear transformation (see Chapter 2 or [28]), one obtains the following constraints in the measurement domain of the rotating fan beam data:

$$\Delta_\theta \le \frac{\Delta_0}{X_0}$$

$$\Delta_\alpha \le \frac{\Delta_0}{R \cos \alpha_0},$$

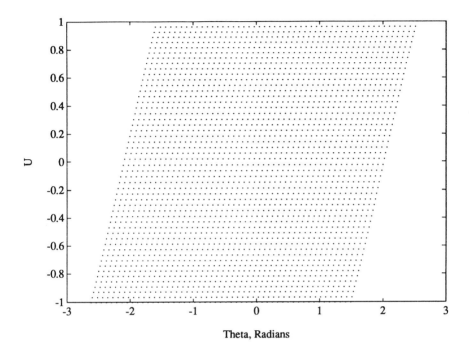

Figure 7.13 Mapping of the rectangular samples from the (θ, α) domain to the (Θ, U) domain.

where Δ_0 is the desired resolution, and the target's support is within the disk of radius X_0.

Finally, in many imaging systems the collected data or their temporal/spatial Fourier transforms provide information regarding the spatial Fourier distribution of the target function. In this book, we have examined a class of those imaging systems that is governed by the properties of propagating waves. There are other imaging systems that result in an inversion in the Fourier domain of the target function. An important example is Magnetic Resonance Imaging (MRI) [19]. The governing principle for developing a system model and inversion for MRI is quite different from the propagating waves phenomenon. Reference [30] provides a discussion on the reconstruction problem in MRI.

PROJECTS

1. Simulate the bistatic imaging systems described in this chapter and develop their inversion algorithms.

2. Establish the equivalence of the signal subspaces for a synthetic array database and its echo-mode bistatic counterpart database via Gram-Schmidt orthogonalization procedure.

REFERENCES

1. *Proc. IEEE*, special issue on *Acoustical Imaging,* vol. 67, no. 4, April 1979.

2. *Proc. IEEE,* special issue on *Computerized Tomography,* vol. 71, no. 3, March 1983.

3. M. Azimi and A. Kak, "Multiple scattering and attenuation phenomena in diffraction imaging," Purdue University Technical Report TR-EE 85-4, February 1985.

4. M. Born and E. Wolf, *Principles of Optics*, 6th edition, New York: Pergamon Press, 1983.

5. R. N. Bracewell, "Strip integration in radioastronomy," *Aust. J. Phys.,* vol. 9, pp. 198-217, 1956.

6. R. N. Bracewell, *The Fourier Transform and its Applications*, 2nd edition, New York: McGraw-Hill, 1978.

7. L. A. Chernov, *Wave Propagation in a Random Medium*, New York: McGraw Hill, 1969.

8. R. L. Fante, "Electromagnetic beam propagation in turbulent media," *Proc. IEEE*, vol. 63, no. 12, December 1975.

9. J. Goodman, *Introduction to Fourier Optics*, New York: McGraw-Hill, 1968.

10. G. T. Herman, *Image Reconstruction from Projections*, New York: Academic Press, 1980.

11. B. Horn, "Density reconstruction using arbitrary ray-sampling schemes," *Proc. IEEE*, 66, p. 551, May 1978.

12. A. Ishimaru, *Wave Propagation and Scattering in Random Media*, Academic Press, 1978.

13. K. Iwata and R. Nagata, "Calculation of three-dimensional refractive index distribution from interferograms," J. Opi. Soc. Am. 60, pp. 133-135, 1970.

14. M. Kaveh, R. Mueller, and R. Iverson, "Ultrasonic tomography based on perturbation solutions of the wave equation," *Computer Graphics and Image Processing*, 9, 105-116, 1979.

15. M. Kaveh, R. Mueller, R. Rylander, T. Coulter and M. Soumekh, "Experimental results in ultrasonic diffraction tomography," *Acoustical Imaging*, vol. 9, K. Wang (Ed.), pp. 433-450, New York: Plenum, 1980.

16. M. Kaveh and M. Soumekh, "Computer assisted diffraction tomography," in *Image Recovery: Theory and Application*, H. Stark (Ed.), pp. 369-413, New York: Academic Press, 1987.

17. J. B. Keller, "Accuracy and validity of the Born and Rytov approximations," J. Opt. Soc. Amer. 59, 1003-1004, August 1969.

18. P. M. Morse and H. Feshbach, *Methods of Theoretical Physics*, New York: McGraw-Hill, Parts 1 and 2, 1953.

19. A. Macovski, *Medical Imaging Systems*, Englewood Cliffs, NJ: Prentice Hall, 1983.

20. R. K. Mueller, M. Kaveh, and G. Wade, "Reconstructive tomography with applications to ultrasonics," *Proc. IEEE*, 67, 567-587, 1979.

21. R. K. Mueller, "Diffraction tomography I: the wave equation," *Ultrasonic Imaging*, 2, pp. 213-222, 1980.

22. D. Nahamoo and A. Kak, "Ultrasonic diffraction imaging," Purdue University Technical Report TR-EE 82-20, August 1982.

23. A. Papoulis, *Systems and Transforms with Applications in Optics*, New York: McGraw-Hill, 1968.

24. S. M. Rytov, "Diffraction of light by ultrasonic waves," *Izv. Akad. Nauk SSSR,* Ser. Fiz. 2, p. 223, 1937.

25. M. Soumekh and M. Kaveh, "A theoretical study of model approximation errors in diffraction tomography," *IEEE Transactions on Ultrasonics, Ferroelectrics, and Frequency Control,* vol. UFFC-33, no. 1, pp. 10-20, January 1986.

26. M. Soumekh, "Echo imaging using physical and synthesized arrays," *Optical Engineering,* vol. 29, no. 5, pp. 545-554, May 1990 (special issue on *Image Restoration and Reconstruction*).

27. M. Soumekh, "Image reconstruction techniques in tomographic imaging systems," *IEEE Transactions on Acoustics, Speech, and Signal Processing,* vol. ASSP-34, no. 4, pp. 952-962, August 1986.

28. M. Soumekh, "Band-limited interpolation from unevenly spaced sampled data," *IEEE Transactions on Acoustics, Speech, and Signal Processing,* vol. ASSP-36, no. 1, pp. 110-122, January 1988.

29. M. Soumekh and J. Choi, "Reconstruction in diffraction imaging," *IEEE Transactions on Ultrasonics, Ferroelectrics, and Frequency Control,* vol. UFFC-36, no. 1, pp. 93-100, January 1989.

30. M. Soumekh, "Reconstruction and sampling constraints for spiral data," *IEEE Transactions on Acoustics, Speech, and Signal Processing,* vol. ASSP-37, no. 6, pp. 882-891, June 1989.

31. H. Stark, J. Woods, I. Paul, and R. Hingerani, "Direct Fourier reconstruction in computer tomography," *IEEE Transactions on Acoustics, Speech, and Signal Processing,,* vol. 29, pp. 237-245, 1981.

32 J. W. Strohbehn, "Line-of-sight wave propagation through the turbulent atmosphere," *Proc. IEEE,* 56, pp. 1301-1318, August 1968.

33. V. I. Tatarski, *Wave Propagation in a Turbulent Medium,* New York: McGraw-Hill, 1961.

34. A. J. Witten, J. Tuggle, and R. Waag, "A practical approach to ultrasonic imaging using diffraction tomography," *Journal of Acoustical Society of America,* 83(4), p. 1645, April 1988.

35. E. Wolf, "Three-dimensional structure determination of semi-transparent objects from holographic data," *Opt. Commun.,* 1, p. 153, 1969 [Born inversion].

Index

A

aerial combat blind-velocity imaging 370-372

Air traffic control/surveillance radar
    211-218
  airborne moving target indication (AMTI)
    215
  bistatic radar 217
    imaging system geometry 214
  electronic scanner 212-215
    system model 213
    inversion 215
  focused beams 212
  imaging system geometry 214
  mechanically rotating scanner 217-218
    imaging system geometry 240
  moving target Doppler (MTD) 215
  moving target indication (MTI) 215
  stereo radar 216-217
    imaging system geometry 214

airborne moving target indication (AMTI) 215
Airy pattern 137
ambiguity function 61-62, 258
analog to digital (Λ/D) convertor 29
angular spectrum 153, 194-196
angular steering 198, 218
array configuration function 491

Arrays
  active 187
  bistatic 505
  passive 440
  physical 187
  phased 188-189
  rotating 239, 519, 535, 544
  synthetic 261-262

attenuation 101, 103, 537

Automatic target detection with ISAR
    420-432
  see Inverse synthetic aperture radar

Autonomous vehicle radar/sonar 96-100
  slant angle 98
  slant range 98
  slant speed 98
  system model 97-100

B

band-limited signals 5

Bandpass signals 5, 27
  coherent processing 27-30
  quadrature representation 27

baseband conversion 27-30
baseband ISAR 324-326
baseband signal 27

Beamforming, generalized 209-211
  see also Dynamic focusing
  radiation pattern 210-211
  relation to digital filter design 211
  weight function 210

Bistatic array imaging
  echo-mode 505-512
  geometrical optics approximation 533-547
  geophysical 527-533
  transmission-mode 513- 527

bistatic radar 217
bistatic SAR 337-339
bistatic transmitter/receiver 35
blind angle 355, 373, 481
Born approximation 513
broadside target scene 266
B-scanner 188

C

Celestial imaging 484-502
  see Passive array imaging
center of mass 54
characteristic equation 148-149